Private Sector Environmental Information and the Law

Current advancements in civil rights and environmental activism emphasise the crucial importance of making environmental information widely available to the public, regardless of whether it is in the hands of the government or of corporations, especially when the information is needed to understand and prevent risks for human health and the environment. In the wake of a resurgence of environmental and civil rights activism, conflicts flare between the right of the people to know and the right of private actors to keep certain information hidden, mostly for commercial reasons. This book offers a detailed comparative analysis of how environmental information is being accessed in different countries and jurisdictions, and how these issues are currently being handled by judges and governments. Focusing on the right of access to environmental information held and produced by private actors and the legal issues that emerge when other values and rights are compromised, this book offers an alternative framework to improve on current legal systems, suggesting a more nuanced and balanced approach that takes both set of interests duly into consideration. Providing an integrated approach to public environmental law and private commercial law, the book integrates the arguments from both sides to establish a common ground, defining shared principles and models that provide a solid basis for a robust new system. Reviewing access to private sector information at a truly international level, this book will be relevant to students, academics and practitioners working in these areas.

Juliana Zuluaga-Madrid holds a PhD in Law and an LLM in Energy and Environmental Law. She has worked for companies in the mining sector, Oil & Gas and is currently Legal Director at Ingema S.A, a company in the energy sector. She combines her legal practice with academic engagements as lecturer and research advisor for Universidad del Rosario (Bogotá).

Routledge Research in International Environmental Law

Enforcement of International Environmental Law
Challenges and Responses at the International Level
Martin Hedemann-Robinson

Marine Pollution, Shipping Waste and International Law
Gabriela Argüello

Compensation for Environmental Damage Under International Law
Jason Rudall

International Environmental Law Compliance in Context
Mechanisms and Case Studies
Belen Olmos Giupponi

Sustainable Fisheries Management and International Law
Marine Fisheries in Bangladesh and the Bay of Bengal
Abdullah Al Arif]

Marine Conservation and International Law
Legal Instruments for Biodiversity Beyond National Jurisdiction
Sarah Louise Lothian

Nature Law and Policy in Europe
Edited by Andrew L.R. Jackson

Environmental Liability and the Interplay between EU Law and International Law
Dr Emanuela Orlando

https://www.routledge.com/Routledge-Research-in-International-Environmental-Law/book-series/INTENVLAW

Private Sector Environmental Information and the Law

Juliana Zuluaga-Madrid

Routledge
Taylor & Francis Group
LONDON AND NEW YORK

First published 2024
by Routledge
4 Park Square, Milton Park, Abingdon, Oxon OX14 4RN

and by Routledge
605 Third Avenue, New York, NY 10158

Routledge is an imprint of the Taylor & Francis Group, an informa business

British Library Cataloguing-in-Publication Data
A catalogue record for this book is available from the British Library

ISBN: 978-1-032-30976-7 (hbk)
ISBN: 978-1-032-31014-5 (pbk)
ISBN: 978-1-003-30761-7 (ebk)

DOI: 10.4324/9781003307617

Typeset in Times New Roman
by Taylor & Francis Books

To my brother, Hugo Alejandro

Contents

Tables

Acknowledgements

The thoughts in this academic work would have never seen the light without the invaluable support of the Promoter of my PhD, Prof. Dr. Geert van Calster, and without the inspiration and encouragement of my dear friend Prof. Dr. Leonie Reins. Thank you for your trust and guidance during all these years.

Thank you, Stephen Marcinuk, for your patience and unconditional support to push me through the finish line. When I had doubts, you were always there to dissipate them and renew my efforts. Thanks to my family, Liana Madrid, Hugo Zuluaga, Sara María Zuluaga, Hugo Alejandro Zuluaga and Alejandra Maya, for sharing with me the hopes, difficulties, and rewards of this academic challenge, and to my dear friend Elsemiek Apers for her constant support and hospitality. Thanks to Gustavo Zambrano, for believing in me from the start.

Thanks to my professors and colleagues at KU Leuven, Georgetown University Law Faculty, Lewis and Clark University and Hebrew University for allowing me to share the ideas of this research and for providing much needed feedback and recommendations. Special thanks to Prof. Dr. Bernard Vanheusden, for always having a moment to discuss my questions and his insightful comments.

Thanks to Gran Colombia Gold, particularly the CEO Lombardo Paredes Arenas and Alejandro Ramírez for making it possible for me to pursue my PhD whilst working at the company; the support and flexibility were a key driver for the successful completion of this book. To my colleagues at the company during my PhD years, Maria Camila Arango, Lucas Velasquez, Paulina Mejía and Elkin Pinto, thank you for providing words of encouragement and an extra hand at work when I needed it.

Finally, special thanks to the members of the Examination Committee, to my supervisors and all the administrative and faculty staff at KU Leuven who were involved in the different steps of the academic process leading to the completion of this research. Thank you to the publishers of this book, for bringing it into the light.

Acronyms and Abbreviations

ACCC	Aarhus Convention Compliance Committee
APA	Administrative Procedure Act
Art.	Article
CBI	Confidential Business Information
CJEU	Court of Justice of the European Union
DTSA	Defend Trade Secrets Act
EC	European Commission
ECHA	European Chemicals Agency
ECHR	European Convention on Human Rights
ECLAC	Economic Commission for Latin America and the Caribbean
ECtHR	European Court of Human Rights
EIA	Environmental Impact Assessment
EMAS	Eco-Management and Audit Scheme
EPA	Environmental Protection Agency
EU	European Union
FOI	Freedom of Information
FOIA	Freedom of Information Act
FTA	Free Trade Agreement
GMO	Genetically Modified Organism
GRI	Global Reporting Initiative
ICHR	Inter-American Court of Human Rights
ICCPR	International Covenant on Civil and Political Rights
IPR	Intellectual Property Rights
NEPA	National Environmental Protection Act
NGO	Non-Governmental Organisation
OAS	Organisation of American States
OECD	Organisation for Economic Cooperation and Development
PRTR	Pollution Releases and Transfers Register
REACH	Regulation No 1907/2006/EC concerning the Registration, Evaluation, Authorisation and Restriction of Chemicals
SEC	Securities and Exchange Commission
TEU	Treaty on European Union
TFEU	Treaty on Function of the European Union

TRIPS	Agreement on Trade-Related Aspects of Intellectual Property Rights
TSCA	Toxic Substance Control Act
UN	United Nations
UNECE	United Nations Economic Commission for Europe
UNEP	United Nations Environment Programme
US	United States
UTSA	Uniform Trade Secrets Act

1 Introduction

In recent times, the concept of transparency has been redefined from the perspective of public governance and legal practice as an instrument to address power unbalances in society. Terms like 'open government', the 'right-to-know' and 'public participation' have thus become commonplace for legal theorists and practitioners, and environmental law is one of the legal disciplines where these ideas have had a stronger impact.

The transparency trend in the field of environmental law takes the form of a generalised right of public access to environmental information, which is typically embedded in a scheme for public participation which also includes a right to participate in decision-making processes and a right of access to justice in environmental matters. The concept was first codified in international environmental law in Principle 10 of the Rio Declaration[1], which reads:

> Environmental issues are best handled with the participation of all concerned citizens, at the relevant level. At the national level, each individual shall have appropriate access to information concerning the environment that is held by public authorities, including information on hazardous materials and activities in their communities, and the opportunity to participate in decision-making processes. States shall facilitate and encourage public awareness and participation by making information widely available. Effective access to judicial and administrative proceedings, including redress and remedy, shall be provided.

This principle was later developed into a structured legal model becoming internationally (regionally) binding through the adoption, in 1998, of the UNECE Convention on public access to information, participation in decision-making and access to justice in environmental matters [the Aarhus Convention].[2]

1 United Nations Conference on Environment and Development Rio de Janeiro, Brazil (1993). *Rio Declaration on Environment and Development*, 3–14 June 1992, Rio de Janeiro, Brazil.

2 Convention on Access to Information, Public Participation in Decision-making and Access to Justice in Environmental Matters, Aarhus, Denmark, 25 June 1998 (entry into force 30 October 2001) 2161 UNTS 447.

DOI: 10.4324/9781003307617-1

Although the right of public access to environmental information in these instruments appeared to affect public authorities only, there is no reason to assume that private entities were *per se* exempted from a duty to provide environmental information. This has become more evident as private companies are increasingly faced with demands for access to information which until quite recently was considered to fall under business (confidential) secrets and out of bounds for public access. Legal instruments are now frequently used to get access to 'private' environmental data, and information channels between the private sector and the general public are emerging in the form of sustainability reports, pollution registers as well as in the framework of environmental impact assessments and registration and approval of chemical substances and products, among others.

However, a consistent approach to regulate public access to privately held environmental data needs further development, especially considering the conflicts between the public right of access to environmental information and the protection of legitimate private interests in confidentiality and intellectual property rights.

Specific information such as known risks of products and projects that are *not* marketed/carried out,[3] the use of natural resources and efficiency indicators,[4] environmental trade-offs negotiated in agreements with public organisations, the results of internal environmental audits and tests, and even research about the environmental characteristics of a geographical zone, could all very well be in the public interest, fall into the definition of 'environmental information', and still never see the public light because they are held by private entities.

Other types of environmental information (publicly and privately held) are routinely being excluded from disclosure requirements on business confidentiality grounds, such as chemical substances identities, inert components of products, tests results, risk assessments, public contracts for environmental services and information about management of natural resources and environmental impacts; largely without clear guidelines that would help companies, government agencies and the public understand when the information should be made available and when it should remain secret.

If private entities were brought into the scope of environmental transparency instruments in an explicit manner, at least in some cases, not only would there be an increase in the public availability and accessibility of environmental information, but it would contribute to open the debate and make room for proposals about issues such as the prevalence of access rights over

3 E.g. a research report from Inside Climate News suggests that Exxon knew about the effects of fossil fuels and GEI on climate change as early as 1977, ten years before the alarms were set off by the international scientific community. See Banerjee, N., Cushman, J.H. (Jr.), Hasemyer, D., & Song, L. (2015). *Exxon: The Road Not Taken*. Inside Climate News.

4 This information is usually included in Sustainability Reports, but rigorous environmental reporting remains largely voluntary.

the protection of business confidentiality and vice versa, the shifting role of private entities in the provision of public services and the power dynamics between corporations and members of the public in the contexts of environmental participation, access to justice and the protection of fundamental rights.

The object of this book is therefore the right of public access to environmental information held by the private sector taking into account the evolution of public participation instruments at the international, regional and national level, and the tensions raised between the principles of transparency and public participation and the protection of the legitimate interests of private actors, with the purpose of understanding the underlying assumptions supporting the current legal structures, their shortcomings and possible ways forward to better articulate the provisions establishing transparency duties upon private entities within legal regimes of access to environmental information.

At the end, a model is formulated extracting the main lessons from the comparative analysis addressing some of the identified shortcomings. The model consists of an updated 'matrix of values' to be applied in the context of public requests of access to environmental information from the private sector and a proposed method of analysis integrating all the different factors that should be considered in specific cases in order to ensure a more certain, predictable, reasoned and fair solution to the conflicts between environmental transparency and business confidentiality.

1.1 Why Now?

Openness and public participation have come to be considered important means for the realisation of sustainable development aims.[5] Establishing effective mechanisms for access to public information is now seen as a key factor to afford the general public the right to scrutinise how public affairs are managed and public resources invested. It is also an important tool to prevent corruption and legitimise state decisions. Moreover, access to information is a precondition for the exercise of other rights, such as participation in decision-making and political rights.

When it comes to environmental matters, two of the aims of sustainable development are *prima facie* served when states provide mechanisms for effective access to environmental information: social inclusion and environmental protection. The challenge would seem to successfully include the third aim, namely economic development, since the exceptions to disclosure of environmental information based on business confidentiality and intellectual property rights

5 Mason, M. (2010). Information Disclosure and Environmental Rights: the Aarhus Convention. *Global Environmental Politics, 10*(3), 10–31, asserting that transparency, expressed as information access, is deemed to be a necessary expression of, and condition for, democratic governance.

may well hinder the effectiveness of public participation mechanisms,[6] but trade secret law and IPR are there to protect legitimate economic interests in the service of a healthy competitive market as well as to incentivise research, scientific development and innovation.

The process of recognising and implementing the public right of access to environmental information regularly involves private entities to a lesser or higher degree, through 'passive' mechanisms such as requirements directed to environmental authorities and environmental audits which hold information originated in the private sector, and 'active' mechanisms like environmental public reporting (mostly voluntary) and eco-labelling by private companies themselves. In recent times, the importance of including private companies as responsible actors of environmental transparency has become more evident, leading to these entities being addressed in transparency regulations more frequently and causing, therefore, an increase in the conflicts emerging from public requests of information that may be exempted on grounds of business confidentiality or intellectual property rights protection.

In this scenario, it is important to analyse how policy and regulatory measures can be implemented to provide more clarity on when and why private environmental information should be made available to the general public in order to guarantee the minimum tools and materials for effective public participation in environmental decision-making, whilst maintaining a reasonable degree of protection of private interests and expectations in confidentiality.

The protection of trade secrets and IP rights are necessary, they serve a legitimate interest of society and are worthy of protection, but they might still be interfering with public access to environmental information and effective public participation. This research is justified by the pressing need to ensure that the application of IP laws will not unduly undermine the right of public access to environmental information or vice versa. The thesis of this book parts from the assumption that, given adequate guidelines, a satisfactory balance can be achieved between these clashing interests, in the benefit of legal certainty for companies, authorities and the public; and contributing to the materialisation of public participation rights.

1.2 Background and Scope

In most democratic states, the protection of business confidentiality in the form of trade or industrial secrets, intellectual property and commercially sensitive information is a recognised and legitimate legal right. This

6 D'Silva, J., & Van Calster, G. (2010). For Me to Know and You to Find Out? Participatory Mechanisms, The Aarhus Convention and New Technologies. *Studies in Ethics, Law, and Technology, 4*(2), cite Aarhus' negotiation process, where these concerns (among others) were brought up by the NGO coalition and Norway, who opposed to the commercial confidentiality exception as well as that for intellectual property [Report on the eighth session: CEP/AC.3/16 (1997:3)].

recognition serves to protect a fair market, the defence of intellectual rights and commercial transactions, which, ultimately, contributes to the general wellbeing of the economy. The prerogative to withhold private information is closely related to the right to private property, as well as the protection of the economy and prevention of financial harm, which could result from the disclosure of privileged commercial and business-related information.

Nevertheless, the role of private corporations must be revaluated in the light of current environmental concerns. Corporations are key agents in environmental governance and transparency.[7] Any attempt to exercise public participation rights aiming for sustainable development and environmental protection needs to consider the role of private corporations in the different processes of environmental governance.[8]

Moreover, environmental information is the prime material of public participation in environmental matters,[9] and the most relevant information will often come from industries and private companies, as they are likely to engage in activities that may have a significant effect on the environment and affect third parties' interests. Furthermore, private entities are increasingly engaging in the provision of public goods and services that used to be in charge of the government, this 'privatisation' trend obstructs the exercise of access rights to the extent that many transparency laws only apply to public sector entities.

In this scenario, transparency instruments across jurisdictions are increasingly extending disclosure obligations to private entities to report to government agencies and, sometimes, directly to the public. The application of these instruments brings about conflicts between public access, on the one hand, and the protection of business confidentiality, on the other.

Current environmental and transparency instruments already acknowledge this tension and address it. The Aarhus Convention provides exceptions for the protection of the legitimate economic interests of private entities. These exceptions would apply to the obligation to disclose any information when such action were to adversely affect:

> "…(d) The confidentiality of commercial and industrial information, where such confidentiality is protected by law in order to protect a

7 For information on the preponderant role of corporations in environmental global governance see Sukhdev, P. (2012). *Corporation 2020: Transforming business for tomorrow's world.* USA: Island Press.

8 United Nations Economic Commission for Europe – UNECE. (2014). *The Aarhus Convention: An Implementation Guide*, 2nd ed., UN Doc. ECE/CEP/72/Rev.1; Aarhus Convention, Recital 13.

9 Rowan-Robinson, J., Ross, A., & Walton, W. A. (1996). Public Access to Environmental Information: A means to what end? *Journal of Environmental Law, 8* (1), 19–42; Gavouneli, M. (2000). Access to Environmental Information: Delimitation of a Right. *Tulane Environmental Law Journal, 13*, 303–327.

legitimate economic interest. Within this framework, information on emissions which is relevant for the protection of the environment shall be disclosed;

(e) Intellectual property rights;[10]

The working plan of the Rio Declaration, Agenda 21, stated that relevant information should be provided to the public to the greatest possible extent, but taking into account legitimate claims for confidentiality.[11]

Against this background, this book evaluates the current framework for access to environmental information held by the private sector. This assessment serves to identify if and how the application of business confidentiality exceptions may be hindering public participation in environmental matters by keeping relevant environmental information out of reach of the public concerned and how this issue can be addressed through regulatory and policy reform. The research aims to keep a balanced position to reconcile, to the greatest possible extent, the necessity for wider access to relevant environmental information with the preservation of legitimate private interests in confidentiality.

The scope of the book includes a comparative legal analysis of the subject in the international landscape, EU law and the domestic jurisdictions of Colombia and the US as examples of the civil law and common law traditions. In each of these realms the following chapters explore how environmental information is being provided and accessed via public authorities or directly from private entities and what level of protection is afforded to trade secrets and intellectual property under the current laws.

The comparative study includes the EU, in consideration to the position of the region as a regulatory frontrunner in the matter of environmental public participation and corporate transparency,[12] but also as a first mover for topics such as Corporate Social Responsibility and voluntary-based initiatives for environmental disclosure.

At the national level, the review of the US legal regime includes the examination of the Freedom of Information Act (FOIA) and how it is being interpreted and applied to access private information; the Emergency Planning and Community Right-to-Know Act (EPCRA), which established the

10 Aarhus Convention, Article 4(d) and 4 (e).

11 United Nations Conference on Environment and Development Rio de Janeiro, Brazil. (1993). *Agenda 21: Programme of Action for Sustainable Development*, 3–14 June 1992, Rio de Janeiro, Brazil. United Nations Dept. of Public Information, 19.16: 'Industry should provide data for substances produced that are needed specifically for the assessment of potential risks to human health and the environment. Such data should be made available to relevant national competent authorities and international bodies and other interested parties involved in hazard and risk assessment, and to the greatest possible extent to the public also, taking into account legitimate claims of confidentiality'.

12 Gavouneli, *Access to Environmental Information*, 2000.

Toxic Release Inventory (TRI);[13] the Pollution Prevention Act (PPA); and the relevant provisions of the Code of Federal Regulations and related Executive Orders.

The US is highly relevant for the proliferation of business-confidentiality and transparency laws alike. As the world's largest market, it has enacted powerful measures for the protection of trade secrets, intellectual property and commercially sensitive information specifically against disclosure on environmental grounds.[14] However, it also promotes new systems to provide public access to environmental information held by the private sector, such as a Greenhouse Gas Reporting Program administered by the Environmental Protection Agency (EPA). In the comparative study, the US is an important point of reference from the common law system.

The study of domestic jurisdictions also includes Colombia, within the specific South America legal background. Colombia's national laws for access to information and public participation follow the legal trends in other South American countries, which share similar levels of development, customs and values.[15] They are also influenced by international initiatives such as the Organisation for Economic Cooperation and Development (OECD),[16] and the emergence of free trade agreements (FTAs) with, in particular, the EU,[17] which are often conditioned to the adoption of certain environmental and social standards. Although transparency regulations are flourishing,[18] the country and the region have a history of sacrificing environmental interests for economic development.

13 The TRI program was established in 1986 and amended by the Pollution Prevention Act in 1990, requiring EPA to collect and make available to the public certain data regarding toxic releases from private industry. The data are collected annually directly from the companies.

14 See *e.g.* Section 40 Code of Federal Regulations, Part 2, Subpart B, regarding the confidentiality of business information in the framework of public information administered by the EPA.

15 Several Supranational organizations have formed in South America based on these similarities and shared interests, including the Andean Community, the Pacific Alliance and the Mercosur. Colombia belongs to the Andean Community and the Pacific Alliance.

16 On 15 April 2014, the OECD issued a first report of environmental recommendations for Colombia, including the implementation of a Pollutant Release and Transfer Register for chemicals and to provide for better access to environmental information and transparency in decision-making. OECD. (2014). *Environmental Performance Reviews: Colombia (2014)*. Retrieved from http://www.oecd.org/env/country-reviews/ColombiaEPR_AssessmentRecommendations.pdf.

17 ECLAC. (2013). *Access to Information, Participation and Justice in Environmental Matters in Latin America and the Caribbean: Situation, Outlook and Examples of Good Practice.* Santiago: United Nations.

18 ELLA-Evidence and Lessons from Latin America. (2012). *Building the Legal Framework to Support Transparency and Access to Information in Latin America.* Retrieved from http://ella.practicalaction.org/wp-content/uploads/files/120209_GOV_TraAccInf_BRIEF3.pdf.

This selection of states and jurisdictions aims to provide a fundamentally diverse legal landscape and a wide-reaching scope, adequate for the subject-matter of the study. The view from international to national and regional perspectives facilitates the observation of the most general principles and the most specific provisions in a contextual way, helping to dissect how mostly universal concepts are interpreted and applied in actual cases and how the particularities of a legal system can affect their ultimate impact. The legal systems of Colombia, the EU and the US differ in fundamental ways, yet they all have set provisions aimed at granting a (limited) right of access to environmental information to the general public and have established protective measures for confidential business information. These commonalities constitute the basis of the comparative study, which is made richer and more prolific by the examination of the aspects that make them different. So, for example, whilst Colombia is a state organised under a centralised government, with a rigid written constitution and of roman civil law tradition, the US is none of these things. This legal diversity is considered advantageous for the present study because it provides a broader view of possible solutions which directly feed into the formulation of sensible recommendations that can be adapted to different types of states and organisations.

From the comparative analysis, points of conflicts and key issues are identified and described in detail, as well as the current tools and mechanisms being employed to tackle these conflicts, in order to propose an alternative to the current approach based on the most recent case-law and best practices aiming to strike a balance between public access to information held by the private sector and the protection of legitimate interests in privacy and confidentiality.

1.3 Normative Framework

The analysis of the right of access to environmental information and the issues arising from the tensions between transparency and confidentiality in the private sector is carried out within the general frame provided by the Aarhus Convention due to its overarching and integrative nature, as well as the wide availability of scholarly works analysing its concepts and case-law in international and national jurisdictions regarding its provisions and implementation. Note that the Aarhus Convention was adopted in the framework of the United Nations Economic Commission for Europe (UNECE) and although it could be joined by outside states, its geographical scope is mostly limited to the UNECE region.

More specifically, the normative framework employed for the research is the process set up in the Aarhus Convention, meaning the core provisions of the Convention as further specified by various follow-up in technical committees, namely the Almaty Guidelines,[19] the works of the Task Force in

19 Almaty Guidelines on Promoting the Application of the Principles of the Aarhus Convention in International Forums. Almaty, Kazakhstan, 25–27 May 2005, II (15).

Public Participation in decision-making,[20] the Bali Guidelines[21] and the implementation guide to the Aarhus Convention.[22]

When choosing the Aarhus Convention as the source of the normative framework, consideration was given to its influence as an international-regional legal instrument, its further development by case law of the Aarhus Compliance Committee and other national and supranational courts, and the fact that the Convention sets a floor, not a ceiling, on the matters it covers (Aarhus Convention, 1998, Article 3(5)). Even with its flaws, the Convention is still considered to reflect international best practice in the matters it covers.[23] It is the furthest any international instrument has come in the legal development of an autonomous right of public access to environmental information and has been widely taken as a frame of reference for the formulation of specific provisions at national and regional levels. Its enforcement and supporting mechanisms such as the Aarhus Convention Compliance Committee, the possibility for the general public to submit complaints and the Work Forces set up by the Committee of the Parties, have helped to consolidate the Aarhus Convention as an authoritative source for any study related to the public right of access to environmental information. It is important to note that the research does not address directly any of the critiques raised against Aarhus, but it only employs its general structure, definitions, rationale, principles and other useful conceptual elements as a reference framework for a logical and comprehensive analysis. Thus, the concepts, elements and indicators of the normative framework are the result of the analysis of the core provisions of the Aarhus Convention setting standards on how access to environmental information should work, particularly in the light of the public participation in decision-making processes, for which access to information is crucial. The conceptual basis of the normative framework also feeds from authoritative commentaries and complementary sources like the Bali Guidelines, the Implementation Guide to the Aarhus Convention and the opinions of the Aarhus Convention Compliance Committee. A comparative point of reference to the Aarhus Convention is the Regional Agreement on Access to Information, Public Participation and Justice in Environmental Matters in Latin America and the Caribbean (The Escazú Agreement),[24] whose provisions are also examined throughout the present study.

20 Task Force on Public Participation in Decision-making of the Aarhus Convention (established by the Meeting of the Parties through decision EMP.II/1).
21 United Nations Environment Programme – UNEP. The Bali Guidelines for Development of National Legislation on Access to Information, Public Participation and Access to Justice in Environmental matters, 26 February 2010.
22 UNECE, *Aarhus Implementation Guide*, 2014.
23 Etemire, U. (2014). Public Access to Environmental Information: a Comparative Analysis of Nigerian Legislation with International Best Practice. *Transnational Environmental Law*, *3*(1), 149–172.
24 United Nations, Regional Agreement on Access to Information, Public Participation and Justice in Environmental Matters in Latin America and the Caribbean, 4 March 2018 (entered into force 22 April 2021), Escazú, Costa Rica.

Generally, the more environmental data is made available to the general public, the better and more effective public participation will be.[25] It can also be stated however that not *all* of the environmental information is *necessary* on any particular matter to achieve effective public participation in decision-making, as defined by the Aarhus Convention and complemented by regulatory best practices identified in additional studies and official reports.[26] When there are other legitimate interests which are protected by non-disclosure, a threshold must be established to determine which information must be made available regardless of the conflicting interest at stake and which must not.

Public access to environmental information is the first and most basic 'pillar' of public participation under the Aarhus Convention. Although information should be given to the public as a matter of good environmental governance and because it is in the public interest to do so, the normative framework for this study examines public access to environmental information as the necessary means for effective public participation in decision-making processes. The Implementation Guide to the Bali Guidelines highlights the instrumental capacity of the right of access to environmental information, stating that 'Information is essential to enable members of the public to participate meaningfully in public affairs and to make informed decisions about their lives'.[27]

Accordingly, in the analysis of the provisions and lessons from each legal framework, the compass is fixed in what it takes to achieve effective public participation in decision-making from the perspective of access to information.

To this effect, the working concept of 'effective public participation' used throughout the analysis is built taking into consideration Aarhus' standards and supporting sources such as the Bali Guidelines, as well as based on the theory and research of scholars on the subject of how to evaluate public participation to measure effectiveness.[28] This definition is used in the analysis of whether a certain scheme for access to environmental information is able to provide the elements that are necessary for effective public participation.

25 D'Silva & Van Calster, *Participatory Mechanisms*, 2010.

26 *i.a.* Almaty Guidelines and Task Force on Public Participation in Decision-making of the Aarhus Convention (established by the Meeting of the Parties through decision EMP.II/1 adopted at its second extraordinary session held at Geneva, April 2010).

27 UNEP (2015). Putting Rio Principle 10: An Implementation Guide for the UNEP Bali Guidelines for the Development of National Legislation on Access to Information, Public Participation and Access to Justice in Environmental Matters. Nairobi, p. 22.

28 See Rowe and Frewer, L. J. (2000). Public Participation Methods: A Framework for Evaluation. *Science, Technology & Human Values, 25*(1), 3–29.

The underlying assumption is that the Aarhus process is designed to ensure that the public participation processes undertaken under its provisions are, in theory, effective; and access to information is key for this purpose. Indeed, the European Commission has recognised the relevance of the general right of access to information for public participation in democratic processes[29] and, regarding environmental information specifically, the Court of Justice of the European Union suggested in a recent judgment that one of the main purposes of access to environmental information in the framework of the Aarhus Convention and EU legislation is to promote more effective public participation, increasing the accountability of decision-making processes.[30]

'Public Participation' has been defined as 'the group of procedures designed to consult, involve, and inform the public to allow those affected by the decision to have an input into that decision'.[31] In this definition the term 'input' is key, as it will distinguish participation from simple communication.[32]

'Effective public participation' will thus be understood as the participation process in which the public concerned is engaged and is able to issue an informed opinion that is pertinent to the decision-making process, which is duly taken into account by the public authority in charge of the decision, in the way the Aarhus Convention conveys. The elements of this definition are:

1 The involvement of the public concerned.
2 An informed opinion of the public, delivered in the appropriate form and in a timely manner.
3 The consideration that the authority taking the decision gives to the public's opinion.

The issuance of an informed opinion by the public concerned presupposes the provision of all the relevant information to the public, for otherwise the opinion may not be informed or pertinent for the decision-making process.

29 European Commission. (2007). Public Access to Documents held by institutions of the European Community (Green Paper), COM (2007)185, p. 11: 'The main purpose of laws on freedom of information is to enable citizens to participate more closely in democratic decision-making'.

30 Case C 673/13 *Commission v Stichting Greenpeace Nederland and PAN Europe* (2016) ECLI:EU:C:2016:889, para 80: 'It is apparent, in essence, from recital 2 of Regulation No 1367/2006 that the purpose of access to environmental information provided by that regulation is, inter alia, to promote more effective public participation in the decision-making process, thereby increasing, on the part of the competent bodies, the accountability of decision-making and contributing to public awareness and support for the decisions taken.' See also Peeters, M. (2018). About Silent Objects and Barking Watchdogs: The Role and Account ability of Environmental NGOs. *European Public Law, 28*(3), 449–472.

31 Smith, L. G. (1983). *Impact assessment and sustainable resource management*; Longman, quoted in Rowe and Frewer (2000), p. 6.

32 Rowe & Frewer, *Public Participation Methods*, 2000, p. 6.

Thus, for the purposes of the present study, a working definition of 'relevant environmental information' is formulated, based on the concept and elements of effective public participation and the provisions of the Aarhus Convention.[33] 'Relevant Environmental Information', in the context of effective participation in specific projects or activities comprises:

a Facts: relate to the context, precedents, description of the project/programme/measure to be taken.
b Impacts: expected consequences of the proposed measure, positive and negative, on the identified problem and, additionally, on the environmental and social aspects.
c Risks: events with negative connotation that have a probability of happening as a result of the adoption of the proposed measure. If known, the probability of occurrence should also be shared.
d Remedies: the proposed actions to be undertaken in order to prevent the materialisation of risks and mitigate or compensate negative impacts.
e Alternatives: other measures or activities that could achieve the purposes of the proposed measure.
f Costs: the price of adopting the proposed measure, as well as the estimated cost of the alternatives. The analysis of costs must include the long-term benefit.

To facilitate the comparative study, the concept of 'effective public participation' was disintegrated into its core elements in the categories of aims, beneficiaries, procedures, contents, timing and technology; identifying indicators to assess the situation of the right of public access to environmental information in each of the jurisdictions in the comparative study (Table 1.1).

33 Aarhus Convention, Article 6(6):

The relevant information shall include at least, and without prejudice to the provisions of article 4:

(a) A description of the site and the physical and technical characteristics of the proposed activity, including an estimate of the expected residues and emissions;

(b) A description of the significant effects of the proposed activity on the environment;

(c) A description of the measures envisaged to prevent and/or reduce the effects, including emissions;

(d) A non-technical summary of the above;

(e) An outline of the main alternatives studied by the applicant; and

(f) In accordance with national legislation, the main reports and advice issued to the public authority at the time when the public concerned shall be informed in accordance with paragraph 2 above.

Table 1.1 **Indicators of the Normative Framework**[34]

Element	*Definition*	*Indicators*
Aims	A regime of access to information must be inspired by participatory aims.	1 There is an explicit recognition of a right enabling access to environmental information. 2 Access to information is integrated within a framework providing for public participation in environmental governance.
Beneficiaries and Providers of information	Subjects of the regulation: Refers to the number and type of agencies or entities that fall under the law and are mandated to provide the information requested and to whom.	1 Access to information in general is provided without discrimination and without having to state an interest. 2 Scope (wideness) of the public and private entities obliged under access to information laws. 3 In the framework of public participation in specific projects, there are tools for the adequate identification and involvement of the public concerned. 4 Minorities, ONGs and affected parties have a way of being especially considered and engaged in the participation processes.
Material Scope	Refers to the amount and substance of the information that can be accessed and used in participatory processes.	1 Scope (broadness) of the definition of 'environmental information' for the purposes of access to information laws. 2 In the framework of public participation in specific projects, "relevant information" is identified and made available to the public concerned.
Mechanisms for Access	Refers to the actual channels available to the public for access to environmental information.	1 There is a specific obligation upon public/private entities to provide environmental information upon request of the public (passive disclosure). 2 There is a specific obligation upon public/private entities to collect and disseminate relevant environmental information to the public (active disclosure). 3 There is a system for the reporting and dissemination of information on the release and transfer of pollutants (PRTRs).

34 Made by the Author following guidelines of: ELLA (2012) and Darbishire, H. (2011). *Proactive Transparency: The future of the right to information?* Retrieved from http://siteresources.worldbank.org/EXTGOVACC/Resources/DarbishireProactiveTransparency.pdf.

Element	*Definition*	*Indicators*
Procedures	Refers to the procedural aspects of the mechanisms for access to information.	1 There is a time limit for entities to respond to requests for information by the public. 2 Information is provided in the way that it was requested, unless it is only available in another format. 3 Requests can be made in various forms and through different channels. 4 Access to information is free or its cost is limited to the cost of the reproduction of the data. 5 Public entities enable free access to internet databases of environmental information. 6 In the framework of public participation in specific projects, there is a timeframe providing for relevant information to be disclosed early in the participation process and that enough time is given for the public to examine the information and issue an informed opinion.
Exceptions	Refers to the cases in which information may be refused under the law.	1 Exceptions are clearly stated in the law. 2 When certain information is covered by an exception, there's a provision for the disclosure of a non-confidential version of the information or partial disclosure. 3 There is an explicit guideline as to what information may be reserved on grounds of business confidentiality. 4 The protection of Intellectual property and industrial secrets is harmonised with provisions for public access to information. 5 There is a system (criteria) for the solution of conflicts arisen in access to information and protection of business secrets cases. 6 Requests of information denied on the grounds of exceptions are adequately addressed expressing the reasons for the refusal.

Element	*Definition*	*Indicators*
Compliance and Enforcement	Refers to the establishment of clear, binding sanctions in case of non-compliance and the institutions to enforce them.	1 There is an administrative mechanism for review in cases of refusal of public/private entities obligated to provide information upon request. 2 There is a judicial or administrative mechanism for review of conflicts arisen in the application of access to environmental information laws in general. 3 There is an agency or institution in charge overseeing the functioning of the mechanisms for access to information.

2 Preliminary Notions of the Right to Know and the Private Sector

2.1. Legal and Historical Precedents of Access to Environmental Information

The right of public access to environmental information, as currently known, was shaped mainly around international instruments of environmental law, which recognised the importance of involving the public in environmental governance and the management of natural resources, from the Declaration of Stockholm in 1972 to the Rio Declaration in 1992.

At national levels, the right of public access to environmental information is not always regulated in an explicit manner, but it is nonetheless exercised through mechanisms for access to public information and in the framework of environmental public participation processes, such as environmental impact assessments.

A primary regulatory achievement at national level would be the explicit recognition of a right of access to environmental information for the public, particularly because the rationale underlying the recognition of the general right of access to public information and the more specific right of access to environmental information are substantially different. The first is generally based in the exercise of political rights[1] (citizens need access to public information to be able to make informed political choices and to hold their governors accountable); access to environmental information, on the other hand, supports the right to live in a safe and healthy environment and, as defended throughout this study, the right to participate effectively in environmental decisions that may affect them.

In this context, the recognition of a subjective right of access to information conferred upon citizens has evolved in the last decades at the international and national levels. The best example is the Aarhus Convention, in force since 2001.[2] Upon its adoption, the Aarhus Convention was described by the United Nations' General Secretary, Kofi Annan, as

1 Stražišar, B., & Kralj, M. (2016). The Aarhus convention in the nuclear sector – right to information versus nonproliferation? *Journal of Radiological Protection*, 36, 160.

2 Convention on Access to Information, Public Participation in Decision-making and Access to Justice in Environmental Matters, Aarhus, Denmark, 25 June 1998 (entry into force 30 October 2001) 2161 UNTS 447.

DOI: 10.4324/9781003307617-2

> by far, the most impressive elaboration of principle 10 of the Rio Declaration, which stresses the need for … access to information on the environment held by public authorities. As such it is the most ambitious venture in the area of 'environmental democracy' so far undertaken under auspices of the United Nations.[3]

To this date, the Aarhus Convention is the most prominent instrument of international law establishing legally binding commitments upon states to provide citizens with tools for effective public participation in environmental matters. It does so through the promotion of three distinguishable environmental rights: access to environmental information, public participation in decision-making and access to justice. Although the Convention has received largely positive feedback since its adoption, the instrument is not without flaws and important critiques have been made on issues as crucial as the scope of public and private entities it does (not) extend to, the discretion allowed to states for the implementation of some of its core provisions, and the actual materialisation of its purported aim to ensure a substantive human right to a healthy environment. Notably, neither the USA nor Russia ratified the Convention despite being members of the UNECE. Their reasons for choosing not to join can hardly be ascertained, although, in the US case, they may have more to do with the political motives of its leaders at the time than to legal challenges or potential disruptions to its domestic regime.[4] The US adopted the Freedom of Information Act (FOIA) in 1966 and has since taken other decisive steps towards improving transparency and public participation in environmental matters at the federal level. Despite the general acceptance of the Aarhus Convention as an effective guide to the implementation of Principle 10 of the Rio Declaration (or perhaps because of it), no other universal instrument of international law was ever adopted for the same purpose. Ultimately, Latin America and Caribbean states opted to negotiate their own regional agreement for the implementation of Principle 10 of the Rio Declaration, resulting in the adoption of the Escazú Agreement in 2018.[5]

3 Quoted in: ECLAC. (2013). *Access to Information, Participation and Justice in Environmental Matters in Latin America and the Caribbean: Situation, Outlook and Examples of Good Practice.* United Nations, p. 18.

4 Reportedly, the US criticised Aarhus' compliance mechanism for the public entitlements to nominate members for the ACCC, submit allegations of non-compliance and to follow up the proceedings, which it considered to be contrary to established multilateral treaty practice. Mason, M. (2014). 'So far but no further? Transparency and disclosure in the Aarhus convention'. In Gupta, A. and Mason, M., (Eds.) *Transparency in Global Environmental Governance: Critical Perspectives. Earth System Governance.* MIT Press, p. 91.

5 United Nations, Regional Agreement on Access to Information, Public Participation and Justice in Environmental Matters in Latin America and the Caribbean, 4 March 2018 (entered into force 22 April 2021), Escazú, Costa Rica.

Notwithstanding its limitations, the Aarhus Convention is still regarded as the best reflection of international best practice principles[6] with the 'potential to drive and encourage countries to "keep up with the best world standards and practices" in relation to public access to information and decision-making processes in general'.[7]

However, the Aarhus Convention was not the first instrument of international law to explicitly recognise the importance of public participation for environmental good governance and practice. The Stockholm Declaration,[8] adopted at the 'earth summit' held in 1972, had already stated that education in environmental matters is 'essential in order to broaden the basis for an enlightened opinion and responsible conduct by individuals, enterprises and communities in protecting and improving the environment in its full human dimension'.

Subsequently, the UN Charter for Nature (1982)[9] recognised the different aspects of public participation, which were later developed by the Aarhus Convention.

Finally, the Rio Declaration[10] established the way in which public participation should be provided for in every state, asserting in Principle 10:

> Environmental issues are best handled with the participation of all concerned citizens, at the relevant level. At the national level, each individual shall have appropriate access to information concerning the environment that is held by public authorities, including information on hazardous materials and activities in their communities, and the opportunity to participate in decision-making processes. States shall facilitate and encourage public awareness and participation by making information widely available. Effective access to judicial and administrative proceedings, including redress and remedy, shall be provided.

The Rio+20 conference, conducted in June 2012 at the 20th anniversary of the Rio Convention, produced the Declaration 'The Future We Want', which

6 Etemire, U. (2016). *Law and practice on public participation in environmental matters: the Nigerian example in transnational comparative perspective.* Routledge.

7 Etemire, *Public Participation in Environmental Matters*, 2016, quoting Jendroska J. (1998). UNECE Convention on access to information, public participation in decision-making and access to justice in environmental matters: towards more effective public involvement in monitoring compliance and enforcement in Europe. *5th International Conference on Environmental Compliance and Enforcement, Ca*, 16–20.

8 United Nations Convention Concerning the Protection of the World Cultural and Natural Heritage. (1972). *Declaration of the United Nations Conference on the Human Environment*, 16 June 1972, Stockholm, Sweden.

9 General Assembly of the United Nations. (1982). *World Charter for Nature*, A/RES/37/7, 28 October 1982, Articles 16 and 23.

10 United Nations Conference on Environment and Development Rio de Janeiro, Brazil. (1993). *Rio Declaration on Environment and Development*, 3–14 June 1992, Rio de Janeiro, Brazil.

again underscores the importance of public participation, access to information and to administrative and judicial remedies for the promotion of sustainable development. The Parties to the summit encourage action at all levels to promote access to information, public information and access to justice in environmental matters as a contribution to this commitment.[11]

The enactment of international instruments fed significantly into the development of national and regional legislation. The EU, for instance, has adopted several Directives and Regulations specifically aimed at expanding transparency among its own institutions and at Member State level, including Directive 2003/4/EC,[12] which aims to implement the EU's obligations on access to information under the Aarhus Convention providing guidelines for the implementation of the Convention's provisions in each of the Member States, Regulation (EC) No 1049/2001[13] on public access to documents of the EU's institutions (European Commission, European Parliament and European Council), and Regulation (EC) No 1367/2006 on the application of the provisions of the Aarhus Convention to Community institutions and bodies.[14]

In addition to the influence that international law (especially binding instruments) is expected to have in national legislation, there may also be an impact on national and regional instruments in the evolution of international law. For instance, Directive 90/313/EEC of the EU on public access to environmental information and the lessons learned from its implementation in Member States reportedly aided the negotiations of the Aarhus Convention;[15]

11 United Nations Conference on Sustainable Development (Rio+20). (2012). *The Future We Want*, General Assembly Resolution 66/288, 27 July 2012, Rio de Janeiro, Brazil.

12 Directive 2003/4/EC of the European Parliament and of the Council of 28 January 2003 on Public Access to Environmental Information and repealing Council Directive 90/313/EEC, [2003] O.J. L 41/26.

13 Regulation (EC) No 1049/2001 of the European Parliament and of the Council of 30 May 2001 regarding public access to European Parliament, Council and Commission documents, [2001] O.J. L 145/43.

14 Regulation (EC) No 1367/2006 of the European Parliament and of the Council on the application of the provisions of the Aarhus Convention on Access to Information, Public Participation in Decision-making and Access to Justice in Environmental Matters to Community institutions and bodies, [2006] O.J. L 264/13.

15 Noteboom, C. (2003). Addressing the External Effects of Internal Environmental Decisions: Public Access to Environmental Information in the International Law Commission's Draft Articles on Prevention of Transboundary Harm. *NYU Environmental Law Journal, 12*, 245, citing as source the Commission Report on Directive 90/313/EEC; Jendrośka, J. (2012). Citizen's Rights in European Environmental Law: Stock-Taking of Key Challenges and Current Developments in Relation to Public Access to Information, Participation and Access to Justice. *Journal for European Environmental & Planning Law, 9*(1), 81; Jendroska, J. (2005). Aarhus Convention and Community Law: the Interplay. *Journal for European Environmental & Planning Law, 2*(1), 19; Directive 90/313/EEC is explicitly mentioned in the reports of the first, third and fifth sessions of the negotiations of the Convention. Retrieved from http://www.unece.org/env/pp/adwg.html.

in another case, the widespread adoption of Freedom of Information (FOI) laws in Europe contributed to the adoption, in 2009, of the Convention on Access to Official Documents of the Council of Europe (Tromsø Convention).[16]

The democratisation of environmental information was influenced by several theories and values that emerged and grew in importance across jurisdictions in the last decades. Among these are the transition to democratic state models, the transparency trend, the 'information governance' in environmental law and the evolution of human rights theory.

2.1.1. Transition to Democratic State Models

Democracy is strongly founded in the public's involvement in government decisions, so it would be incompatible with a democratic state model to refuse the public the information they need to form an opinion and participate effectively in the political processes.

The European Court of Human Rights (ECtHR) stated in the *Lingens* case: 'Freedom of the press affords the public one of the best means of discovering and forming an opinion of the ideas and attitudes of political leaders. More generally, freedom of political debate is at the very core of the concept of a democratic society'.[17]

Furthermore, the Declaration on the Freedom of Expression and Information, adopted in 1982 by the Committee of Ministers of the Council of Europe, asserts that freedom of expression and information is a fundamental element of the principles of genuine democracy, the rule of law and respect for human rights.[18]

Krämer relates the concept of transparency as an inherent quality of an 'open society'.[19] The open society is a political concept first used by the philosopher Karl Popper and refers to the society where it is acknowledged that nobody is the holder of the absolute truth, thus policy-makers and legislators

16 Convention on Access to Official Documents CETS No. 205, Council of Europe, 18 June 2009, Tromsø, Norway. See also Council of Europe. (2009). *Explanatory Report to the Council of Europe Convention on Access to Official Documents.* Retrieved from https://rm.coe.int/CoERMPublicCommonSearchServices/DisplayDCTMContent?documentId=09000016800d3836; Schram, F. (2011). From a General Right of Access to Environmental Information in the Aarhus Convention to a General Right of Access to All Information in Official Documents. In M. Pallemaerts (Ed.), *The Aarhus Convention at ten: interactions and tensions between conventional international law and EU environmental law*, p. 440. Groningen: Europa Law Publishing.

17 *Lingens v Austria*, App. 9815/82 (1986), para 42.

18 Hugelier, S. (2011). Freedom of expression and transparency: two sides of one coin. *Jura Falconis, 47*(1), 61–90, quoting 'The Council of Europe (C of E) in 1982: European Convention on Human Rights' (1987) European Yearbook C of E, 25–27.

19 Krämer, L. (2013). The EU, Access to Environmental Information and the Open Society. *ERA Forum*, 14(4), 463–474.

must carry out their duties in the open, promoting dialogue and discussion with the public.[20] On the contrary, a closed society would be one where most political decisions and laws are made behind closed doors, with little, if any, knowledge or involvement of the general public. According to Krämer, 'the closed society-concept is not compatible with democracy, with rights of the individuals and with transparent decision-making procedures'.[21]

In the EU, the Treaties of Lisbon assert the community's adhesion to the principles of an open society: Article 1 of the Treaty on European Union (TEU) states: 'This Treaty marks a new stage in the process of creating an even closer union among the peoples of Europe, in which decisions are taken as openly and as closely as possible to the citizen'.[22] Other references are found in Articles 9(3) and 11(2) TEU and Articles 15(1) and 298 of the Treaty on the Functioning of the European Union TFEU,[23] referring specifically to the EU's institutions. Transparency was thus enshrined as a fundamental principle of the Union.[24]

Regarding environmental information specifically, the Organisation for Economic Cooperation and Development (OECD) defines 'environmental democracy' as 'encompassing the availability of, and access to, environmental information, opportunities for participation and partnerships of individuals, firms and NGOs in environmental decision-making, and access to courts'.[25] This suggests that Principle 10 of the Rio Declaration (a direct precedent of the Aarhus Convention) basically establishes the conditions for 'environmental democracy'.

2.1.2. The Transparency Trend

Transparency is defined, for the purposes of this book, the disclosure of information to the public.[26] Generally speaking, *access to information* is the most visible form of transparency from a regulatory perspective, and both concepts may be used indistinctly for legal purposes.[27]

The right of access to information is materialised through Freedom of Information Acts (hereinafter FOIAs), which implement the subjective right of the public to request and obtain access to information.

20 Krämer, *Open society,* 2013, p. 465. Krämer refers to the book *The open society and his enemies,* by Karl Popper, published in 1945.
21 Krämer, *Open society,* 2013, p. 466.
22 Consolidated Version of the Treaty on European Union (TEU), [2012]. O.J. C 326/13.
23 Consolidated Version of the Treaty on the Functioning of the European Union (TFEU) [2012]. O.J. C 326/47.
24 Krämer, *Open society,* 2013.
25 OECD. (2001). *Environmental Outlook*, p. 255. Retrieved from http://dev.ulb.ac.be/ceese/CEESE/documents/ocde%20environment%20outlook.pdf.
26 Mol, A. P. J. (2010). Epilogue: The Future of Transparency: Power, Pitfalls and Promises. *Global Environmental Politics, 10*(3), 132–143. Mason (2010) also refers to transparency in terms of access to information.
27 Hugelier, *Freedom of Expression*, 2011.

Most FOIAs are usually based in one or both of the following precepts: (i) the idea of a transparent governmental model which involves anti-corruption measures improving accountability levels of public entities before other state (controlling) authorities and the public and (ii) the recognition of a subjective right of the people to access public information as part of the right of Freedom of Expression.

The first traces of transparency in the form of FOI laws are found in Sweden, with the adoption of the first FOIA in 1766, promoted by congressman Anders Chydenius, who was, in turn, inspired by Chinese practice. The act required that official documents be made available immediately upon request to the public at no charge.[28]

Interestingly, some authors consider the Colombian 'Political and Municipal Organisation Code', Law 149 of 1888, as the world's second act providing access to public information.[29] This law allowed citizens to request public documents from government entities, unless otherwise provided for by the law.[30]

After the adoption of the Universal Declaration of Human Rights in 1948, other countries followed suit. However, the actual 'explosion' of FOI laws occurred after 1990, when in a lapse of 15 years over 50 countries passed FOI laws, 40 of them between 1999 and 2005.[31] The shifting to greater openness in government coincides with the 'third wave' of transitions to democracy, a period between the mid 1970s and early 1990s in which several countries adopted free and fair elections to choose their governors.[32] As of today, over 100 states have adopted FOI laws.[33]

28 Ackerman, J. M., & Sandoval-Ballesteros, I. E. (2006). The Global Explosion of Freedom of Information Laws. *Administrative Law Review, 58*(1), 90.

29 Banisar, D. (2004). *Freedom of Information And Access to Government Record Laws Around the World.* Retrieved from https://www.ndi.org/files/2044_ww_freeinfo_010504.pdf; Ackerman & Sandoval-Ballesteros, *Global Explosion*, 2006.

30 Article 357: 'Every individual has a right to be given copies of the documents held in the Secretaries and files of the administrative offices, provided that (i) the documents are not reserved, (ii) the requester supplies the paper to be employed and pays the copyist, and (iii) the copies can be obtained under the supervision of an office employee and without overburdening their work. No employee shall give simple copies of reserved documents or authenticated copies of any documents without an order of the chief of the office' (translation by the author).

31 Ackerman & Sandoval-Ballesteros, *Global Explosion*, 2006.

32 Huntington, S. P. (1993). *The Third Wave: Democratization in the late twentieth century.* University of Oklahoma Press; Ackerman & Sandoval-Ballesteros, *Global Explosion*, 2006.

33 The list retrieved from Freedominfo.org, reported the FOI law of South Sudan (2014) as 102nd in the world. Retrieved from http://www.freedominfo.org/regions/global/foi-regimes/. The Center for Law and Democracy also publishes a list with a rating for each country. Retrieved from http://www.rti-rating.org/country-data. Additional information can be found at http://www.access-info.org/standards-laws.

This trend supports the idea that transparency is no longer only a political goal for democratic states, but a seed of the Right to Information, which is in turn an attribute of citizenship that can be exercised and must be guaranteed by states. Some authors go further to argue that the right to information is not only a faculty but a duty of citizens in a democracy. According to Roberts, 'citizen participation in holding government to account is not just a productive possibility under democracy. It is a duty and a responsibility'.[34]

Transparency as a democratic value and as a standard is highly relevant from the perspective of procedural environmental rights. The laws providing free public access to information are routinely used to access environmental information. Conversely, the provisions on access to environmental information are frequently based on principles of transparency and the general aim to make public authorities more accountable to the public for the environmental decisions they adopt and the management of public resources allocated to environmental matters.

The objectives generally stated in FOI laws clearly coincide and support the aims attributed to good environmental governance. In many ways, transparency legal instruments and environmental laws can be mutually supportive. Some of the main purposes found in FOI laws are:

- Greater involvement and awareness of the public in political affairs and the activities of the government, participation in policy-making and public surveillance of democratic processes.[35]
- More reliable economic systems that foster foreign investments and contribute to keep a healthy market.[36]
- Less corruption in public administration and better government practices, efficiency in public administration.[37]
- Greater transparency also leads to greater legitimacy for the administration, as it becomes more accountable.[38]

The previous review reveals how transparency is considered an essential component of a democratic society, and the specific right of access to

34 Roberts, A. (2001). Structural Pluralism and the Right to Information. *The University of Toronto Law Journal, 51*(3), 243–271, esp 245.

35 Bovens, M. (2002). Information Rights: Citizenship in the information Society. *The Journal of Political Philosophy, 10*(3), 317–341.

36 Vishwanath, T., & Kaufmann, D. (2001). Toward Transparency: New Approaches and Their Application to Financial Markets. *The World Bank Researcher Observer, 16*(1), 41–57.

37 Rose-Ackerman, S. (1999). *Corruption and Government: Causes, Consequences and Reform.* Cambridge University Press, asserting that increasing transparency has also been used to improve legitimacy of private organisations.

38 Savino, M. (2011). *The Right to Open Public Administrations in Europe: Emerging Legal Standards.* Retrieved from http://www.epsa2011.eu/files/Themes_2011/OECD Administrative Transparency 1010.pdf.

information is increasingly being recognised at national and international level, though not without challenge.

2.1.3. 'Informational Governance' and Environmental Reform

In close connection with the above, a trend towards 'information governance' has been detected as the result of the increased value of information for political, economic and social processes. Environmental governance has been greatly affected by these new informational dynamics.

Mol defends the idea of 'informational governance' as a system in which information, its processes and technologies play a central role.[39] In his theory about environmental governance reform, the advent of new information technologies, the recognition of a general right-to-know (and its implementation in national regulations providing access to public information held by state entities), paired with the increased participation of private actors in transparency-driven initiatives (mostly voluntary), has produced a shift in environmental governance where information is the new power currency.

According to Langley, the rise of transparency as an organising principle in global environmental governance is closely associated with the partial privatisation of that governance, evident in the growth of voluntary forms of information disclosure (*e.g.* environmental auditing and management systems).[40]

The impact of the 'informational governance' from an environmental perspective has been examined, for example, as a driver for consumer behaviour towards more sustainable products and as an enhancer for environmental activism,[41] but it may very well be at the core of more profound structural changes regarding the role of the state, the non-profit sector and private entities in environmental governance.

Arguably, the new era of information influenced a shift from passive disclosure to what can be called proactive transparency, exemplified by the adoption of Pollutant Releases and Transfers Registers (PRTRs) and the disclosure of information to the public and not only to government agencies.

According to a World Resource Institute Report, three main forces have triggered the growing worldwide demand for public access to environmental information: (i) the urgency and scope of environmental problems, which called for wide support and thus information sharing; (ii) the increased activism in civil society and (iii) the developments and spreading in information technology and communication means.[42]

39 Mol, A. P.J. (2008). *Environmental Reform in the Information Age: the Contours of Informational Governance.* Cambridge University Press.

40 Langley, P. (2001). Transparency in the Making of Global Environmental Governance. *Global Society 15 (1), 73–92*; quoted by Mason, M. (2010). Information Disclosure and Environmental Rights: the Aarhus Convention. *Global Environmental Politics, 10*(3), 10–31.

41 Mol, *Environmental Reform*, 2008.

42 Mol, *Environmental Reform*, 2008.

Much of the change in the demand and control of environmental information has happened in the realm of private organisations: company environmental reporting, eco-label schemes, certification procedures (*e.g.* ISO series), the adoption of pollutant releases registers, transparency requirements from the stock markets regulators and voluntary initiatives are some examples. It is only logical, then, that some of the main challenges and opportunities of the information era for environmental governance will touch upon private interests and, furthermore, they are likely to occur in the ambit of private relations between the public and the private entities, where states will only play a minor role or will be cut out of the information transaction and its consequences.

2.1.4. The Evolution of Human Rights Theory

The recognition of a universal right to freedom of expression paved the way for the enactment of FOIAs and laws for access to environmental information, but this was not achieved in a straightforward manner.

The first trace that resembled what is today understood as 'freedom of expression' was the English Bill of Rights, adopted in 1689, which granted 'freedom of speech in parliament'.[43] One century later, the French National Assembly's Declaration of the Rights of Man and of the Citizen issued in 1789, in the context of the French Revolution, included the right to freedom of expression in the following terms:

> Article 11: The free communication of ideas and opinions is one of the most precious of the rights of man. Every citizen may, accordingly, speak, write, and print with freedom, but shall be responsible for such abuses of this freedom as shall be defined by law.[44]

The international status of the right to freedom of expression was formally settled with its inclusion in the Universal Declaration of Human Rights in 1948, and the International Covenant on Civil and Political Rights (ICCPR), adopted in 1966.

The former introduced freedom of expression in Article 19, stating:

> Everyone has the right to freedom of opinion and expression; this right includes freedom to hold opinions without interference and to seek, receive and impart information and ideas through any media and regardless of frontiers.[45]

43 Bill of Rights, England, 1689: 'That the Freedome of Speech and Debates or Proceedings in Parlyament ought not to be impeached or questioned in any Court or Place out of Parlyament'.

44 La Déclaration Universelle des Droits de l'homme et du Citoyen, 26 August 1789, Article 11.

45 Universal Declaration of Human Rights, 12 December 1948, G.A. Res. 217A, UN GAOR, 3d Sess., 1st plen. mtg., UN Doc A/810., Article 19.

Article 19 of the ICCPR, in turn, states that

> Everyone shall have the right to freedom of expression; this right shall include freedom to seek, receive and impart information and ideas of all kinds, regardless of frontiers, either orally, in writing or in print, in the form of art, or through any other media of his choice.[46]

With a similar wording, the right of expression can also be found in the European Convention on Human Rights (Article 10),[47] the Inter-American Convention on Human Rights (Article 13)[48] and the African Charter on Human and People's Rights (Article 9),[49] establishing a worldwide-accepted attribute of the human person.

The recognition of this right must be construed to not only preclude arbitrary forms of government control or censorship, but to impose an obligation on states to guarantee the effective exercise of the right to information, thus requiring positive actions for this purpose.[50]

The positive recognition of a subjective right to freedom of expression entails the possibility to enforce this right before state authorities and others. The possibility of enforcement is, arguably, what transforms principles into rights,[51] thus the explicit recognition of the right of expression in international, regional and national legislation has positively influenced the enactment of freedom of information laws, the expansion of the existing transparency-aimed regulations and the abolishment of barriers to access public (and even private) information.

One of the reasons for the far-reaching impact of freedom of expression is that it has been construed to include several expression-related liberties:

- The right to seek information and ideas.
- The right to receive information and ideas.
- The right to impart information and ideas.[52]

46 International Covenant on Civil and Political Rights, 16 December 1966 (entered into force on 23 March 1976), 999 UNTS 171.

47 Convention for the Protection of Human Rights and Fundamental Freedoms (European Convention on Human Rights, as amended), 4 November 1950 (entered into force on 3 September 1953).

48 Inter-American Convention on Human Rights, 21 November 1969 (entered into force on 18 July 1978), 1144 UNTS 123.

49 African Charter on Human and Peoples' Rights, Organization of African Unity (African Union), Banjul, Gambia, 27 June 1981 (entered into force on 21 October 1986).

50 Ackerman & Sandoval-Ballesteros, *Global Explosion*, 2006.

51 Banisar, D., Parmar, S., de Silva, L., & Excell, C. (2012). Moving from Principles to Rights: Rio 2012 and Access to Information, Public Participation, and Justice. *Sustainable Development Law & Policy*, Spring.

52 Hugelier, *Freedom of Expression*, 2011.

The right to 'seek' information as part of the right of expression is clear in the wording of the ICCPR, which explicitly mentions it, unlike Article 10 of the ECHR, which does not contain this specific word. Although freedom of expression is part of the core democratic principles prevalent in most European countries which are Parties to the ECHR, the European Court of Human Rights (hereinafter ECtHR) was reluctant at first to accept that Article 10 includes the right to seek information and the correlative obligation of state authorities to provide it, but it seems to have moved past its former reservations and recent case-law points unequivocally to the existence of a right of access to public information within Article 10 'Freedom of expression' of the ECHR.[53] Access to information is thus a key component of the right to freedom of expression, which is, in turn, a cornerstone in any democracy.[54] The ECtHR has stated that 'Freedom of expression constitutes one of the essential foundations of a democratic society and one of the basic conditions for its progress and each individual's self-fulfilment'.[55]

The rights to private property, business confidentiality and intellectual property, among others, when explicitly protected by law in the specific jurisdictions, act as a counterweight to freedom of expression rights.

This delicate balance is made explicit in FOI laws and other pieces of legislation providing for access to environmental information, which usually include a list of exceptions to the general rule of disclosure. In these cases, human rights courts are faced with the task of interpreting and limiting the application of the exceptions to the right of freedom to expression. The ECtHR, for instance, stated that the exceptions to freedom of expression 'must be narrowly interpreted and the necessity for any restriction must be established convincingly'.[56] Any interference must also be proportionate and national authorities must give relevant and sufficient justification for it.[57]

53 For the former interpretation see *Leander v Sweden*, App. 9248/81 (1987); *Gaskin v UK,* App. 10454/83 (1989); and *Guerra and others v Italy,* App. 14967/89 (1998). For the more recent trend see *Sdruženi Jihoðeské Matky v Czech Republic*, App. 19101/03 (2006), para 10–11; *Társaság a Szabadságjogokért v Hungary*, App. 37374/05 (2011); *Kennedi v Hungary,* App. 31475/05 (2009); *Gillberg v Sweden,* App. 41723/06 (2013); *Shapovalov v Ukraine*, App. 45835/05 (2012); *Youth Initiative for Human Rights v Serbia, App. 48135/06 (2013); Österreichische Vereinigung zur Erhaltung, Stärkung und Schaffung eines wirtschaftlich gesunden Land- Und Forst-Wirtschaftlichen Grundbesitzes v Austria*, App. 39534/07 (2013).

54 Alexander Meiklejohn argues that the concept of democracy is that of self-government by the people and in order for it to work, requires an informed electorate. For people to be properly informed there must be no constraints on the free flow of information and ideas. See Meiklejohn, A. (1948). *Free Speech and Its Relation to Self-Government*. The Lawbook Exchange, p. 46.

55 *Lingens v Austria, 1986*.

56 *The Observer and Guardian v UK*, App.13585/88 (1991). See also Hugelier, *Freedom of Expression*, 2011.

57 Van Dijk, P., van Hoof, F., van Rijn, A., & Zwaak, L. (2006). *Theory and Practice of the European Convention on Human Rights* (4th ed.). Intersentia.

A fairly unexplored human rights theory in support of access to environmental information is the recognition of a fundamental right to a healthy environment.[58] The Aarhus Convention states in its preamble that 'every person has the right to live in an environment adequate to his or her health and well-being', and cites several international declarations expressing the need to ensure a healthy environment for the well-being of the individuals,[59] but this premise is not fully reflected in the contents of the Convention's provisions, which focus almost exclusively on procedural guarantees. The actual coupling between the procedural provisions of the Convention and the substantive right to a healthy environment has been questioned in the past.[60]

The Escazú Agreement, on the contrary, includes among its provisions an explicit recognition of the substantial right to a healthy environment and the correlative obligation of states to guarantee it. Article 4(1) states: 'Each Party shall guarantee the right of every person to live in a healthy environment and any other universally-recognized human right related to the present Agreement.' This would be the first international (regional) binding instrument establishing an explicit obligation upon states to ensure the right to a healthy environment for the people. Since the Escazú Agreement only entered into force in April 2021, it is yet to be seen how this provision will impact the implementation process and the exercise of participatory rights in the states that ratified the agreement.

In examining the international instruments up until the adoption of the Escazú Agreement, it can be argued that a human right to access environmental information may have a stronger standing in human rights theory than the substantive right to a healthy environment. As a procedural right, it is seen as a natural expression of longstanding civil and political liberties, supported on the premise of balancing the interests of government and society,[61] whilst the existence of a human right to a healthy environment was, until recently, a largely unsettled matter.[62] It must be noted, however, that

58 Roesler suggests that this could be explained by the collective nature of the right to a healthy environment. Roesler, S. M. (2012). The Nature of the Environmental Right to Know. *Ecology Law Quarterly, 39*, 989–1040.

59 Among them the UN World Charter of Nature (1982) and the European Charter on Environment and Health (1989), World Health Organisation (WHO).

60 See Mason, *Information Disclosure*, 2010.

61 Fitzmaurice, M. (2002). Some Reflections on Public Participation in Environmental Matters as a Human Right in International Law. *Non-State Actors and International Law*, 2, 1. See also Pedersen, O. W. (2009). European Environmental Human Rights and Environmental Rights: A Long Time Coming? *The Georgetown International Environmental Law Review*, 21, 73; arguing that a substantive right to the environment in international law is, at best, emerging.

62 See Lewis, B. (2012). Environmental Rights or a Right to the Environment? Exploring the Nexus between Human Rights and Environmental Protection. *Macquarie Journal of International and Comparative Environmental Law, 8*(1), 36–47; Turner, S. (2004). The Human Right to a Good Environment – The sword in the stone. *Non-State Actors and International Law, 4*(3), 277–301; Shelton, D. (2006). Human Rights and the Environment: What Specific Environmental

recognising a subjective individual right to a healthy environment can have far-reaching consequences in favour of the right of public access to environmental information. In Colombia and South Africa people have been able to access information from private entities because it was needed for the protection of their fundamental rights, including the right to a healthy environment as recognised in their respective constitutions.[63]

2.2. Fundamental Notions of Private Entities

2.2.1. Public v Private

The origin of the differentiation between the public and the private can be traced back to two fragments of Justinian's *Institutions* (Corpus iuris). They define public law as *what is referred to the condition of the Roman State*, and private law as *what concerns the individual's utility.*[64]

The terms 'public' and 'private' have been widely used in different scientific fields such as political sciences, economics and social studies, where they are construed to include a wide array of phenomena, but they usually have in common the plural connotation of what is 'public' and the singularity of what is 'private'. Similarly, 'public' usually implies a common use or finality, while 'private' points out to a particular interest, perhaps in opposition to the interests of others.

Bobbio explains the dichotomy as two complementary spheres of a universe, which are mutually exclusive and exhaustive. This means that every entity can be categorised in one of the spheres, but no entity can be included in both. This also means that the definition of one of the terms carries an implicit definition of the other, as the negation of the first, *e.g.* 'peace' means no-war.[65]

In the legal field, the division between both concepts is founded in the general notion of utility: to the individual utility is opposed the common utility. The notion can be clearly appreciated in the modern concepts of 'public' and 'private' interest. The state is the quintessential administrator of the 'common' interests, representing the collective, the society organised under the law. Therefore, 'public' becomes state-related and, by exclusion, private is everything outside the state's scope of intervention and action, often concerned with individual interests only.

Rights Have Been Recognised? *Denver Journal International Law and Policy, 35*, 129–174.

63 See Zuluaga Madrid, J. (2017). Access to Environmental Information from Private Entities: A Rights-Based Approach. *Review of European, Comparative and International Environmental Law, 26*(1), 38–53.

64 Bobbio, N. (1989). *Estado, Gobierno y Sociedad.* Mexico: Fondo de Cultura Económica, pp. 11–12.

65 Guerrero, O. (2003). Lo Privado versus lo Público: La Administración Pública entre Escila y Caribdis. *Revista Signos Públicos*, 4(8), 45–86. (Translation by the author.)

Based on the previous conceptions, 'public law' is usually defined as the corpus of legal dispositions aimed at regulating the relations between the state and its citizens, or in-between states; and 'private law' is the part of the legal framework aimed at regulating relations in-between private citizens.

Public law as a systematic group of legal norms was born later than private law. The main institutions of the private law in the Roman State were family, property, contracts and testaments, which were included in Justinian's *Digest* (AD 530–533). Public law made its appearance as an independent and coherent corpus of law by the time the modern state was conceived, in approximately the 16th century.[66]

The modern state's ideals called for a powerful governmental apparatus, one that could effectively intervene to regulate the behaviour of the citizens. Hegel considered the absorption of civil society by the state as a form of progress, in the same way as the modern era was conceived as a time of progress, when the relentless development of the state dominated over individualisms.[67]

Greater state intervention is clearly reflected in the economic sector, as the states become the exclusive providers of many services for the citizens and operate directly the countries' most important industries. According to Bobbio, the *publicization* of the 'private' is one of the facets of the changing process for the most advanced industrial societies.[68]

Nowadays, the opposite process is predominating in western societies. Private companies are increasingly performing functions that used to be controlled by governments, such as the provision of public utilities, nature resources exploitation and the construction of public infrastructure. This phenomenon has been widely referred to as 'privatisation'.[69]

Privatisation is said to undermine the effectiveness of FOI laws, when they have been designed to apply to government or government-adjacent agencies, because the information related to the services and activities that are passed to private bodies escapes the orbit of the law and it can no longer be publicly accessed. There is also the well-founded fear that these entities do not conform to the transparency standards set out to public authorities and agencies.[70]

But what exactly makes a company 'private' or 'public'? It is ultimately up to each state to determine in their domestic legislation (and sometimes in the statutes of each legal field) what is to be referred to as 'public' or 'private' entities. Some of the usual factors considered to determine if a certain organisation is public or private in nature, are the following:

66 Guerrero, *Privado vs Público*, 2003.
67 Guerrero, *Privado vs Público*, 2003.
68 Guerrero, *Privado vs Público*, 2003.
69 Ebbesson, J. (2011). Public Participation and Privatisation in Environmental Matters: An Assessment of the Aarhus Convention. *Erasmus Law Review, 4*(2).
70 Roberts, *Structural Pluralism*, 2001.

- Origin of the company's funds.
- Legal nature of the people who are part of the organisation (*e.g.* state agencies or individuals).
- Aims: general or individual interests pursued by the organisation.
- Objectives: if the activities performed by the organisation can be considered of public service or utility.
- The level of autonomy of the organisation, *i.e.* if it's controlled by the government or by any state authority.

Based on these or similar general criteria, laws and statutes define, for the purposes of a certain legal matter, what is to be understood as 'public' and 'private' entities.

The specific laws that determine this division in each jurisdiction are reviewed to analyse the scope of the legislation, however, the elements considered by legislators and policymakers in defining these terms are at the core of the present research and will be given special attention.

The boundaries seem to be less than clear considering new types of organisations such as cooperatives, foundations and NGOs which, despite being formed by private or individual persons, pursue 'public' aims, defend collective interests and, sometimes, are financed with public monies and perform public functions.

Calland refers to the distinction between public and private entities for the purposes of access to public information as a 'false divide', which is 'increasingly irrelevant and confusing given the blurred lines between the two sectors and the transfer of power, functions and responsibilities from one to the other'.[71]

Indeed, the continuous exchange of public powers and administrative functions between government agencies and private corporations, added to the similarity in the potential impact of public and private institutions alike over public interests and rights, makes us wonder if a distinctive treatment regarding obligations of transparency and disclosure of public interest information is still justified.

2.2.2. Definition of Private Entities

For the purposes of this book, the term 'private entities' will refer to physical or legal persons who, under national law, are not considered public entities, and which engage in business, professional activities or the provision of services, acting in that capacity.

For illustrative purposes only, it can be ascertained that private entities generally enjoy the following prerogatives:

- Autonomy in the direction of its business or social purpose, within the limits of the law.

71 Calland, R. (2007). Prizing Open the Profit-Making World. In A. Florini (Ed.), *The Right to Know: Transparency for an Open World*. Columbia University Press, p. 239.

- Their financial resources do not originate in public funds, thus are not usually subject to public financial accountability rules.[72]
- Liberty to enter contracts by exercising their freedom of will and not subject to procurement regulations.
- They may serve private or for-profit purposes or non-profit ideals as well.
- They may act in regulated or non-regulated markets but are not under the administrative control of any public authority.

The terms 'private company' and 'private corporation' will be used to refer specifically to commercial, for-profit organisations.

The term 'public company' will refer to companies that are listed in the common stock market exchange, in accordance with the US law definition,[73] but, unless otherwise stated, this type of companies will also be included in the general expression 'private companies' as far as they can be identified according to the general pointers set above.

2.2.3. *Public and Private Information*

The question about what can be considered public or private information can be interpreted and responded to in different ways. A first, simple parameter to classify information as public or private is whether the information has been published and thus is in the public domain, as opposed to information which is held by private persons and entities for their own use and kept from the general public. This way to look at the question does not present a lot of controversy but is not very helpful to determine what information *should* be disclosed or *belongs* in the public domain.

Another criterion to establish the public or private character of a piece of information may be by identifying the *ownership* of that information. In general, information which is formed, collected and processed by public authorities, using public resources, is deemed to be a public possession,[74] while the

72 The obvious exception being public listed companies subject to the supervision of public authorities such as the Securities Exchange Commission (SEC) in the US, which nevertheless is not equivalent to the level of public scrutiny usually afforded to entities managing public resources.

73 According to 12 CFR 363.1 [Title 12 – Banks and Banking; Chapter III – Federal Deposit Insurance Corporation; Subchapter B – Regulations and Statements of General Policy; Part 363 – Annual Independent Audits and Reporting Requirements]: '[P]ublic company means an insured depository institution or other company that has a class of securities registered with the U.S. Securities and Exchange Commission or the appropriate Federal banking agency under Section 12 of the Securities Exchange Act of 1934 and non-public company means an insured depository institution or other company that does not meet the definition of a public company'.

74 Open Society Justice Initiative and others (2008). *Written Comments on the Case of Társaság a Szabadságjogokért v. Hungary.* Retrieved from https://www.opensocietyfoundations.org/sites/default/files/hungary_20080901.pdf.

production of private individuals or enterprises is private property and, in principle, its divulgation cannot be forced by the state or by others outside the scope of specific reporting obligations. Private information is generally considered a private possession and, as such, it is subject to special protection under the law preventing its unduly divulgation and exploitation by others. Intellectual property laws assume that the rightful owner of a certain information should be able to profit from it and maintain its exclusive rights. However, information of private origin submitted to a public authority in the framework of a public administrative procedure becomes public from the perspective of ownership, *e.g.* applications for environmental permits.

From the viewpoint of the contents of a document and the legal possibility to obtain access, the Colombian Constitutional Court has drawn distinctions between public, private, and semi-private information. *Public* information is all the information that can be freely obtained and disseminated without restrictions, it doesn't matter if it can be considered personal or general, such as official documents, court rulings and information about the civil state of people and family conformation; *semi-private* information is defined as records, personal or non-personal, not considered public, in which a sector of society may have a legitimate interest, whose access is subject to minimum restrictions, thus can only be obtained or offered by instruction of an administrative authority acting within its functions or in the framework of private data management regulations (*e.g.* social security data, financial behaviour, income data). Conversely, *private information* is out of bounds of the public sphere and can only be accessed by virtue of a judicial order, a notable example being the business books holding commercial transactions, documents and other data related to the day-to-day functioning of businesses.[75] On top of this, the Court distinguishes *classified or secret information*, which refers to personal information closely related to the fundamental rights of the person such as intimacy and dignity, which cannot be publicly accessed, not even through a judicial order, as it belongs strictly in the private ambit of the holder. Examples of this last category are information about sexual preference and genetic data.[76] Notwithstanding the didactic value of this classification to help Colombian legal operators to correctly apply the rules about public access to information, this is not as helpful as it could be for the present analysis because it poses the question of the public character of the information from an *ad hoc* perspective based on existing legislation, and as a result, it does not offer many pointers to decide whether a specific environmental information *should be* public, private or something else.

The Aarhus Convention does not distinguish between private and public information for the purpose of public access. It does however exclude

75 Colombian Constitutional Court, Case T-238/18, Judgment of 26 June 2018, M. P. Gloria Stella Ortiz Delgado.

76 Colombian Constitutional Court, Case T-729/02, Judgment of 5 September 2002, M.P. Eduardo Montealegre Lynett.

information which the public authority does not hold from the duty of disclosure, in a much more practical approach than defining which information is considered public on top of the other provisions establishing when the public should get access.

For the purposes of this study, it will be understood that information held by public authorities or on their behalf is *prima facie* public, unless explicitly labelled otherwise. An assumption will be made that even when there are actual definitions of 'public' versus 'private' or even 'semi-private' information, this issue is only marginally relevant when there are more specific legal provisions establishing if certain information can be accessed by the public and which information is exempted. This is because when the law provides a right of public access, it matters very little if the information was initially labelled 'private' or 'public'.

The 'public' or 'private' quality of the information will only be used as an auxiliary criterion for the purposes of the present study, since most of the legal instruments omit this analysis to focus instead on the nature of the authority *holding* the information and whether it can be exempted from disclosure for the protection of public or private interests.

2.2.4. The Protection of Business Confidentiality

The protection of business confidentiality is usually expressed in general terms due to the lack of a global definition of what is a 'business secret' and is, consequently, worth of special protection against disclosure. Not even in domestic legislation is always possible to find an explicit definition of the concept.[77]

Other terms for the same concept are 'trade secrets', 'commercially sensitive information' and 'confidential business information', all of them equally obscure. Trade secrets are usually not protected under intellectual property laws because they constitute a different category that is rather complementary to intellectual property rights.[78] They can be found at the origin of patents, copyrights, designs or other intangible rights but are not considered intellectual property rights (IPR) themselves.[79]

Notwithstanding the lack of a generally accepted definition of 'business secret', some efforts have been made to set criteria that allow identifying which information should be considered in this category for the purposes of legal protection against its undue divulgation.

77 Czapracka, K. A. (2008). Antitrust and Trade Secrets: The US and the EU Approach. *Santa Clara Computer & High Tech L.J.*, 24(207), 231.

78 Some authors have defended the conceptual advantages of defining trade secret law as a component of Intellectual Property Law. See Lemley, M. A. (2011). The Surprising Virtues of Treating Trade Secrets as IP Rights. In R. Dreyfuss, P. Newman, & K. J. Strandburg (Eds.) *The Law and Theory of Trade Secrecy*, Edward Elgar Publishing, p. 640.

79 Gabel, D. (2014). *The proposed Directive on Trade Secrets in the EU.* Retrieved from http://www.whitecase.com/publications/article/proposed-directive-trade-secrets-eu.

On 8 June 2016, following a proposal from the European Commission, the European Parliament and the Council adopted a Directive 'on the protection of undisclosed know-how and business information (trade secrets) against their unlawful acquisition, use and disclosure'.[80] The Directive defines 'trade secrets' as information that (i) is secret in the sense that it is not generally known among or readily accessible to persons within the circles that normally deal with the kind of information in question (ii) has commercial value because it is secret (iii) has been subject to reasonable steps under the circumstances, by the person lawfully in control of the information, to keep it secret. This definition echoes the definition of 'undisclosed information' in the Agreement on Trade-related Aspects of Intellectual Property Rights – TRIPS and is also similar to the definition in the US Uniform Trade Secrets Act.[81]

Article 339 of the Treaty on the Functioning of the European Union (TFEU) establishes a limitation for EU's institutions to divulge business secrets in the following terms:

> The members of the institutions of the Union, the members of committees, and the officials and other servants of the Union shall be required, even after their duties have ceased, not to disclose information of the kind covered by the obligation of professional secrecy, in particular information about undertakings, their business relations or their cost components.

Furthermore, Council Regulation 1/2003, setting rules on the enforcement of competition rules, provides in Article 27 (2) that parties concerned shall have access to the file 'subject to the legitimate interest of undertakings in the protection of their business secrets', which, however, will not preclude the Commission from 'disclosing and using information necessary to prove an infringement'.[82]

However, neither the text of the TFEU nor that of Regulation 1/2003 identifies which types of information are intended to be protected by the obligation of professional secrecy and neither provide a definition of 'business secrets'.[83]

80 Directive (EU) 2016/943 on the protection of undisclosed know-how and business information (trade secrets) against their unlawful acquisition, use and disclosure, [2016] O.J. L 157/1.

81 Agreement on Trade-Related Aspects of Intellectual Property Rights [TRIPS], Annex 1C of the General Agreement on Tariffs and Trade (GATT), World Trade Organisation, 1994, Article 39 (2); US Uniform Trade Secrets Act [UTSA] § 1 (amended 1985), 14 U.L.A. 437 (2006).

82 Council Regulation (EC) 1/2003 of 16 December 2002 on the implementation of the rules on competition laid down in Articles 81 and 82 of the Treaty, [2003] OJ L1/1.

83 See Jellema, C. P. (2002). The Redheaded Stepchild of Community Competition Law: The Third Party and its Right to be Heard in Competition Proceedings. *Boston University International Law Journal*, 20, 211.

The CJEU has used a definition of 'business secrets' as 'information of which not only disclosure to the public but also mere transmission to a person other than the one that provided the information may seriously harm the latter's interests',[84] a rather general definition that may or may not actually relate with the business. In the case of *Bank Austria,* the same court set out criteria for the definition of confidential information in general (business secrets and other confidential information) establishing the following conditions:

a That the information should be known only to a limited number of persons;
b That disclosure of the information must be liable to cause serious harm to the person who has provided that information or to third parties; and
c That the interests liable to be harmed by disclosure must objectively be worthy of protection.[85]

The third condition clearly indicates the need to undertake a balancing test to assess the weight of the interests endangered by disclosure, which will be analysed considering 'the public interest that the activities of the EU's institutions take place as openly as possible'.[86] This assessment should not be undertaken in this instance, however, but rather when the information has effectively been identified as 'confidential'. It is in this scenario where a decision must be made on whether the information must remain secret or if there are other interests that outweigh the owner's interest in withholding it.[87]

From a Common Law perspective, the definition of 'trade secret' in the US is adopted in the Uniform Trade Secrets Act (UTSA). It defines trade secret as:

[I] Information, including a formula, pattern, compilation, program device, method, technique, or process, that:
Derives independent economic value, actual or potential, from not being generally known to, and not being readily ascertainable by proper means by, other persons who can obtain economic value from its disclosure or use, and

84 CJEU (First Instance), Case T-353/94, *Postbank NV v Commission*, Judgment of 18 September 1996, para 87.
85 CJEU (First Instance), Case T-198/03, *Bank Austria Creditansalt AG v Commission*, Judgment of 30 May 2006, para 71.
86 *Bank Austria Creditansalt AG v Commission*, 2006, para 71.
87 See Carlton, R., Lawrence, J., & Mcelwee, M. (2008). Confidentiality and Disclosure in European Commission Antitrust Proceedings – The Case for Clarity. *European Competition Journal*, 4(401), 405: 'If, in the act of deciding whether a particular item of information constitutes business secrets or other confidential information, a case-by-case balancing test is conducted, the apparent protection against disclosure in the legislative texts is stripped of meaning'.

Is the subject of efforts that are reasonable under the circumstances to maintain its secrecy.[88]

In conclusion, the definition of 'business secret' or 'trade secret', for the purposes of the protection of the legitimate economic interests of a legal or natural person which could be harmed by disclosure, is mostly a formal concept that must be given substance on a case by case basis following the general criteria set by the judges and administrative authorities.

Based on the preliminary exam of the applicable norms in the EU and the US, essential attributes of the 'business secrets' would be (i) the confidential nature of the information, that is, the information is not in the public domain and the owner takes appropriate measures to keep it secret; and (ii) this circumstance represents a competitive advantage to the owner of the information (*i.e.* its disclosure would entail an economic harm to the owner).

The terminology is quite important for the interpretation of the rules containing exceptions to the general right of access to information to prevent undermining the effectiveness of the general right of access. Within the scope of the Aarhus Convention, grounds for refusal to disclosure are to be interpreted in a restrictive way (Aarhus Convention, Article 4(4)), thus an open-ended concept of 'business secret' is hardly compatible with the spirit and aims of the Convention.[89]

2.3. The Aarhus Convention: Fundamental Concepts and Contribution

The Aarhus Convention was adopted at the Fourth Ministerial 'Environment for Europe' Conference, held in Aarhus, Denmark, in June 1998. It entered into force on 30 October 2001, on the 90th day after its 16th ratification.

The objective of the Convention, as stated in Article 1, is to provide for each Party to establish the rights of access to information, public participation in decision-making, and access to justice in environmental matters in order to contribute to the protection of the right of every person of present and future generations to live in an environment adequate to his or her health and well-being.

To materialise its objective, the Convention establishes procedural measures, which would enable citizens to participate by exercising the three essential rights of public participation: (i) access to Information, (ii) participation in decision-making and (iii) access to justice in environmental matters.

88 The UTSA has been so far adopted in forty six states. See more in Czapracka, *Antitrus and Trade Secrets*, 2008.

89 UNEP. (2015). *Putting Rio Principle 10: An Implementation Guide for the UNEP Bali Guidelines for the Development of National Legislation on Access to Information, Public Participation and Access to Justice in Environmental Matters.* Nairobi, p. 34. Retrieved from https://wedocs.unep.org/bitstream/handle/20.500.11822/11201/UNEP%20MGSB-SGBS%20BALI%20GUIDELINES-Interactive.pdf?sequence=1&isAllowed=y: 'Clear definitions of terms such as "commercial business information" are very important in establishing fair, balanced and enforceable regimes'.

The most representative precedent of the principles comprised in the Aarhus Convention is the Rio Declaration (1992), the non-binding manifesto adopted at the United Nations Conference on Environment and Development carried out in Rio de Janeiro, Brazil, in June 1992.

Principle 10 of the Rio Declaration explicitly states the importance of public participation in the planning and management of environmental resources, establishing three main ways to allow such participation: to provide access to information concerning the environment that is held by public authorities, the opportunity to participate in decision-making processes and effective access to judicial and administrative procedures including redress and remedy.

One of the fundamental concepts adopted in the Aarhus Convention and related to the research is the concept of 'public authority', which includes government agencies and other entities performing public administrative functions and others in charge of environmental services under their control. Notably, the Convention adopts a functional approach in the definition of public authority, extending the scope of the provisions to reach persons and entities not usually defined as 'public', either because they are funded with private capital or otherwise governed by private law. The Aarhus Implementation Guide explains about the inclusion of private entities:

> Recent developments in privatized solutions to the provision of public services have added a layer of complexity to the definition. The Convention tries to make it clear that such innovations cannot take public services or activities out of the realm of public information, participation or justice.[90]

Other important concepts are the definition of 'environmental information' for the purposes of the right of access (thoroughly examined in Chapter 4) and the terms 'public' and 'public concerned', which limit the scope of beneficiaries and cases in which preferential access to information must be given to the public directly affected by a decision. Examples are found in Article 6(2): 'The public concerned shall be informed, either by public notice or individually as appropriate, early in an environmental decision-making procedure, and in an adequate, timely and effective manner, inter alia, of…'; Article 6(6): 'Each Party shall require the competent public authorities to give the public concerned access for examination, upon request where so required under national law, free of charge and as soon as it becomes available, to all information relevant to the decision-making referred to in this article…'; and Article 9(2): 'Each Party shall, within the framework of its national legislation, ensure that members of the public concerned (…) have access to a review procedure before a court of law and/or another independent and impartial body established by law, to challenge the substantive and procedural legality of any decision, act or omission subject to the provisions of article 6…'

90 United Nations Economic Commission for Europe – UNECE (2014). *The Aarhus Convention: An Implementation Guide*, 2nd ed., UN Doc. ECE/CEP/72/Rev.1., p. 46.

Finally, the exceptions regime found in Article 4(4) of in the Aarhus Convention constitutes an important referent of the limitations to the right of access to environmental information, especially the exceptions for the protection of business confidentiality and the protection of intellectual property in the context of this research.

2.3.1. Environmental Participation under Aarhus

As previously mentioned, the Convention is structured around three procedural rights: access to environmental information, participation in decision-making in environmental matters and access to justice. The first pillar, access to information, is conceived as an autonomous guarantee, but also as a prerequisite for the effective exercise of the other two procedural rights.

The right of access to environmental information as prescribed in the Aarhus Convention will be taken throughout the study as a point of reference to compare with the other regimes in aspects such as conditions for access, exceptions, scope of the information and the obligated subjects. The provisions regarding the right to participate in decision-making in environmental matters will be taken as a guide to determine what information is needed to ensure effective public participation, to act as an auxiliary criterion in resolving potential conflicts between public access and confidentiality claims. The details of these procedural rights are thoroughly examined in the next Chapters.

2.3.2. Contribution and Innovative Features

At the time of its adoption, the Convention included several innovative features that have largely contributed to its wide-spread recognition and are worth discussing.

First, the Convention adopted a rights-based rationale which went beyond the establishment of commitments from the state-parties to achieve the aims of the international community, recognising instead rights for citizens, capable of being exercised and defended at the national level.

This can be appreciated in Article 1 of the Convention, which links the procedural rights to 'the right of every person of present and future generations to live in an environment adequate to his or her health and well-being'. In fact, the objective of the Convention refers to the duty of each Party to guarantee the three basic rights developed in the Convention: access to information, public participation in decision-making and access to justice in environmental matters, constituting the first multilateral environmental agreement to focus on the obligations of the states towards their own citizens.[91]

91 Pedersen, O. W. (2009). European Environmental Human Rights and Environmental Rights: A Long Time Coming? *The Georgetown International*

At the time of the adoption of the Aarhus Convention, the existence of a human right to a healthy environment was not quite recognised in the international legal landscape, but procedural rights like access to information, participation in decision-making and access to justice had certain recognition at the international level and their instrumental and specific nature made them easier to codify and enforce.[92]

The Aarhus Convention incorporated a human rights dimension by acknowledging that human beings are entitled to live in an adequate environment as a precondition for the effectiveness of other human rights, and a procedural approach, by establishing clear legal procedures to be enabled by each of the state parties for its citizens.[93] This feature strengthens the Convention as it balances out the more abstract values associated with environmental protection and the specific rights of the public to participate effectively in environmental matters.[94]

Closely linked to the above, an important feature of the Convention is the procedural approach chosen as the mechanism to better implement the aims of public participation.

Public participation in practice involves a series of actions, thus, the Convention established the procedures that should be enabled in each state party to guarantee the different pillars of the public participation principle, aiming for effectiveness and harmony.

The establishment of concrete procedural norms in Aarhus set a benchmark for public participation with potentially global effects, laying down the grounds for the development of public participation provisions at national and international levels.

A third important characteristic was the design of its own compliance mechanism. Kravchenko referred to the Aarhus Convention's compliance mechanism as 'an ambitious effort to bring democracy and participation to the very heart of compliance itself'.[95] In many ways, the Convention's compliance mechanism embodies its founding principles in an innovative way.[96]

Environmental Law Review, 21, 73; Kravchenko, S. (2007). The Aarhus Convention and Innovations in Compliance with Multilateral Environmental Agreements. *Colo. J. Int'l Envtl. L. & Pol'y*, 18(1), 1.

92 See, generally, Pedersen, *Environmental Human Rights*, 2009, p. 93: 'the Aarhus Convention is the first multinational environmental agreement (MEA) which specifically links human rights with environmental protection'.

93 Birnie, P. W., & Boyle, A. E. (2002). *International Law and the Environment* (2nd ed.). Oxford University Press.

94 Davies, S. (2007). In Name or Nature? Implementing International Environmental Procedural Rights in the Post-Aarhus Environment A Finnish Example. *Environmental Law Review, 9*, 190.

95 Kravchenko, S. (2005). Strengthening Implementation of MEAS: The Innovative Aarhus Compliance Mechanism. In D. Zaelke, D. Kaniaru, & E. Kruzikova (Eds.) *Making Law Work Environmental Compliance & Sustainable Development*, Cameron May, pp. 245–254.

96 Wates, J. (2005). The Aarhus Convention: a Driving Force for Environmental Democracy. *Journal European Environmental and Planning Law*, 2(1).

The Aarhus Convention Compliance Committee (ACCC) was adopted at the First Meeting of the Parties to the Convention, which took place in Lucca, Italy, in October 2002.[97]

The Committee is a collegiate body composed of nine independent experts, instead of the usual state representatives. The members of the ACCC do not have to adjust their views depending on diplomatic or political goals and they are expected to rely on their knowledge and experience in issuing an opinion.[98] Notably, members of the Committee can be nominated by environmental non-governmental organisations within the scope of Article 10(5) of the Convention, and not only by Parties and Signatories.

The Committee's action may be triggered by communications from the Parties to the Convention, referrals by the Secretariat and, most importantly, from communications by the public, including NGOs, about alleged non-compliance (Aarhus Convention, Article 15). This feature has already proved quite effective in bringing claims of non-compliance before the ACCC, as there have already been 137 communications from the public, whilst there have been only two communications by the Parties and no referrals by the Secretariat (2015 data).[99]

The ACCC issues recommendations aimed at ensuring that the Convention's provisions are duly applied and are not disregarded over erred interpretations or assumptions by the parties or national authorities in charge of their application. However, these recommendations are not binding to the parties. They are sent to the Meeting of the Parties (to the Aarhus Convention) where government representatives endorse them before issuing a communication to the party involved in the matter.

Notwithstanding the non-binding nature of its recommendations, the ACCC's opinions provide an authoritative interpretation of the provisions of the Convention.[100] In fact, the Committee's outcomes are often referred to as 'case-law' or 'jurisprudence',[101] and have significant potential to influence future interpretation of the Convention's provisions.

The action of the ACCC has significantly contributed to the uniform interpretation of the Aarhus Convention in academic spheres as well as its application by governments and other organisations. Furthermore, by interpreting the Convention's principles as they should apply to new situations and challenges, the ACCC upholds the validity and relevance of the Convention's provisions through time.

97 Meeting of Parties (MOP) Decision I/7, doc. ECE/MP.PP/2002/2 (Add.8).

98 Kravchenko, *Strengthening Implementation*, 2005.

99 UNECE. (2015). *Communications from the Public*. Retrieved from http://www.unece.org/env/pp/pubcom.html.

100 Jendroska, J. (2011). Aarhus Convention Compliance Committee: Origins, Status and Activities, *Journal European Environmental and Planning Law, 8*(4), 301–314.

101 Marsden, S. (2012). Direct Public Access to EU Courts: Upholding International Law via the Aarhus Convention Compliance Committee. *Nordic Journal of International Law, 81*, 175–204.

The achievements of the Compliance Committee so far suggest that the mechanism has been successful in aiding the implementation of the Aarhus Convention by the parties, it has also helped with the divulgation and promotion of the procedural rights established in the Convention among the public in general and, by operating under principles of maximum access and no standing requirements,[102] it is also contributing to the broader discussion of access to justice in environmental matters, particularly visible at the EU and Member State levels.

Finally, it is worth mentioning that the definition of 'Public Authorities' adopted in the convention is quite far-reaching and comprehensive, as it even extends to private persons when they perform public functions or are under control of a public entity.

Despite public authorities acting in a legislative or judicial capacity being excluded from the definition, the Convention's Preamble stipulates 'the desirability of transparency in all branches of government' and calls on legislative bodies to implement the principles of the Convention in their proceedings on a voluntary basis (Preamble, para 11).

Understanding 'public authority' as the manifestation of the unilateral authority of the state (exercised by an entity or person) as opposed to the basic principle of individual self-determination, constituted, and limited by the rule of law,[103] it is fair to attribute the exercise of public authority to a wide array of institutions, including private entities.

In this sense, the Aarhus Convention early recognised the phenomenon of diffusion and privatisation of public power which used to be vested only in traditional governmental entities but is now exercised by entities of a different legal nature.

102 Regarding the recognition of environmental NGOs as interested parties to submit claims and stand before judicial authorities, see UNECE, Economic and Social Council, Meeting of the Parties to the Convention on Access to Information, Public Participation in Decision Making and Access to Justice in Environmental Matters, Compliance Committee, Thirty-second meeting, Geneva, 11–14 April 2011, Report of the Compliance Committee Addendum, Findings and recommendations with regard to communication ACCC/C/2008/32 (Part I) concerning compliance by the European Union. 14 April 2011, ECE/MP.PP/C. 1/2011/4/ Add.1. Retrieved from http://www.unece.org/fileadmin/DAM/env/pp/compliance/CC32/ece.mp.pp.c.1.2011.4.add.1_as_submitted.pdf; Marsden (2012, p. 195). Other cases regarding compliance of the Member States in reference to NGOs standing before national courts are: Decision V/9b on compliance by Austria (ECE/MP.PP/2014/2/Add.1); Decision V/9d on compliance by Bulgaria (ECE/MP.PP/2014/2/Add.1); Decision V/9f on compliance by the Czech Republic (ECE/MP.PP/2014/2/Add.1) and Decision V/9h on compliance by Germany (ECE/MP.PP/2014/2/Add.1).

103 Von Bogdandy, A., Wolfrum, R., von Bernstorff, J., Dann, P., & Goldmann, M. (Eds.) (2009). *The Exercise of Public Authority by International Institutions: Advancing International Institutional Law.* Springer.

3 Characterisation of the Right to Access Environmental Information

3.1. Recognition of the Right to Information as a Human Right

The right of access to public information or simply, 'right to information' is defined for the purposes of the present research as the general right of the people to access information held by public entities without having to state any particular interest.[1] Villanueva argues that if there was a need to show a particular interest to access public information, the information would not really be 'public'.[2]

Evidence points to an increased acceptance of the human right status of the right to information at the international level. This is visible, for instance, in several 'soft law' instruments such as the Principles on the Right of Access to Information by the OAS Inter-American Judicial Committee, which starts by recognising 'the right to information as a fundamental right which ensures access to the information controlled by public organs…'[3] and the Declaration of Principles on Freedom of Expression in Africa, which explicitly states that 'Public bodies hold information not for themselves but as custodians of the public good and everyone has a right to access this information, subject only to clearly defined rules established by law'.[4] The UN Special Rapporteur on Freedom of Opinion and Expression has also stated clearly that the right of

1 The right to information is commonly understood as the right to access information held by public bodies. Mendel, T. (2009). *The Right to Information in Latin America. A Comparative Legal Survey,* UNESCO. Retrieved from http://portal.unesco.org/ci/en/files/26159/12054862803freedom_information_en.pdf/freedom_information_en.pdf.

2 Villanueva, E. (2006). Tendencias en el Reconocimiento Constitucional del Derecho de Acceso a la Información Pública. In S. López-Ayllón (Ed.) *Democracia, transparencia y constitución: propuestas para un debate necesario.* Universidad Autónoma de México.

3 Organisation of American States – Inter-American Juridical Committee, Principles on the Right of Access to Information, CJI/RES.147 (LXXIII-O/08). Retrieved from http://www.oas.org/en/sla/dil/docs/CJI-RES_147_LXXIII-O-08 eng.pdf.

4 Declaration of Principles on Freedom of Expression in Africa, African Commission on Human and Peoples' Rights, 32nd Session, Banjul, The Gambia, 17–23 October 2002. Retrieved from http://www.refworld.org/docid/4753d3a40.html.

DOI: 10.4324/9781003307617-3

freedom of expression includes the right to access information held by the state in his annual reports to the UN Commission on Human Rights,[5] and the United Nations Human Rights Committee adopted General Comment No. 34 (2011), on Article 19 of the International Covenant on Civil and Political Rights, stating that the right to freedom of expression includes a general right of access to information held by public bodies.

The finding of a right to access public information within the more generally recognised right to freedom of expression, automatically grants human right status to the first, contributing to its positioning at the international level in view of the general inclusion of the right to freedom of expression in international and regional human right instruments such as the UN Universal Declaration of Human Rights and the International Covenant in Civil and Political Rights.[6] Table 3.1 shows how the right of freedom of expression has been integrated into several such agreements.

In addition to the 'soft law' instruments establishing the right to information as a human right (either independently or as part of the right to expression), there is a global trend among states for the adoption of 'Freedom of Information' laws, which are often the regulatory instruments to implement and guarantee citizens' rights to information in domestic jurisdictions.[7]

International and regional human rights courts have also contributed significantly with the legal development of the right to information as a full-fledged human right at the international level. The European Court of Human Rights [ECtHR] ascertained the existence of a right to receive information within Article 10 on 'freedom of expression' as early as 1979, in the judgment of *Sunday Times v UK* (1979).[8] In its ruling, the Court held that

> (…) Whilst the mass media must not overstep the bounds imposed in the interests of the proper administration of justice, it is incumbent on them to impart information and ideas concerning matters that come before the courts just as in other areas of public interest. Not only do the media have the task of imparting such information and ideas: the public also has a right to receive them.[9]

5 Report of the Special Rapporteur, *Promotion and protection of the right to freedom of opinion and expression*, UN Doc. E/CN.4/1998/40, 28 January 1998, para. 14. See also Mendel. *Legal Survey*, 2009.

6 Universal Declaration of Human Rights, 12 December 1948, G.A. Res. 217A, U. N. GAOR, 3d Sess., 1st plen. mtg., UN Doc A/810., Article 19, International Covenant on Civil and Political Rights, 16 December 1966 (entered into force on 23 March 1976), 999 UNTS 17.

7 As of 2019, over 100 countries have adopted freedom of information laws. See Freedominfo.org. (2016). *FOI Regimes.* Retrieved from http://www.freedominfo.org/regions/global/foi-regimes/.

8 ECtHR *The Sunday Times v The United Kingdom*, App. 6538/74 (1979).

9 *Sunday Times v UK*, paras 65–66.

Table 3.1 Freedom of Expression in International Human Rights Conventions

Freedom of Expression in International Human Rights Conventions
United Nations Universal Declaration of Human Rights (UN, 1948)
Article 19: Everyone has the right to freedom of opinion and expression; this right includes freedom to hold opinions without interference and to seek, receive and impart information and ideas through any media and regardless of frontiers.
American Convention on Human Rights (OAS, 1969)
Article 13: Freedom of Thought and Expression
Everyone has the right to freedom of thought and expression. This right includes freedom to seek, receive, and impart information and ideas of all kinds, regardless of frontiers, either orally, in writing, in print, in the form of art, or through any other medium of one's choice (…)
African Charter on Human and People's Rights (OAU, 1982)
Article 9: Every individual shall have the right to receive information. Every individual shall have the right to express and disseminate his opinions within the law.
International Covenant in Civil and Political Rights (UN, 1966)
Article 19: 1. Everyone shall have the right to hold opinions without interference. 2. Everyone shall have the right to freedom of expression; this right shall include freedom to seek, receive and impart information and ideas of all kinds, regard less of frontiers, either orally, in writing or in print, in the form of art, or through any other media of his choice. 3. The exercise of the rights provided for in paragraph 2 of this article carries with it special duties and responsibilities. It may therefore be subject to certain restrictions, but these shall only be such as are provided by law and are necessary: (a) For respect of the rights or reputations of others; (b) For the protection of national security or of public order (order public), or of public health or morals.

Interestingly, after the *Sunday Times v UK* case, the ECtHR adopted a consistent interpretation of Article 10 of the ECHR according to which the right to receive information basically prohibited a government from restricting the public from receiving information that others wished to impart to them, but did not confer upon an individual person a right to request access, nor implied an obligation on the government to impart information.[10] The exception to this rule was in cases of dangerous activities, where the Court sustained that 'public access to clear and full information is viewed as a basic human right'.[11]

However, the ECtHR conceded that access to information could be justified for the protection of other rights, such as the right to privacy and family life in Article 8 of the ECHR and the right to a fair hearing in Article 6.[12] The case of *Guerra v Italy* (1998) is an example of this reasoning, and it was related with access to environmental information. In this case, the ECtHR dismissed the argument that Article 10 of the ECHR implied an obligation of

10 See *Leander v Sweden*, App. 9248/81 (1987); *Gaskin v UK*, App. 10454/83 (1989) and *Roche v UK*, App. 32555/96 (2005).

11 *Öneryildiz v Turkey* [GC], App. 48939/99 (2004), para. 62.

12 See *Guerra et al v Italy*, App. 14967/89 (1998); *MGinley Egan v UK*, App. 21825/93 (1998); *Odievre v France*, App. 42326/98 (2003); *Lopez Ostra v Spain*, App. 16798/90 (1995); *Giacomelli v Italy*, App. 59909/00 (2008), where the court found that the applicant's deprivation of any effective right of participation as provided under domestic law amounted to a violation of Article 8 ECHR.

the authorities to disseminate information, but conceded that failure by the authorities to release crucial information about the environmental risks posed by a chemical factory close to the petitioners' residence was in violation of Article 8 of the ECHR, as it had prevented the applicants from properly assessing the risk that they were being exposed to, in violation of their right to privacy and family life.

In recent years, however, the court changed this approach and has now explicitly recognised a right to information on grounds of Article 10 of the ECHR. The transition started with the case of *Matky v Czech Republic* (2006), in which the ECtHR conceded for the first time that denying access to administrative documents constituted an interference with the right to receive information included in Article 10 of the ECHR. The interference was justified in this case, however, because it was found that the information requested (mostly technical information about a nuclear plant) was not in the public interest and its withholding by the state on grounds of national security, public health and the protection of third parties' interests was justified.[13]

Afterwards, in *Társaság a Szabadságjogokért v Hungary* (2011), the ECtHR stated: 'the Court has recently advanced towards a broader interpretation of the notion of "freedom to receive information"... and thereby towards the recognition of a right of access to information' (para. 35) but also warned that 'the right to freedom to receive information basically prohibits a Government from restricting a person from receiving information that others wish or may be willing to impart to him' pointing that the situation in case 'essentially concerns an interference – by virtue of the censorial power of an information monopoly – with the exercise of the functions of a social watchdog, like the press, rather than a denial of a general right of access to official documents' (para. 36).

In *Youth Initiative for Human Right v Serbia* (2013),[14] the shift towards the recognition of a right to access information held by public authorities within Article 10 of the ECtHR is more clearly appreciated, as the Court claimed that denial by an intelligence agency to disclose public information to an NGO was a violation to the right to freedom of expression in Article 10, considering the role of the NGO as a contributor to the public debate. Notably, Judges Sajó and Vučinić state in their concurring opinions that 'in the world of the Internet, the difference between journalists and other members of the public is rapidly disappearing. There can be no robust democracy without transparency, which should be served and used by all citizens'.[15] This

13 See *Sdruženi Jihočeské Matky v Czech Republic*, App. 19101/03 (2006); *Társaság a Szabadságjogokért v Hungary*, App. 37374/05 (2011); *Kennedi v Hungary*, App. 31475/05 (2009); *Gillberg v Sweden*, App. 41723/06 (2013); *Shapovalov v Ukraine*, App. 45835/05 (2012); *Österreichische Vereinigung zur Erhaltung, Stärkung und Schaffung eines wirtschaftlich gesunden Land- Und Forst-Wirtschaftlichen Grundbesitzes v Austria*, App. 39534/07 (2013).

14 *Youth Initiative for Human Rights v Serbia*, App. 48135/06 (2013).

15 Joint Concurring Opinion of Judges Sajó and Vučinić. (2013). *Youth Initiative for Human Rights v Serbia Judgment – separate Opinion.*

statement suggests that the ECtHR may take a more open approach in future cases.

In the Americas, the case of *Claude Reyes v Chile* (2006) before the Inter-American Court of Human Rights (ICHR) is paradigmatic; in its ruling, the Court explicitly recognised that the right of access to public information was comprised within the right of expression as it was stated in the Inter-American Convention on Human Rights, which uses similar wording as other international human rights instruments.[16]

The case involved a group of citizens (NGO representatives) who requested information about a logging project named 'Proyecto Rio Condor' to the Chilean Committee of Foreign Investments, a public entity. The petitioners argued that the project could cause damage to the environment and thwart sustainable development in Chile. The information was partially denied without providing any reasons or legal support for the refusal.

The ICHR assumed that the right of expression in Article 13 of the American Convention on Human Rights includes not only the right and liberty to express one's own mind but also the right and liberty to 'seek, receive and disseminate information and ideas of any kind'.[17]

The Court held the need for public authorities in any democratic society to uphold the principle of maximum access, which establishes a presumption that all the information is accessible, subject to a restricted exceptions system.[18]

A final and significant argument for the international recognition of a human right to access information from public authorities is the Convention on Access to Official Documents adopted by the Council of Europe in the city of Tromsø, Norway, in June 2009, which entered into force on 1 December 2020.[19]

This Convention is the first binding instrument of international law to explicitly recognise a general right of access to information held by public authorities,[20] taking into account international human rights instruments and the Aarhus Convention.[21] The Convention builds upon the assumption 'that

16 See Table 3.2 Freedom of Expression.

17 *Claude Reyes v Chile*, (ser. C) No. 151 (2006), para. 77.

18 Article 13.2 of the American Convention on Human Rights allows restrictions necessary to ensure 'respect for the rights and reputation of others" or "the protection of national security, public order, or the public health and morals'.

19 Convention on Access to Official Documents CETS No. 205, Council of Europe, 18 June 2009 (entered into force on 1 December 2020), Tromsø, Norway.

20 Komanovics, A. (2010). Transparent Europe? The Council of Europe Convention on Access to Official Documents. *Boletín JADO, 19*, 141–170.

21 Tromsø Convention, Preamble (para. 3): 'Bearing in mind, in particular, Article 19 of the Universal Declaration of Human Rights, Articles 6, 8 and 10 of the European Convention for the Protection of Human Rights and Fundamental Freedoms, the United Nations Convention on Access to Information, Public Participation in Decision-making and Access to Justice in Environmental Matters (Aarhus, 25 June 1998) and the Convention for the Protection of Individuals with

all official documents are in principle public and can be withheld subject only to the protection of other rights and legitimate interests'.[22]

The Tromsø Convention aims to establish minimum core provisions, rather than an ideal model for the right of access to public information. In fact, it has been criticised for its lack of decisive mandate on issues as crucial as the timeframes within which public authorities must process citizen's requests, the narrow scope of public authorities to which it applies, and its failure to make a general statement on the right of access to information.[23] Despite these shortcomings, there is a binding international treaty aiming to guarantee the right of access to public information, which is a powerful indicator of the existence of a human right at the international level.

As long as environmental information is still 'information', there is actually an implicit human right of access to environmental information held by public entities at the international level reflected in the Tromsø Convention.

3.1.1. The Right to Access Environmental Information in International Law

The right of access to environmental information is found explicitly in international law instruments as well. Procedural environmental rights, encompassing general rights of the people to participate in environmental governance, have had widespread support in diverse international and regional environmental law instruments, from the paradigmatic Principle 10 of the Rio Declaration, swiftly comprising what public participation in environmental matters is about, to more specific and binding instruments such as the Convention on Biological Diversity (Article 14),[24] the UN Framework Convention on Climate Change (Article 6)[25] and the UNECE Convention on EIA in a Transboundary Context (Espoo Convention).[26]

The Escazú Agreement, recently adopted with the purpose of implementing Principle 10 of the Rio Declaration in Latin America and the Caribbean, proclaims the objective of guaranteeing full and effective implementation of the rights of access to information, public participation in decision-making and access to justice in environmental matters (Article 1),[27] implying the

regard to Automatic Processing of Personal Data of 28 January 1981 (ETS No. 108)'.

22 Tromsø Convention, Preamble, para. 7.

23 Komanovics, *Transparent Europe*, 2010.

24 United Nations Convention on Biological Diversity, 5 June 1992 (entered into force on 29 December 1993), 1760 UNTS 79.

25 United Nations Framework Convention on Climate Change, 5 June 1992 (entered into force on 21 March 1994), 1771 UNTS 107.

26 UNECE Convention on Environmental Impact Assessment in a Transboundary Context, 25 February 1991 (entered into force on 10 September 1997), 1989 UNTS 309.

27 United Nations, Regional Agreement on Access to Information, Public Participation and Justice in Environmental Matters in Latin America and the Caribbean, 4 March 2018 (entered into force 22 April 2021), Escazú, Costa Rica.

functional and autonomous character of these rights, and their ability of being regulated and enforced at national level.

On top of these examples, the best evidence of the existence of a right of access to environmental information is, clearly, the Aarhus Convention itself. The level of specificity, clarity and enforceability of the procedural environmental rights found in the Aarhus Convention, as well as their evolution and support by other sources of international law provide enough substance to be employed as a normative framework for the present study.

3.1.2. Influence of International Law in Regional and National Jurisdictions

Noting the increasing recognition of a right of access to public information, mainly built over 'freedom of expression' rights and widespread values like transparency, democracy and public participation, it is interesting to see how the right of access to information is taking hold at regional and national levels.

At the EU level, the right to access information held by the EU institutions has not only been explicitly recognised in the constituting treaties and the EU Charter of Fundamental Rights but it has been subject to further regulation and promotion at Member State level, as transparency is increasingly recognised as a cornerstone of EU governance.

The EU Charter of Fundamental Rights,[28] adopted in 2000, aims to collect and give visibility to human rights recognised by the EU and to which EU law is bound. It guarantees 'the right of every person to have access to his or her file' (Article 41) and the right of access to documents of EU's institutions (Article 42). The Charter acquired binding status with the entry into force of the Lisbon Treaty in 2009.[29]

The right of expression contained in the Charter is a recollection of the same right in the European Convention on Human Rights. Accordingly, it may be interpreted as having the same scope and limitations as Article 10 of the ECHR,[30] and in reference to the case law of the ECtHR.[31]

28 European Charter of Human Rights (final text), [2007] O.J. C303/1.

29 Article 6(1) of the TEU, as amended by the Lisbon Treaty, states: 'The Union recognises the rights, freedoms and principles set out in the Charter of Fundamental Rights of the European Union of 7 December 2000, as adapted at Strasbourg, on 12 December 2007, which shall have the same legal value as the Treaties'.

30 European Charter of Human Rights (2007), Article 52: '3. In so far as this Charter contains rights which correspond to rights guaranteed by the Convention for the Protection of Human Rights and Fundamental Freedoms, the meaning and scope of those rights shall be the same as those laid down in the said Convention. This provision shall not prevent Union law providing more extensive protection'.

31 Wils, W. P. J. (2011) EU Anti trust Enforcement Powers and Procedural Rights and Guarantees: The Interplay between EU Law, National Law, the Charter of Fundamental Rights of the EU and the European Convention On Human Rights. *World Competition, 34*(2), 189–213.

Consequently, the ECtHR interpretation of Article 10 of the ECHR as including the right of access to public information held by the state, supposes the same expansive interpretation of the respective provision on the right of freedom of expression in the EU Charter, which complements the right to access documents held by the EU institutions set out explicitly in Article 42 of the Charter.[32]

Moreover, Article 7 of the Charter (respect for private and family life) has the same meaning and scope as Article 8 ECHR thus, in the same logic, it could be validly applied in cases of environmental participatory rights within the limits and conditions established by the ECtHR.[33]

Along the same lines, the Lisbon Treaty recognises access to information from EU institutions as a subjective right. Article 15 TEU establishes that 'in order to promote good governance and ensure the participation of civil society, the Union institutions, bodies, offices and agencies shall conduct their work as openly as possible', and reaffirms that 'any citizen of the Union, and any natural or legal person residing or having its registered office in a member state, shall have a right of access to documents of the Union's institutions, bodies, offices and agencies, whatever their medium'.[34]

This right was implemented through Regulation No. 1049/2001 regarding access to documents held by the EU institutions.[35] Up until the adoption of this regulation, access to information from the EU institutions was largely determined by codes of conduct implemented by each of the institutions.[36] At Member State level, the matter of access to administrative documents has been mostly left to each of the national governments,[37] but there is evidence that a fundamental right of access to administrative information is contained in the national legislation of virtually all of the EU Member States.[38]

The recognition and evolution of a right of access to environmental information at EU level has run in parallel with that of the general right of access to public information, intertwining at some points. Access to environmental

32 European Charter of Human Rights (2007), Article 42: 'Any citizen of the Union, and any natural or legal person residing or having its registered office in a Member State, has a right of access to documents of the institutions, bodies, offices and agencies of the Union, whatever their medium'.

33 See *Guerra v Italy* (1998) and *Taşkin and Others v. Turkey*, App. 46117/99 (2005).

34 Consolidated Version of the Treaty on European Union (TEU), [2012]. O.J. C 326/13.

35 Regulation (EC) No 1049/2001 of the European Parliament and of the Council of 30 May 2001 regarding public access to European Parliament, Council and Commission documents, [2001] O.J. L 145/43.

36 Code of Conduct 93/730/EC concerning Public Access to Council and Commission Documents, [1993] O.J. L 340/41 and Commission Decision 94/90/ESCS/EC/Euratom, [1994] O.J. L 46/58.

37 Harden, I. (2009). The Revision of Regulation 1049/2001 on Public Access to Documents. *European Public Law, 15*(2), 239–256.

38 Gavouneli, M. (2000). Access to Environmental Information: Delimitation of a Right. *Tulane Environmental Law Journal*, 13, 303.

information can be found in several pieces of EU's environmental law instruments, such as the 1975 Council Directive concerning the quality of bathing water,[39] and the Environmental Impact Assessment (EIA) Directive adopted in 1985.[40]

In 1990, Directive 90/313 on access to information on the environment[41] was adopted, providing for Member States to enable public access to environmental information held by public authorities, which were defined as any public administration body at national, regional or local level with responsibilities relating to the environment, except bodies acting in judicial or legislative capacity (Article 2). This Directive was taken into consideration in the negotiation of the Aarhus Convention's provisions on access to environmental information.[42] Notably, regarding Member States' authorities, while there is specific EU legislation for access to environmental information, there are no EU laws providing for access to public information in general.

Following the adoption and entry into force of the Aarhus Convention,[43] to which the Union and each of the Member States is a party, the EU amended its legislation to better conform with the Convention provisions. Regarding the right of access to environmental information in the Member States, Directive 2003/4 on Public Access to Environmental Information repealed and replaced Directive 90/313 going even further than the Convention by adding items to the definition of 'environmental information' to which the public has access (Recital 10).[44]

39 Council Directive Concerning the Quality of Bathing Water EEC/76/160, [1975] O.J. L 31/1.

40 Council Directive 85/337 of 27 June 1985 on the assessment of the effects of certain public and private projects on the environment [1985] O.J. L 175/40 codified with amendments by Directive 2011/92/EU of the European Parliament and of the Council, [2012] O.J. L. 26/1, as amended by Directive 2014/52/EU of the European Parliament and of the Council, [2014] O.J. L. 124/1.

41 Council Directive 90/313/EEC of 7 June 1990 on the freedom of access to information on the environment [1990] O.J. L158/56/90.

42 At a special session on 17 January 1996 in Geneva, the Committee on Environmental Policy (CEP) set up an Ad Hoc Working Group for the negotiations of the Aarhus Convention. See Report of the CEP- Special Session - ECE/CEP/18 (1996). The reports of the Ad Hoc Working Group for the first, second and third sessions make reference to the relevant community directives, particularly Directive 90/313. See Report on the first session of the Ad Hoc Working Group, CEP/AC.3/2 (1996:8); Report on the second session of the Ad Hoc Working Group, CEP/AC.3/4 (1996:4,6); Report on the third session of the Ad Hoc Working Group, CEP/AC.3/6 (1997:6).

43 The Aarhus Convention entered into force on 30 October 2001, the EU ratified the Convention on 17 February 2005. Council Decision 2005/370/EC of 17 February 2005 on the conclusion, on behalf of the European Community, of the Convention on access to information, public participation in decisions-making and access to justice in environmental matters, [2005] O.J. L 124/13.

44 Directive 2003/4/EC of the European Parliament and of the Council of 28 January 2003 on Public Access to Environmental Information and repealing Council Directive 90/313/EEC, [2003] O.J. L 41/26.

Regarding the EU institutions specifically (not those of Member States), Regulation No. 1367/2006[45] was the instrument used to align EU law with the Convention's provisions, although its application in combination with Regulation No. 1049/2001 has revealed some discrepancies between the EU's legislation and the Convention's provisions, affecting in practice the right of access to environmental information held by EU institutions.[46] Wolf argues that the approach taken by the EU was not the best way to guarantee compliance with the Convention, particularly regarding the application of exceptions, since the EU legislation 'lack coherence and clarity (...) and the combined provisions breach the Convention in a number of key respects'.[47]

In theory, both regulations must be applied in a complementary manner, considering that Regulation 1367/2006 is *lex specialis* concerning access to environmental information. Therefore, in case of conflicting interpretations, this regulation prevails over the general access regime in cases of access to environmental information.[48] This is important because Regulation 1367/2006 has been found to provide a broader scope and to be more specific regarding the application of exceptions than Regulation 1049/2001.[49]

In Latin America and the Caribbean, the right of access to information has been actively promoted by the Organisation of American States (OAS), through the adoption of non-binding guidelines, such as the Principles on Access to Public Information[50] and the OAS Model Law on Access to Information,[51] in which the influence of the Inter-American Court of Human Rights is clearly visible: both instruments are based on the right to information as a part of the right to freedom of expression as the Court interpreted it in the *Reyes v Chile* judgment.

45 Regulation (EC) No 1367/2006 of the European Parliament and of the Council on the application of the provisions of the Aarhus Convention on Access to Information, Public Participation in Decision-making and Access to Justice in Environmental Matters to Community institutions and bodies, [2006] O.J. L 264/13.

46 Wolf, S. (2013). Access to EU environmental information: EU compliance with Aarhus Convention. *ERA Forum, 14*(4), 475–491. See also Jendrośka, J. (2012). Citizen's Rights in European Environmental Law: Stock-Taking of Key Challenges and Current Developments in Relation to Public Access to Information, Participation and Access to Justice. *Journal for European Environmental & Planning Law, 9*(1), 71–90.

47 Wolf, *EU Environmental Information*, 2013, p. 476.

48 CJEU (Court of First Instance), Case T-29/08 *Liga para Protecção da Natureza (LPN) v European Commission*, Judgment of 9 September 2011, 105.

49 Von Unger, M. (2007). Access to EU Documents: An end at Last to the Authorship Rule? *Journal European Environmental and Planning Law, 6*, 440–448.

50 Organisation of American States - Inter-American Juridical Committee, Principles on the Right of Access to Information, CJI/RES.147 (LXXIII-O/08).

51 Organisation of American States (OAS), Model Inter-American Law on Access to Information, Doc. AG/RES. 2607 (XL-O/10), 8 June 2010. Retrieved from http://www.oas.org/en/sla/dil/docs/access_to_information_Text_edited_DDI.pdf.

Regarding a subjective right of access to environmental information, the adoption of the Escazú Agreement certainly positions the access rights enshrined in Principle 10 of the Rio Declaration as independent, full-fledged human rights at the international-regional level in the region. The substantive right to a healthy environment also gains in visibility. Article 4 of the Agreement explicitly provides that 'Each Party shall guarantee the right of every person to live in a healthy environment and any other universally-recognized human right related to the present Agreement', in what could be the first binding instrument of international law to recognise the right to live in a healthy environment as a human right. This provision, along with the IACtHR Advisory Opinion OC 23/2017, position the right to live in a healthy and adequate environment as an enforceable human right in the Inter-american Human Rights System.[52]

3.1.3. Statutory and Constitutional Recognition of the Right to Information

In many states, there is an explicit recognition of the right to information in the national Constitution, establishing in a straightforward manner its status as a human right within that jurisdiction. Right2info refers to at least 59 countries which have incorporated the right to information in their national constitutions, including 12 countries in America and 18 in Europe.[53]

The Colombian Political Constitution (1991) gave constitutional status to the right of access to documents by including the following provision in Article 74: 'Every person has a right of access to public documents except in cases established by law. Professional secrets are inviolable'.

Complementing this provision, Article 23 reads: 'Every person has the right to present respectful petitions to the authorities for the general or private interest and to secure their prompt resolution. The legislative authority may regulate the filing of petitions to private organisations in order to guarantee fundamental rights'.[54]

The 'right of petition' established in Article 23 of the Colombian Constitution is a fundamental right, which can be protected by an expeditious and preferential judicial mechanism named the *tutela* action, which is analogous to an *amparo* procedure in other Latin American countries and in Spain. This right was regulated through Law 1755 of 2015 (Right of Petition Law),

52 Inter-American Court of Human Rights. (2017). *Advisory Opinion oc-23/17 of November 15, 2017 Requested by the Republic of Colombia*. Retrieved from https://www.corteidh.or.cr/docs/opiniones/seriea_23_ing.pdf.

53 Right2info.org. Retrieved from http://www.right2info.org/constitutional-protections. See also Karanicolas, M. & Mendel, T. (2012). *Entrenching RTI: An Analysis of Constitutional Protections of the Right to Information*. Centre for Law and Democracy, Halifax, Ca.

54 Political Constitution of the Republic of Colombia, 4 July 1991.

which established the terms and conditions for its exercise by the citizens, including the scope of obligated subjects, exceptions and remedies.[55]

Regarding the legal nature of this right, the Colombian Constitutional Court explained that the Right of Petition is the 'gender', and the right of access to public information is the 'species', meaning that the latter is included in the first. In fact, the Right of Petition goes much further than providing access to information and public documents, as it is also the suitable mechanism to demand action from the authorities or the recognition of a particular right outside the courts. According to the Constitutional Court, the right of access to public documents, the right to information and the right of petition share the same axiological core.[56]

The Colombian Constitutional Court has further stated that the right of every person to access public documents is indeed a fundamental right, because it is intrinsically connected to undisputed fundamental rights like the Right of Petition.[57]

Meanwhile, in the US federal legislation, the existence of an actual right of access to public information is not a clear-cut issue. Notwithstanding a long tradition of 'open society' and transparent government, as shown by the early adoption of the Freedom of Information Act – FOIA in 1966,[58] the US Supreme Court has been reluctant to interpret the First Amendment of the Constitution, which guarantees the freedom of speech, as implying a full right of public access to information.[59] The US catalogue of fundamental rights is a combination of the rights explicitly enshrined in the Bill of Rights and the Constitution and those that have been interpreted by the Supreme Court to be implicit in the listed guarantees, such as the right of association and the right to privacy. Freedom of Speech is, arguably, one of the rights that most needed to be interpreted and further elaborated to constitute an effective guarantee for citizens, because it was initially defined in the First Amendment only as a negative liberty: 'Congress shall make no law abridging the freedom of speech or of the press'. Most of the 'implicit' human rights were recognised in the

55 Law 1755 of 2015, 'Regulating the Fundamental Right of Petition and repealing a Title of the Code of Administrative Procedure', 30 June 2015.

56 Colombian Constitutional Court, Case T-672/00, Judgment of 9 June 2000, M.P. Alejandro Martínez Caballero and Case T-605/96, Judgment of 13 November 1996, M.P. Jorge Arango Mejía.

57 Colombian Constitutional Court, Case T-524/93, Judgment of 10 November 1993, M.P. Hernando Guerrero Vergara, Case T-621/96, Judgment of 14 November 1996, M.P. Antonio Barrera Carbonell and Case T-074/97 Judgment of 18 February 1997, M.P. Fabio Moron Díaz.

58 The US was the fourth country ever to pass a FOI law. Ackerman, J. M., & Sandoval-Ballesteros, I. E. (2006). The Global Explosion of Freedom of Information Laws. *Administrative Law Review, 58*(1), 90.

59 *Houchins v KQED*, Inc., 438 U.S. 1, 16 (1978): 'Neither the First Amendment nor the Fourteenth Amendment mandates a right of access to government information or sources of information within the government's control'. See also *Travis v Reno*, 163 F.3d 1000, 1007 (7th Cir. 1998).

1960s and 1970s, during the 'activist' phase of the Supreme Court, and the right of access to public information was not among them. However, the Supreme Court has openly acknowledged that the reason for the recognition of implicit fundamental rights is because they are deemed 'indispensable to the enjoyment of rights explicitly defined'.[60] In this logic, it should be a matter of time before a fundamental right of access to information is recognised by the US Supreme Court.

On the other hand, a Constitutional right of privacy has been found to be implicit in the First Amendment of the US Constitution. In a case of *Mobile Oil Company v The Washington Post* (1984), the appellant (Mobile) submitted libel against the decision of the District Court to unseal 38,000 pages of deposition transcripts and other documents of the discovery materials that were not used in trial. On appeal, the court reversed the unsealing because

> [the] appellant had a **constitutionally protected privacy interest** in the unsealed information, and there was no overriding reason to disclose the information. The presumptive openness of discovery materials not used at trial derived only from the Federal Rules of Civil Procedure, and **no right of access to such materials could be found in the common law or the U.S. Constitution**. Further, appellant had provided sufficient reasons for non-disclosure because the information if revealed would have harmed its competitive position (emphasis added).[61]

Notwithstanding the position of the Supreme Court, a right of access to information in certain governmental proceedings, specifically in criminal cases, has been recognised as a constitutional right, at least for the press.

The US Supreme Court protected public access to criminal procedures in defence of the First Amendment (freedom of speech) because of the long-standing tradition of openness that had characterised judicial procedures, recognising further that

> Public scrutiny of a criminal trial enhances the quality and safeguards the integrity of the factfinding process, with benefits to both the defendant and to society as a whole. Moreover, public access to the criminal trial fosters an appearance of fairness, thereby heightening public respect for the judicial process. And in the broadest terms, public access to criminal trials permits the public to participate in and serve as a check upon the judicial process – an essential component in our structure of self-government.[62]

Notwithstanding the apparent reluctance of US courts to acknowledge the existence of a fundamental right of access to information (derived of the

60 *Richmond Newspapers v Virginia,* 448 U.S. 555. 100 S. Ct. 2814 (1980).
61 *Tavoulareas v Washington Post Co.,* 724 F.2d 1010 (D.C. Cir. 1984).
62 *Globe Newspaper Co. v Superior Court,* 457 U.S. 596, 605–06 (1982).

freedom of speech right in the First Amendment or otherwise), the Freedom of Information Act (FOIA) does provide for public access to records held by federal agencies, stating that

> Except with respect to the records made available under paragraphs (1) and (2) of this subsection, and except as provided in subparagraph (E), each agency, upon any request for records which (i) reasonably describes such records and (ii) is made in accordance with published rules stating the time, place, fees (if any), and procedures to be followed, shall make the records promptly available to any person.[63]

The FOIA has been used to access environmental information with some success.[64] Other statutes provide for additional mechanisms of active and passive access to environmental information, such as the Clean Air Act (CAA), the Clean Water Act (CWA), the Emergency Planning and Community Right to Know Act (EPCRA), among others.

A key for the interpretation of the evolution of transparency and public participation legislation in the US is to observe that the FOIA and the Administrative Procedure Act (APA), adopted in 1946,[65] conceded a public right to know about the way the government was carrying out its public functions as a matter of public hygiene, to prevent corruption and injustice by public agencies acting under a veil of secrecy.[66] The US is a long defender of the right of the public to get information from the government to be able to scrutinise public decision-making in general, and as a necessary tool for people's 'self-government', one of the principles of American constitutionalism.[67] It is in this transparency-friendly scenario where disclosure of environmental data by public and private entities emerges in the form of specific duties in

63 Freedom of Information Act of July 4, 1966 [FOIA], Public Law No. 89–487, 80 Stat. 250, codified as amended at 5 U.S.C. § 552 (1994), para. 552(a)(3)(A).

64 Vladeck, D. C. (2007). Information Access - Surveying the Current Landscape of Federal Right-to-Know Laws. *Texas Law Review*, 86, 1987.

65 The Administrative Procedure Act (APA) was passed by the U.S. Congress in 1946 to serve four basic purposes: 1. to require agencies to keep the public currently informed of their organization, procedures, and rules (sec. 3); 2. to provide for public participation in the rulemaking process (sec. 4); 3. to prescribe uniform standards for the conduct of formal rulemaking (sec. 4 (b)) and adjudicatory proceedings (sec. 5), i.e., proceedings that by statute are required to be made on the record after opportunity for an agency hearing (secs. 7 and 8); and 4. to restate the law of judicial review (sec. 10). Resources for the Future (2001). *Public Access to Environmental Information and Data: Practice Examples and Lessons from the United States, the European Union, and Central and Eastern Europe*, Washington D.C.

66 For an account of American transparency at the onset, see Roberts, A. (2001). Structural Pluralism and the Right to Information. *The University of Toronto Law Journal, 51*(3), 243–271.

67 Rubenfeld, J. (2003). Of Constitutional Self-Government. *Fordham Law Review, 71*(5), 1749–1765.

order to preserve state goals like human health and safety (*e.g.* release of toxic chemicals), the quality of natural resources (*e.g.* reports on water and air quality), consumers' trust (*e.g.* risk of contamination in the food change, risks of products) and the stability of exchange markets (*e.g.* reports to the Securities and Exchange Commission).[68] Reportedly, only in the mid 1990s, information disclosure, right-to-know and environmental reporting were accounted as tools for good environmental governance, until then they were mostly consequences of implementing democratic and transparency ideals.[69]

The EU, on the other hand, recognised early in the regulatory process free public access to environmental information as a tool for good governance and transparency, as exemplified by the Council Directive on the quality of bathing water (1975), the Environmental Impact Assessment (EIA) Directive (1985), and the relatively pioneering Directive 90/313 on Access to Environmental Information (1990).

The issue of constitutional recognition takes relevance in this context because jurisdictions with a strong constitutional tradition can more easily accommodate new reforms and legislation that find direct support in their respective constitutional texts. In the case of the right of public access to information, the constitutional support may be found in formulations of Freedom of Speech and 'self-government', like in the US;[70] the Right of Petition and access to public documents, as in Colombia; or in the principles of 'open government' and the right of access to documents held by public institutions, as in the EU.

From the perspective of enforcement and remedies, the constitutional status of the right to access public information in the Colombian case entails the possibility of accessing quick judicial remedy through the *tutela* action. It also places the right of access above other legally protected interests, which is relevant when examining the application of exceptions to disclosure in a case-by-case basis; and ensures that legal instruments of lower status do not abridge the right. The lack of such a distinct recognition in the US could arguably entail practical difficulties in accessing public information, exceptions to disclosure may be applied more severely and there could be increased barriers to judicial remedy.

3.1.4. The Right of Access to Environmental Information at National Level

When a general right of access to public information is recognised, environmental information that falls within the scope of the right can then be publicly accessed under the same terms.

68 Environmental Law Institute. (1984). *Environmental Audit Issue Paper: Duties to Report or Disclose Information on The Environmental Aspects of Business Activities.* Washington D.C.

69 Mol, A. P. J. (2010). Epilogue: The Future of Transparency: Power, Pitfalls and Promises. *Global Environmental Politics, 10*(3), 132–143.

70 Roesler, S. M. (2012). The Nature of the Environmental Right to Know. *Ecology Law Quarterly, 39*, 989–1040.

The Colombian General Environmental Law of 1993 was adopted after the Rio Conference (1992), and explicitly mentions the Rio Declaration in Article 1.[71] This law provides for public access to certain environmental information on request, without having to state any particular interest:

> Right of Petition of Information. Every natural or legal person has the right to formulate a direct request of information in relation with the elements capable of producing pollution and the dangers that these elements may pose to human health in accordance with Article 16 of the Law 23 of 1973. This request must be attended in 10 business days. Additionally, any person may invoke his right to be informed about the quantities and utilisation of the financial resources destined to the preservation of the environment (Article 74).

In the EU, provisions for public access to environmental information are found in several regulatory instruments dating back to the 1970s. The 1996 Directive on Integrated Pollution Prevention and Control, for instance, states

> Member States shall ensure public access to applications for permits to enable it to comment on them before the authority reaches its decision, as well as access to the results of monitoring of releases.

This article also mandates for a report on the principal emissions and responsible sources to be published every three years.[72] Its successor, the Industrial Emissions Directive (Directive 2010/75/EU), prescribes the application of the Aarhus Convention to permit procedures in Member States (Article 24), whilst the Directive on the Assessment of the Effects of Certain Plans and Programs on the Environment (2001) provides for Member States to make plans and programmes available to the public prior to their adoption to receive comments,[73] and the Framework Water Directive (2000) mandates public access to information regarding river basin management plans during their establishment.[74]

In the US, several statutes mandate disclosure of specific environmental information, mostly to the government, such as the Emergency Planning and

71 Law 99 of 1993, 'Creating the Minister of the Environment, organising the public sector in charge of the management and conservation of the environment and the renewable natural resources, organising the National Environmental System (SINA), and other dispositions', 22 December 1993.

72 Council Directive 96/61/EC concerning Integrated Pollution Prevention and Control, [1996] O.J. L 257/26, Article 15.

73 Directive 2001/42/EC of the European Parliament and of the Council of 27 June 2001 on the assessment of the effects of certain plans and programmes on the environment, [2001] O.J. L 197/30, Article 6.

74 Directive 2000/60 establishing a framework for Community action in the field of water policy, [2000] O.J. L 327/1, Article 14.

Community Right-to-Know Act (ECPRA, 1986) establishing the Toxic Release Inventory (TRI), the Clean Air Act, the Safe Drinking Water Act (1996), requiring public water companies to inform their customers when they violate contamination standards, among others.[75] Information submitted to the public authorities may be accessed through the federal FOIA and the equivalent state laws.

Despite the identification of these statutory provisions, access to environmental information as a subjective right of the public is only explicitly recognised at the international level (The Aarhus Convention), in the EU legal framework, and in Colombia. In the US, on the other hand, neither is access to public information a constitutional right, nor is access to environmental information a legally recognised subjective right of the people.

The status of codification of the rights of access analysed above is summarised in Table 3.2.

Table 3.2 Legal Instruments Providing Access to Information

	International	*EU*	*US (federal)*	*Colombia*
Access to **public Information** (transparency)	Tromsø Convention Human Rights Conventions (as freedom of expression). Soft Law instruments.	TEU TFEU EU Charter Regulation 1049/2001 (EU institutions)	FOIA (1966) 1st Amendment (Freedom of Speech, in some cases)	Constitution (Arts. 74 and 23) Transparency Law (1712/2014) Right of Petition Law (1755/2015)
Public access to **Environmental Information**	Aarhus Convention (1998) Kiev Protocol (2009) Bali Guidelines (2010) Escazú Agreement Other treaties and 'soft law' international instruments. (UNFCC, CBD, Cartagena Protocol on Biosafety, Espoo Convention).	Directive 2003/4 Regulation 1367/2006 (on the application of the Aarhus Convention by EU institutions) Directive 2010/75/EU (Industrial Emissions Directive)	National Environmental Policy Act (NEPA) EPCRA (Toxic Release Inventory) Clean Air Act Safe Drinking Water Act Federal Insecticide, Fungicide and Rodents Act Other Environmental Statutes	General Environmental Law (99/93) Single Environmental Decree (1076/2015) Natural Resources Code (Decree 2811/1974)

75 See further in Echeverria, J. D., & Kaplan, J. B. (2003). Poisonous Procedural 'Reform': In Defense of Environmental Right-to-Know. *Kansas Journal of Law and Public Policy, 12*(1), 579.

3.2. Systems for Public Participation in Environmental Matters

In a logical next step of the analysis, it will be examined whether the rights of access to information identified in the last section are framed within a scheme of public participation in environmental governance. The underlying assumption is that access rights integrated this way will have more visibility, the ability to be reinforced by other procedural rights and overall better chances to be used effectively in achieving the general goals of democratic participation and transparency.

The right of access to environmental information established at the international level in the Aarhus Convention is clearly integrated in a framework providing for public participation in environmental matters, along with the rights to public participation in decision-making and access to justice.

The relationship between the three distinguishable participatory rights is one of interdependence and mutual support. Each right, contemplated alone, would not have the scope and importance it gains when working together with the other two.[76]

It is not by accident that Article 10 of the Rio Declaration portrayed public participation in environmental matters as a three-pronged principle, instead of establishing separate principles for each of the participatory rights.

At the EU level, the implementation of the Aarhus Convention in the Member States was planned through the adoption of different instruments for each of these rights. Directive 2003/4 focuses on access to environmental information and Directive 2003/35/EC provides for public participation in respect of the drawing up of certain plans and programmes relating to the environment,[77] although Aarhus provisions are also integrated within specific environmental legal instruments, such as the Industrial Emissions Directive (2010) and the Water Framework Directive (2000). Regarding the third pillar of the Aarhus Convention on access to justice, the EU has been unable so far to pass legislation regulating this delicate matter, which is considered a weakness of EU compliance with the Convention.[78]

76 United Nations Economic Commission for Europe – UNECE. (2014). *The Aarhus Convention: An Implementation Guide*, 2nd ed., UN Doc. ECE/CEP/72/Rev.1.

77 Directive 2003/35/EC of the European Parliament and of the Council providing for public participation in respect of the drawing up of certain plans and programmes relating to the environment and amending with regard to public participation and access to justice, [2003] O.J. L 156/17.

78 The Commission made a proposal to the European Parliament and Council for a Directive on access to justice in environmental matters in 2003, which was withdrawn in 2014 having failed to achieve the necessary support to be adopted. Reportedly, this is the only time besides the withdrawal of the proposal for a Soil Directive that the Commission withdrew a proposal in environmental law. See Proposal for a Directive of the European Parliament and of the Council on access to justice in environmental matters /* COM/2003/0624 final - COD 2003/0246 */. Retrieved from http://eur-lex.europa.eu/legal-content/EN/TXT/?uri=CELEX:52003PC0624. See also re issues of EU compliance with the third pillar of the

In this case, even though the EU has guided the implementation of the environmental procedural rights in Member States through separate instruments, they all aim to implement the Aarhus Convention, which provides the common framework for public participation in environmental matters and ensures that there is a 'system' supporting these different participatory rights.

Perhaps the lack of a general compass is one of the reasons for the absence of such a system in Colombia, where access to environmental information is not integrated with public participation schemes, which until very recently were virtually non-existent. Public participation in decision-making processes still can only be found in isolated provisions which do not complement each other and lack in specificity, seriously undermining their effectiveness. Examples of the mechanisms in place are the prior consultation process under the ILO Convention 169,[79] which only applies to ethnic communities (indigenous and African-Colombian, mainly), the Environmental Impact Assessment procedure, which is fairly ineffective in practice as a tool for public participation because it fails to impose any specific obligations upon project operators aimed at promoting public participation in the decision-making process such as public hearings, mandatory public disclosure of relevant information or protocols to receive and properly consider public comments; and the special mechanisms for participation in administrative procedures, which need to be triggered by an interested member of the public and are still rather limited.[80] None of these participation procedures is regulated in detail. The Colombian Environmental Licence Authority, however, in an attempt to establish minimum guidelines for public participation in EIA procedures, adopted in 2018 a *Guide of Citizen Participation in Environmental Licencing*,[81] which proposes methodological and procedural guidelines to engage communities in EIA processes, sets minimum requirements of access to information and indicates the way participatory activities must be documented and supported. These guidelines are not binding, however, and their enforcement depends on the regional environmental authorities exercising their discretion to make specific requirements to project operators on an *ad hoc* basis. In sum, these provisions fail to materialise an actual right of public participation in decision-making processes, lacking most if not all of the

Convention: D'Silva, J., & Van Calster, G. (2010). For Me to Know and You to Find Out? Participatory Mechanisms, The Aarhus Convention and New Technologies. *Studies in Ethics, Law, and Technology, 4*(2) and Oliver, P. (2013). Access to Information and to Justice in EU Environmental Law: The Aarhus Convention. *Fordham International Law Journal, 36*(1423), 1456.

79 Convention concerning Indigenous and Tribal Peoples in Independent Countries ILO C169, International Labor Organisation, 76th session, 27 June 1989 (entered into force 5 September 1991), Geneva.

80 Colombian General Environmental Law, Articles 72–74.

81 National Agency of Environmental Licences - ANLA. (2018). *Guia de Participación Ciudadana en el Licenciamiento Ambiental*. Retrieved from http://portal.anla.gov.co/guia-participacion-ciudadana.

elements discussed in the normative framework about what makes public participation effective.

Public participation in Colombia could be improved if there were specific rules on why, how, when, with whom and for what public participation procedures should take place, ideally framed in a system that considers principles of environmental law and human rights in a regional context.

Colombia was recently admitted as a member to the Organisation for Cooperation and Economic Development (OECD), after several years in a process that included the assessment of environmental policies and legislation. The OECD 2014 Environmental Performance Review on the country made specific recommendations to increase public participation in environmental matters and access to information, including the establishment of a Pollutant Release and Transfer Register.[82] The somewhat insufficient governance landscape seems to be changing, however: in August 2018 the government created the 'Inter-sectoral Board for Environmental Democracy', a multidisciplinary task group with the participation of environmental public authorities, private sector, universities, environmental institutes and NGOs entrusted to aid with the formulation of legislative and public policy instruments for the implementation or Principle 10 of the Rio Convention, taking in consideration the recently adopted Escazú Agreement.[83]

Regarding access to justice, Colombian law establishes an *actio popularis* allowing anyone to file a judicial recourse for the protection of the environment, and an action for annulment which can be filed against administrative acts granting permits or environmental licences, when the act or the procedure leading to its adoption are found to be defective under the law. However, these judicial remedies are not specifically designed for environmental cases, and they are certainly not integrated with other public participation mechanisms.

In the US, public participation in decision-making is only integrated with access to information provisions in subject-specific acts, such as the Clean Water Act, which mandates 'the use, assistance, and encouragement of public participation in the development, revision, and enforcement of any regulation at federal and State levels'[84] and further requires carrying out consultation and cooperation actions with interested organisations and persons and recognised experts as well as the development of minimum standards for public participation in cooperation with the states.[85] However, as a matter of policy, EPA's mission includes ensuring that 'all parts of society – communities, individuals,

82 OECD. (2014). *Environmental Performance Reviews: Colombia (2014)*. Retrieved from http://www.oecd.org/env/country-reviews/ColombiaEPR_AssessmentRecommendations.pdf.

83 Resolution 1496 of 2018 'Creating the Intersectoral Board for Environmental Democracy (MIDA) and other dispositions', Ministry of Environment and Sustainable Development, 3 August 2018.

84 Clean Water Act, 33 U.S.C. Par. 1254 (a) (2006).

85 Toth, B. (2010). Public Participation and Democracy in Practice - Aarhus Convention Principles as Democratic Institution Building in the Developing World. *Journal of Land Resources and Environmental Law, 30*(2), 306.

businesses, and state, local and tribal governments – have access to accurate information sufficient to effectively participate in managing human health and environmental risks',[86] recognising the necessary interdependency of access to information rights and other components of public participation in environmental governance.

Additionally, the Administrative Procedure Act (APA) establishes the possibility of an 'interested person' (broadly defined to include individuals, partnerships, associations, corporations and public or private entities in general) to petition for the issuance, amendment or repeal of a rule,[87] through the mechanism of 'notice-and-comment' rulemaking for the general public participation in regulatory decisions of state agencies. This consists of a 90-day timeframe (60-day comment and 30-day reply) during which proposals for administrative rules are published and open for public comments. Though with some limitations, this mechanism allows for public participation in decision-making and gives legitimacy to the agencies' regulatory functions.

Regarding access to justice, the US legal system provides for several ways to challenge actions and decisions that may be against environmental laws or that may be thwarting the exercise of public participation rights. Refusals to information requests under FOIA, for instance, may be appealed to the head of the concerned agency and thereafter before a federal court. Additionally, many environmental statutes provide US citizens with automatic standing to sue for the implementation and enforcement of the law, even when they have not suffered direct harm or are not able to claim a direct interest. This is based on the public trust doctrine and the conception of a general right to a clean environment.[88] The Clean Water Act (2006), for example, allows for standing in suits against the Environment Protection Agency (EPA) or the state equivalent for failure to carry out their obligations under the act.[89] Other statutes however only allow 'affected parties' to bring lawsuits under the act, such as Federal Insecticide, Fungicide and Rodenticide Act FIFRA.[90] Outside the scope of environmental regulations, APA's 'open meetings' requirement allows 'any person' to challenge agency implementation of the statute before the Court.[91]

In conclusion, there is no 'public participation system' as such in the US either, but a varied array of provisions allowing limited exercise of participatory rights in environmental governance.

86 Environmental Protection Agency. Retrieved from https://www.epa.gov/aboutepa/our-mission-and-what-we-do.

87 Administrative Procedure Act [APA], 5 USC Par. 553 (e) (2006).

88 Lamdan, S. (2017). *Environmental Information: Research, Access and Environmental Decisionmaking*. Environmental Law Institute.

89 Toth, *Public Participation*, 2010, citing Congressional Research Service (2008), *Clean Water Act: A Summary of the Law* 1, 7.

90 Federal Insecticide, Fungicide, and Rodenticide Act (attended in 1972 and 2003) 7 U.S.C. §§ 136 et seq. (1947).

91 US APA, para. 552 b (h).

4 Scope of the Laws Providing Access to Information

4.1. Scope of Beneficiaries: Is Access to Information Provided Without Discrimination and Without Having to State an Interest?

As previously explained, an inherent characteristic of the general right of access to information is that it should be afforded to any member of the public, without having to prove any particular interest or even explain their motives. This is so because in the theoretical foundations of the right there is the underlying assumption that public information belongs to the public and it should be made available for its own sake.[1]

This argument is present in the motives and considerations of most FOI laws, expressing, in general terms, that people should be entitled to access public information because it is necessary in a democratic state and it contributes to strengthen state legitimacy and administrative good practice.

Furthermore, where access to public information is recognised as a human right, its exercise should never be restricted for reasons of domicile, nationality, gender, race, citizenship or any other status of the human person.

Private entities are also entitled to access environmental information and any public information under the FOI laws. Although the focus of this research places them in the other extreme of the information stream, it should be noted that they are also entitled to exercise 'freedom of expression' related liberties such as the right 'not to speak' which is the counterpart of the right of access (to compel speech), the right to privacy and the right of property over their private information, from which the protection of business confidentiality and trade secrets often derives. Legal entities are also entitled to assert their rights of due process and a fair trial, and rights to a good name and reputation. Many a times, access to information may be provided as the instrument to materialise these high-standing values, which are not exclusive attributes of the natural person.

1 Villanueva, E. (2006). Tendencias en el Reconocimiento Constitucional del Derecho de Acceso a la Información Pública. In S. López-Ayllón (Ed.) *Democracia, transparencia y constitución: propuestas para un debate necesario.* Universidad Autónoma de México.

DOI: 10.4324/9781003307617-4

That being said, extended privileges regarding the right of access to environmental information may entail certain restrictions in the scope of the beneficiary public. The Aarhus Convention, for instance, provides preferential access to information in the framework of participation in decision-making on specific projects to the 'public concerned' (Article 6).[2] This is defined in the Convention as public 'affected or likely to be affected, or having an interest in, the environmental decision-making' (Article 2(2)). Importantly, under the Aarhus Convention, Environmental NGOs complying with applicable requirements under national law will always be deemed to have an interest, thus will be considered 'public concerned'.

Articles 6, 7 and 8 of the Aarhus Convention deal with public participation in decision-making in three different scenarios: specific projects or activities; environmental plans, programmes and policies; and the preparation of binding normative instruments. In these cases, access to environmental information serves the specific purpose of facilitating the exercise of the right to participate in the decision-making processes. Within this context, the competent authority may (and should) identify the public concerned and provide the necessary information to ensure their ability to input an informed opinion.

The privileges afforded to the 'public concerned' under these provisions should not be construed to entail any limitations for the public in general to access environmental information. The Aarhus Convention contains among its general provisions a non-discrimination rule, which warns against restricting participatory rights for reasons of nationality, citizenship or domicile (Article 3(9)). At the International level, this rule can be complemented by the provisions of the Espoo Convention regarding Environmental Impact Assessments in a transboundary context.[3]

In this regard, the Escazu Agreement may present shortcomings due to its definition of 'public' as natural persons and organisations (and groups thereof) that are nationals or are subject to the national jurisdiction of a state Party to the Agreement,[4] hence limiting the participation of the public from other states that could be affected by transboundary projects. On the other

2 Convention on Access to Information, Public Participation in Decision-making and Access to Justice in Environmental Matters, Aarhus, Denmark, 25 June 1998 (entry into force 30 October 2001) 2161 UNTS 447.

3 UNECE Convention on Environmental Impact Assessment in a Transboundary Context, 25 Feb 1991 (entered into force on 10 September 1997), 1989 UNTS 309. For a more detailed analysis of the non-discrimination principle in international law see Mason, M, 'Citizenship beyond National Borders? Identifying Mechanisms of Public Access and Redress in International Environmental Regimes', *Global Governance: A Review of Multilaterialism and International Organizations,* 12 (2006), 283–303.

4 United Nations, Regional Agreement on Access to Information, Public Participation and Justice in Environmental Matters in Latin America and the Caribbean, 4 March 2018 (entered into force 22 April 2021), Escazú, Costa Rica, Article 2.

hand, a step forward may be the Agreement's acknowledgement of 'persons and groups in vulnerable situations', defined as

> (…) those persons or groups that face particular difficulties in fully exercising the access rights recognized in the present Agreement, because of circumstances or conditions identified within each Party's national context and in accordance with its international obligations.[5]

The Agreement mandates that Parties shall take measures to ensure effective access to vulnerable persons or groups

> establishing procedures for the provision of assistance, from the formulation of requests through to the delivery of the information, taking into account their conditions and specificities, for the purpose of promoting access and participation under equal conditions.[6]

This could be achieved, for example, providing training to public officials in charge of information requests that would allow them to identify persons or groups in vulnerable situations, assess the context in which the information is being sought and offer especial assistance in obtaining the correct information, interpreting it when necessary and facilitating its utilisation.

Unlike the Aarhus Convention, the Escazú Agreement does not have a specific definition of 'public concerned'. However, it provides that state Parties shall identify the 'public directly affected' by specific projects or decisions in order to engage with them in public participation processes; and shall also take the necessary measures to facilitate their understanding and participation when they speak a language which is not the official language of the country.[7]

The protection established in the Escazú Agreement for defenders of environmental human rights deserves a special mention. Parties shall ensure that they have an enabling environment to exercise their rights, and shall take effective measures to 'recognize, protect and promote all the rights of human rights defenders in environmental matters, including their right to life, personal integrity, freedom of opinion and expression, peaceful assembly and association and free movement'.[8]

The EU follows closely the conditions of the Aarhus Convention regarding the scope of beneficiaries of access to information rights. Directive 90/313 already expressed the duty of Member States to 'ensure that public authorities are required to make available information relating to the environment to any natural or legal person at his request and without his having to prove an

5 Escazú Agreement, Article 2 (e).
6 Escazú Agreement, Article 4.
7 Escazú Agreement, Article 7(11).
8 Escazú Agreement, Article 9(2).

interest'.[9] The same provision is replicated in Article 3 of Directive 2003/4 repealing this Directive to comply with Aarhus' standards.[10]

Although the Directives omit any specific rule banning discrimination for the purposes of the rights of access, they must be read in accordance with the general rules and principles found in the EU Treaties which forbid any discrimination on grounds of nationality and the case-law of the ECtHR.[11]

In contrast, Regulation No. 1049/2001 on public access to European Parliament, Council and Commission documents,[12] establishes the obligation to allow access to documents to 'any citizen of the Union, and any natural or legal person residing or having its registered office in a Member State' (Article 2(1)) but leaves to the discretion of the institutions whether to grant access to persons not residing or not having their registered office in a Member State. This does not apply to documents containing environmental information otherwise included in the scope of Directive No 2003/4. Regulation No 1367/2006 on the application of the provisions of the Aarhus Convention to Community institutions and bodies[13] states that 'the rights guaranteed by the three pillars of the Aarhus Convention are without discrimination as to citizenship, nationality or domicile' (Recital 6) and explicitly extends the application of Regulation No 1049/2001 to any request by an applicant for access to environmental information held by Community institutions without discrimination as to citizenship, nationality or domicile (Article 3).

In Colombia, the constitutional Right of Petition, the main mechanism to request access to information, is established in favour of *any person*, including non-nationals acting under Colombian jurisdiction, and so is the right of access to public documents enshrined in Article 74 of the Constitution.[14] Access to environmental information under the General Environmental Law is likewise in favour of 'any natural or legal person'.[15]

9 Council Directive 90/313/EEC of 7 June 1990 on the freedom of access to information on the environment [1990] O.J. L158/56/90, Article 3.

10 Directive 2003/4/EC of the European Parliament and of the Council of 28 January 2003 on Public Access to Environmental Information and repealing Council Directive 90/313/EEC, [2003] O.J. L 41/26.

11 ECtHR, Council of Europe (2011). *Handbook on European Non-Discrimination Law.* Retrieved from https://www.refworld.org/pdfid/4d886bf02.pdf,

12 Regulation (EC) No 1049/2001 of the European Parliament and of the Council of 30 May 2001 regarding public access to European Parliament, Council and Commission documents, [2001] O.J. L 145/43.

13 Regulation (EC) No 1367/2006 of the European Parliament and of the Council on the application of the provisions of the Aarhus Convention on Access to Information, Public Participation in Decision-making and Access to Justice in Environmental Matters to Community institutions and bodies, [2006] O.J. L 264/13.

14 Political Constitution of the Republic of Colombia, 4 July 1991.

15 Law 99 of 1993 'Creating the Minister of the Environment, organising the public sector in charge of the management and conservation of the environment and the renewable natural resources, organising the National Environmental System (SINA), and other dispositions', 22 December 1993, Article 74.

Neither rule demands that the applicant must show any particular interest or state the motives of their request and they should all be applied under the premise of non-discrimination found in the Constitution (1991, Article 13). Furthermore, the General Transparency Law establishes the principle of maximum disclosure, stating that all information held, controlled or under custody of an obligated entity is public and cannot be withheld unless otherwise provided in the law or the Constitution.[16] Article 3 of the same statute establishes a principle of 'non-discrimination', stating that obligated entities shall provide information to any person requesting it on equal conditions and without demanding a reason or motive for the request.

An exception to this rule is in cases of exercising the Right of Petition before private entities for the protection of the petitioner's fundamental rights, which implies a direct connection between the applicant and the information sought, hence the need to state a motive. This mechanism, found in the Constitution and implemented through the Right of Petition Law,[17] allows access to information held by private entities and natural persons, which is otherwise excluded from the scope of the general right of access to public information and the right of access to environmental information, as long as it is required for the exercise or protection of the petitioner's fundamental rights, such as the right to a healthy environment and the right to privacy and family life.

In the US case, access to information under the Freedom of Information Act can be exercised by anyone, citizens or non-citizens, and there is generally no need to state any reason or to prove interest in the information.[18] Associations, foreign governments and NGOs may also employ the FOIA to request environmental information from federal government agencies. The Supreme Court has recognised this far-reaching scope in the case of *National Archives & records Administration v Favish* (2004), stating: 'The disclosure does not depend on the identity of the requester. As a general rule, if the information is subject to disclosure, it belongs to all'.[19]

A partial exception to this rule is the case of agencies which are an *element of the intelligence community* as defined by the National Security Act of 1947; they are forbidden to make any record available to any foreign government entity or representative.[20]

The scope of beneficiaries becomes almost irrelevant in relation to the mechanisms for active dissemination of information by public authorities and other obligated entities. The information is usually made available through

16 Law 1712 of 2014 'Creating the Law of Transparency and of the Right of Access to National Public Information and other dispositions', 6 March 2014, Article 2.

17 Law 1755 of 2015 'Regulating the Fundamental Right of Petition and repealing a Title of the Code of Administrative Procedure', 30 June 2015.

18 Freedom of Information Act of July 4, 1966, Public Law No. 89–487, 80 Stat. 250, codified as amended at 5 U.S.C. § 552 (1994), Article (a)(3).

19 *Nat'l Archives & Records Admin. v Favish*, 541 U.S. 157, 172 (2004).

20 US Freedom of Information Act, Section (a)(3)(E).

electronic databases with unrestricted access to the public. The point can be made, though, that disadvantaged groups may have difficulties in accessing information through electronic means and practical factors such as distance, communication technologies, mobility, and other socio-economic issues may stand in the way of effective access to information. In this regard, provisions similar to the Escazú Agreement's on 'persons or groups in vulnerable situations' may help to ensure equality in access, for instance by enabling reading rooms in distant locations, promoting free access to internet and IT education in particularly vulnerable communities, and improving communication channels between the authorities and the public.

4.2. Material Scope: What Information Can be Accessed?

The material scope refers to the *object* that can be accessed through the different access to information laws. When the law focuses on environmental information, this is the definition that should be analysed for the comparative study. In cases where the law applies to general information (not only environmental), it is worth paying attention to the *format* of the information and any other conditions that may restrict access on the basis of the nature, situation, status or location of the records.

4.2.1. Data, Information and Knowledge

Going from general to specific, it is worth noting that some authors[21] have made an important distinction between data, information and knowledge. 'Data' is a broad concept that can encompass different types of content, most importantly 'raw' data, or unfinished pieces of information. Figures, numbers, datasheets, laboratory reports and test results that have not been organised in an intelligent manner can be called 'raw data'. 'Information' most often refers to data that has undergone some processing to make it useful. It is more significant than raw data because it has been organised in a logical manner and can therefore be more easily identifiable and tracked. Information regularly appears as 'documents' and in many legal instruments both terms are used indistinctively. Finally, 'knowledge' is the result of access to information in a specific context and in relation to a particular question.

Most access to information legislation provides public access to 'information' or 'documents', and only in some cases to raw or unprocessed data. When discussing 'access to information' in this book, the term will not extend to raw data or 'knowledge' unless noted.

21 The following conceptual construction is based on the distinction made by Jimenez-Beltran (1995) and Esty (2004) as referenced in Mol, A. P. J. (2008). *Environmental Reform in the Information Age: the Contours of Informational Governance.* Cambridge University Press.

4.2.2. Restrictions Based on Format

The Aarhus Convention, in its definition of 'environmental information' refers to 'any information in written, visual, aural, electronic or any other material form', meaning that no information can be restricted from disclosure based on its material format. This is also the case in the Escazú Agreement.[22]

The issue is relevant in the case of the EU, where Regulation No 1367/2006 was enacted to implement the Aarhus Convention for EU institutions and bodies, thus it applies in cases of access to 'environmental information', whilst access to public information in general (not environmental) from the same institutions is determined by Regulation No 1049/2001, providing access only to 'official documents'. The European Court of First Instance ruled in case T-264/04, *WWF-EPO v Council of the European Union* (2007), that the 'concept of document must be distinguished from that of information'.[23] Thus, under Regulation No 1049/2001, the EU institutions only must disclose information held as formal documents, as opposed to '... any information in written, visual, aural or electronic or any other material form' as defined in the Aarhus Convention. By the time of this decision, however, the Aarhus Convention was not yet in force in the EU, and Regulation No 1367/2006 had not yet been adopted.

Regulation No 1367/2006 (Article 4) mandates that 'Regulation No 1049/2001 shall apply to any request by an applicant for environmental information held by [EU] institutions and bodies'. As previously noted, both regulations must be applied in a consistent manner, considering that Regulation No 1367/2006 is *lex specialis* concerning access to environmental information. Therefore, in case of conflicting interpretations, the Aarhus Regulation prevails over the general access regime.[24] This means that the EU institutions, when faced with requests of environmental information, should provide access to 'information' regardless of whether it is contained in a document or not.

On the other hand, the US FOIA employs the term 'record' to refer to the information that can be accessed under the act. This statute establishes that the public shall have access to:

> (A) any information that would be an agency record subject to the requirements of this section when maintained by an agency in any format, including an electronic format; and
> (B) any information described under subparagraph (A) that is maintained for an agency by an entity under Government contract, for the purposes of records management.[25]

22 Escazú Agreement, Article 2(c).
23 CJEU, Case T-264/04, *WWF-EPO v. Council of the European Union*, Judgment of 25 April 2007.
24 CJEU (Court of First Instance), Case T-29/08 *Liga para Protecção da Natureza (LPN) v European Commission*, Judgment of 9 September 2011. 105.
25 US Freedom of Information Act, Sec. 552(f)(2).

The term 'record' was not given any definition until the amendment to FOIA in 1996. After the amendments, Section 552(f)(2) defined 'record and any other term used in this section in reference to information' as 'any information that would be an agency record subject to the requirements of this section when maintained by an agency in any format, including an electronic format.'[26]

The scope of the statute is not so much determined by the definition of 'record' but by the that of 'agency record'.

The Supreme Court has developed some guidance to interpret these statutes to assert when certain information is an 'agency record'. A two-part test was formulated which required that the records were (i) obtained or produced by an agency and (ii) under the control of the agency at the time of the request.[27] Assuming that the gist of the matter depends on what can be defined as 'control', the Supreme Court defined four indicators to determine when a record is under control of the agency:

> (1) the intent of the document's creator to retain or relinquish control over the record []; (2) the ability of the agency to use and dispose of the record as it sees fit; (3) the extent to which agency personnel have read or relied upon the document; and (4) the degree to which the document was integrated into the agency's record systems or files.[28]

The definition of 'control' is relevant for this study because it is also the criteria to determine when information held by an agency's contractor can be accessed under the US FOIA. In this matter, the Supreme Court has stated that a record held by a private contractor is an 'agency record' when it 'is maintained for an agency by an entity under government contract, for the purposes of records management'.[29]

The US Supreme Court has also clarified that the public's right of access under FOIA does not include a duty of the agency to elaborate a document or to organise information, but only to provide copies of existing documents or information that can be retrieved from an electronic database without any additional processing.[30]

26 Electronic Freedom of Information Act [EFOIA], 5 U.S.C. Sec. 552(f)(2) (Supp. II 1996).

27 *Dep of Justice v Tax Analysts*, 492 U.S. 136, 144–45 (1989). U.S. DOJ, Department of Justice Guide to the Freedom of Information Act 2 (2016) Retrieved from https://www.justice.gov/sites/default/files/oip/legacy/2014/07/23/procedural-requirements.pdf#p9.

28 *Burka v. HHS,* 87 F.3d 508, 515 (D.C. Cir. 1996) (quoting *Tax Analysts v. DOJ,* 845 F.2d 1060, 1069 (D.C. Cir. 1988)), cited in U.S. DOJ, Department of Justice Guide to the Freedom of Information Act 2 (2016) Retrieved from https://www.justice.gov/sites/default/files/oip/legacy/2014/07/23/procedural-requirements.pdf#p9.

29 US DOJ, *Guide to the Freedom of Information Act*, 2016.

30 US DOJ, *Guide to the Freedom of Information Act*, 2016.

The additional requisite of 'possession' by an obligated subject, of the record or the piece of information requested, can also be found in the transparency instruments of the other jurisdictions. Regulation No 1049/01 applies to 'all the documents held by an institution, that is to say, documents drawn up or received by it and in its possession',[31] meanwhile, the Colombian Transparency Law establishes a general principle according to which 'all information in the possession, under the control, or in the custody of an obligated subject is public and can only be classified or restricted by a constitutional or legal provision'[32] and the Aarhus Convention also provides an exception to disclosure when the information requested is not held by the authority to whom the petition was addressed.[33]

Resuming the analysis of format, the Colombian Transparency Law defines 'information' as the 'organised collection of data contained in any document that the obligated subjects generate, obtain, acquire, transform or control'.[34]

The same law provides definitions of 'open data' and 'document in construction', stating:

> … j) Open Data: It is all primary or unprocessed data found in standard and inter-operative formats to facilitate access and utilisation thereto, which is under the custody of public or private entities performing public functions and is made available to any citizen, freely and unrestricted, with the purpose of being reused by third parties and to create services derived from it.
>
> k) Document in construction: Preliminary and non-definitive information, belonging to a deliberative process of an obligated entity. It shall not be considered public information.[35]

Whilst the reference to 'document' and 'organised collection' in the definition of 'information' seems to restrict the concept, the law explicitly covers 'raw data', which can be reused, even for commercial purposes. Unfinished documents, on the other hand, seem to be explicitly excluded from the Transparency Law. However, the Constitutional Court conditioned the interpretation of this definition stating that 'the possibility of an obligated subject to withhold preliminary information is conditioned on the decision serving a constitutionally legitimate purpose and the measure being reasonable, proportional and necessary'.[36]

From the above, the following conclusions can be drawn:

31 EU Regulation No. 1049/01, Article 2(3).
32 Colombian General Transparency Law, Article 2.
33 Aarhus Convention, Article 4 (3)(a).
34 Colombian General Transparency Law, Article 6(a).
35 Colombian General Transparency Law, Article 6 (j)–(k).
36 Colombian Constitutional Court, Case C-274/13, Judgment of 9 May 2013, M.P. Maria Victoria Calle Correa.

i The terms 'documents', 'information' and 'records' should not be interpreted narrowly to unduly restrict the rights of public access enshrined in the transparency laws. The most modern laws generally define the scope of the accessible information as the data available in any format, including electronic records and unprocessed data.

ii The scope of the right is limited to the information that is in possession or under control of the obligated subjects. To prevent this rule from undermining the effectiveness of the right to information, the obligated subjects must have a duty to produce, obtain and keep all the information they need for their functions in an appropriate manner (organised, updated, indexed etc.). This also means that information held by third parties (*i.e.* private contractors) may eventually be accessed even if they are not specifically obligated under the law.

4.2.3. The Definition of 'Environmental Information'

The Aarhus Convention's definition of 'Environmental Information' is quite far-reaching and comprehensive. Article 2(3) of the Convention defines it as:

> (…) any information in written, visual, aural, electronic or any other material form on:
> (a) The state of elements of the environment, such as air and atmosphere, water, soil, land, landscape and natural sites, biological diversity and its components, including genetically modified organisms, and the interaction among these elements;
> (b) Factors, such as substances, energy, noise and radiation, and activities or measures, including administrative measures, environmental agreements, policies, legislation, plans and programmes, affecting or likely to affect the elements of the environment within the scope of subparagraph (a) above, and cost-benefit and other economic analyses and assumptions used in environmental decision-making;
> (c) The state of human health and safety, conditions of human life, cultural sites and built structures, inasmuch as they are or may be affected by the state of the elements of the environment or, through these elements, by the factors, activities or measures referred to in subparagraph (b) above;

According to the Aarhus Convention Implementation Guide the definition is not exhaustive but rather provides three different categories with illustrative examples.[37] It should be interpreted considering the stated purposes of the Convention to make the scope as broad as possible.

Conversely, the Escazú Agreeement defines 'environmental information' as

37 UNECE, *Aarhus Implementation Guide*, 2014, p. 38.

> '… any information that is written, visual, audio, and electronic, or recorded in any other format, regarding the environment and its elements and natural resources, including information related to environmental risks, and any possible adverse impacts affecting or likely to affect the environment and health, as well as to environmental protection and management'.[38]

The literal interpretation of both definitions seems to suggest a broader scope of the Aarhus Convention in comparison to the Escazú Agreement. Aspects such as economic risk assessments, information about cultural sites and other factors affecting the conditions of human life and human safety may fall outside the definition in the latter instrument. It can be argued however that a broad abstract definition is preferable to prevent the unduly restriction of the scope of the right. This could be the case if there is a specific rule that mandates the broad interpretation of the provision and a default presumption of inclusion so that, if in doubt, the information will be deemed to be accessible under the Agreement's provisions.

Back to the analysis of Aarhus' definition, it is important to note that many of the terms included could be interpreted considering other relevant legal instruments, as suggested in the Implementation Guide, namely EU Directive 2008/50/EC for 'air and atmosphere'; the Convention on Biological Diversity for the term 'biological diversity' and EU Directive 2001/18/EC for the term 'Genetically Modified Organisms' (GMO).

The definition in the Convention mentions 'factors… affecting or likely to affect the elements of the environment' – which may be understood as agents capable of exercising an influence – activities or measures that may affect the elements of the environment within the scope of the first category, as well as any economic analysis or assumptions used in environmental decision-making.

A non-exhaustive list of examples can be construed from the Implementation Guide and the findings of the Aarhus Convention Compliance Committee (ACCC). On this basis, factors, measures and activities are likely to include environmental permits and licences, public policy documents, legislation, plans, programs and environmental agreements, administrative contracts affecting the environment[39] and information about land use and planning.[40]

The interpretation of economic analysis and assumptions used in environmental decision-making can benefit from the list of 'relevant information' in Article 6(6), which refers to the information that should be made available to

38 Escazú Agreement, Article 2(c).

39 Aarhus Convention Compliance Committee, Case ACCC/C/2008/30 (Republic of Moldova), ECE/MP.PP/C.1/2009/6/Add.3.

40 Aarhus Convention Compliance Committee, Case ACCC/C/2004/08 (Armenia), ECE/MP.PP/C.1/2006/2/Add.1.

the public concerned for the decision-making process regarding specific activities or projects. The Implementation Guide rightly points out that

> As economic analyses may have a great impact on whether or not a particular project will go ahead, it is important to be able to examine the thinking that went into them (…) It is therefore also important to be able to analyse the assumptions behind economic modelling used in environmental decision-making.[41]

The third category listed refers to the state of human health and safety and conditions of human life, cultural sites and structures that could be affected by the two previous categories. In this case, the Convention is concerned with the effects of the elements of the environment and the factors that may affect them into the wellbeing of communities, public health issues and the natural consequences of the conditions of the environment in human life.

This analysis reveals a complementary and logical interrelationship between the categories of 'environmental information' in the Aarhus Convention establishing a material delimitation to the object of the public right of access to information. When access to environmental information is subject to regulation in the different jurisdictions, a definition of 'environmental information' would be key to the application of information rights, but this is not the case when access to environmental information is granted in the framework of a law providing access to public information in general.

Noting that neither the US nor Colombia has specific laws on access to environmental information, access to this type of information is not limited by the definition of the term (which is absent in this jurisdictions), instead it is determined by the definitions of 'public' vs. 'private' information, the scope of obligated entities, what constitutes 'document' or 'agency record', and the delimitation of the exceptions to disclosure in general access regulations.

4.2.4. Access to 'Relevant' Environmental Information in Decision-Making Processes

The inclusion of a specific analysis about the availability of 'relevant environmental information' besides the more general concept of 'environmental information', is aimed to show that a more nuanced approach to the types of environmental information that may be necessary for effective public participation in decision-making can contribute to the resolution of conflicts arising from business confidentiality claims.

The rationale here is that not all of the environmental information included in public access laws is equally important from the perspective of the public interest and effective public participation in decision-making. Considering that one of the instruments to determine when disclosure should prevail over

41 UNECE, *Aarhus Implementation Guide*, 2014, p. 54.

confidentiality is a 'balancing test' between the interests protected, knowing the actual importance of the environmental information for the applicant would be key to assess if the adverse effect of disclosure over the legitimate interests protected with an exception outweighs the public interests in disclosure. This approach generally takes after the *interest theory of rights* developed by Joseph Raz, aimed at identifying rights by inquiring into the ultimate values or interests that support them in order to define the correlative duties associated with them.[42]

The need for all relevant information to be made public during a decision-making process has been widely recognised as a natural component of the participation process. Guideline 10 of the 'Bali Guidelines' specifically states:

> States should ensure that all information relevant for decision-making related to the environment is made available, in an objective, understandable, timely and effective manner, to the members of the public concerned.[43]

Moreover, the concept has found support in the principles of 'natural justice' and 'fair administrative process'. According to Morrison-Saunders & Early the primary requisites for upholding these legal principles are that the decision-maker operates without bias and that third persons likely to be affected by the decision are given an opportunity to be heard.[44] In EIA processes this translates into the need to apply a 'test of significance' to the information used in the decision-making process in order to make it available for comments, if it raises substantive issues, before the decision is made; even if this is *after* a public consultation process has been carried out.[45]

Faircheallaigh also suggests that it may be only through effective public participation that all of the *relevant* information about a specific project or policy measure can be obtained. This author points out that information about the potential consequences of the proposed actions should include the fears and hopes of the people's predictions of the likely effect of projects, which are an important part of social impact, thus the benefits may come from a double direction: public participation feeds into better information

42 Raz, J. (1986). *The Morality of Freedom*, Oxford University Press, pp. 165–192. Examples of this approach are found in Roesler, S. M. (2012). The Nature of the Environmental Right to Know. *Ecology Law Quarterly, 39*, 989–1040 and Roberts, A. (2001). Structural Pluralism and the Right to Information. *The University of Toronto Law Journal, 51*(3), 243–271.

43 United Nations Environment Programme – UNEP. The Bali Guidelines for Development of National Legislation on Access to Information, Public Participation and Access to Justice in Environmental matters, 26 February 2010.

44 Morrison-Saunders, A., & Early, G. (2008). What Is Necessary to Ensure Natural Justice in Environmental Impact Assessment Decision-Making?. *Impact Assessment and Project Appraisal*, 26, 29–42.

45 Morrison-Saunders & Early, *Natural Justice*, 2008.

gathering and sharing; and access to relevant information, in turn, sustains effective public participation.[46]

In Chapter 1 a working definition of 'relevant environmental information' was introduced, based on the concept of effective public participation. This definition encompasses the most important information that must be made available to ensure meaningful public participation in decision-making process regarding specific activities, measures or projects. It includes:

a Facts: relate to the context, precedents, and description of the project/programme/measure to be taken.
b Impacts: expected consequences of the proposed measure, positive and negative, on the identified problem and, additionally, on the environmental and social aspects.
c Risks: events with negative connotation, which have a probability of happening as a result of the adoption of the proposed measure. If known, the probability of occurrence is also relevant.
d Remedies: the proposed actions to be undertaken in order to prevent the materialisation of risks and mitigate or compensate negative impacts.
e Alternatives: other measures or activities, which could achieve the purposes of the proposed measure.
f Costs: the price of adopting the proposed measure, as well as the estimated cost of the alternatives. The analysis of costs must include the long-term benefit.

This working definition was drawn based on Article 6(6) of the Aarhus Convention, which lists the information that must be disclosed to the public concerned as soon as it becomes available for their participation in decision-making regarding specific projects or activities.

At the international level, the Espoo Convention also establishes access to *relevant* information in the framework of transboundary environmental impact assessment. Article 3(5) establishes that the 'Party of origin' (of a project with transboundary impacts) shall provide to the 'Party affected', upon receipt of a notice indicating the latest desire to participate in the EIA,

> … (a) Relevant information regarding the environmental impact assessment procedure, including an indication of the time schedule for transmittal of comments; and
> (b) Relevant information on the proposed activity and its possible significant adverse transboundary impact.

46 O'Faircheallaigh, C. (2010). Public Participation and Environmental Impact Assessment: Purposes, Implications, and Lessons for Public Policy Making. *Environmental Impact Assessment Review*, 30.

Article 4 further specifies the documentation that must be submitted to the competent authority for the EIA evaluation and which shall be distributed to the public in the areas likely to be affected, contained in Appendix II of the Convention.

At the EU level, Directive 2003/4/EC on access to environmental information replicates almost exactly Article 2(1) containing the definition of 'Environmental Information' of the Aarhus Convention, which logically exceeds the scope of what we call 'relevant environmental information'. The definition of the Directive reads:

> 'Environmental information' shall mean any information in written, visual, aural, electronic or any other material form on:
>
> (a) the state of the elements of the environment, such as air and atmosphere, water, soil, land, landscape and natural sites including wetlands, coastal and marine areas, biological diversity and its components, including genetically modified organisms, and the interaction among these elements.
> (b) factors, such as substances, energy, noise, radiation or waste, including radioactive waste, emissions, discharges and other releases into the environment, affecting or likely to affect the elements of the environment referred to in (a);
> (c) measures (including administrative measures), such as policies, legislation, plans, programmes, environmental agreements, and activities affecting or likely to affect the elements and factors referred to in (a) and (b) as well as measures or activities designed to protect those elements.
> (d) (d) reports on the implementation of environmental legislation;
> (e) cost-benefit and other economic analyses and assumptions used within the framework of the measures and activities referred to in (c); and
> (f) the state of human health and safety, including the contamination of the food chain, where relevant, conditions of human life, cultural sites and built structures inasmuch as they are or may be affected by the state of the elements of the environment referred to in (a) or, through those elements, by any of the matters referred to in (b) and (c).[47]

The broad categories established therein clearly encompass information on specific projects or activities that may have an effect in the elements of the environment (Article 2(1), Paragraph c), including the factors that produce such effects and their interactions (Paragraph b), the risks and actual impacts of the activity on the environment and human living conditions (Paragraphs. a, b and f) as well as the analysis of alternatives and costs that justifies the project (Paragraph e).

Furthermore, environmental impact studies and risk assessments concerning the elements of the environment (as defined in Paragraph (a) of the

47 EU Directive 2003/4/EC, Article 2(1).

definition of 'environmental information') should be actively disseminated by public authorities at Member State level (Article 6 (2) (g)).

In the framework of EIA processes, Directive 2011/92/EU (EIA Directive) provides in Article 5 the minimum information that the developer of a project shall provide, which largely includes the categories of description, effects, features and measures envisaged to control the impacts and a description of reasonable alternatives to the project.[48]

Outside the scope of EIA procedures, the IPPC Directive, recast by Directive 2010/75/EU on industrial emissions (Directive on Industrial Emissions),[49] mandates in Article 24 that the following information regarding permit procedures is made available to the public: the content of the decisions, the results of any consultations, technical information on the 'Best Available Techniques', reference documents relevant for the activity, relevant information on the measures taken by the operator upon cessation of activities, and the results of emissions monitoring, among others, without prejudice to the application of the exceptions established in Directive 2003/4/EC. Article 23 of the Industrial Emissions Directive specifically provides for the disclosure of the reports issued by the authorities upon an environmental inspection, which shall be made publicly available within four months of the visit. In this case, the application of exceptions to disclosure is not explicitly stated. Additional rules providing access to information in the framework of permits for specific activities are found in Articles 65 (subject to the restrictions of Article 4, Directive 2003/4/EC) and Article 72 (regarding a summary of the inventories submitted by combustion plants).

In Colombia, there is no regulation clearly stating the information that must be made available to the public in EIA contexts. The *Guide of Citizen Participation in Environmental Licencing*[50] adopted by the Colombian Environmental Licences Authority in 2018 is a legitimate attempt to improve this, establishing among its (non-binding) recommendations that the public gets access to the following information to participate in the EIA processes:

- The technical characteristics, activities and scope of the project.
- Purpose and scope of the environmental studies to be carried out in the framework of the licencing procedure.

48 Council Directive 85/337 of 27 June 1985 on the assessment of the effects of certain public and private projects on the environment [1985] O.J. L 175/40 codified with amendments by Directive 2011/92/EU of the European Parliament and of the Council, [2012] O.J. L. 26/1, as amended by Directive 2014/52/EU of the European Parliament and of the Council, [2014] O.J. L. 124/1. A more detailed list is provided in Annex IV with basically the same items.

49 Directive 2010/75/EU of the European Parliament and of the Council of 24 November 2010 on industrial emissions (integrated pollution prevention and control), [2010] O.J. L 334.

50 National Agency of Environmental Licences - ANLA. (2018). *Guia de Participación Ciudadana en el Licenciamiento Ambiental.* Retrieved from https://www.anla.gov.co/01_anla/documentos/biblioteca/guia_participacion_ciudadana.pdf

- Characteristics and differences between the phases of the project, works or activity, if applicable.
- Environmental laws applicable to the process (environmental licencing procedures, environmental authorities, among others).
- Purpose of the public participation in the elaboration of the environmental study.
- Methodological procedure of the participatory process.[51]

During the Environmental Licensing procedure certain mechanisms for public participation may be enabled to improve public's access to relevant information, such as a public hearing, which can be requested by the General Ombudsman or its delegate for environmental affairs, the Minister of the Environment, the general directors of other environmental authorities, local governors or mayors, or at least one hundred people or three NGOs.[52] Members of the public may also request to be recognised as an interested party in the administrative procedure, getting access to the file.[53]

It is important to note, however, that the Colombian Constitutional Court has upheld claims of confidentiality over certain parts of EIA studies, thus access to the file does not ensure full access to all the relevant information about a specific project.[54]

The US system has few points in common with the other legal systems regarding access to information in the framework of effective public participation, starting with the EIA scheme.

The National Environmental Policy Act of 1969 (NEPA) first introduced the duty upon federal agencies to submit Environmental Impact Statements (EIS) for actions which 'significantly affect the quality of the human environment'.[55] Later, the Council on Environmental Quality issued regulations implementing the Act.[56] The US Environmental Protection Agency (EPA) serves as a repository for the EIS prepared by federal agencies and provides notice of its availability in the Federal Registry.

The EIS requirement implies, in principle, the need to report a considerable amount of *relevant* environmental information including an assessment of *all* the environmental consequences of the proposed action, *all* reasonably foreseeable

51 ANLA, Guía de Participación Ciudadana, 2018, p. 11.

52 Decree 1076 of 2015, 'Single Regulatory Decree for the Environmental Sector', 26 May 2015, Article 2.2.2.4.1.5.

53 Colombian General Environmental Law, 1993, Article 69.

54 Colombian Council of State, Case 11001-03-15-000-2016-0194301, *Maria Cristina Ferrucho Porras v Tribunal Administrativo de Antioquia*. Judgment of 15 March 2018, M.P. Stella Jeannette Carvajal Basto.

55 National Environmental Policy Act of 1969, 42 U.S.C. §4321 et seq. (1969).

56 Council on Environmental Quality, 40 CFR Parts 1500–1508 (reprint 2005). Retrieved from https://www.energy.gov/sites/prod/files/NEPA-40CFR1500_1508.pdf. NEPA established the Council on Environmental Quality (CEQ) within the Executive Office of the President to ensure that Federal agencies meet their obligations under NEPA. See https://ceq.doe.gov/.

alternatives to that action and mitigation measures necessary to reduce any adverse environmental impacts.[57]

NEPA provides that Federal Agencies must

> (c) include in every recommendation or report on proposals for legislation and major federal actions significantly affecting the quality of the human environment a detailed statement by the responsible official on:
>
> (i) the environmental impact of the proposed action,
> (ii) any adverse effects which cannot be avoided should the proposal be implemented,
> (iii) alternatives to the proposed actions,
> (iv) the relationship between local short-term uses of man's environment and the maintenance and enhancement of long-term productivity, and
> (v) any irreversible and irretrievable commitments of resources which would be involved in the proposed action should it be implemented.[58]

This information must be made available to the President, the Council of Environmental Quality and to the public in the terms of the FOIA (on a request basis).

An important point of criticism of the EIS is that these documents have become extremely burdensome, complex and lengthy due to the aim of federal agencies to avoid any possibility of judicial reversal for not having considered all factors and alternatives of an action. Public access to this type of documents can hardly aid better public participation since the *relevant information* remains buried among thousands of pages of not-so-important data.[59]

In the EU and Colombia, EIA guidelines require the inclusion in the study of an executive or a non-technical summary (*e.g.* Directive 2011/92/EU, Article 5(c)). In Colombia, the National Authority of Environmental Licences or the Ministry of the Environment adopts specific guidelines through a regulation for EIA studies for different types of projects (*i.e.* underground mining, oil exploration, infrastructure, hydropower plants etc.), these include the precise components of the study in each case, always requiring an executive summary.[60] Meanwhile, in the US, the details of the EIS are largely left for the agencies to define. In some cases, executive summaries are indeed

57 US Council on Environmental Quality, 2005.
58 US NEPA, Sec. 4332 (c).
59 Hourdequin, M., Peter L., Hanson, M.J., & Craig, D. (2012). Ethical Implications of Democratic Theory for U.S. Public Participation in Environmental Impact Assessment, *Environmental Impact Assessment Review*, 35, 37–44.
60 See *e.g.,* Resolución 1519 of 2017 'Adopting the terms of reference for the elaboration of the Environmental Impact Study required for obtaining the Environmental Licence for projects on the construction and operation of plants generating hydroelectric power'.

found in some EIS, but since there is no specific rule on the subject, it can be expected that many others will lack one.[61]

Equally important, neither NEPA nor the regulations of the Council on Environmental Quality clarify which actions 'significantly affect the quality of the human environment', thus agencies can get away without producing an EIS by simply issuing an 'environmental assessment' (EA) containing just enough information to justify a 'Finding of No Significant Impact' (FONSI).[62]

Reportedly, agencies often supplement these FONSIs at an early stage of projects introducing mitigation measures to avoid going above the threshold of 'significant impact' that would require the production of an EIS. This is not a negative outcome if projects are being adjusted to improve their environmental aspects even if only to avoid the bureaucracy and hassle involved in the EIS process,[63] but comes with a high cost in terms of transparency and public involvement.

Projects and activities exempted from the requirement of an EIS can easily fall out of the public radar and relevant information about their impacts and environmental consequences remain out of reach for the public and perhaps even for the authorities in charge of the decision-making. This is not a minor issue considering that each year federal agencies produce about 50.000 Environmental Assessments leading to FONSIs and only about 500 EISs.[64] Although projects that do not need an EIS are deemed to have only insignificant environmental impacts, it is undeniable that environmental information in these projects and activities will be significantly more difficult to access, if at all possible. On top of this, agencies are authorised to establish 'categorical exclusions' for actions which allegedly do not, individually or cumulatively, produce a significant effect on the human environment, and for which, therefore, neither an environmental assessment nor an environmental impact statement shall be required.[65] If access to relevant information from projects or activities that only have an EA is difficult, environmental information about *categorically excluded* actions is virtually non-existent.[66]

Several conclusions can be drawn from the previous analysis. The first is that the concept of 'relevant environmental information' in the framework of effective public participation in decision-making is not a strange concept,

61 See *e.g.* the Executive Summary of EPA's study on the Impacts from the Hydraulic Fracturing Water Cycle on Drinking Water Resources. Retrieved from https://www.epa.gov/hfstudy/executive-summary-hydraulic-fracturing-study-final-assessment-2016.

62 Karkkainen, B. C. (2004). Whiter NEPA? *New York University Environmental Law Journal*, 12.

63 Karkkainen, *Whiter NEPA*, 2004.

64 NEPA. (2012). *Environmental Impact Statements Filed Through 2012*. Retrieved from https://ceq.doe.gov/docs/get-involved/combined-filed-eiss-1970-2012.pdf.

65 US Council on Environmental Quality, 2005.

66 Karkkainen, *Whiter NEPA*, 2004.

especially at the international and EU levels. Complete categories of environmental information are being selected and customised in EIA laws, which mandate their public disclosure following a purposive approach: to ensure effective public participation in decision-making. The actual contents of the concept slightly differ among the studied jurisdictions, but their core components are generally the same.

Second, 'relevant environmental information' in the framework of specific projects and activities will be, in most cases, produced and/or controlled by the project developer. Most statutes therefore provide that the information shall be made available by the project developer, not by the public authority. This may increase the risk that relevant environmental information remains outside the scope of FOI laws or, even if held by public authorities, that it is withheld from the public on grounds of business confidentiality.

4.3. Scope of Obligated Subjects

The first thing to note is that transparency regimes across different jurisdictions and levels of government may vary greatly when it comes to define the scope of their obligated subjects, more so than about the definition of 'documents' or the general entitlements associated with a public 'right to know'.

At first glance, an idea of uniformity may emerge from the fact that most general transparency laws are addressed to 'public entities' or 'government agencies', but this impression may be deceiving, as each statute usually adopts its own definition of 'government', 'public authority' or 'agency'.

The international regime, exemplified by the Aarhus Convention and the Tromsø Convention on Access to Official Documents, introduces a broad interpretation of 'public authorities' effectively extending the scope of obligated subjects beyond government in the strict sense.

The Tromsø Convention gets the credit for being the first international convention providing for a general right of access to public information, but it has been subject to criticism for the narrow range of public bodies to which it applies.[67] Article 1 defines 'public authorities' as government at national, regional and local level, judicial or legislative authorities performing administrative functions and natural or legal persons exercising administrative authority. Most national FOI laws in Europe go further than this in the scope of obligated subjects.[68]

The Aarhus Convention provides a more comprehensive definition of 'public authorities' but excludes entities acting in a judicial or legislative capacity. Article 2(2) defines 'public authorities' as including:

67 Komanovics, A. (2010). Right to Information in Europe: The Council of Europe Convention on Access to Official Documents, *Studia Iuridica Auctoritate Universitatis Pecs*, 147, 75.

68 Coliver, S. (2015). The Right to Information and the Expanding Scope of Bodies Covered by National Laws since 1989. In P. Molnár (Ed.) *Free Speech and Censorship Around the Globe*. Central European University Press, pp. 187–210.

a Government at national, regional and other level;
b Natural or legal persons performing public administrative functions under national law, including specific duties, activities or services in relation to the environment;
c Any other natural or legal persons having public responsibilities or functions, or providing public services, in relation to the environment, under the control of a body or person falling within subparagraphs (a) or (b) above;
d The institutions of any regional economic integration organization referred to in article 17, which is a Party to this Convention.
This definition does not include bodies or institutions acting in a judicial or legislative capacity.

This definition has been adopted almost literally by the EU through Directive No 2003/4, directed to Member States; and implemented by Regulation No 1367/2006 on the application of the Aarhus Convention by the EU institutions and bodies. The scope of public authorities for the purposes of access to information in the EU therefore extends to at least the executive branch of public power in each Member State, including any person performing public administrative functions and those providing public services or having public responsibilities in relation to the environment under control of any of the above. By virtue of Regulation No 1367/2006, the existing transparency duties of the European Commission, Parliament and the Council under Regulation No 1049/2001 were extended to all other EU institutions and bodies regarding access to environmental information. Although the EU could have chosen to exclude authorities acting in a legislative capacity such as the European Parliament and the Council, it did not.[69] It is important to note that before the EU's adherence to the Aarhus Convention, Regulation No 1049/2001 already established public access to official documents of the EU institutions, and this act is still regarded as the 'framework' transparency regime for the EU's institutions;[70] hence, environmental information held by the European Commission, the European Parliament and the Council was already being accessed under this regulation and it would have been regressive to exclude the European Parliament or the Council from transparency duties under subsequent regulations based on the Aarhus Convention.

In contrast to the Aarhus Convention, the Escazú Agreement does not provide an explicit exclusion of public bodies acting in a judicial or legislative capacity. Article 2 determines the scope of the obligated authorities by the following definition:

69 Mason, M. (2010). Information Disclosure and Environmental Rights: the Aarhus Convention. *Global Environmental Politics, 10*(3), 10–31, asserting that transparency, expressed as information access, is deemed to be a necessary expression of, and condition for, democratic governance.

70 CJEU, Case C-673/13 P *Commission v Stichting Greenpeace Nederland and PAN Europe*, Judgment of 23 November 2016.

'Competent authority' means, for the purposes of articles 5 and 6 of the present Agreement, any public body that exercises the powers, authority and functions for access to information, including independent and autonomous bodies, organizations or entities owned or controlled by the government, whether by virtue of powers granted by the constitution or other laws, and, when appropriate, private organizations that receive public funds or benefits (directly or indirectly) or that perform public functions and services, but only with respect to the public funds or benefits received or to the public functions and services performed;

It is noteworthy that the definition of 'competent authorities' for the purposes of access to information is more detailed and generally broader than for the other participatory rights addressed in the Escazú Agreement. A clear difference with the Aarhus Convention is that the definition of 'competent authority' in the Escazú agreement does not assimilate private entities to public bodies, but rather recognises that these entities are bound by transparency duties when they receive, directly or indirectly, public funds or benefits or when they perform public functions or services. Even if this distinction has no consequence in practice, there is still a noteworthy symbolic meaning in imposing transparency obligations to private entities explicitly. The clear language sends the message that private entities can be indirect subjects of international law, and, in a more substantive way, that their private nature should not be used as an excuse to rule out transparency obligations, at least in the environmental realm. In fact, private entities are explicitly mentioned in several provisions of the Escazú Agreement, speaking of the importance of including private actors in environmental governance instruments.

At the national level, the scope of the laws gets even more nuanced. In Colombia, the constitutional Right of Petition can be exercised against any public entity, in any branch of public power, which includes government-related bodies, decentralised agencies, public corporations (city councils and provincial legislatures), state-owned companies, autonomous agencies and controlling organisms, but also against private entities (natural or legal persons) when the information is necessary for the exercise of the petitioner's fundamental rights.[71]

Furthermore, an independent right of access to public information derived from the Right of Petition was regulated in the General Transparency Law. Under this statute, the term 'public authority' is broadly defined to include:

1 Any public entity in each of the branches of public power at all levels of state structure.
2 Government autonomous organs and entities (control organs and other agencies).

71 Colombian Right of Petition Law, Article 32.

3 Natural and legal persons, public or private, performing public functions or providing public services regarding the information directly related thereto.
4 Any natural or legal person performing public functions or exercising public authority regarding the information directly related to their performance of such functions and authority.
5 Political parties and groups.
6 Entities administering public funds.
7 Public enterprises created by law, state undertakings and corporations in which the state has any participation.[72]

In contrast, under the US FOIA, the public has access to information from federal agencies only. An 'agency' is defined as any

> ...executive department, military department, government corporation, government controlled corporation, or other establishment in the executive branch of the government, or any independent regulatory agency.[73]

Within this scope, some persons are exempt. For instance, although FOIA applies to the Executive Office of the President, it does not apply to the president himself, his immediate staff and the entities within the office that provide advising and assistance to the President, such as the vice president, the National Security Advisor, the National Security Council and the White House Council.[74] The Council of Environmental Quality, however, has been found to fall within the scope of FOIA because its investigatory, evaluative and recommendatory functions exceed merely advising the president.[75]

State authorities are out of the scope of this federal regulation. The disclosure of information to the public by state authorities is subject to the special regulations in each state. Reportedly, all of the states of the U.S.A and the District of Columbia have adopted Freedom of Information Laws,[76] which in and of themselves present significant variations on their own definitions of 'public authorities'.[77]

72 Colombian General Transparency Law, Article 5.
73 US Freedom of Information Act, Sec. 552(e).
74 Resources for the Future (2001). *Public Access to Environmental Information and Data: Practice Examples and Lessons from the United States, the European Union, and Central and Eastern Europe*, Resources for the Future.
75 *Pac. Legal Found. v Council on Envtl. Quality,* cited in US DOJ, *Guide to the Freedom of Information Act*, 2016.
76 Coliver, *Expanding Scope*, 2015.
77 See Feiser, C. D. (2000). Protecting the Public's Right to Know: The Debate over Privatization and Access to Government Information under State Law. *Florida State University Law Review*, 27, 825–64; and Capeloto, A. (2014). Transparency on Trial: A Legal Review of Public Information Access in the Face of Privatization. *Connecticut Public Interest Law Journal*, 13, 19–42.

FOIA also restricts access to information to the executive branch of government, but this includes the Environmental Protection Agency (EPA).[78] This is extremely relevant for the purposes of access to environmental information, because the EPA oversees most environmental programs in the US, delegating only some of its functions to state authorities that oversee local projects in concert with the federal authority. Reportedly, with the proliferation of environmental statutes since EPA's inception in 1970, the agency now creates and collects more data than ever through its regulatory programs and environmental studies.[79]

The original definition of federal 'agency' under FOIA was amended by the US Congress in 1974 beyond the definition of 'agency' contained in the APA, with the aim of including entities that 'perform governmental functions and control information of interest to the public'.[80] Sec. 551(1) of the FOIA defines 'agency' as 'any authority of the Government of the United States, whether or not it is within or subject to review by another agency'. The standing definition of 'agency' (under APA) was 'any administrative unit with substantial independent authority in the exercise of specific functions'.[81] The amendment of the Congress may have been short-sighted however, because the judicial and administrative interpretation of FOIA, as it stands today, generally leaves out contractors of federal agencies, even when they are effectively performing core functions of these agencies.[82] Only when the records in question can be considered 'agency records' because they are under their 'control', have these records been publicly accessible under the US FOIA.[83]

The obligations under FOIA extend to private entities when the perform public functions belonging to a federal agency with a high degree of independence, virtually acting on behalf of the agency (the 'functional equivalent' theory) and also when a federal agency exerts strong control on the day-to-day activities of the private entity (the 'control' criteria).[84] Environmental information held by private entities in one of the previous scenarios will be available under FOIA, provided it falls within the definition of 'agency record' which requires that there is sufficient link between an 'agency' and the requested record.[85] The criteria to determine this were developed by the US Supreme Court in the absence of a statutory definition.

78 US Freedom of Information Act, Sec. 551(1).
79 Lamdan, S. (2017). *Environmental Information: Research, Access and Environmental Decisionmaking*. Environmental Law Institute.
80 Feiser, C. D. (2000). Privatization and the Freedom of Information Act: An Analysis of Public Access to Private Entities Under Federal Law, *Federal Communications Law Journal*, 52, 21–62 (citing p. H.R. REP. No. 93–876 (1974)).
81 *Soucie v David*, 448 F.2d 1067, 1073 (D.C. Cir. 1971).
82 Feiser, *Privatization*, 2000; Capeloto, *Transparency on Trial*, 2016.
83 Roberts, *Structural Pluralism*, 2001; Feiser, *Privatization*, 2000.
84 Feiser, *Privatization*, 2000.
85 *Forsham v Harris*, 445 U.S. 169, 100 S. Ct. 977 (1980).

Overall, setting aside the issue of private entities, Colombia has the most comprehensive interpretation of public entities under its transparency regime, extending to authorities in all branches of public power (executive, legislative and judicial), in all levels of government (national, regional, local) and covering extensively entities performing public functions, receiving public funds, controlled by a government entity, or otherwise engaged in public interest activities (*e.g.* political parties, public utility companies, health services providers, etc.). The US FOIA at the federal level is relatively the most restrictive, applying only to federal agencies and only in the executive branch of public power. Note that transparency does not end with the federal FOIA, as each state has established its own FOIA with varying interpretations of the public agencies covered.

The Aarhus Convention and the EU offer comparable definitions and scope of the obligated subjects covered under their transparency provisions, each within its specific subject-matter. These relatively early laws focused strongly on the definition of government/government functions as the main criteria to establish the scope of the obligated subjects, as opposed to public funding or the provision of public services employed in more recent instruments. This change may be related to the privatisation phenomenon and increased demands of transparency led by civil society organisations.[86] The more modern approach is observed in the Escazú Agreement, which not only includes private entities openly but also adopts a broad definition of public entities (for the purposes of access to information) including:

> independent and autonomous bodies, organizations or entities owned or controlled by the government, whether by virtue of powers granted by the constitution or other laws, and, when appropriate, private organizations that receive public funds or benefits (directly or indirectly) or that perform public functions and services.[87]

According to the Implementation Guide to the Bali Guidelines, it is considered good practice to define ‘public authorities’ broadly. The document asserts that

> States should carefully define the term ‘public authorities’ to include not just agencies, ministries, institutions, departments and other bodies of government at any level (national, regional, local), but also certain other bodies or persons. In general, the definition could extend to any natural or legal person with public responsibilities or functions or providing public services. Such a definition would ensure that privatization, outsourcing or other such changes would not result in a lessening of responsibility and accountability towards the public.[88]

86 Roberts, *Structural Pluralism*, 2001.
87 Escazú Agreement, Article 2.
88 UNEP (2015). *Putting Rio Principle 10: An Implementation Guide for the UNEP Bali Guidelines for the Development of National Legislation on Access to*

However, the scope of obligated subjects will depend greatly on the interpretation in each jurisdiction of key terms such as 'under control' and 'administrative functions', vastly employed to establish the level of dependence between government agencies and other entities justifying the imposition of transparency duties upon the latter. A detailed analysis of these concepts is included in Chapter 5.

4.4. Scope of Exempted Information

Under the European Convention on Human Rights, specifically Article 10 (Freedom of Expression), the ECtHR considered that information could be withheld, stating: 'when the law to exercise the right to receive information can impair the rights of others, public safety or public health, the extent of the right to access information in cause is limited by Article 10(2) of the Convention'.[89]

Although this convention does not list specific exceptions, the ECtHR found in this article sufficient legal basis to derogate from the general right of access in certain cases. More detailed regulations on the right of access usually include specific exceptions to the general rule of disclosure.

Colombia's Transparency Law and Right of Petition Law contain a large catalogue of the information that can be exempted from disclosure to protect other interests. The Transparency Law establishes exceptions in two articles, one for the protection of private interests and another for the protection of public interests. Article 18 establishes that 'public classified information' is all public information whose access can be denied (in written and providing proper motivation) because it can be harmful for the rights to intimacy, the people's right to life, health or safety, or any commercial, industrial, and professional secrets. Information about investment projects of state-owned commercial and industrial companies[90] may also be exempted from disclosure.

Article 19, on the other hand, provides for exceptions to disclosure for the protection of public interests, including national security, international relations, the right to due process and a fair trial, the rights of minors, the country's economic stability and public health. Documents containing opinions or concepts that are part of a deliberative process of public servants are also exempted. However, these exceptions shall not exceed a period of 15 years. All obligated subjects must have an updated index of all the exempted information that they hold, including the name of the document, the basis on

Information, Public Participation and Access to Justice in Environmental Matters. Nairobi, p. 29. Retrieved from https://wedocs.unep.org/bitstream/handle/20.500.11822/11201/UNEP%20MGSB-SGBS%20BALI%20GUIDELINES-Interactive.pdf?sequence=1&isAllowed=y.

89 UNEP, *Bali Guidelines Implementation Guide*, 2015, p. 11.

90 This is a category of public entity that operates with public funds but in under the same legal and market conditions as private corporations.

which it is exempted from public access and a reference to the legal act by which it was classified. It is important to note that exceptions to disclosure may operate in respect of a document's content, but never on the information about the document's existence or possession by a public entity.

Article 21 establishes rules for the application of the previous exceptions: when only a part of a document can be exempted, a public version must be made available that conceals only the classified parts. Exceptions will not apply to information about the violation of human rights or crimes against humanity. Notably, any act of concealing, destroying or otherwise altering public information, after it has been subject to a request for information, is a criminal offense.

The Colombian Right of Petition Law also establish exceptions to protect, generally, the same public and private interests (Article 24). Notably, the law specifically states that 'Commercial and industrial secrets, and strategic plans of public utility companies' are exempted from disclosure.

Concerning the exceptions regime, the Constitutional Court established specific guidelines for their regulation. Restrictions to the right of access to public information will only be constitutionally legitimate, according to the Court, when

> They aim to protect fundamental rights or constitutionally valuable interests such as (i) national security, (ii) public order, (iii) public health and (iv) fundamental rights; and they are appropriate (adequate to protect a constitutionally legitimate purpose) and necessary for that purpose, hence, the measures establishing an exception to the diffusion of public information must the subject to a proportionality test.[91]

These guidelines were explicitly included in the Transparency Law (Article 28).

All the transparency laws examined in this book list the cases in which information may be refused to protect other private or public interests, except the Escazú Agreement. Although several versions of the text during negotiations included a comprehensive exceptions regime, the final agreement generally left the issue to the domestic legislation of each state, establishing only a subsidiary provision to be applied in cases where there is no exceptions regime in the country's domestic legislation. Article 5(6) states

> Access to information may be refused in accordance with domestic legislation. In cases where a Party does not have a domestic legal regime of exceptions, that Party may apply the following exceptions: (a) when disclosure would put at risk the life, safety or health of individuals; (b) when

91 Colombian Constitutional Court, Case T-889/09, Judgment of 1 December 2009, M.P. Luis Ernesto Vargas Silva and Case T-511/10, Judgment of 18 June 2010, M.P. Humberto Antonio Sierra Porto.

disclosure would adversely affect national security, public safety or national defence; (c) when disclosure would adversely affect the protection of the environment, including any endangered or threatened species; or (d) when disclosure would create a clear, probable and specific risk of substantial harm to law enforcement, prevention, investigation and prosecution of crime.

Notwithstanding the lack of a binding exceptions regime, the Escazú Agreement provides some mandatory guidelines to the regulation and application of exceptions to disclosure at national level (Article 5).

Under the Aarhus Convention, parties may provide for the refusal of information requests when disclosure may adversely affect:

a The confidentiality of the proceedings of public authorities, where such confidentiality is provided for under national law;
b International relations, national defence or public security;
c The course of justice, the ability of a person to receive a fair trial or the ability of a public authority to conduct an enquiry of a criminal or disciplinary nature;
d The confidentiality of commercial and industrial information, where such confidentiality is protected by law in order to protect a legitimate economic interest. Within this framework, information on emissions which is relevant for the protection of the environment shall be disclosed;
e Intellectual property rights;
f The confidentiality of personal data and/or files relating to a natural person where that person has not consented to the disclosure of the information to the public, where such confidentiality is provided for in national law;
g The interests of a third party which has supplied the information requested without that party being under or capable of being put under a legal obligation to do so, and where that party does not consent to the release of the material; or
h The environment to which the information relates, such as the breeding sites of rare species.[92]

The scope of the information exempted under this regime largely depends on the implementation of the provisions by each of the Parties. They should be careful, however, to not undermine the Convention's objectives. The ACCC has stated that establishing full categories of information as exempted is against Article 3(1) and Article 4(4) of the Convention.[93]

The US FOIA, finally, establishes nine different grounds for exemptions to the right of public access: (i) national defence and foreign relations; (ii)

92 Aarhus Convention, Article 4(4).
93 ACCC/C/2008/30 (Republic of Moldova).

information related solely to the internal rules of an agency; (iii) information specifically exempted in other statutes (such as the TSA); (iv) trade secrets and CBI *obtained from a person and privileged or confidential*; (v) *inter* and *intra* agency correspondence; (vi) personnel and medical files and others whose disclosure would affect personal privacy; (vii) records compiled for law enforcement purposes (with several qualifying criteria); (viii) records of agencies in charge of regulation and supervision of financial institutions; and (ix) geological and geophysical data concerning wells.

The 2016 amendments to the US FOIA introduced some limitations to the application of the exemptions, including a time limit of 25 years for exemption number 5 and a general 'foreseeable harm' test.[94] The actual scope of the exceptions regime, again, will largely depend on the policies of the agency and/or of the acting president. The US FOIA has been severely criticised in the past for allowing too much information to be kept secret at the discretion of the public servants.[95]

Exceptions to disclosure for the protection of different private or public interests also apply to mechanisms for active access to information, thus similar provisions are found in the Kiev Protocol (Article 12),[96] the E-PRTR Regulation (Article 11)[97] in the EU, and the US ECPRA establishing the Toxic Release Inventory (TRI). This last statute, in Section 11022(d)(2)(A)-(F), allows the government to withhold 'second tier' information about chemicals, at the request of the submitter, which includes: 'A) The chemical name or the common name of the chemical as provided on the material safety data sheet. (B) An estimate (in ranges) of the maximum amount of the hazardous chemical present at the facility at any time during the preceding calendar year. (C) An estimate (in ranges) of the average daily amount of the hazardous chemical present at the facility during the preceding calendar year. (D) A brief description of the manner of storage of the hazardous chemical. (E)

94 FOIA Improvement Act of 2016, Public Law No. 114–185 (2016).

95 Vladeck, D. C. (2007). Information Access – Surveying the Current Landscape of Federal Right-to-Know Laws. *Texas Law Review*, 86, 1987; Wilcox, W. A. J. (2001). Access to Environmental Information in the United States and the United Kingdom. *Loyola of Los Angeles International and Comparative Law Review, 23* (2), 121.

96 Protocol on Pollutant Release and Transfer Registers to the UNECE Convention on Access to Information, Public Participation in Decision-making and Access to Justice in Environmental Matters, 21 May 2003 (entered into force on 9 October 2009), Doc. MP.PP/2003/1, Article 12: 'Each Party may authorize the competent authority to keep information held on the register confidential where public disclosure of that information would adversely affect: (…)(c) The confidentiality of commercial and industrial information, where such confidentiality is protected by law in order to protect a legitimate economic interest; (d) Intellectual property rights'.

97 Regulation (EC) No 166/2006 of the European Parliament and of the Council of 18 January 2006 concerning the establishment of a European Pollutant Release and Transfer Register and amending Council Directives 91/689/EEC and 96/61/EC, [2006] O.J. L 33/1.

The location at the facility of the hazardous chemical. (F) An indication of whether the owner elects to withhold location information of a specific hazardous chemical from disclosure to the public under section 11044 of this title'.[98]

Note that active access instruments apply mostly to information about releases into the environment and substances that represent a risk to human health, therefore, the application of exceptions should be particularly rigorous. Exemptions for the protection of trade secrets under the US EPCRA allowing operators to withhold information about toxic substances that should be made publicly available in the TRI, would not be sustained under the Aarhus Convention and the EU legislation which specifically provide that information about emissions into the environment shall not be kept from the public for the protection of trade secrets or on grounds of business confidentiality.

Establishing exceptions to public disclosure in transparency legal instruments is a common practice that finds strong support in international human rights instruments, national constitutions, jurisprudence, and doctrine. Best practice dictates that these exceptions should be carefully drafted; they must be clear, limited, and reasonable to avoid excessive interference with the rights of public access. This is a first step. The way in which the exceptions are to be interpreted and applied is equally if not more important for the effectiveness of access to information rights.

Some universal rules have been formulated as examples of good practice to guide the application of exceptions to disclosure in the framework of transparency legislation, such as:

- Exceptions must be narrowly defined and restrictively applied.
- The burden of proof belongs to the entity refusing access.
- The adverse effects for the interests protected with the exception must be reasonably foreseeable and not purely hypothetical, and it should be weighed against the adverse effects on the public right of access (harm test).
- An overriding public interest in the disclosure of the information supersedes the application of the exception (public interest test).[99]

These general guidelines and sometimes more specific ones can be found within each of the studied legal systems.

98 Emergency Planning and Community Right-to-Know Act of 1986, 42 U.S.C. §§ 11001–11050 (2012).

99 These rules can be found in one or more of the following sources: The Aarhus Convention and its Implementation Guide, the Bali Guidelines and its implementation Guide, national guidelines such as the UK's DEFRA guidelines on the application of the Environmental Information Regulations, jurisprudence of the European Court of Justice referring to the rules in the Aarhus Convention and the EU instruments implementing it, International Human Rights Courts in reference to the right to freedom of expression and, finally, scholarly research.

At EU level, the CJEU has developed a solid body of case-law on the application of the exceptions to the right of access to documents of the EU institutions under Regulation No 1049/2001 and, to a lesser extent, to access environmental information under Regulation No 1367/2006 and regarding the implementation of Directive No 2003/4 at Member State level.

The General Court's judgment in *Turco* (2008)[100] set a framework for the application of the exceptions which demanded 'reasonable, foreseeable, specific and effective' harm to the interest protected with the conditional exceptions set in Regulation No 1049/2001 to legally withhold the information from the public, considering the particularities of every case.[101] Subsequent decisions[102] have revealed certain categories of information which can be presumed to be exempted from disclosure under EU legislation, for which no 'harm test' or 'balancing exercise' would have to be carried out in order to refuse access:

- Documents relating to State Aid procedures (Regulation 659/1999 does not grant interested parties an access right to files in state aid review cases);
- The submissions lodged in pending proceedings before the EU courts;
- The documents in merger control proceedings;[103]
- The documents relating to proceedings under Article 101 TFEU;
- The documents relating to an infringement procedure during its pre-litigation stage, including pilot procedures.

However, in a recent development, the CJEU Grand Chamber set aside a decision of the General Court that had all but established a new presumption of non-disclosure of documents in the framework of the European Commission legislative action. The case in question, *ClientEarth v European Commission,*[104] related to a request for information lodged by the NGO ClientEarth before the European

100 CJEU Joined Cases C-39 & 52/05 P, *Sweden and Turco v Council*, Judgment of 1 July 2008.

101 Adamski, D. (2012). Approximating a Workable Compromise on Access to Official Documents: The 2011 Developments in the European Courts. *Common Market Law Review, 49*, 521–558.

102 CJEU Case C-139/07 P, *Commission v Technische Glaswerke Ilmenau GmbH,* Judgment of 29 June 2010; *Liga para Protecção da Natureza (LPN) v European Commission.*

103 Commission Regulation No. 802/2004 implementing Council Regulation (EC) No. 139/2004 on the control of concentrations between undertakings, [2004] O.J. L 133/1. Article 17(3) provides: 'The right of access to the file shall not extend to confidential information, or to internal documents of the Commission or of the competent authorities of the Member States. The right of access to the file shall equally not extend to correspondence between the Commission and the competent authorities of the Member States or between the latter'.

104 CJEU, Case C-57/16, *ClientEarth v. European Commission*, Judgment of 4 September 2018.

Commission in 2014 to obtain access to the impact assessment reports drafted for the Commission about possible legislative action to adopt a directive on access to justice in environmental matters and regarding environmental inspections. The Commission refused to disclose the documents based on Article 4(3) of Regulation No 1049/2001 (the ongoing decision-making process exception), arguing that such disclosure would affect the decision-making process and the Commission's independence in the role of pursuing the general interest.[105]

The Grand Chamber found that the withholding of such documents interfered with the public's ability to participate effectively in decision-making processes in the framework of the legislative action of the European Commission. The fact that the information was related to the environment and was produced in the context of the legislative functions of the Commission may have also contributed to balance the scale in favour of transparency. The Court affirmed:

> Although the submission of a legislative proposal by the Commission is, at the impact assessment stage, uncertain, the disclosure of those documents is likely to increase the transparency and openness of the legislative process as a whole, in particular the preparatory steps of that process, and, thus, to enhance the democratic nature of the European Union by enabling its citizens to scrutinise that information and to attempt to influence that process. As is asserted, in essence, by Client Earth, such a disclosure, at a time when the Commission's decision-making process is still ongoing, **enables citizens to understand the options envisaged and the choices made by that institution** and, thus, to be aware of the considerations underlying the legislative action of the European Union. In addition, **that disclosure puts those citizens in a position effectively to make their views known regarding those choices before those choices have been definitively adopted**, so far as both the Commission's decision to submit a legislative proposal and the content of that proposal, on which the legislative action of the European Union depends, are concerned.[106] (emphasis added)

The Court's position in this case brings into discussion a new argument and point of reference to help balance the application of exceptions to disclosure in the framework of the EU transparency framework: the relevance of the information to enable effective public participation in decision-making. This argument can be easily applied in cases of access to environmental information where the right of public access to information is supported in a system that includes the right to public participation in decision-making processes

105 Ankersmit, L. (2018). *Case C-57/16P Client Earth v. Commission: Citizen's Participation in EU Decision-Making and the Commission's Right of Initiative.* Retrieved from http://europeanlawblog.eu/2018/10/22/case-c-57-16p-clientearth-v-commission-citizens-participation-in-eu-decision-making-and-the-commissions-right-of-initiative/.

106 *ClientEarth v European Commission*, para 92.

and access to justice, such as the frameworks provided in the Aarhus Convention, EU legislation and the Escazú Agreement. Notably, this is not the first time that the CJEU brings up effective public participation in decision-making in deciding cases of access to information, the cases of *Stichting Greenpeace Nederland* (2016) and *Bayer CropScience* (2016)[107] hinted this way in assessing the scope of the definition of 'emissions into the environment' for the purposes of the application of the exception of business confidentiality.

From the review above, it can be concluded that the case-law of the CJEU is still evolving to develop clearer guidance for the application of exceptions in the framework of the general transparency regime (Regulation No 1049/2001) and, indirectly, for access to environmental information as well. The judicial doctrine supporting general presumptions of confidentiality seems to be at odds with the legal mandate of maximum disclosure and the safeguards against the indiscriminate reliance on exceptions that unduly affects the public's right to information, such as the 'harm test' and the 'public interest test'. An interesting counterargument, however, is the purposive approach adopted by the CJEU in the case of *ClientEarth,* where considerations of the possible interference with the Commission's decision-making process came secondary to the fact that the information in question was required for the effectiveness of public participation in the decision-making process, one of the main purposes of the right of access to information to begin with. This development is extremely relevant in the context of this study.

In Colombia, the Constitutional Court has set guidelines for the interpretation and application of restrictions to the right of access to public information. Among them is the condition that the public servant who refuses information must express the motives in writing and adequately justify the decision, and the restriction must abide by reasonability and proportionality principles.[108]

Under Article 28 of the Transparency Law, when the public authority refuses to disclose information, it bears the burden of proof to demonstrate the reasons that justify the refusal. Furthermore, the authority must state whether the disclosure of the information would cause *present, probable* and *specific* harm to the protected interest, which exceeds the public interest in accessing the information (harm test). In this context, it is pertinent to consider the purposes of the right of access to public information, as determined by the Constitutional Court: (i) to ensure democratic participation and the exercise of political rights; (ii) to enable the exercise of other constitutional rights by allowing the public's knowledge of the conditions necessary for their

107 CJEU, Case C-442/14 *Bayer CropScience and Stichting De Bijenstichting*, Judgment of 23 November 2016.

108 Colombian Constitutional Court, Case C-491/07, Judgment of 27 June 2007, M. P. Jaime Córdoba Triviño.

realisation; and (iii) to ensure transparency of public administration, by constituting a citizen control mechanism for the state's activity.[109]

Along the same lines, US courts have construed the FOIA to require a very narrow interpretation of the exceptions,[110] and even when the information may fall within one of the statute's exemptions, agencies may still release it to the public if there is no compelling reason to withhold it.[111]

However, the application of FOIA's exemptions has been decisively influenced by the specific policy of each of the acting presidents. In 1993, President Clinton issued a first Memorandum largely supporting a presumption of open access and the application of a 'foreseeable harm' test to the withholding of information under FOIA's exemptions,[112] which was then replaced under the administration of President George W. Bush following the terrorist attacks of September 2001. The office of the US Attorney General issued Memorandum of October 12, 2001, stating that the Department of Justice would defend decisions to withhold records 'unless they lacked a sound legal basis or present an unwarranted risk of adverse impact on the ability of other agencies to protect other important records'. This effectively translated into a presumption of secrecy, instead of a presumption of access.[113] President Obama reversed some of the previous government's policies issuing a Memorandum on January 21, 2009, his first full day in office, stating:

> The Freedom of Information Act should be administered with a clear presumption: In the face of doubt, openness prevails. The Government should not keep information confidential merely because public officials might be embarrassed by disclosure, because errors and failures might be revealed, or because of speculative or abstract fears. Nondisclosure should never be based on an effort to protect the personal interests of Governmental officials at the expense of those they are supposed to serve.[114]

These guidelines were codified by the FOIA Improvement Act of 2016, signed into law by President Obama on 30 June 2016, coinciding with the 50th

109 Colombian Constitutional Court, Case C-274/13, Judgment of 9 May 2013, M.P. Maria Victoria Calle Correa.

110 *Air force v. Rose*, 425 U.S. 352, 361 (1976) and *Welford v. Hardin*, 444 F. 2d 21 (4th Cir. 1971).

111 *Charles River Park 'A' INC. v HUD*, 519 F 2d. 935 (D.C. Cir. 1975) and *Chrysler Corp v Brown*, 441 U.S. 181, 285 (1979).

112 A general analysis and links to the relevant documents is available at the US Department of State Website: https://www.justice.gov/oip/blog/foia-update-president-and-attorney-general-issue-new-foia-policy-memoranda.

113 US Attorney General. (2001). *Memorandum*. Retrieved from https://www.justice.gov/archive/oip/011012.htm.

114 Office of the President of the United States. (2009). *Freedom of Information Act*. Federal Register Vol. 74, No. 15. Retrieved from https://www.transportation.gov/sites/dot.gov/files/docs/Presidential%20Memorandum%20of%20January%2021%2C%202009.pdf.

anniversary of the original FOIA. Among the main changes, the presumption of openness was officially incorporated into the law as well as the 'foreseeable harm' standard for the application of the exemptions.

The US Supreme Court has also asserted that FOIA exemptions are discretionary, not mandatory.[115] This means that an agency may make 'discretionary disclosures' of exempt information where they are not otherwise forbidden from doing so, but these discretionary powers do not operate to all the exemptions, since some categories of exempted information are otherwise protected from disclosure under different statutes, such as trade secrets under the Trade Secrets Act.

The application of the exceptions protecting business confidentiality are explored in more detail in Chapter 6.

115 *Chrysler v. Brown.*

5 Access to Private Sector Environmental Information

This chapter contains the comparative analysis of the passive and active mechanisms found in the studied jurisdictions related to environmental information held by private entities. The analysis examines the way these instruments work in practice *vis-à-vis* access to information in general and the levels of state transparency, complementing the previous sections related to the scope and nature of the right of access to information. But before embarking on the analysis of the substantive rules, the justification for the inclusion of a right of public access to environmental information held by private entities underlying many of these mechanisms will be explored.

5.1. Why Increase Access to Private Sector Environmental Information?

Private actors, especially for-profit corporations, have come to claim an important position in environmental governance. First, for the type of activities they engage in, which may have significant environmental impacts: not every company carries out environmentally relevant activities, but virtually all high-impact activities are carried out either by the state or by private companies. Second, due the 'privatisation' of state functions, private companies are increasingly performing activities that used to be monopolised by the state, such as waste management, provision of water and electricity and environmental standard-setting, like the ISO 14000 series of Environmental Management Systems.[1] Third, private companies have a significant influence in environmental regulation and state control through lobbying activities, international associations and self-regulatory initiatives, among others.[2]

Some authors raise concerns about the effectiveness of government environmental regulations to control private companies' performance in

1 Falkner, R. (2003). Private Environmental Governance and International Relations. Exploring the Links. *Global Environmental Politics, 3*(2), 72–87.
2 Sukhdev, P. (2012). *Corporation 2020: Transforming business for tomorrow's world.* Island Press.

DOI: 10.4324/9781003307617-5

'privatised' economies. It has been argued that this scheme favours industry self-regulation and market-based mechanisms over effective government control. This is also called 'free market environmentalism' and involves a more relaxed attitude from the government to allow the natural forces of the market to regulate environmental performance, by making it *too expensive* to keep perverse environmental practices and to be inefficient in the use of natural resources. Detractors argue that environmental costs are not being properly accounted for in the products' final pricing, thus invalidating the market-based logic of regulation.[3]

In the specific case of environmental transparency, it has been brought up as a criticism to existent regulations that they generally exclude private entities from mandatory duties of disclosure, weakening the information access rights of the public. Mason argues that the general exclusion of private entities from mandatory transparency obligations reflects a structural imbalance in the Aarhus Convention between social welfare and market liberal perspectives.[4]

Many FOI laws are designed exclusively for public authorities and anti-corruption programs rarely include private sector companies.[5] The reasons for the generalised exclusion of private entities may be attributed to a traditional logic of the legal protection afforded to private actors in liberal markets preventing excessive state interference.[6]

One of the most common ways to extend transparency obligations to private entities is by drafting a broad definition of 'public authorities' to cover these entities in certain cases. Notably, Bünger and Schomerus attribute to privatisation the evolution of the concept of public authorities to include private bodies under some circumstances.[7] The Aarhus Convention Implementation Guide explains, referring to the definition of 'public authorities' of the Convention, the following:

3 Ebbesson, J. (2011). Public Participation and Privatisation in Environmental Matters: An Assessment of the Aarhus Convention. *Erasmus Law Review, 4*(2), pp. 71–72; Richardson, B. J. (1999). Changing Regulatory Spaces: The Privatization of New Zealand Environmental Law. In K. Bosselmann & B. J. Richardson (Eds.) *Environmental Justice and Market mechanisms: Key Challenges for Environmental Law and Policy.* Kluwer Law International, p. 209.

4 Mason, M. (2014). 'So far but no further? Transparency and disclosure in the Aarhus convention'. In: Gupta, A. and Mason, M., (Eds.) *Transparency in Global Environmental Governance: Critical Perspectives. Earth System Governance.* MIT Press, pp. 83–106.

5 Coliver, S. (2015). The Right to Information and the Expanding Scope of Bodies Covered by National Laws since 1989. In P. Molnár (Ed.), Free Speech and Censorship Around the Globe (pp. 187–210). Central European University Press.

6 Mason, M. (2010). Information Disclosure and Environmental Rights: the Aarhus Convention. *Global Environmental Politics, 10*(3), 10–31.

7 Bünger, D., & Schomerus, T. (2011). Private Bodies as Public Authorities under International, European, English and German Environmental Information Laws. *Journal for European Environmental & Planning Law, 8*(1), 62–81.

> Recent developments in privatized solutions to the provision of public services have added a layer of complexity to the definition. The Convention tries to make it clear that such innovations cannot take public services or activities out of the realm of public information, participation or justice.[8]

Ebbesson argues that the privatisation trend is leading to a 'privatisation of environmental law': since the performance of environmental functions, use and control of resources pertain to public interests, values and wealth; and privatisation shifts 'the arbiter of value from a political process focused on defining collective ambitions and aspirations to an individual deciding whether something is good in his or her own (more or less selfish, hedonistic, and materialistic) terms',[9] then, public decision-making processes are 'eroding under the influence of property rights doctrines, market devolution and commercial imperatives'.[10] He asserts that the broad approach taken by the Aarhus Convention by including private entities performing public administrative functions or providing services in relation with the environment ensures that participatory rights are resilient to privatisation processes, but this will still depend on the way domestic laws regulate the provision and performance of such services.[11]

Privatisation affects government's transparency in general, as critical services closely related to what we call 'state goals', such as ensuring access to basic conditions of life and social protection, are being 'outsourced' to third parties. The risks and perils of privatisation for the effectiveness of the public's right-to-know have been vastly documented and studied.[12] In this context, it has been pointed out that only few disclosure laws establish a right to obtain documents created by contractors while working for government agencies (reportedly, New Zeland's and Ireland's),[13] contractors have little incentive to make any information public by themselves, and enforcement authorities and controlling agencies frequently lack powers to intervene when these entities refuse public requests for access. When governments have taken

8 United Nations Economic Commission for Europe – UNECE. (2014). *The Aarhus Convention: An Implementation Guide*, 2nd ed., UN Doc. ECE/CEP/72/Rev.1, p. 46.

9 Ebbeson, *Public Participation Environmental Matters,* 2011 citing M. H. Moore. (2002). Introduction [to the Symposium: Public Values in an Era of Privatization]. *Harvard Law Review*, 5 (2002–3), 1215, pg. 73.

10 Ebbeson, *Public Participation Environmental Matters,* 2011, p. 73 citing Richardson, *Changing Regulatory Spaces*, 1999, p. 209.

11 Ebbeson, *Public Participation Environmental Matters,* 2011, pp 74–77. See also Lee M., & Abbot, C. (2003). The Usual Suspect? Public Participation Under the Aarhus Convention, *Modern Law Review, 66*(1), 80.

12 See *i.e.* Roberts, A. (2006). *Blacked Out: Government Secrecy in the Information Age.* Cambridge University Press; Drache, D. (Ed.) (2001). *Market or Public Domain? Global Governance and the Asymmetry of Power.* Routledge.

13 Roberts, *Blacked Out,* 2006.

steps to assign transparency obligations to some private entities by virtue of their public functions, many have been successful in lobbying their way out of such impositions by arguing a competitive disadvantage to enter the market, as it happened in the UK and Canada in the case of utilities providers.[14]

Besides these issues, there are some reported benefits of increased public disclosure of environmental information from private actors:

- Catalysing improvements in environmental performance.
- Leverage market forces to achieve environmental improvements.
- Disclosure of environmental liabilities and penalties provides specific deterrents to future violations.
- Incentives for companies to address environmental problems more expeditiously.
- Correcting information asymmetries.
- Empower environmental group efforts and the work of public 'watchdogs'.
- Incentivise community organisation.[15]

From the perspective of the efficacy of access to information legislation, there are strong arguments in favour of assigning responsibilities to private entities to deliver environmental information directly to the public.

Firstly, because high impact activities are being carried out by private corporations, information about the magnitude of the impacts, the measures being taken to mitigate them, the costs and alternatives available and the safeguards implemented to protect environmental resources is produced and held by the private companies themselves, and it is not certain that all of it is being submitted to public authorities (to be accessed by the public through traditional channels). Flournoy, Halter & Storz point out that 'Under a regulatory scheme that prohibits conduct if adverse effects are proven, the proponent of an action has little incentive to generate or produce information about adverse effects'.[16]

Secondly, indirect access to the information can be problematic in a number of ways: private entities may fail to report all the relevant information to the public authorities in due time, public authorities may find it difficult to enforce reporting obligations, the processing of the information will necessarily extend the time between the moment the information is available and its disclosure to the interested public, etc.[17]

14 Roberts, *Blacked Out,* 2006.

15 Case, D. W. (2005). Corporate Environmental Reporting as Informational Regulation: A Law and Economics Perspective. *Colorado Law Review*, 76, 379.

16 Flournoy, A. C., Halter, H., & Storz, C. (2008). Harnessing the Power of Information to Protect Our Public Natural Resource Legacy. *Texas Law Review, 86*(1), 1575, p. 1597.

17 See Etemire, U. (2012). Public Access to Environmental Information Held by Private Companies, *Environmental Law Review, 14*, 7–25, for a more detailed analysis of these and other reasons.

Thirdly, voluntary schemes of disclosure, as helpful as they may be to increase the idea of transparency or the legitimacy of high-impact industrial activities,[18] are not sufficient to ensure access to the most relevant, sensitive or incriminatory environmental information, which is precisely what the public should be ordinarily entitled to under a transparency regime.[19]

Although there is a strong case to extend transparency obligations to private entities, opposing arguments point out that this would result in an excessive interference with the rights to private property and privacy of the companies, that increased transparency may lead to competitive disadvantages and ultimately affect the economic interests of the state, or that research and innovation may be halted on account of the risks that such legislation may entail for the protection of trade secrets and intellectual property rights.

Beyond the debate, evidence shows that access to environmental information held by the private sector is already happening through different channels, which are explored next.

5.2. Indirect Access Through Public Authorities

In all the studied jurisdictions, the public may access environmental information originated in private entities indirectly through the mechanisms for access to information by public authorities when they hold the information. The efficacy of this type of access is significantly influenced by two aspects that are closely examined in this study: (i) the comprehensiveness of the reporting duties placed upon private entities to deliver environmental information to the public authorities, and (ii) how the exceptions for protection of business confidentiality and intellectual property rights operate in that jurisdiction.

In the US, most legal instruments establishing mandatory reporting obligations afford private entities the right to assert confidentiality over the information they deliver to the public agencies, which, in turn, are required to withhold the information from the public, unless there is a specific statutory exception to the duty of confidentiality, as is in fact the case for emission data under the Clean Air Act.[20]

A clear example of indirect access to environmental information from private entities is found in the framework of the Environmental Impact Assessment processes or environmental permitting procedures, in which the private operator interested in carrying out a specific activity or project must submit substantial environmental information to the authorities in order to obtain a

18 Ebbeson, *Public Participation Environmental Matters,* 2011. See also Morrison, J., & Roth-Arriaza, N. (2007). Private and Quasi private Standard Setting. In D. Bodansky et al. (Eds.) *The Oxford Handbook of International Environmental Law,* 498, p. 526.

19 Etemire, *Private Companies*, 2012.

20 US Clean Air Act [CAA], 42 U.S.C, 7401 et seq. (1970), Sec. 7607.

permit or environmental licence. The information can then be made available to the public by the public authority through active or passive disclosure.

Another example in the US are the reporting duties for Public Companies (publicly traded corporations) to the Securities and Exchange Commission (SEC), which include environmental information such as the material effects of compliance with environmental provisions and any legal proceedings arising from them, as well as any known events that may result in a material change of the Company's liquidity (*e.g.* environmental-related lawsuits) and the company's environmental policies to the extent that they may cause fines or penalties with an estimated cost.[21] Since the SEC is a federal agency, the information in its possession can be accessed through a FOIA request.

At the EU level, a Directive on the disclosure of non-financial information by certain large undertakings was adopted in 2014, covering environmental information specifically.[22] The Directive provides for Member States to impose obligations on to some public-interest large undertakings (more than 500 employees) to report details on the foreseeable impacts of the undertaking's operations on the environment, the use of renewable energy, GEI emissions, the use of water and air pollution.

This section surveys the mechanisms of active transparency that result in indirect public access to environmental information from private entities through the reporting, gathering, organising, and disseminating actions of government authorities.

5.2.1. Active Disclosure: From the Private Duty to Report to the Public Obligation to Inform

Active access to public information, also referred to as 'proactive transparency',[23] encompasses activities to actively collect, organise, and disseminate information of public interest. Typical examples of active access to environmental information are the Pollution Release and Transfer Registers – PRTRs

21 US Securities Exchange Act (1934), Regulation S-K Items 101, 103 and 303. 15 U.S.C. § 78a. See also Love Simons, A. (2006). Loopholes in Corporate Environmental Reporting and What Is Being Done to Close Them: A Recent GAO Study Examines the Status of Environmental Reporting to the SEC and Suggests Improvements, *Villanova Environmental Law Journal*, 17, 331, and the originating report by the GAO:

U.S. Government Accountability Office, Environmental Disclosure: Sec Should Explore Ways To Improve Tracking And Transparency Of Information 1 (July 2004). Retrieved from http://www.gao.gov/new.items/d04808.pdf.

22 Directive 2014/95/EU of the European Parliament and of the Council of 22 October 2014 amending Directive 2013/34/EU as regards disclosure of non-financial and diversity information by certain large undertakings and groups, [2014] O.J. L 330/1.

23 Darbishire, H. (2011). Proactive Transparency: The future of the right to information? Retrieved from http://siteresources.worldbank.org/EXTGOVACC/Resources/DarbishireProactiveTransparency.pdf.

(which gather information about emissions into the environment and toxic substances releases and organise it in publicly available databases), reporting obligations of public or private entities regarding their environmental performance, systems of environmental alerts (*e.g.* in cases of risk to human health), periodical reports on the state of the environment and the publication of environmental laws, policies and decisions.

Active public access to environmental information may be observed as the result of two distinct actions. First, the collection of information by the entity and/or system in charge. In this stage, environmental reporting obligations have a crucial role from the private sector perspective, and, from the public sector viewpoint, it includes the production of reports on the state of the environment and results of periodical monitoring and follow-up carried out by regulators.

Better active access systems need to establish clear standards for information collection, production and organisation and enable mechanisms to facilitate compliance, such as e-reporting. The quality, accuracy, completeness and timeliness of the information will depend greatly on these mechanisms in the first stage of active disclosure.

The second phase is the dissemination to the public. From this perspective, it is possible to observe best practices or innovative strategies to make the information known and accessible to the public, for example by using electronic databases, periodical reports, massive media, and other means of communication based on new technologies.

The specifics of the most representative schemes are examined next.

5.2.1.1. Pollutants Release and Transfer Registers (PRTRs)

The previously mentioned Kiev Protocol to the Aarhus Convention on Pollutant Release and Transfer Registers, adopted in 2003 and in force since 2009,[24] was the first legally binding international instrument of this kind, established with the objective of enhancing public access to information.[25]

The PRTRs are inventories of emissions into the environment of certain substances of interest and the facilities where they are generated. These systems are designed to make the information publicly available and easily accessible by location, allowing the public to assess the levels of pollutant emissions in their hometown or even directly from a specific facility.

The United States was one of the first jurisdictions to enable a PRTR through the Emergency Planning and Community Right to Know Act

24 Protocol on Pollutant Release and Transfer Registers to the UNECE Convention on Access to Information, Public Participation in Decision-making and Access to Justice in Environmental Matters, 21 May 2003 (entered into force on 9 October 2009), Doc. MP.PP/2003/1.

25 D'Silva, J., & van Calster, G. (2010). For Me to Know and You to Find Out? Participatory Mechanisms, The Aarhus Convention and New Technologies. *Studies in Ethics, Law, and Technology, 4*(2).

(EPCRA),[26] which created the Toxic Release Inventory (TRI) as a response to the Bhopal tragedy in India in 1984.[27]

The TRI database compiles data required by the EPCRA about potential chemical hazards including emergency notification, material safety data sheets, emergency and hazardous chemical inventory and toxic chemical release forms. The precise location of the hazardous materials, however, may be withheld from the public for the protection of the operator's trade secrets.[28] The toxic chemical release reporting only applies to facilities employing more than ten full-time employees. These forms include the name, location, principal business activity of the facility, specific information about the toxic chemical and the annual quantity of emissions.[29] The TRI is available through the EPA's website.[30]

PRTRs usually feed from the information gathered through specific reporting obligations of industrial facilities. The US Clean Air Act, for instance, establishes a reporting requirement for stationary sources releasing chemicals.[31] The Safety Drinking Water Act, in turn, requires pollution reporting to the public: a consumer confidence report must be distributed to customers by the water companies showing if there are pollutants in the water supply exceeding the maximum levels and the correlated health concerns.[32]

The EU, on the other hand, signed the Kiev Protocol on 21 May 2003 and established in 2006 its own PRTR through Regulation (EC) 166/2006 as an electronically accessible database (E-PRTR).[33] This tool provides significant environmental information to the public on pollutant releases with the ultimate purposes of contributing to reduce environmental pollution and to facilitate public participation in environmental decision-making.[34] Before the E-PRTR, there was a European Pollutant Emission Register (EPER) adopted

26 Emergency Planning and Community Right-to-Know Act of 1986, 42 U.S.C. §§ 11001–11050 (2012).

27 D'Silva & van Calster, *Participatory Mechanisms*, 2010.

28 US EPCRA, Sec. 11022(d)(2)(F).

29 US EPCRA, Sec. 11023(g).

30 Available online at: https://www.epa.gov/toxics-release-inventory-tri-program.

31 US Clean Air Act, Sec. 7412(r). Stationary sources means any buildings, structures, equipment, installations, or substance emitting stationary activities. See also Chekouras, K. (2007). Balancing National Security with a Community's Right-to-Know: Maintaining Public Access to Environmental Information Through EPCRA's Non-Preemption Clause. *Environmental Affairs Law Review*, 34, 107.

32 US Safe Drinking Water Act, 42 U.S.C. § 300i-2(a)(3)., 300g-3(c)(4) (1996).

33 Regulation (EC) No 166/2006 of the European Parliament and of the Council of 18 January 2006 concerning the establishment of a European Pollutant Release and Transfer Register and amending Council Directives 91/689/EEC and 96/61/EC, [2006] O.J. L 33/1.

34 Bünger, D. (2010). What's Up and What's Next in the Arena of Pollution Control? The New E-PRTR as a Tool towards Innovative Climate and Environmental Conservation Approaches, *Journal of European Environmental and Planning Law*, 7, 177.

in 1996[35] following the United Nations Conference on Environment and Development in Rio de Janeiro and the recommendations in Agenda 21,[36] but the current database is more comprehensive, monitoring emissions of about 100 chemicals, including more activities, releases to land, from diffuse sources and off-site transfers. The regulation is binding and directly applicable to Member States and the operators.[37] The E-PRTR reportedly contains information from over 30.000 industrial facilities covering 65 economic activities across Europe.[38] A facility must report data if it is dedicated to one of the 64 economic activities listed in Annex I of Regulation 166/06 and exceeds at least one of the applicable capacity thresholds. The reports must be submitted annually to the national competent authority including:

i Releases to air, water and land of any pollutant specified in Annex II exceeding the thresholds set therein,
ii Off-site transfers of hazardous waste exceeding 2 tonnes per year or non-hazardous waste of 2000 tonnes or more per year,
iii Off-site transfers of any pollutant in Annex II in wastewater to be treated, if they exceed the threshold value.[39]

Other environmental reporting requirements under EU law are the National Emissions Ceiling Directive,[40] the Emissions Trading System, which established the Greenhouse Gas Registry;[41] the Urban Waste-water Treatment Directive[42] and the Waste Statistics Regulation.[43]

One of the shortcomings of Regulation 166/06 relates to the lack of harmonisation with the information requirements of the Integrated Pollution Prevention and Control (IPPC) Directive, recast in the Industrial Emissions Directive (IED).[44]

35 Commission Decision 2000/479/EC on the Implementation of a European Pollutant Emission Register (EPER).
36 Agenda 21, United Nations Conference on Environment & Development, Rio de Janeiro, Brazil, 3 to 14 June 1992, Chapters 19.40 (b), 19.44, 19–49 (b), 19.60 and 19.60 and 19.61 (c).
37 Bünger, *The New E-PRTR*, 2010.
38 E-PRTR Webpage, Available online at http://prtr.ec.europa.eu/#/home.
39 Regulation 166/06, Article 5,
40 Directive 2001/81/EC of the European Parliament and of the Council of 23 October 2001 on national emission ceilings for certain atmospheric pollutants, [2001] O.J. L 309/22.
41 Directive 2003/87/EC establishing a Scheme for Greenhouse Gas Emission Allowance trading within the Community and amending Council Directive 96/6i/EC, [2003] O.J. L 275/32.
42 Council Directive 91/271/EEC of 21 May 1991 concerning urban waste-water treatment, [1991] O.J. L 135/40.
43 Regulation (EC) No 2150/2002 of the European Parliament and of the Council of 25 November 2002 on waste statistics, [2002] O.J. L 332/1.
44 Directive 2010/75/EU of the European Parliament and of the Council of 24 November 2010 on industrial emissions (integrated pollution prevention and control), [2010] O.J. L 334.

Article 12 lists the information that the applicant for a permit must submit to the competent authority, including data on the materials used by the installation, the sources of emissions and their effects on the environment, the technology used to prevent or reduce such emissions, among other relevant information. Article 24, similarly, lists information that must be made available in the process of obtaining or updating a permit, and Article 14, referring to the minimum permit conditions, asserts that it should include all measures necessary for compliance with environmental quality standards and the prevention of pollution. There is an overlap of information between the reporting requirements of Regulation 166/06 and the IED Directive for permit holders, this shows an opportunity to supplement the information reported under both laws to better contribute to the objectives of public participation and pollution reduction, but the mechanisms have not been properly integrated yet.[45]

On the matter of environmental reporting in the EU, the European Commission issued a report in 2017 consisting in a 'fitness check' of the current system. The Commission found about 181 specific environmental reporting obligations contained in 58 pieces of environmental legislation;[46] some of them applying to businesses and others to the Member States, reporting either to the Commission itself or to the European Environmental Agency (EEA). Among the findings, the Commission reported that 76% of the obligations rely mainly on textual information, which is the most difficult to process and organise in standardised databases, and about 86% of the legislative requirements could be improved by the implementation of indicators. Acknowledging the importance of effective dissemination of the information reported, one of the proposed actions was to develop a Guidance and Best Practices document by 2018 with examples and strategies to improve public access to data in easy-to-understand ways.[47]

On the other hand, Colombia does not have an established PRTR. In fact, the Organisation for Economic Co-operation and Development – OECD published an Environmental Performance Review of Colombia in 2014 recommending the implementation of a national emission inventory to reinforce the efforts to reduce the health impacts of urban pollution.[48] Another suggestion is to improve the national environmental information systems by increasing the coherence among the different monitoring networks and

45 Bünger, *The New E-PRTR*, 2010.

46 European Commission. (2017). *Actions to Streamline Environmental Reporting*. COM (2017) 312 final, pg. 3.

47 European Commission, *Streamline Environmental Reporting*, 2017.

48 OECD. (2014). *Environmental Performance Reviews: Colombia* (2014). Retrieved from http://www.oecd.org/env/country-reviews/ColombiaEPR_AssessmentRecommendations.pdf; Ministerio de Ambiente y Desarrollo Sostenible de Colombia (MADS) (2016). *Modelo Conceptual para la implementación del Registro de Emisiones y Transferencia de Contaminantes (RETC) en Colombia*. Retrieved from http://www.andi.com.co/Ambiental/SiteAssets/Paginas/default/Modelo%20conceptual%20RETC_2016.pdf.

registers and disseminating environmental information to decision-makers and the public more frequently.[49]

In June 2017, however, the Ministry of Environment and Sustainable Development published a 'Conceptual Model for the Implementation of the Pollutant Release and Transfers Register of Colombia', in order to get feedback from stakeholders in the regulatory process to follow.[50] The document takes into consideration the Guidance Manual for Governments issued by the OECD in 1996[51] and the Guide Document adopted by UNITAR in 1997 on the design of national PRTRs.[52] The proposed PRTR for Colombia would initially include emissions to water and air from point sources, unlike the European PRTR, which includes information from diffuse sources where already available at Member State level (Regulation (EC) No. 166/2006, Article 3). A total of 127 substances would initially be included in the PRTR, of which 55 (43%) are currently included in national air and water quality laws and 72 (57%) are found in international instruments ratified by Colombia, namely The Kyoto Protocol to the United Nations Framework Convention on Climate Change, the Montreal Protocol on ozone-depleting substances, the Minamata Convention on mercury, the Stockholm Convention on Persistent Organic Pollutants, and the Rotterdam Convention on the Prior Informed Consent Procedure for certain Hazardous Chemicals and Pesticides in International Trade.[53]

The list would be updated as the international and domestic legal instruments get modified or as necessary.[54] The PRTR information shall be of a public character but access thereto may be restricted based on the exceptions set in the Transparency Law to protect public and private legitimate interests. Within this context, information about the identity and location of facilities and the amount of their emissions or transfers for dangerous substances will always be public.[55]

Under the proposed Colombian PRTR, private operators cannot withhold information that they are obligated to report to the public authorities, but

49 OECD, *Environmental Performance Reviews: Colombia,* 2014.

50 Ministerio de Ambiente y Desarrollo Sostenible de Colombia (MADS). (2016). *Modelo Conceptual para la implementación del Registro de Emisiones y Transferencia de Contaminantes (RETC) en Colombia*, 155. Retrieved from http://www.andi.com.co/Ambiental/SiteAssets/Paginas/default/Modelo%20conceptual%20RETC_2016.pdf.

51 OECD (1996). *Pollutant Release and Transfer Registers (PRTRs): A Tool for Environmental Policy and Sustainable Development; Guidance Manual for Governments*, Paris.

52 United Nations Institute for Training and Research (UNITAR) (1997). *Implementación del Proyecto para el Diseño de un RETC Nacional, Guidance Document.* Retrieved from http://cwm.unitar.org/publications/publications/cbl/synergy/pdf/cat2/prtr/prtrgdsp.PDF.

53 OECD, *Environmental Performance Reviews: Colombia*, 2014.

54 MADS, *Modelo Conceptual para RETC*, 2016.

55 MADS, *Modelo Conceptual para RETC*, 2016.

they can submit a confidentiality claim specifying if the generic name of a substance must be kept confidential, and the environmental authorities shall take the appropriate measures to restrict public access. The publicly accessible database shall specify which information has been kept confidential for each facility and the reasons.[56]

5.2.1.2. Public Databases

Colombia has established a System of Environmental Information (SIAC), which has its origins in the Code of Renewable Natural Resources of 1974,[57] but was only properly established in 2006. The system includes information about the state of the environment as well as policy responses to threats and other general information. The following is a non-exhaustive list of the information to be found:

a Cartographic information
b Hydrological and climatic information
c Edaphological information
d Geological information
e Non-agricultural uses of land
f Forestry inventory
g Fauna inventory
h Legal information (Natural Resources code)
i Levels of pollution by region
j Emissions sources and pollution inventory.

Colombia's very first freedom of information piece of legislation provided in 1985 that this type of information should be made freely available to the public when held by state-entities and, further, that it should be regularly disseminated if it could be of public interest.[58]

The SIAC comprises two different subsystems: the Environmental Information System (SIA) and the Environmental Planning and Management Information System (SIPGA). The SIPGA focuses on monitoring government environmental projects, plans and programs, whilst the SIA refers mostly to the state of the natural resources and the pressures of anthropogenic activities on the environment. Within the SIA, there is a Renewable Resources Use Information System (SIUR), an Integrated Environmental Register (RUA) and a Hazardous Waste Register (RESPEL). The RUA regularly collects information from operators and facilities about the use of water, amount and

56 MADS, *Modelo Conceptual para RETC*, 2016.
57 President of Colombia, Decree – Law 2811 of 1974 'Code of Renewable Natural Resources', 18 December 1974, Article 20.
58 Law 57 of 1985 on Public Dissemination of Official Acts and Documents, 5 July 1985, Articles 22–24.

quality of discharges, energy consumption, emissions, and waste (a good starting point for a PRTR). However, it does not identify the emitted substances under an international coding system, nor does it make the information available to the public.[59]

In 2006, the European Union adopted Regulation No 1907/2006/EC concerning the Registration, Evaluation, Authorisation and Restriction of Chemicals (REACH Regulation),[60] with the purpose, among others, of ensuring a high level of protection of human health and the environment in relation to chemicals. The Regulation provides for the gathering and communication of information about the risks, properties, safety and the effects on the environment and human health of chemical products to allow producers, distributors, and consumers to use them safely. Part of the information is made available online by the European Chemical Agency (ECHA), an entity created by the same Regulation, which oversees its implementation,[61] and other data could be accessible through requests of access to information under transparency legislation (the ECHA website makes available yearly figures on the exercise of the right of access to documents).[62] The ECHA is currently undergoing a process to update its transparency approach to better ensure public participation and access to environmental information.[63]

Public access to information under the REACH regulation may be hampered by the complexity of the data, the general lack of awareness about the availability of such data and the provisions in the same regulation allowing companies to claim confidentiality over some of the information submitted to the public agencies.

The US equivalent to these e-databases are the electronic information repositories administered by the EPA. EPA currently administers around 33 different environmental programs, receiving information from public and private origin in accordance with the provisions of the main US environmental statutes: informational and planning laws (NEPA and ECPRA), pollution control laws (CAA and CWA), resource management laws (Endangered Species Act – ESA), chemical tracking laws (TSCA, RCRA, FIFRA) and liability laws (CERCLA).[64] Some of the subject-specific databases available through the EPA website are the National Emissions Inventory (NEI), providing estimates of air emissions from stationary and mobile sources, released

59 MADS, *Modelo Conceptual para RETC*, 2016.

60 Regulation No 1907/2006/EC concerning the Registration, Evaluation, Authorisation and Restriction of Chemicals, [2006] O.J. L 396/1.

61 EU REACH Regulation, Article 119.

62 The 2018 report is available online at: https://echa.europa.eu/documents/10162/13604/adt_2018-key-figures_en.pdf/686ca66d-a5f9-ed9c-604e-0c696e44a7b3.

63 See ECHA's Management Board report on Transparency Achievement and Goals for 2019–2020 at https://echa.europa.eu/documents/10162/27476116/FINAL_MB_16_2019_Update_Transparency_Approach_MB53.pdf/6eefe67f-7f08-508b-eb9b-011302cf447c.

64 Lamdan, S. (2017). Beyond FOIA: Improving Access to Environmental Information in the United States. *The Georgetown Environmental Law Review, 29*, 481.

every three years; the Permit Compliance System (PCS) and Integrated Compliance Information System (ICIS) databases covering facilities holding National Pollutant Discharges Elimination System permits,[65] the information collected from the Resource Conservation Recovery Act (RCRA);[66] the Risk Management Plan implemented pursuant to the Clean Air Act for extremely hazardous substances;[67] and the Greenhouse Gas Reporting Program (GHGRP) providing information about greenhouse gas emissions for facilities and suppliers.[68] The information reported, processed and categorised is also made available through the EPA webpage.

Some of the issues affecting the use and benefits of these databases relate to the overwhelming amount of information available, information may not be up to date, the website is confusing, and, despite the vast amounts of data, there are still inaccuracies and missing information due to deficiencies of self-reporting systems and because the information collection is limited to private entities in regulated sectors.[69]

One of the most significant weaknesses of active mechanisms like open databases and PRTRs relates to the deficiencies of the self-reporting system employed to collect the data. One study following TRI data collection found that regulated entities violate reporting requirements both intentionally, by underestimating pollution levels and even submitting false data to avoid pollution controls, and unintentionally, due to ignorance of the law and lack of expertise.[70]

5.2.1.3. Public Reporting and Notice Duties

The General Environmental Law of Colombia provides for the publicity of administrative decisions regarding environmental permits through each environmental agency's official gazette. A notice about a specific decision is also given to anyone who has requested to be a part in the administrative

65 Permit Compliance System (PCS) and Integrated Compliance Information System for the National Pollutant Discharge Elimination System (ICIS-NPDES). Available online at: http://echo.epa.gov/ and www.epa.gov/enviro/facts/pcs-icis/search.html.

66 Resource Conservation and Recovery Act Information database (RCRAInfo). Available online at: http://echo.epa.gov and www.epa.gov/enviro/facts/rcrainfo/search.html. RCRA Biennial Report (BR) data, a subset of RCRAInfo is available at: www.epa.gov/epawaste/inforesources/data/biennialreport/index.htm.

67 Available in EPA Federal Reading Rooms. For details, see: www.epa.gov/oem/content/rmp/readingroom.htm.

68 GHG Reporting Program data are available online at: http://ghgdata.epa.gov/ghgp/main.do, www.epa.gov/enviro/facts/ghg/search.html and http://www.epa.gov/ghgreporting/ghgdata/reportingdatasets.html.

69 Lamdan, *Beyond FOIA*, 2017.

70 Lamdan, *Beyond FOIA*, 2017 quoting Abell, D. J. (1994). Emergency Planning and Community Right-to-Know act: The Toxic Release Inventory, 47 *SMU Law Review, 581*, 592–93.

procedure for the environmental permit, a right that may be exercised by anyone without stating any particular interest.[71]

With the adoption of the Transparency Law in 2014,[72] the diffusion of state information of public interest was taken to the next level: a broad range of public and private entities are obligated under this law to make available public interest information in their website, including information about the entity's structure, a directory of public servants, procurement processes, internal policies and laws, procedures and decisions adopted by the entity, any auditing, management or other sort of monitoring reports, and information on how to engage in the formulation of policies, laws or other of the entity's public functions.[73] Furthermore, all the obligated subjects must implement a publication system and enable a 'Registry of Information Assets' for public consultation.[74]

The Colombian Constitution (1991) additionally established the obligation of the Contraloría General de la República, the public spending watchdog, to issue annual reports on the state of the environment. The report for 2016–2017, for instance, included some of the abovementioned aspects and also specific chapters on the protection of moorland ecosystems, the environmental impacts of illegal mining and the institutional capacity to face the environmental challenges brought about by the implementation of the Colombian peace accords.[75] The 2018 report evaluates the regional progress of the environmental programs contained in the National Development Plan, the public environmental spending, and reviews the efficacy of economic instruments like the carbon and plastic bags taxes.[76]

Active access to information is also exercised in the processes of issuing new regulatory instruments. Under a 2017 regulation, the Ministry's initiatives must be published in its website for 15 days for public consultation and comments before their enactment,[77] although it was already common practice to publish draft legislation among stakeholders to receive comments.

71 Law 99 of 1993 'Creating the Minister of the Environment, organising the public sector in charge of the management and conservation of the environment and the renewable natural resources, organising the National Environmental System (SINA), and other dispositions', 22 December 1993, Article 71.

72 Law 1712 of 2014 'Creating the Law of Transparency and of the Right of Access to National Public Information and other dispositions', 6 March 2014.

73 Colombian Transparency Law, Article 4.

74 Colombian Transparency Law, Articles 9–12.

75 Contraloría General de la República. (2017). *Informe sobre el estado de los Recursos Naturales y del Ambiente 2016–2017*. Bogotá D.C.

76 Contraloría General de la República (2018). *Informe sobre el estado de los Recursos Naturales y del Ambiente 2017–2018*. Bogotá D.C.

77 Resolution 2443 of 2017 'Establishing terms for the publication of regulation projects', Ministry of Environment and Sustainable Development, 27 November 2017.

Under the US FOIA,[78] federal agencies also have obligations of proactive disclosure of information, including administrative adjudication orders and opinions, agency guidance and, notably, copies of all records that have been released to any person via a previous FOIA request.[79] This information must be made publicly available in a 'reading room', but nowadays many agencies have much of the contents of the reading room available on their websites.[80]

Other environmental specific statutes in the US provide for public notice requirements. The EPCRA requires facilities to submit information about any hazardous materials in order to help communities plan for accidental releases,[81] although the effectiveness of this scheme to allow the public to take additional measures to protect their health and safety has been called into question because the information made available is not sufficient to determine public exposure to the hazardous substances and it is also not intended to inform the public but rather to comply with the reporting requirements.[82]

Under de US National Environmental Policy Act (NEPA),[83] Environmental Impact Statements (EIS) drafted by the federal agencies for activities that may have a significant impact into the environment must be published. The draft version is subject to public comments for a period, and, sometimes, the final versions as well. The CAA and the CWA also provide for reporting obligations about pollution into the environment, which is made publicly available. The CWA created the National Water Quality Inventory Report and the Assessment and Total Maximum Daily Load Tracking and Implementation System (ATTAINS),[84] both containing information about water quality and pollution.

On the other hand, much of the information collected by the EPA under the reporting obligations of the CAA is also published in the agencies' databases, including trends of the main air pollutants, atmospheric emissions and air quality.[85] Both laws also provide that information about permits that allow polluting emissions into air and water must be publicly accessible (the CWA provides for CWA permit searching in its National Pollution Discharge

78 Freedom of Information Act of July 4, 1966, Public Law No. 89–487, 80 Stat. 250, codified as amended at 5 U.S.C. § 552 (1994).
79 US FOIA, Sec. 552(a)(2)(A).
80 Lamdan, *Beyond FOIA*, 2017.
81 US EPCRA, Sec. 11002, 11004, 11023.
82 Roesler, S. M. (2012). The Nature of the Environmental Right to Know. *Ecology Law Quarterly, 39*, 989–1040.
83 National Environmental Policy Act of 1969, 42 U.S.C. §4321 et seq. (1969).
84 Assessment and Total Maximum Daily Load Tracking and Implementation System (ATTAINS), EPA, Available at: http://www.epa.gov/waterdata/assessment-and-total-maximum-daily-load-tracking-and-implementation-system-attains; National Water Quality Inventory Report to Congress, EPA, Available at https://www.epa.gov/waterdata/national-water-quality-inventory-report-congress
85 See EPA, *National Air Quality: Status and Trends of Key Air Pollutants.* Retrieved from www.epa.gov/air-trends.

Elimination System – NPDES).[86] Though virtually all of the main federal environmental statutes provide for some kind of reporting obligations, it is important to note that these provisions were not intentionally designed with public disclosure and access to information as their main goals, but instead as means to determine minimal compliance with regulatory standards. Therefore, direct public access and review of this information has been found to be difficult, burdensome, and costly.[87] However, the data has been used by certain stakeholders, such as NGOs, to organise and publicise information about the environmental performance of the reporting entities, an example is the US organisation Environmental Defense, which operates an environmental 'Scorecard' internet website (www.scorecard.org).[88]

Public notices and reports on the state of the environment are commonly used in international environmental instruments as well. The Aarhus Convention provides that Parties shall ensure that a report on the state of the environment is published every three or four years.[89] These reports, along with other general environmental information of public interest such as legislation, policies, plans, etc., shall be made progressively available through electronic databases.[90] These obligations were implemented at the EU level by means of Regulation No 1367/2006,[91] which generally extends the duty of proactive disclosure through databases by the EU institutions and bodies to include data derived from the monitoring activities affecting the environment, environmental authorisations and agreements, EIAs and risk assessments concerning environmental elements, and progress reports on the implementation of international and community environmental legislation.[92] The Commission is charged to ensure that the reports on the state of the environment are published at regular intervals not exceeding four years.[93] In practice, however, the European Environmental Agency publishes its assessment of the European environment's state every five years.[94] Subject-specific reports, however, are issued at more regular intervals on topics such as waste

86 Lamdan, *Beyond FOIA,* 2017.
87 Case, *Corporate Environmental Reporting*, 2005.
88 Case, *Corporate Environmental Reporting*, 2005.
89 Convention on Access to Information, Public Participation in Decision-making and Access to Justice in Environmental Matters, Aarhus, Denmark, 25 June 1998 (entry into force 30 October 2001) 2161 UNTS 447, Article 5(4).
90 Aarhus Convention, Article 5(3).
91 Regulation (EC) No 1367/2006 of the European Parliament and of the Council on the application of the provisions of the Aarhus Convention on Access to Information, Public Participation in Decision-making and Access to Justice in Environmental Matters to Community institutions and bodies, [2006] O.J. L 264/13.
92 EU Regulation No 1367/2006, Article 4(2) .
93 EU Regulation No 1367/2006, Article 4(4) .
94 The EEA's 'European environment – state and outlook' report. The sixth (and latest) SOER was released on 4 December 2019. Retrieved from https://www.eea.europa.eu/publications/soer-2020/at_download/file.

management, air quality, carbon emissions, water pollution etc.[95] Additionally, many European legislative instruments require Member States to produce and report relevant environmental information. For example, under the Water Framework Directive, Member States must produce information about the management plans of river basins and inform the European Commission, other Member States, and the public.[96]

To summarise, legal instruments at every level establish obligations to provide basic environmental information like the reports on the state of the environment, to give proper notice to concerned members of the public when there is an increased health or environmental risk, and to voluntary disclose other information to facilitate public participation in environmental matters. Public agencies' obligations to give notice and to issue regular reports on environmental information of public interest are an effective way to diminish the administrative burden associated with processing individual requests for information. The use of electronic databases and other technological tools is perceived to increase the effectiveness of proactive disclosure, and it should be widely implemented as a matter of good public governance.

However, there is still some room for improvement of the existing systems. The information reported to public entities under mandatory systems may not be suited for public disclosure in an easy-to-understand way. Awareness campaigns could go a long way in educating the public about the availability of the information promoting the utilisation of the active mechanisms. Proactive disclosure initiatives could be customised for specific communities and/or contexts, enhancing their all-inclusive capacity and reaching the people who would benefit from access the most. The different mechanisms could be standardised and even combined using technological tools to increase clarity, accessibility and usability of the released information.[97]

Regarding the impact of these instruments *vis-à-vis* access to information from the private sector, they may constitute important means for diffusion of key environmental information improving public participation in decision-

95 The reports are available at the EEAs website: https://www.eea.europa.eu/publications.

96 Directive 2000/60 establishing a framework for Community action in the field of water policy [2000] O.J. L 327/1, Article 15.

97 *E.g.* the Escazú Agreement provides as a general rule: 'For the implementation of the present Agreement, each Party shall encourage the use of new information and communications technologies, such as open data, in the different languages used in the country, as appropriate. In no circumstances shall the use of electronic media constrain or result in discrimination against the public'(Article 4(9)). Regarding environmental databases specifically, the Agreement says: 'Each Party shall guarantee that environmental information systems are duly organized, accessible to all persons and made progressively available through information technology and georeferenced media, where appropriate' (Article 6(3)). United Nations, Regional Agreement on Access to Information, Public Participation and Justice in Environmental Matters in Latin America and the Caribbean, 4 March 2018 (entered into force 22 April 2021), Escazú, Costa Rica.

making, but this will largely depend on the effectiveness of the mechanisms to collect the relevant information from private entities, the capacity of the public entity to process it and to finally communicate it in a useful, timely and trustworthy manner. Notably, the additional effort put by the public entities in this process may be compensated by a decrease of public requests for information.

5.2.2. Passive Access: Indirect Access by Request to a Public Authority

Indirect access to private information held by public authorities operates in the same way and under the same general procedural conditions of the right of access to public information, thus the information may be withheld if it falls in one of the categories exempted from disclosure that protect private interests, such as personal privacy, business confidentiality, professional secrecy, and intellectual property rights.

Generally, transparency instruments cover information 'held' by public authorities, no matter its origin. Private information submitted to a public agency is therefore presumed to be public, unless it is covered by an exception under the general access regime.

An interesting example is the US Toxic Substance Control Act (TSCA),[98] which requires firms producing chemicals for commercial use to test their products and supply information about the risks associated with them to the EPA to obtain approval before beginning to manufacture. In 2016, an amendment to this act[99] created new safety standards based on the risk assessments, making more detailed procedures for review and approval of chemical substances, and increasing transparency of the process by banning unwarranted claims of confidentiality over chemical information,[100] the reform may have been at least partially influenced by the EU's equivalent to the TSCA, the REACH regulation.[101]

The EPA is now required to assess and make determinations on most confidentiality claims for chemical identity and over a representative subset of at least 25% of other CBI claims within 90 days of the receipt of the claim. Under the (amended) TSCA, CBI is classified in three groups: (i) Presumptive CBI, this is information broadly recognised as commercially sensitive and is therefore exempted from substantiation (*i.e.* trade secrets): manufacturing processes and chemical formulae, 'proprietary information', production volumes, customers or suppliers, specific uses (a generic use must

98 Toxic Substances Control Act, 15 U.S.C. § 2613(b) (2000).

99 Frank R. Lautenberg Chemical Safety for the 21st Century Act, Public Law No. 114–182 (2016).

100 Lamdan, *Beyond FOIA*, 2017.

101 For a thorough comparison between these statutes see: Jones Day (2017). An Assessment and Comparison of New TSCA and REACH – White Paper. Retrieved from file:///Users/kzjuliana/Downloads/Assessment%20Comparison%20New%20TSCA%20REACH.pdf.

be provided);[102] (ii) CBI requiring substantiation, is any other information claimed as confidential by the submitter, not falling into any of the other two categories, for which the EPA requires specific information justifying the petition of confidentiality at the time of submission.[103] The substantiation must be framed in the eventual harm to the submitter's commercial interests if the information were publicly disclosed. The information must also be secret, and the submitter must be careful to demonstrate that reasonable measures are being taken to preserve its confidentiality; and, (iii) information which cannot be claimed to be confidential, *i.e.* health and safety studies used by EPA to determine whether chemical substances pose an unreasonable risk of injury to human health or the environment.[104]

The EPA makes the final decision on the approval or denial of the confidentiality claims. In case of denial, submitters of the information may file an appeal before a US District Court.[105] Once the information has been classified as CBI under the TSCA, the EPA may still disclose it in certain circumstances, but it must carefully monitor this release. The amended act authorises access to CBI to certain persons in special circumstances, such as first respondents in an emergency spill of a chemical substance or state public health officials that may need it for their functions, but the duty of confidentiality extends to them, and the agency must ensure that an agreement of confidentiality is signed by these persons (before the 2016 amendment to the TSCA only federal employees or contractors had access to this type of CBI).[106]

Similarly in the EU, under REACH, information submitted to the European Chemical Agency (ECHA) for approval of a substance may also be claimed as confidential and similar rules apply regarding substantiation of confidentiality claims and the impossibility to make such claims over certain safety and health chemical data.[107] Article 119(1) of the REACH regulation mandates the dissemination of certain information about the registered chemical substances for which no confidentiality claims can be made, including, among others, the

102 US TSCA, Sec 14(c)(2).

103 US TSCA, Sec 14(c)(3). On 17 January 2018, EPA published a notice of its interpretation of the revised TSCA section 14(c)(3) as requiring substantiation of non-exempt CBI claims at the time the information claimed as CBI is submitted to EPA. Retrieved from https://www.govinfo.gov/content/pkg/FR-2017-01-19/pdf/2017-01235.pdf.

104 Engler, R., Bergeson & Campbell P. C., Podcast 'All Things Chemical', Confidential Business Information under TSCA, 29 November 2018, Retrieved from https://poddtoppen.se/podcast/1439928193/all-things-chemical/confidential-business-information-under-tsca.

105 US TSCA, Sec. 14(g)(2)(D).

106 Engler, Bergeson & Campbell, *All Things Chemical*, 2018.

107 European Union REACH Regulation, Article 119. See also European Chemicals Agency (ECHA). (2018). *Dissemination and Confidentiality under the REACH Regulation*. Retrieved from https://echa.europa.eu/documents/10162/22308542/manual_dissemination_en.pdf/7e0b87c2-2681-4380-8389-cd655569d9f0.

classification and labelling of the substance, physicochemical data and on pathways and environmental fate, the result of each toxicological and ecotoxicological study and information about analytical methods which make it possible to detect a hazardous substance when discharged into the environment and to determine direct exposure to humans.

In the field of chemicals and substance law, the regulations of the different jurisdictions have more probability to interact or affect one another. In fact, this is an area of cooperation between the US and EU regulatory agencies.[108] It is important to note, incidentally, that information that is submitted to the ECHA for the approval of a substance in the EU and which is not claimed as confidential, cannot later be claimed as CBI before the EPA, because the information would be presumed to be already in the public domain.

The practical consequence of claiming confidentiality under the TSCA or any other statute in the framework of passive access to information is that the EPA is required to notify the submitter when it receives a FOI request for information protected as CBI and is considering releasing it. The submitter is then given the opportunity to present additional arguments opposing to disclosure.[109] The agency makes the final decision following legal and internal policy guidelines, including by conducting a 'foreseeable harm test' in certain cases.[110]

If the agency decides to disclose the information, the submitter of the information may still recur to the courts using a 'reverse FOIA suit', which has been defined by the US courts as

> One in which the 'submitter of information – usually a corporation or other business entity' that has supplied an agency with data on its policies, operations or products – seeks to prevent the agency that collected the information from revealing it to a third party in response to the latter's FOIA request.[111]

In a reverse FOIA suit, the party seeking to avoid the disclosure of information has the burden of proof, and the judicial review is carried out based on the administrative record, in accordance with the 'arbitrary and capricious' standard established in the Administrative Procedure Act.[112]

108 The US EPA and the EU ECHA signed a statement of cooperation in December 2010. Retrieved from https://echa.europa.eu/documents/10162/13558/soi_us_echa_usepa_en.pdf/c371c7e4-2cf4-4ec5-9caa-d0fd2d7080a1.

109 US Executive Order No. 12,600, 5 U.S.C. § 552 note (2006), Sec. 3. This Executive Order defines 'submitter' as 'any person or entity from whom the Department obtains business information, directly or indirectly', Sec. 3.

110 FOIA Improvement Act of 2016, Public Law No. 114–185 (2016).

111 U.S. DOJ. (2016). *Department of Justice Guide to the Freedom of Information Act* 2. Retrieved from https://www.justice.gov/sites/default/files/oip/legacy/2014/07/23/procedural-requirements.pdf#p9.

112 US DOJ, *Guide to the Freedom of Information Act,* 2016, pg. 872. Review on the administrative record is a 'deferential standard of review [that] only requires that

In the EU process, applicants for confidentiality have access to a review procedure if ECHA rejects their confidentiality claims.[113] The final decision of the review procedure can ultimately be challenged before the General Court of the CJEU.[114] Unlike in the US, public bodies are not required to give notice to the submitters of information claimed as confidential when they receive a public request for access, since the protection is deemed to exist when the agency accepts the claim as valid upon submission. This does not mean, however, that information claimed as CBI will never be publicly disclosed, as other legal exceptions may apply in certain cases, for instance, when the EU institution considers that the information relates to emissions into the environment, in accordance with article 6(1) of Regulation No. 1367/2006.

None of the other legal systems under review provides a scheme for the protection of proprietary information held by public entities with this level of detail. A positive outcome of this approach is that a more careful consideration is taken on a case-by-case basis to public requests of information that may be covered by legal exemptions to protect third parties' interests, which can favour disclosure in a favourable political environment for openness and restrict the application of exceptions to the information that should be protected, and no more. A negative aspect is that it can make access procedures more burdensome for agencies, submitters and petitioners, insofar as additional time is required to process the request, it may increase processing costs and there is a higher risk of uncertainty to the outcome.

In most cases, public agencies apply the rules of disclosure over the information they hold with no distinction between public or private origin. Any of it could eventually be covered by a legal exception, although certain grounds for exceptions will clearly apply predominantly over information of public origin (*e.g.* national security) and others over information submitted by private persons (personal privacy, commercial confidentiality). Colombia may be the exception. According to the Constitutional Court, when assessing requests for information, public authorities must consider the origin of the information they hold (among other factors) to determine whether the information can be disclosed. The Court expressed that, depending on the classification of the information between personal, interpersonal, public, private, semi-private or confidential, the following rules apply:

(i) Personal confidential information contained in public documents cannot be disclosed;
(ii) Access to public documents containing private or semi-private information can only be granted indirectly through the corresponding judicial or administrative authorities and following their respective procedures;

a court examine whether the agency's decision was "based on a consideration of the relevant factors and whether there has been a clear error of judgment".'

113 EU REACH Regulation, Article 118(3).

114 ECHA, *Dissemination and Confidentiality,* 2018.

(iii) Public documents containing public personal information are free to access;
(iv) The confidentiality of information may be held against members of the public but it cannot be an obstacle for institutional, political or legal control over the public actions to which the classified information refers. In any case, there is a principle of pre-eminence of the right of access to information when there are conflicting rules or lack of regulation.[115]

As mentioned in a previous chapter, the actual utility of the classification to provide clarity is doubtful because more specific rules establishing a presumption of public access over all the information *held* by public authorities and the exceptions to the rule are established in the Transparency Law and the Right of Petition Law.[116]

As in the EU and unlike the US, in Colombia there are no provisions requiring public agencies to notify and/or communicate to private submitters of information when there is a public request or when the agency is planning to disclose the information to third parties. In a recent case, a request of public access to an EIA study held by an environmental authority was refused on grounds of business confidentiality, the petitioner ultimately filed a *tutela* action for the protection of their right to public access, but these procedures were annulled and had to be restarted because the original submitter of the EIA was not notified and was thus deprived of the opportunity to defend its interest in the tutela procedure.[117]

5.2.2.1. Concluding Remarks

This section explored some of the situations and provisions in the different jurisdictions taking effect when public authorities are faced with public requests of access to information of private origin.

The field of chemical substances and registration of products provides a rich source of examples of these cases. As a highly regulated subject, there are many sources of information about how public requests are managed by the regulatory agencies. The EU and the US have the more sophisticated systems for submission of proprietary information to regulatory agencies, procedures, and requirements to determine which information is confidential, and how to deal with public requests. The US provides the added advantage of establishing clear rules to give notice to the submitter of the information when the

115 Colombian Constitutional Court, Case T-221/16, Judgment of 4 May 2016, M.P Alberto Rojas Ríos.

116 Law 1755 of 2015, 'Regulating the Fundamental Right of Petition and repealing a Title of the Code of Administrative Procedure', 30 June 2015.

117 Colombian Council of State, Case 11001-03-15-000-2016-0194301, *Maria Cristina Ferrucho Porras v Tribunal Administrativo de Antioquia*. Judgment of 15 March 2018, M.P. Stella Jeannette Carvajal Basto.

agency has decided to disclose it, enabling them to put forward arguments in defence of their confidentiality interest.

In most cases, however, no such specific rules exist for other types of private information held by public authorities like environmental reports, studies submitted in the context of environmental permitting procedures, and even environmental information provided on a voluntary basis. In all these cases the general rules for access to public information apply, and the corresponding regime of exceptions will be the main point of reference to determine when certain information of private origin must be withheld.

5.3. Direct Access to Environmental Information Held by Private Entities

Direct access to information from private entities refers to the possibility of members of the public to directly request access to environmental information held by private entities (*i.e.* without the involvement or intermediation of a public authority) either because (i) they fall into the definition of public authorities under the applicable transparency legislation, or (ii) because they have the legal imposition to disclose information to the public regardless of their involvement in the public sphere. For conceptual clarity, both scenarios will be explored separately, using examples and comparisons from the studied jurisdictions along the way.

Direct public access to information from private entities can also occur through active disclosure, most frequently in the shape of voluntary schemes and eco-labelling and notice requirements.

Both passive and active mechanisms will be examined, in the following order: (i) passive access to information from private entities assimilated to public authorities, (ii) passive access to private entities not assimilated to public authorities, and (iii) private entities proactive disclosure.

5.3.1. Private Entities Included in the Definition of 'Public Authorities'

Providing a broad definition of 'public authorities' in transparency instruments is a common technique to prevent public information from escaping public scrutiny in cases when a *prima facie* private entity is performing public functions or exercising public authority. The rationale is that these public functions have traditionally been carried out by government agencies and nothing justifies removing the information from the public sphere only because they are now being 'decentralised' to the private sector.[118]

118 UNEP. (2015). *Putting Rio Principle 10: An Implementation Guide for the UNEP Bali Guidelines for the Development of National Legislation on Access to Information, Public Participation and Access to Justice in Environmental Matters.* Nairobi. Retrieved from https://wedocs.unep.org/bitstream/handle/20.500.11822/11201/UNEP%20MGSB-SGBS%20BALI%20GUIDELINES-Interactive.pdf?sequence=1&isAllowed=y; Roberts, A. (2001). Structural Pluralism and the Right to Information. *The University of Toronto Law Journal, 51*(3), 243–271.

Table 5.1 Public Authorities covered in Transparency Laws

	Instrument/Definition includes private entities when they are…	*Performing public functions*	*Exercising administrative powers*	*Under Control of a state agency*	*Receiving public funds*	*Providing public services*	*Notes*
International	Aarhus Convention	✓	✓	✓*		✓* (under the control of government)	* Related to the environment
	Tromso Convention		✓				
	Escazú Agreement	✓*	✓*	✓	✓*	✓*	*Only in relation to the services/functions/funds. Additionally, entities owned by the government.
The EU	Directive 2003/4	✓	✓	✓*		✓* (under the control of government)	* Related to the environment.
US	Federal FOIA	✓*	✓*	✓		✓*	* Acting on behalf of a federal agency.
	Connecticut, Florida Maryland, Oregon	✓		✓	✓		Flexible approach, the presence of any factor results in access.[119]
	New York, Georgia, Ohio, California	✓					Includes contractors of public agencies.
	Colorado, Maine, and Minnesota						Laws operate over 'public records' no matter who holds them.[120]
	Arkansas, Michigan, and South Dakota				✓		Strict approach, only this factor results in access (Feiser, 2000a).
	Pennsylvania, New Jersey, and West Virginia						Entities created by law or previously determined to be subject to FOIA.[121]

	Instrument/Definition includes private entities when they are…	*Performing public functions*	*Exercising administrative powers*	*Under Control of a state agency*	*Receiving public funds*	*Providing public services*	*Notes*
Colombia	Transparency Law	✓*	✓		Administering public funds[122]	✓*	*Only in relation to the public functions or services. Additionally: Political Parties Companies with any Government participation.
	Right of Petition Law	✓	✓	✓	✓	✓	Additionally: State-owned Companies. Any private entity for the protection of individual rights.

119 The analysis of US state legislation is largely based in: Feiser, C. D. (2000a). Protecting the Public's Right to Know: The Debate over Privatization and Access to Government Information under State Law. *Florida State University Law Review*, 27, 825–64; and Capeloto, A. (2014). Transparency on Trial: A Legal Review of Public Information Access in the Face of Privatization. Connecticut Public Interest Law Journal, 13, 19–42.

120 A record can be considered public when it is used for governmental purposes or directly relates to public business. Feiser (2000a) quoting 24 Media L. Rep. (BNA) 1792, 1795 (Me. Super. Ct. 1995).

121 Pennsylvania Legislature passed a more expansive FOI law in 2008, which was applied by a lower court in 2010 adopting the more flexible "nature of the records" approach, where records directly related to government function are subject to disclosure even if in the possession of a third parties (Capeloto, 2014).

122 *E.g.* private entities ascribed to the Colombian Social Security System, which includes health services providers, pension funds and certain insurance companies.

In Chapter 4, the scope of obligated subjects under each transparency regime was examined. Building on the previous analysis, the present section reviews the rationale behind the most common arguments used to determine when private entities should be assimilated to public authorities.

As an introduction, Table 5.1 summarises private entities' 'coverage' by the definitions of 'public authorities' (or equivalent) in the main transparency instruments examined, plus a comparative view of the main factors used by US states to illustrate just how varied the approaches can be, even in the same country.

5.3.1.1. Noncumulative Factors for the inclusion of private entities in definitions of 'Public Authority'

With the backdrop of privatisation, many statutes employ different conceptual resources and develop criteria to determine when non-state entities should be subject to transparency requirements as equivalents to public authorities. This section examines some of the most frequent factors determining the scope of these laws. Usually, the occurrence of a single determinant factor would be enough to categorise private entities as public authorities.

5.3.1.2. Performing Public Administrative Functions

Private entities are said to be included in the definition of public authorities under the Aarhus Convention and EU Directive 2003/4[123] when they perform 'public administrative functions under national law'.[124] Under the US FOIA, if an entity performs a public function in place of a government agency, it is considered a 'functional equivalent' to a federal agency and is therefore covered by the FOIA, but this definition of 'public function' is more restricted than Aarhus' because it requires that the entity holds substantial independent authority in performing a clearly defined government function on behalf of an agency.[125]

An early attempt to identify entities that may be acting in the place of the government and should be considered as government for certain purposes, was the theory of the 'emanation of state', defined by the CJEU in *Foster* as

> … a body, whatever its legal form, which has been made responsible, pursuant to a measure adopted by the State, for providing a public service under the control of the State and has for that purpose special

123 Directive 2003/4/EC of the European Parliament and of the Council of 28 January 2003 on Public Access to Environmental Information and repealing Council Directive 90/313/EEC, [2003] O.J. L 41/26.

124 Aarhus Convention, Article 2(2)(b).

125 *United States v. Orleans*, 425 U.S. 807, 814 (1976); *Washington Research Project inc. v. Department of Health, Education and Welfare,* 504 F.2d 238 (D.C. Cir. 1974).

> powers beyond those which result from the normal rules applicable in relations between individuals.[126]

Following this precedent, the European Court found in *Griffin v South West Water*,[127] that water companies could be considered 'emanations of the state' under the Directive, despite their private nature. However, these two decisions did not take place in the context of public access to information.

Directly applicable to this study, in *Fish Legal*,[128] the British Upper Tribunal made a reference to the CJEU asking for guidelines to define if water utility companies were considered 'public authorities' under Directive 2003/4 and the Aarhus Convention. The case in question involved sewage and water utility companies, which in England and Wales are private companies appointed by the government to provide those services in a certain area. These companies are conducted as private corporations, they are run by Boards of Directors, accountable to their shareholders, run on normal commercial principles with the aim of generating profit and they do not receive public subsidies or other special benefits from the government.[129] In interpreting Article 2(2) of Directive 2003/4, the CJEU held that the concept of 'public administrative functions' should be harmonised at EU level, but the attribution of such functions to specific entities should be assessed against the provisions of the domestic legislation of each Member State. The Advocate General (AG) offered in his Opinion that 'public administrative functions' are 'functions by virtue of which individuals have imposed on them a will the immediate effectiveness of which, albeit subject to review, does not require their consent'. The Court largely agreed with the AG adding, as a general guideline, that 'public authorities' were

> legal persons governed by public law or by private law, which are entrusted, under the legal regime which is applicable to them, with **the performance of services of public interest**, inter alia in the environmental field, and which are, for this purpose, vested with **special powers** by national law, beyond those which result from the regular rules applicable in relations between persons governed by private law.[130] (emphasis added)

Following the CJEU guidelines, the UK Upper Tribunal ruled that water companies were public authorities under the Environmental Information

126 CJEU, Case C-188/89, *Foster and others v British Gas plc.* Judgment of the Court of 12 July 1990, para. 20.

127 UK, *Griffin v South West Water* [1995] IRLR 15 (25 August 1994).

128 CJEU, Case C-279/12 *Fish Legal & Emily Shirley v. The Information Commissioner United Utilities, Yorkshire Water and Southern Water*, Judgment of 19 December 2013.

129 Van Calster, G., & Reins, L. (2017). *EU Environmental Law.* Edward Elgar Publishing.

130 *Fish Legal*, para. 52.

Regulations (EIRs)[131] by virtue of the *special powers* they had vested in them.[132]

The reference offered by the CJEU in *Fish Legal* comes to fill a vacuum in the interpretation of Directive 2003/4 (and indirectly of the Aarhus Convention) at EU level.[133] Following this ruling, the UK Information Commissioner's Office issued a detailed guidance document regarding the application of the definition of a public authority under the EIRs. The document presents a non-exhaustive list of what could constitute 'special powers' in the context of the CJEU decision to help the organisations to determine whether they fall into the definition, including the following:

1 Compulsory purchase (of land).
2 Access to and use of private property.
3 Creating new laws and criminal sanctions.
4 Special levels of influence or advisory roles.
5 Susceptibility to judicial review.[134]

Arguably, this definition of 'public authority' may be disruptive at Member State level when internal administrative laws depart from the approach adopted by the CJEU. In France, for instance, there is a clear distinction between 'public authorities' and private entities entrusted with public responsibilities, even when the latter are vested with special powers by virtue of the public functions they perform. Under French administrative law, these private entities remain private for all legal purposes.[135]

131 Statutory Instrument 2004 no. 3391 (England, Wales and Northern Ireland) 'The Environmental Information Regulations', 2004.

132 UK Upper Tribunal, Case No. GIA/0979/2011, *Fish Legal and Emily Shirley v Information Commissioner, United Utilities Water plc, Yorkshire Water Services Ltd, Southern Water Services Ltd and the Secretary of State for the Environment, Food and Rural Affairs*

133 See Bünger, D., & Schomerus, T. (2011). Private Bodies as Public Authorities under International, European, English and German Environmental Information Laws. *Journal for European Environmental & Planning Law, 8*(1), 62–81.

134 UK Information Commissioner's Office (ICO). (2014). *Public Authorities under the EIR*, pp. 7–8. Retrieved from https://ico.org.uk/media/1623665/public-authorities-under-eir.pdf.

135 Platon, S. (2015).The notion of "public authority" in the recent case law of the European Court of Justice and its impact on French administrative law. *Montesquieu Law Review*, (1), 1–6, pg. 5: 'The definition of private entities entrusted with public service tasks is currently set by the Conseil d'Etat's decision in A.P.R. E.I. The following are now considered to be private entities entrusted with public service tasks: "any private entity entrusted with tasks of general interest, monitored by the Administration AND having *prérogatives de puissance publiques* (the equivalent under French law of "special powers")" or, in the absence of such powers, any private entity "where, in light of the general interest of its activity, the circumstances of its creation, its organisation or its operation, the duties imposed on it as well as the measures adopted in order to verify whether the aims assigned to it have been achieved, it appears that the Administration intended to

Colombia follows the French legal tradition in administrative law. 'Public function' is defined as any activity exercised by the organs of the state for the fulfilment of its aims. Private legal and natural persons can perform public administrative functions by virtue of delegation from public authorities according to the Constitution, without losing their private legal nature. However, when private entities are vested with the faculty of exercising public authority, they will be constrained by the rules applicable to public authorities as regards their performance of those public functions, with all the prerogatives and burdens associated with the exercise of public power.[136] Not all contracts with a state entity will result in the exercise of 'public authority', even if the contractor is carrying out activities of public interest or utility, but public authorities can and do delegate their power to private entities through contracts, for example under concession contracts, for the provision of public services that are the responsibility of the state, or for the collection and administration of public funds and property. The Constitutional Court has pointed out that the exercise of public functions can be identified by the exteriorisation of prerogatives inherent to the state, such as regulating conduct, issuing unilateral decisions, and exercising coercive powers.[137]

The Colombian Transparency Law applies to public servants and private persons exercising public power, providing public services, or otherwise performing public functions, but only in respect to the information related to the performance of those functions, the public services provided, or the public power exercised.[138]

The Constitutional Court's theory of the 'exteriorisation of prerogatives inherent to the state' clearly resembles the CJEU theory of 'special powers', but it would be hasty to assert their overall equivalence.

The previous analysis suggests that the concept of 'public administrative functions' is not limited to a strictly functional approach to what can be considered 'state functions', but rather to the exercise of public power, which is objectively verifiable in reference to each state's structure, especially in comparison to the faculties resulting from the application of private law between private actors.

5.3.1.3. 'Under Control of a Government Agency'

Private entities providing public services related to the environment 'under control' of a government agency or another entity performing public

entrust such tasks to it"'. Conseil d'Etat (CE), Sect., 22 January 2007, Association du Personnel Relevant des Etablissements pour Inadaptés (A.P.R.E.I.), Application n° 264541.

136 Colombian Constitutional Court, Case C-135/16, Judgment of 17 March 2016, M.P. Luis Ernesto Vargas Silva.

137 Colombian Constitutional Court, Case C-037/03, Judgment of 28 January 2003, M.P. Alvaro Tafur Galvis.

138 Colombian Transparency Law, Article 5.

administrative functions are also covered by the obligations of the Aarhus Convention and EU Directive 2003/4. According to the ACCC, this provision includes, at a minimum, all publicly-owned companies.[139] Following the CJEU reasoning in *Fish Legal*, to be 'under control' means that the private entity '…is not autonomous in determining the way in which it performs its environmental functions since a public authority is in a position to exert decisive influence on the entity's action'.[140]

The 'control' criterion applies in the US to the definition of 'state controlled corporation' of the FOIA, which was initially thought to include corporations that received federal funds.[141] The US Supreme Court held in the case *Forsham v Harris*[142] that a federal grantee could not be considered a federal agency for the purposes of FOIA if the government did not exert substantial control over the entity's day-to-day operations and decision-making processes.[143] Conversely, the Court of Appeals found in *Rocap v Indiek* that the Federal Home Loan Mortgage Corporation was a 'government-controlled corporation' under the FOIA because '(i) it was chartered under federal law; (ii) it was controlled by federal statute; (iii) its employees were federal employees; (iv) it operated solely on federal funds and (v) it was subject to the complete control of federal officials'.[144]

The 'control' theory in the US has a long-standing tradition, with the first FOIA judgments dating back to the 1970s. The application of an equivalent standard under the Aarhus Convention and Directive 2003/4 in the EU may need further development. The standard set by the CJEU in *Fish Legal* leaves considerable room for interpretation. The way in which public authorities exert control could vary; regulatory control, for instance, could be anything from special obligations to enter contracts with customers or to guarantee supply, to the obligation to offer its services under fixed tariffs. Other types of control may result from public authorities influencing the entity's administrative decisions by means of participation as shareholders, naming members of the board of directors or exercising voting rights to which they may be entitled.[145]

139 Case ACCC/C/2004/4 (Hungary), ECE/MP.PP/C.1/2005/2/Add.4, para 10. A publicly owned company established for the construction of highways qualifies as a public authority under the Aarhus Convention. Case ACCC/C/2004/01 (Kazakhstan), ECE/MP.PP/C.1/2005/2/Add.1: A State-owned enterprise with responsibilities for the atomic power industry falls under the definition of 'public authorities'.

140 *Fish Legal,* para. 68.

141 Feiser, C. D. (2000). Privatization and the Freedom of Information Act: An Analysis of Public Access to Private Entities Under Federal Law, *Federal Communications Law Journal, 52*(21–62), 32.

142 *Forsham v. Harris*, 445 U.S. 169, 100 S. Ct. 977 (1980).

143 US DOJ, *Guide to the Freedom of Information Act*, 2016, p. 872.

144 *Rocap v Indiek* 539 F.2d 174 (D.C. Cir. 1976), para. 176.

145 UNECE, *Aarhus Implementation Guide*, 2014.

The Aarhus Convention Implementation Guide has pointed out that regulatory control falls within this concept of 'under the control', but it seems unlikely that any private entity acting in a regulated market would be a 'public authority' under Aarhus.[146] Notably, the UK Upper Tribunal interpreted the CJEU decision in the *Fish Legal* case finding the 'control test' to be a very demanding one and decided that water utility companies could not be deemed to be under the control of public authorities despite being subject to relatively heavy regulation.

The UK Courts had previously considered the issue of control through regulation, stating:

> State regulation if anything points against the body regulated being a public authority. Increased privatisation has led to increased regulation, because of the need for activities that have passed from the public sector to the private sector to be subject to a measure of public control. It is the regulator, not the regulated, who exercises a public function.[147]

Even though several transparency instruments aim to provide public access to information held by entities under control of the government, the actual scope of this right depends greatly on the definition and application of the 'control' criteria adopted by each state. The analysis suggests that the threshold of public involvement is a high one: there must be an effective interference in the decision-making processes of the private entity and its overall capacity to autonomously determine the way in which it operates. However, public interference can take very different forms, therefore, a systemic analysis on case-by-case basis may be recommended.

5.3.1.4. 'Receiving Public Monies and/or Benefits'

Some modern transparency instruments extend their definitions of 'public authorities' to entities receiving public funds or some other form of state aid. The Colombian Transparency Law is a clear example, extending the scope of transparency obligations to companies with any participation of the government and entities administering public funds,[148] and the scope of access is not limited to the information related to the public resources. The Constitutional Court has asserted that the public must be able to access all the information related to the administration and use of public funds, in order to exercise public control and increase accountability.[149] Conversely, the US Supreme

146 UNECE, *Aarhus Implementation Guide*, 2014.

147 *R (Heather) v Leonard Cheshire Foundation* [2001] EWHC Admin 429 (2001) 4 CCLR 211. Cited in: Denny, A. (2005). Utility Companies and the Public / Private Divide. *Judicial Review, 10*(65), 66.

148 Colombian Transparency Law, Article 5.

149 Colombian Constitutional Court, Case C-273 of 2013, Judgment of 9 May 2013, M.P. Alberto Rojas Ríos.

Court sustained that merely receiving a federal grant was not a factor for an entity to be considered an 'agency' under the federal FOIA, unless it was subject to day-to-day control by the government.[150]

The Escazú Agreement explicitly extends its definition of 'competent authorities' for the purposes of the public right of access to environmental information to private entities that receive public funds or benefits, directly or indirectly, but only with respect to these funds or benefits.[151]

Arguably, the general right of access to public information should 'follow the [public] money' as a matter of administrative good hygiene and government accountability, regardless of the legal nature of the person administering it. Public funds are the 'property' of the public, after all.

Notably, several US states provide in their respective state FOIA that entities receiving a certain amount of public funds will be subject to the transparency regulation, going beyond the federal FOIA in this aspect.[152]

Determining a threshold in the amount of public funds that trigger public transparency obligations may be an effective tool to control excessive administrative burdens whilst preserving the spirit of the legislation.

5.3.1.5. 'Providing Public Services'

Many of the examined instruments extend transparency obligations to entities providing public services, but most of them attach some conditions.

The Aarhus Convention and Directive 2003/4 apply to entities providing public services *in relation with the environment and under control* of another public authority; only the information related to these public services must be disclosed.[153] The Escazú Agreement and the Colombian Transparency Law apply to entities providing public services regardless of their environmental nature, but access is limited to the information related to the provision of these services. The US FOIA does not apply to entities providing public services *per se*, only to the extent that they are acting on behalf of a federal agency or under their control, thus, entities falling into one of the previous categories.

The definition of 'public services' in this context may be thorny. It appears to be simple enough to transmit the idea of a state-performed activity, but if it is going to be employed as a criterion to bring private entities into the public realm, a more precise definition is necessary. An exegetical analysis of the provision tells us that the term 'public services' is not subsumed into 'public functions' because that would make it redundant and meaningless, and it probably refers to something different than the mere provision of public *utility* services, because if that were the case, the text would say as much.

150 *Forsham v. Harris.*

151 Escazú Agreement, Article 2.

152 Florida, Oregon, Maryland, Connecticut, Arkansas, Michigan and South Dakota have explicitly used this factor. Feiser, *Access to Government Information*, 2000.

153 Aarhus Convention, Article 2(2)(c).

Roberts employs 'public services' to generally refer to public interest activities that used to be the responsibility of governments but are now being outsourced to the private sector;[154] 'critical public services' would be those affecting basic rights.[155] Ebbesson lists 'public services' as an area of privatisation, providing as examples water and energy supply, transport, sewage treatment, and security.[156] Rosenbloom uses the term 'public services', in the US legal framework, as synonym of the expression 'government services once performed by public authorities'.[157]

In the absence of relevant case-law applicable to this definition, 'public services' could be interpreted in accordance with each state's constitutional framework. In the Colombian case, 'public services' are those for which access must be guaranteed by the government to all, in fulfilment of the state's constitutional aims, examples are water supply, electricity, public transportation, health care and basic education.

Regarding this interpretation, we agree with Ebbesson that

> (...) in practice, the distinction between carrying out public administrative functions and other functions under public administrative control is far from clear-cut, and rather contextual. Yet, in many situations, this definition includes private corporations to whom resources, services and functions are transferred.[158]

From the previous lines a common thread emerges suggesting that the definition of 'public services' relates to activities that were transferred from government entities, originally (or currently) entrusted to public authorities, which, additionally, are clearly in the public interest. The definition, therefore, will depend more on the public origin of the services in question than on the actual nature of those services.

A more extensive interpretation of the term 'public services' through the lenses of the maximum disclosure principle would probably include entities carrying out activities of high public interest, such as private hospitals, schools, and prisons.[159] These examples, however, do not fall far from the tree of 'public origin' activities mentioned before. In Colombia, the Transparency Law applies to political parties and 'significant groups of citizens.' During the law's constitutionality control process, the Court was asked to declare the unconstitutionality of this provision because the inclusion of these entities

154 Roberts, *Structural Pluralism*, 2001, p. 243.
155 Roberts, *Structural Pluralism*, 2001, p. 264.
156 Ebbesson, *Privatisation in Environmental Matters*, 2011, p. 79.
157 Rosenbloom, J. D. (2009). Is the private sector really a model of efficiency and independence? Re-evaluationg the use of public authorities during recessionary times. *Government Law and Policy Journal, 11*(2), 6–11, 10.
158 Ebbesson, *Privatisation in Environmental Matters*, 2011, p. 81.
159 Ackerman, J. M., & Sandoval-Ballesteros, I. E. (2006). The Global Explosion of Freedom of Information Laws. *Administrative Law Review, 58*(1), 90.

meant that private citizens would be charged with obligations that so far were exclusive to public servants. The Court upheld the provision arguing that these organisations could not be considered merely private persons considering the function they fulfil in a democracy, the fact that they receive public funding, and that they perform a constitutionally relevant function that should be subject to public scrutiny.[160]

The concept of 'public interest' is an elusive one however, with poorly defined confines. In the analysis of the current toolbox for the balanced application of exceptions to the right of public access to information, this concept is revisited.

5.3.1.6. Other Criteria for the Extension of 'Public Authority' Concepts

Some less frequently applied criteria are the following:

5.3.1.6.1. ENTITIES CREATED BY A LAW OR STATUTE

In the US, the states of Pennsylvania, New Jersey and West Virginia have used this factor to determine when the state FOIA extends to entities other than the government. This parameter alone however would be insufficient to qualify an entity as an obligated subject under other states' laws. An example is the figure of 'public authorities' in the states of New York and California, which are especial corporations created by law for the provision of certain public services or the administration of public infrastructure and are still considered private entities for legal purposes (including transparency obligations).[161]

5.3.1.6.2. ENTITIES OWNED BY THE STATE OR IN WHICH THE STATE HAS PARTICIPATION

Insofar as an entity owned by the state does not fall into one of the main categories of 'public authority' described above, this entity is very likely to have a primarily commercial or for-profit purpose.

In Colombia, these state companies are obligated subjects under transparency legislation, but they are exempt from providing their own information that can be of a proprietary, industrial, or commercial nature.[162]

Issues of protection of intellectual rights or CBI are more likely to appear in relation to this type of 'public entities' than to any other.

160 Colombian Constitutional Court Case C-273/13.

161 Public authorities are generally created to provide one public service or undertake one public project. Some well-known examples include the Port Authority of New York & New Jersey, the Tennessee Valley Authority, and the Housing Authority of the City of Los Angeles (Rosenbloom, *Re-evaluationg the use of public authorities,* 2009).

162 Colombian Transparency Law, Article 5.

5.3.1.6.3. ENTITIES SPECIFICALLY DESIGNATED BY STATUTE TO BE INCLUDED AS 'PUBLIC AUTHORITIES'

In exceptional cases, an entity may be determined to be a 'public authority' for the purposes of a FOI law only by virtue of a statute. This is the case of Amtrak, in the US, which was designated an obligated subject under the FOIA by the Rail Passenger Service Act in 1970.[163]

5.3.1.6.4. ENTITIES CONTRACTING WITH THE STATE

Few FOIAs apply unconditionally to entities contracting with the state,[164] it is more common to find cases where state contractors are obligated under transparency laws by virtue of another concurring circumstance: because an agency is delegating public powers onto them (*e.g.* public parks administrators, external auditors, register offices, public notaries etc.), they are acting on behalf of a public authority (the US 'functional equivalent' figure), they are holding public records under control of a public authority (these would be 'agency records' under US federal law), or providing 'public services' as government contractors (*e.g.* private prison administrators, health care providers, public transportation, postal services etc.).

Notably, in the case of public contractors, barriers to the right of public access to information are more easily remediated than in other cases: the contract terms themselves can establish specific obligations of information disclosure upon the contractor which are in line with the legal obligations of the contracting entity under transparency legislation, customised according to the nature of the activity, the level of public interest and the needs of confidentiality of the private person.[165] However, this is a double-edged sword because, with the same flexibility, confidentiality clauses can be included in these contracts, interfering with the right of public access to the information held by the public authority related to that particular contract.[166] It seems

163 Feiser, *Access to Government Information*, 2000.

164 Ireland, New Zealand and the state of Western Australia reportedly extend the scope of their FOI laws to cover contractor records (Roberts, *Structural Pluralism*, 2001).

165 Ebbeson, *Privatisation in Environmental Matters*, 2011, p. 81; 'The risk that privatisation of a service results in less information for the public can be reduced by an adequate legal framework (e.g. regulations, procurement or other contractual conditions) surrounding the transfer, and obliging the corporation in charge of the service to gather and provide certain environmental information related to its activity'.

166 Roberts reports that the government of the Australian state of Victoria regularly included confidentiality clauses in its contracts with private providers confounding later attempts to get access to contract information through FOI laws (Robert, *Structural Pluralism*, 2001, p. 249).

that, in practice, it is more likely to find confidentiality clauses than safeguards for access rights in public contracts.[167]

Based on the previous considerations, Table 5.2 summarises the questions to ask when defining if an entity is considered a public authority for the purposes of transparency legislation considering each of the examined main factors:

Table 5.2 Questions Used to Define What is a Public Authority

Factor	*Question*	*Relevant in…*
Performing public administrative functions	Does the entity hold special powers beyond those granted to parties in a private legal relationship to perform a service of public interest?	The EU
	Does the company enjoy the following prerogatives: • Compulsory purchase of land • Access to and use of private property • Creating new laws and criminal sanctions • Special levels of influence or advisory roles • Susceptibility to judicial review.	UK (cumulative test)
	Does the company enjoy the following prerogatives: • Regulating conducts • Imposing its unilateral will onto others • Exercising coercive power	Colombia (cumulative test)
	Is the entity clearly performing a government function on behalf of a government agency?	US
Under control of a government agency	Is the entity publicly owned?	Aarhus' jurisdiction, the EU.
	Is the entity under 'regulatory' control? (very high threshold)	Aarhus' jurisdiction, the EU.
	Does a public entity exercise 'decisive influence' over the entity by virtue of a statute, contract, or any other cause?	UK
	Is the entity unable to determine in an autonomous manner the way it provides its services because of the interference exerted by a public entity?	The EU
	• Are the day-to-day operations of the company controlled by a public agency? • Is it chartered under federal law? • Is it controlled by federal statute? • Are its employees federal employees? • Does it operate solely on federal funds?	US (cumulative factors)

167 Several authors refer to the unconventionality of such provisions in public contracts (Roberts, *Structural Pluralism*, 2001, p. 266).

Factor	*Question*	*Relevant in…*
Receiving public funds	Is the entity receiving public funds or benefits directly or indirectly?	Escazú's jurisdiction
	Is the entity publicly funded or administering public funds?	Colombia
Providing public services	Were the services that the entity provides once provided by the state?	Non-determinant indicator.
	Are the services provided by the entity in the 'public interest'?	The EU, Aarhus's jurisdiction (under the factor of public functions)
	Are the services that the entity provides ensured by the state under national laws?	Colombia

5.3.1.6.5. CONCLUDING REMARKS

This section provides important insights into the different rationales being used to extend the definition of 'public entity' to other quasi-public or private entities for the purposes of public access to information. Additional criteria not specifically mentioned such as special powers to issue tax-exempt bonds, ability to exercise compulsory purchase of land, regulatory agency, imposition of tariffs over the services the entity provides, unilateral definition of contractual terms etc. can be generally subsumed in the main categories examined, following the reasoning of the courts that revert the analysis of whether a person is 'performing public functions' or 'exercising administrative authority' to the analysis of whether the entity in question is vested with 'special powers'.

From the analysis it becomes apparent that the main reason for regulators to employ these different criteria in their FOI laws relates to the phenomena associated with the increased privatisation of services and functions weakening the public right of access to information. From this perspective, it is only logical that the common thread of the different rationales is the connection between the private entity and the public sphere, which, as we have seen, can take various and different forms.

This crucial element of the analysed factors is also the key difference between this section and the next. The following part looks at situations where private entities are assigned with transparency duties in direct benefit of the public regardless of their connection to the government, their administrative powers, or the public functions they (do not) perform.

In the more general analysis of whether to extend transparency duties to private organisations, merely formal considerations about the origin of the services being provided by an entity, its structural similarities to government agencies, or the level of government control have been criticised in the past as insufficient and 'unprincipled'.[168] They do not offer a satisfactory answer to the question of *why* should these entities be subject to transparency duties. An alternative view suggests considering the possible harm to fundamental interests that the lack of transparency can produce.[169] In Roberts' words:

> The critical question in determining information rights is not whether an organisation 'looks governmental' or whether it performs a function that was once assigned to a government agency. Rather, the important questions are whether an organisation's conduct could cause unjustifiable harm to fundamental interests, and whether transparency requirements may avoid such harm.[170]

In this author's opinion, 'a concern for basic interests will result in the imposition of access requirements even on private organisations operating in competitive markets'.[171]

The following section departs from the government-centred reasoning of the previous factors to explore alternative approaches to extend transparency obligations to private organisations.

5.3.2. Private Entities Not Included in the Definition of 'Public Authorities'

The following mechanisms implement a direct approach to the question of whether the public should be able to ask private entities directly for environmental information. Evidence suggests that a lot of the information regularly gathered and produced by private firms about the environment and regarding their own impacts remains out of bounds for the public and sometimes also for the authorities, part of it on justified grounds such as business confidentiality, protection of IPR and third's parties interests (e.g. private privacy), but other categories of privately held environmental information, we argue, should be made publicly available under certain circumstances and for different reasons.

A first example would be information about the environment produced during research which is at least partially publicly funded. Even if the company does not fall within the definition of 'public authority' under transparency laws, and thus it is not legally required to disclose this information, a

168 Roberts, *Structural Pluralism*, 2001, pp. 253–254.

169 The 'interest theory of rights', based on Raz is mentioned throughout the study as a tool that may be used not only to determine in which cases private entities should be subject to transparency duties but also in the balancing exercise between the right of access and the protection of confidentiality. Raz, J. (1986). *The Morality of Freedom*, Oxford University Press, 165–192.

170 Roberts, *Structural Pluralism*, 2001, p. 271.

171 Roberts, *Structural Pluralism*, 2001, p. 259.

strong argument can be made that the information is a public good because it was at least partially paid with tax-payers money and it is also of public interest because of its subject-matter. In the US, as of April 2000, the so-called 'Shelby Amendment'[172] requires government agencies to publicly disclose the results of federally funded research, subject to personal privacy protections. A key element for the adoption of this law was the debate over the scientific basis of EPA's regulations to strengthen national ambient air quality standards. Before the Shelby Amendment, private performers of federally funded research were not required to provide federal agencies with raw data and related information in response to FOIA requests.[173]

A second example is information gathered and produced in risk assessments for new products and projects. Not all of this information will eventually be submitted to the government either because the company desists of the project/product or because it is not required. This information should be made publicly available if it reveals potential risks for the public or for the environment as a matter of corporate responsibility, considering the high public interest in environmental information. Broad access to environmental information is essential for environmental management[174] and important participants in risk management like researchers, journalists, people who are exposed to pollution and the doctors that treat them, need to be able to access the known information to contribute to better decision-making in a global scale.

A third category would be environmental information for which there is a pressing *need* in the specific context. This would include environmental information *necessary* to ensure effective public participation in decision-making about specific projects and activities that is not already included in the categories that the law mandates to disclose and information required for the protection of the petitioner's rights. Lyndon documented, for example, the case of Cathy Behr, a nurse in Colorado who fell seriously ill after treating a worker that had suffered injuries in a chemical spill. The manufacturer of the chemicals refused to release the full ingredients of the substance, making it difficult for her to obtain adequate diagnosis and treatment.[175] In circumstances such as these, private companies should not be able to refuse the

172 Omnibus Consolidated and Emergency Supplemental Appropriations Act of 1999, Pub. L. No. 105–277, 112 Stat. 2681.

173 Fischer, E.A. (2013). *Public Access to Data from Federally Funded Research: Provisions in OMB Circular A-110*. Congressional Research Service. Retrieved from https://fas.org/sgp/crs/secrecy/R42983.pdf.

174 Lyndon, M. (2011). Trade Secrets and Information Access in Environmental Law. In R. Dreyfuss & K. J. Strandburg (Eds.), *The Law and Theory of Trade Secrecy: A Handbook of Contemporary Research* (pp. 443–466). Edward Elgar Publishing, pg. 452.

175 Lyndon, *Trade Secrets and Information*, 2011, p. 455, quoting Layton, L. (2010). Use of Potentially Harmful Chemicals Kept Secret Under Law. *Washington Post*, 4 January 2010, A1.

disclosure of environmental information, even if it can be considered their private property, trade secrets or IPR.

The fourth category of privately generated information which should always be made available to the public are the indicators of the company's environmental performance (resource use, waste production, energy efficiency, carbon print etc.) because only in this way could the full benefits of regulation by disclosure for environmental protection be achieved.[176] In the words of Case, 'the ability to enable environmental performance monitoring is the most critical element to the potential efficacy of environmental informational regulatory rules'.[177] Some of this information is already publicly accessible through PRTRs and other public databases, and is also included in voluntary sustainability reports disclosed by companies.[178] A serious obstacle to public databases however is that the information may take a long time to be collected, organised and publicised.[179] Delayed release of information can sometimes be just as ineffective as no release at all.

Bringing private entities into the open as direct subjects of transparency obligations also contributes to the debate of confidentiality *versus* disclosure of environmental information by exposing the real interests protected in each regime without the artificial distinction between public and private entities, which is, arguably, unprincipled and increasingly confusing. If most proprietary or commercially sensitive information is inaccessible anyway because of the default exclusion of private entities from transparency laws, useful discussions about when trade secrets should prevail over the right of public access and vice versa may not appear as relevant and could be set aside.

Finally, the arguments regularly raised by advocates of environmental transparency in conflicts with business confidentiality are in many cases relevant and transferable to the debate of private sector transparency in general. The argument that focuses on the *nature* of the information, for instance, defending that certain environmental information is just too important to remain hidden from the public (*e.g.* information about hazardous substances, emissions into the environment, risks for the public health and the environment) can be extended to argue that the information should be released as soon as it is available, in a complete, clear, and reusable manner, and therefore the public should be entitled to elicit disclosure directly from the producers/holders of the information, regardless of their public or private nature.

176 The argument of the 'regulation by disclosure' is the potential improvement of environmental practices as a result of social, political and market pressures triggered by the disclosure of a firm's environmental performance indicators. See Fung, A., Graham, M., & Weil, D. (2007). *The Perils and Promise of Transparency*. Cambridge University Press.

177 Case, *Corporate Environmental Reporting*, 2005, p. 433.

178 Case, *Corporate Environmental Reporting*, 2005.

179 TRI data is up to 18 months old by the time it is publicly released by EPA, which makes it already outdated at the time of its release (Case, *Corporate Environmental Reporting*, 2005).

It is important to note that direct access to information from private entities is likely to come with its own issues of enforcement, practical implementation and, notably, tensions with legitimate private interests and conflict over the confidentiality of the information. Many of these issues may also appear in cases of indirect access to private entities' information through public authorities and in cases of entities assimilated to public bodies, but access to remedies and tools for conflict resolution could, arguably, be more readily available in 'semi-public' or 'public' judicial and administrative instances than in the horizontal relationship between two private actors (applicant and respondent).

Looking at the different jurisdictions, it should be noted that transparency obligations directly assigned to private organisations when they are not 'involved' with government activities are rare in international and national legislation. Soft law instruments, understandably, may be somewhat more progressive and propose wider scope for access to information rights, such as the Declaration of Principles on Freedom of Expression in Africa, adopted by the African Commission on Human and People's Rights, which explicitly proclaims a right to access information from private entities when it is required for the exercise of other rights.[180]

The most progressive approach from an access perspective comes in this case from Colombian domestic legislation, where a right of access to information from private entities is constitutionally established when the information is needed to exercise or protect the applicant's fundamental rights, but a special mention should be made of the provisions of the Escazú Agreement that address access to information directly from private entities. Article 6(10) emphasises access to information from private entities by establishing that 'Each Party shall ensure that consumers and users have official, relevant and clear information on the environmental qualities of goods and services and their effects on health, favouring sustainable production and consumption patterns'; and Article 6(12), in a softer language, commends Parties to 'take the necessary measures (…) to promote access to environmental information in the possession of private entities, in particular information on their operations and the possible risks and effects on human health and the environment'. Notwithstanding the non-binding language of this provision, it is remarkable because it places the interest of disclosure on the nature of the information regardless of the legal status of the entity holding it, which, in a way, objects to the notion of private property over the information held by private entities and implicitly disregards presumptions of confidentiality over business-related information that is also environmental information and that is relevant to assess the risks and impacts of the company's operations on human health and the environment.

180 Declaration of Principles on Freedom of Expression in Africa, African Commission on Human and Peoples' Rights, 32nd Session, Banjul, The Gambia, 17–23 October 2002.

This analysis supports the argument that access rights in environmental matters should not be primarily determined according to the traditional organic criterion that distinguishes between public and private organisations because phenomena like privatisation, increased involvement of civil society and emerging forms of legal organisation pose new challenges to the traditional elements employed in defining when certain entity is considered public and when it is not. In the new 'informational society', these criteria seem to be growing obsolete. Other factors, such as the nature of the information, the context in which it is requested, and the purpose of disclosure in terms of the protected interests should be employed in place of, or at least concurrently with, the organic criterion.

5.3.2.1. Access to Information for the Protection of Rights: The Colombian Example

Colombia does not have a specific legal instrument dealing with access to environmental information, thus requests for this kind of information are generally handled under the Right of Petition Law.

The right of petition is a constitutional right of citizens to submit respectful petitions to the authorities and obtain a clear, complete, and timely reply. According to Article 23 of the Colombian Political Constitution (1991), this right can be exercised by anyone to ask information directly from private entities which is required for the protection of their fundamental rights.

Though very few jurisdictions share a similar provision,[181] this concept is not strange to human rights legal theory. Authors across the legal spectrum have pointed out the instrumentality of access to information as a necessary precondition for the exercise of basic human rights.[182] A clear example is the fundamental right to security and the correlated need to access information about potential threats to health and safety, which has been defended by the ECtHR in several landmark decisions (*i.a. Guerra v Italy* and *McGinley and Egan v UK*). Access to information is also clearly linked to political participation rights, usually read in conjunction with the fundamental right of freedom of expression.[183] For the Colombian Constitutional Court, two of the

181 Similar provisions can be found in Kenya's Constitution (2010), Section 35.1, which guarantees a right of access to any information that is held by any 'person' and that is 'required' for the exercise or protection of any right; Rwanda's Law No. 04/2013 of 08/02/2013 Relating to Access to Information, Article 2.4, applies to a private body that holds information relevant to 'rights and freedoms of people', and South Africa's Constitution (1996) which provides that 'Everyone has the right of access to (a) any information held by the State and; (b) any information that is held by another person and that is required for the exercise or protection of any rights'.

182 See examples in Zuluaga Madrid, J. (2017). Access to Environmental Information from Private Entities: A Rights-Based Approach. *Review of European, Comparative and International Environmental Law, 26*(1), 38–53.

183 Roberts, *Structural Pluralism*, 2001.

three identified purposes of the right of public access to information are instrumental: (i) to ensure democratic participation and the exercise of political rights and (ii) to enable the exercise of other constitutional rights by allowing the public's knowledge of the conditions necessary for their realisation. The third purpose is the increase of administrative accountability through public control.[184] Notably, the CJEU has recently asserted the right of access to environmental information as a necessary precondition for effective public participation in decision-making, deciding, on these grounds, to grant access to the impact assessment reports drafted for the Commission about possible legislative action to adopt a directive on access to justice in environmental matters and regarding environmental inspections. This information had previously been refused to the NGO ClientEarth under the argument that its disclosure could interfere with the Commission's decision-making process.[185]

The idea of granting access to information from private entities when it is necessary for the exercise of other fundamental rights can be observed in practice in Colombia's domestic legislation.

The right to ask information directly from private entities is established in the Constitution. The Constitutional Court has explained about this provision:

> The right of petition against private organisations (…) enables individuals to oppose abuses in which they may incur armed by their dominant position in a legal relationship. It constitutes an instrument of democratic participation because it allows the people to inquire and protect themselves from the activities carried out by private organisations when they interfere, for any reason, with their subjective or collective sphere, through acts of power. It is also a means to demand respect for fundamental rights from private persons.[186]

The constitutional provision was implemented through the Right of Petition Law which, in Article 32, provides that

> Any person shall be able to exercise the right of petition to guarantee his/her fundamental rights before private entities with or without legal personality such as (commercial) societies, corporations, foundations, associations, religious organisations, cooperatives, financial institutions, or clubs.
>
> (…)

184 Colombian Constitutional Court Case C-273/13.

185 CJEU, Case C-57/16, *ClientEarth v. European Commission*, Judgment of 4 September 2018.

186 Colombian Constitutional Court, Case T-001/98, Judgement of 16 January 1998, M.P. Antonio Barrera Carbonell.

> The private organisations may only invoke the confidentiality of the information in the cases explicitly established in the Political Constitution and in the law.
>
> (…)
>
> Par. 1: This right can also be exercised before natural persons when the petitioner is in a position of defencelessness, subordination or under the dominant function or position of the natural person.

This article can be relied upon to request access to information held by any private organisation and natural persons in the cases mentioned above, even if the entity or person does not have any connection with government functions, funds, or regulatory control, independently of their aims and regardless of the public interest nature of their activities.

The general inclusion of private entities as obligated subjects of the right of petition can potentially result in a wider access to environmental information for the public in Colombia, compared to the other jurisdictions. Direct access to environmental information from private entities could be justified for the protection of the petitioner's fundamental rights to life, health and a healthy environment, all of them with constitutional status. Furthermore, the Right of Petition Law explicitly extends to public utility companies and financial and stock-market institutions,[187] going further in coverage than the Aarhus Convention and EU legislation. In the UK, the question of whether privatised utility companies were public authorities under the Aarhus Convention and Directive 2003/4 was only resolved after a judgment in 2015, finally establishing that these companies were considered public authorities by virtue of the special powers vested in them.[188]

Inquiring into the rationale behind these provisions in the Colombian system, Colombian courts have interpreted and applied the constitutional right of petition from private entities mostly through judgments produced in the exercise of the *tutela* action, an expeditious judicial procedure to stop the violation of fundamental rights. According to the Constitutional Court, the reasoning behind the establishment of the right of petition before private persons is the asymmetry of powers between members of a community, a discrepancy that sometimes may be greater than that between the state and its citizens. This situation requires the establishment of mechanisms for the protection of people's rights in relation with others that hold greater political, social, or economic power.[189] It is the Court's opinion that respect for the fundamental rights of others is an obligation of private citizens (and corporations), and not only of the government. To ensure this, the equality of

187 Colombian Right of Petition Law, Article 33.

188 *Fish Legal*, para. 68. See analysis by Randhawa, R. K. (2015). *Rights of Access to Environmental Information from Privatised Companies*. Gowling WLG.

189 Colombian Constitutional Court, Case C-951 of 2014, Judgment of 4 December 2014, M.P. Gloria Stella Ortiz Delgado (regarding the constitutionality of the legislative proposal for a statutory law of the Right of Petition).

private relationships needs to be preserved, which is why allowing the exercise of the right of petition by the weak part of a private relationship helps to remediate the power unbalance and enables individuals to assume a real defence of their interests.[190]

Access to information from private persons is conditioned to the need of the information for the protection of the petitioner's fundamental rights. Under Colombian law, these include the basic attributes of the human person, civil and political liberties, and several social guarantees such as the right to health and the right to education. The Colombian catalogue of fundamental rights is considerably broad and open to new inclusions, as international Human Rights treaties entered by Colombia automatically become a part of the Constitution. Insofar as the Escazú Agreement can be considered a 'human rights treaty', its provisions will have constitutional status once the Agreement enters into force for Colombia, and the protection of the rights enshrined therein can be invoked as grounds to request access to information held by private actors.[191]

Additionally, the Colombian Constitutional Court is considered one of the most active in the Latin American region and is vested with broad powers to interpret the Constitution and international human rights treaties ratified by Colombia to extend the constitutional protection to a vast array of social, economic and other rights.[192] In a 1998 judgment, for example, the Court ordered the production of a document attesting about the labour relationship between a private entity and the petitioner to protect the petitioner's right contained in the Substantive Labour Code, which is not a 'fundamental' right *stricto sensu*, but relates indirectly with the right to work.[193] In a 2007 case, the Court ordered a private organisation that collected unpaid debt to respond to a request as it was deemed necessary to guarantee the effectiveness of the petitioner's right of habeas data and the right of personal and family privacy.[194] Like these cases, the Constitutional Court has found justified the right of petition before private entities for the protection of the right to intimacy and family life, the right to a good name and reputation and the right to work and social security.

Regarding access to environmental information specifically, the judicial doctrine of the Constitutional Court has confirmed that the right to enjoy a healthy environment, enshrined in Article 79 of the Constitution, is a

190 Colombian Constitutional Court, Case T-689/13, Judgment of 30 September 2013, M.P. Jorge Ignacio Pretelt Chaljub.

191 The Colombian Congress approved the ratification of the Escazú Agreement through Law 2273 of 5 November 2022.

192 Lizarazo Rodríguez, L. et al. (2014). Constitutional Aspects of FTAs: A Colombian Perspective. *European Law Journal, 20*(6), 824.

193 Colombian Constitutional Court, Case T-111/02, Judgment of 15 February 2002, M.P. Manuel Jose Cepeda Espinosa.

194 Colombian Constitutional Court, Case T-798/07, Judgment of 27 September 2007, M.P. Jaime Córdoba Triviño.

fundamental right due to its intrinsic connection to the very fundamental rights to life and health.

The Court stated:

> The right to the [healthy] environment cannot be separated from the people's right to life and health. In fact, the disturbing factors of the environment cause irreparable damage to human beings, thus it must be ascertained that the environment is a fundamental right for the existence of humanity. The Court has come to this conclusion when it has evaluated the influence of the environment in the life of men and this is why, in previous tutela judgments, it has been affirmed that the right to the environment is a fundamental right...[195]

But the protection of the right to a healthy environment is not the only plausible basis to request environmental information. The Court has also recognised the right to privacy and family life as a fundamental right on its own, and environmental conditions can have a significant effect in the effective exercise of these rights as well. The Court has made this link explicit in the following terms:

> The natural or private person who, taking advantage of the public authorities inaction, pollutes the air and causes nuisance to the people at their homes to a degree that they are not obligated to suffer, violates simultaneously the right to a healthy environment and the fundamental right to privacy. The production of bad odours as part of industrial activities is arbitrary when, despite the existence of sanitary rules and due to the deficient control of the public authorities, it causes a significantly disproportionate annoyance to a person to the degree of impeding the exercise of his right to privacy.[196]

This shows that access to environmental information held by private entities should be provided for the protection of the right to a healthy environment or any other fundamental rights such as the right to privacy and family life. There are many documented *tutela* cases dealing with requests of access to information from private entities for the protection of fundamental rights, but to this point, there are no specific cases dealing with environmental information. This does not mean that the mechanism is not active however, only that the cases involving environmental information have not reached the courts. An interesting example of the application of an equivalent provision is found in South Africa, where the rights of access to information can also be

195 Colombian Constitutional Court, Case C-671/01, Judgment of 28 June 2001, M. P. Jaime Araújo Rentería, Sec 4.4.1.

196 Colombian Constitutional Court, Case T-219/94, Judgment of 4 May 1994, M.P Eduardo Cifuentes Muñoz.

exercised against private persons for the protection of rights.[197] In this case, an environmental NGO obtained access to the 'environmental master plan' and additional documents from the private company ArcellorMittal, on the basis of the protection of their right to a healthy environment and the rights to 'have the environment protected', to monitor the company's operations and, generally, to exercise their public participation rights.[198]

Based on the above, it is possible to assert the great potential for a rights-based approach to access environmental information directly from private entities. Indeed, had a similar provision been available in the US, Ms. Cathy Behr would have been able to request the information about the identity of the chemicals that made her ill and could have received the best medical treatment for her condition. This is a clear hypothetical example of public access to environmental information from private entities for the protection of fundamental rights.

As a final note, the Colombian Constitutional Court has made it clear that public access to information directly from private entities does not preclude the protection of the company's trade secrets or other commercial or business information kept by the entity in confidentiality, not even when the information is required for the protection of the petitioner's fundamental rights. Furthermore, the private information disclosed in this context can only and exclusively be used by the recipient for the protection of their fundamental rights.[199]

5.3.2.2. Access to Specific Categories of Information

Another perspective of transparency rights that disregards the difference between private and public entities justifies public access when the information in question is of the upmost importance for the public, or its disclosure protects higher state values.

Regarding public access to information, Roberts defends the adoption of a criterion of 'harm to fundamental interests', explained as

> [A] method of reasoning about the boundaries of access law that builds on explicit propositions about the good that could be produced by

197 South Africa's Constitution (1996), providing that 'Everyone has the right of access to (a) any information held by the State and; (b) any information that is held by another person and that is required for the exercise or protection of any rights', further regulated in the South African Promotion of Access to Information Act, Act 2 of 2000.

198 South Africa Supreme Court, *Company Secretary of ArcelorMittal South Africa v. Vaal Environmental Justice Alliance* (69/14) [2014] ZASCA 184 (26 November 2014). See analysis in Zuluaga Madrid, *Environmental Information from Private Entities*, 2017.

199 Colombian Constitutional Court, Case T-317/19, Judgment of 15 July 2019, M.P. Diana Fajardo Rivera; Colombian Constitutional Court, Case T-103/19, Judgment of 11 March 2019, M.P. Diana Fajardo Rivera.

> improved transparency. A better method of reasoning would focus on the deleterious effects of opacity: the harms that may be caused when access to information is denied (…) In particular, we can refer to harm to a citizen's fundamental interest and more specifically, those interests that undergird the set of generally recognized basic human rights.[200]

This perspective could be used in support of access to information for the protection of rights, as described in the previous title, but it also fits neatly as the justification for access to specific categories of information when such disclosure would prevent harm to public values or private persons' fundamental interests, as observed in the following cases.

1 Information about emissions into the environment. PRTRs are the embodiment of this. They are directed to private or public industries emitting polluting substances, and the importance of this information for the protection of the environment and public health is sufficient to extend the obligation to private persons regardless of their connection to government without any further considerations. Additionally, there is an argument that emissions cease to be private when they enter the public environmental domain, thus access to information about them is supported on the general right of access to public information.[201]
2 Information about hazards to public health and safety. Several international and national laws impose onto private entities the obligation to disclose information that is necessary to protect the public's health and safety from imminent risks. It is evident in this case the prevalence of the public interest and the right to safety. Employers are usually required to disclose information about any risks to their employees. Private entities also choose to actively disclose information of relevance for the safe use of their products or services as a matter of due diligence, especially in common law jurisdictions where tort laws allow for the imposition of heavy fines and punitive damages to companies omitting their due diligence obligations.[202]
3 Information about violation of human rights and crimes against humanity. Several regulations establish a prohibition to exempt information related to these issues from public access regimes;[203] they also invalidate private confidentiality agreements regarding information of this kind, and

200 Roberts, *Structural Pluralism*, 2001, p. 256.
201 UNECE, *Aarhus Implementation Guide*, 2014.
202 Environmental Law Institute. (1984). *Environmental Audit Issue Paper: Duties to Report or Disclose Information On The Environmental Aspects of Business Activities*. Washington D.C.
203 Colombian Transparency Law, Article 21. Similar provisions are found in the laws of Albania, Brazil, Guatemala, India, Mexico, Peru, Romania and Uruguay (Coliver, *Expanding Scope*, 2015).

foresee protection mechanisms for whistle-blowers.[204] Arguably, if proven that a private entity holds this kind of information, there would be a strong argument to make it available under the general right of access.

4 Environmental, health and safety (EHS) information. Some authors hold the opinion that EHS information should be disclosed, as a general rule, regardless to the nature of the entity holding it or any commercial confidentiality considerations.[205] NGOs advocating for transparency also defend wider access to this kind of information, even from private entities.[206] A strong case can be made for the disclosure of EHS information that is necessary to conduct the appropriate risk assessment of a substance, product, project or activity.

5.3.2.3. CONCLUDING REMARKS

The rationale of a right of access to information directly from private entities when it is necessary for the protection of fundamental rights departs from the perspective of a right of public access depending on the public nature of an entity or its link with the public sphere.

This mechanism is also different from the general right of access to information in fundamental ways. Firstly, one of the main attributes of the right of public access to information is its universal availability: anyone has the right to request public information from their government, sometimes nationality or residency is not even an issue. In this case however, only persons with a direct interest in the information in question may exercise the right of petition. Logically, the direct interest is the necessary link. Secondly, persons exercising the right of public access to information do not need to prove an interest, not even to state a motive. In this case, however, a crucial part of the request is the justification by the applicant as to why the information is necessary for the protection or exercise of their fundamental rights.

These differences point to the fact that access to information from private persons does not have to operate in the same terms as access to information from public authorities. The Colombian Constitutional Court made this clear when deciding about the constitutionality of a paragraph in Article 32 of the Right of Petition law making a remission to the general rules of procedure operating to the Right of Petition before public entities. The Court considered that such a provision would introduce unbalances to the application of the principle of liberty and the autonomy of private will governing relations between private persons. It therefore found it unacceptable to extend the

204 US Defend Trade Secrets Act, Public Law 114–153 (2016), specifically provides protection for whistleblowers denouncing misconduct, even if they incur in violation of private confidentiality agreements.

205 Case, *Corporate Environmental Reporting*, 2005, p. 433.

206 Article 19. (1999). *The Public's Right to Know: Principles on Freedom of Information Legislation*. Retrieved from http://www.article19.org/pdfs/standards/righttoknow.pdf.

entirety of the obligations of public authorities regarding petitions to private persons.[207]

Public access to information directly from private entities can also be granted for certain categories of information representing a prevalent public or private interest. Note that in this case, again, the general right of access to information is not the rule, because these entities would only be required to disclose the information in question and not all the information that they hold.

Finally, it is important to note that the examined situations in which access to information held by private entities is justified, the same reasons can be brought up to override exceptions of business confidentiality.

5.3.3. Private Entities' Active Disclosure

5.3.3.1. Voluntary Schemes

Most of the active disclosure from private entities directly to the public is in the form of voluntary sustainability reporting.

A coalition of KPMG International, the United Nations Environment Programme (UNEP), the Global Reporting Initiative (GRI) and the Centre for Corporate Governance in Africa published four reports titled 'Carrots & Sticks', accounting for the status of sustainability reporting on a global scale since 2006.[208] By 'sustainability reporting instruments' the study refers to 'any instrument, mandatory or voluntary, that requires or encourages organizations to report on their sustainability performance'.[209] The 2016 report included information of the reporting instruments in 64 countries showing a significant increase in both mandatory and voluntary instruments in the last ten years. Only since 2013, there was an increase of more than 100%, with 180 instruments identified in 44 countries for the 2013 report and 383 instruments identified in 64 countries for the 2016 study. Of the 383 instruments, 65% are mandatory and 35% voluntary. The numbers suggest that sustainability reporting is now mainstream, with more than 90 of the world's largest 250 companies and 70 of the largest 100 companies within 45 countries disclosing their sustainability performance.[210]

According to the 2016 'Carrots & Sticks' report, there were more than ten reporting instruments identified in the US and between five and nine in

207 Colombian Constitutional Court Case C-951/14

208 Bartels, W., Fogerlberg, T., Hoballah, A., & Van der Lugt, C. (2016). *Carrots & Sticks: Global Trends in Sustainability Reporting Regulation and Policy.* Retrieved from https://home.kpmg.com/xx/en/home/insights/2016/05/carrots-and-sticks-global-trends-in-sustainability-reporting-regulation-and-policy.html.

209 Bartels, Fogerlberg, Hoballah & Van der Lugt, *Carrots & Sticks,* 2016, p. 6.

210 KPMG. (2015). *Survey of Corporate Responsibility Performance.* Retrieved from https://home.kpmg.com/xx/en/home/insights/2015/11/kpmg-international-survey-of-corporate-responsibility-reporting-2015.html.

Colombia. All of the EU Member States have sustainability reporting instruments in place, but Spain, France, Italy and the Scandinavian states lead the way, followed by Germany and Portugal. The amount of reporting instruments in European countries almost doubled between 2013 (80) and 2016 (155). Some of the new instruments relate to the transposition into national law of the EU Non-Financial Reporting Directive (Directive 2014/95/EU) and there are also new reporting requirements related to energy efficiency and greenhouse gas emissions.

The regions under study present interesting variations in the proportion between mandatory and voluntary reporting instruments. In the Latin America region, voluntary instruments account for 42% of the total, whilst this percentage is only 20% in the US. In Europe, more than one third (38%) of reporting instruments are voluntary and the rest are mandatory.

The main characteristic of voluntary self-regulatory initiatives by the private sector is precisely the impossibility to enforce their obligations to guarantee the desired outcomes. However, while compliance for specific purposes could certainly be improved through binding regulations, some topics might be better tackled through voluntary initiatives, which may offer a more flexible approach, be faster and easier to adopt, and respond more accurately to the needs and capacities of the specific sector.

Whilst the number of voluntary initiatives by the private sector aimed to improve environmental performance and transparency have considerably increased among almost all economic sectors, there is significant disagreement as to their actual effectiveness and the way they may contribute to environmental governance.[211]

The following transparency related international voluntary initiatives have been subscribed to by industry actors in some of the countries being studied:

i The Global Reporting Initiative (GRI), international guidelines for reporting on economic, environmental and social performance. 'Sustainability Reporting' generally refers to the reporting of information relative to the 'triple bottom line' of social, environmental and economic impacts of a corporation's activities.[212] This international organisation pioneered on sustainability reporting since 1997, its core product is the Sustainability Reporting Standards, which have been continuously developed for 20 years.[213]

211 Ebbesson, *Public Participation Environmental Matters,* 2011; Morrison & Roth-Arriaza, *International Environmental Law,* 2007; Etemire, *Private Companies,* 2012.

212 Case, *Corporate Environmental Reporting*, 2005.

213 Global Reporting Initiative (GRI) official website: https://www.globalreporting.org/information/about-gri/gri-history/Pages/GRI's%20history.aspx. See also Global Reporting Initiative (2016). *Forging a Path to Integrated Reporting.* Retrieved from https://www.globalreporting.org/resourcelibrary/GRI-CLG_IntegratedReporting.pdf.

ii The Global Chemicals Industry voluntary initiative 'Responsible Care' (some 60 chemical companies in the US have joined), aimed to improve their environmental, health and safety performance.[214]

iii The Extractive Industries Transparency Initiative (EITI): This is a 'global standard to promote the open and accountable management of oil, gas and mineral resources' (Colombia joined in 2014, Germany is also a party). The EITI standard requires countries and companies to disclose specific information on the key steps in the governance of oil, gas and mining revenues and how they are allocated.[215]

iv The Environmental Management Standard ISO 14001. The most recent environmental management systems standard was adopted in 2015 providing practical tools for organisations of any sector to manage their environmental responsibilities.[216]

v The EU Eco-Management and Audit Scheme (EMAS): similar in purpose to ISO 14000, EMAS is a voluntary environmental management instrument adopted by the European Commission in 1993.

Private sector voluntary initiatives to improve transparency and/or environmental performance may vary significantly: some of them, like the ISO 14001, provide concrete standards of performance, whilst others, such as the GRI standards, only provide guidelines for reporting. The disparity makes it difficult to compare them in terms of efficacy, legitimacy and the overall accomplishment of their stated goals. In fact, one of the main arguments in support of mandatory public reporting relates to the need of a harmonised reporting process to satisfy multiple stakeholders and objectives,[217] which would also allow meaningful comparisons and facilitate the use of the information in participatory processes.

There is no consensus on the actual regulatory value of voluntary initiatives, but most authors agree that they are most useful when employed as a complement to enforceable environmental and transparency legislation, and not as a substitute thereof,[218] or perhaps as the basis for the adoption of a formal mandatory reporting system in place of the piecemeal approach to environmental reporting that seems to prevail in most jurisdictions.[219]

214 International Council of Chemical Associations, https://www.icca-chem.org/responsible-care/.

215 Information available at the EITI official website: https://eiti.org/.

216 International Standard Organisation – ISO official website: https://www.iso.org/iso-14001-environmental-management.html.

217 Emtairah, T. (2002). *Corporate Environmental Reporting: Review of Policy Action in Europe*, Lund, pg. 13.

218 Thorp, T. (2012). The Right to Know and the Duty to Disclose: Pathways to Effective Monitoring, Reporting, and Verification within the Constitutionalism of Climate Justice. *Pace Environmental Law Review*, 30, 140.

219 For a thorough analysis of the potential of voluntary reporting systems to serve as the framework for the enactment of mandatory reporting requirements and the

Some of the main elements that may enhance the contribution of voluntary mechanisms for the achievement of policy goals are the following:

1 The voluntary agreements are formulated in a framework of existing legislation, but their goals and commitments go *beyond* the regulation in place. EMAS, for instance, requires compliance with all the applicable environmental laws and also integrates the environmental management standards ISO 14001, but goes even further than both regulatory schemes.
2 There are specific targets, deadlines, and actions to be implemented by the subscribing parties, and there are mechanisms in place for continuous monitoring, updating and correcting of the initial commitments. Independent audits and overseeing bodies are a plus, particularly if there is involvement of the civil society.[220]
3 The voluntary agreement is entered into by a great majority of the actors in the regulated industry.
4 There are enforcement mechanisms to promote maximum compliance.

Despite the criticism, self-regulatory initiatives which comply with the minimum standards of (i) legitimacy, (ii) external verification, (iii) harmonisation with current legislation, and (iv) overall endorsement by companies, may play a significant role at improving environmental democracy and safeguarding legitimate confidentiality interests in the process. Although these voluntary initiatives should not come as substitutes of the necessary legislative framework to ensure a minimum of environmental transparency, they may significantly contribute to the implementation of transparency standards within a specific industrial sector by establishing roadmaps for compliance and self-monitoring strategies that could make any further regulation unnecessary. The industry itself is also in the best possible position to account for the confidentiality issues that may come with increased transparency and suggest the best ways forward. This would prevent wasting time and public resources on the protection of supposedly confidential business information that may be off target with the actual needs and strengths of the industry.

5.3.3.2. Eco-labelling

The Aarhus Convention mentions eco-labelling as a possible means, where appropriate, to provide relevant environmental information about products put in the market by private sector enterprises to consumers (Article 5(6)). Private eco-labelling schemes in forestry, fisheries or organic food are part of the 'third wave' in environmental governance, based on information

benefits from a legal and economic regulatory perspective, see Case, *Corporate Environmental Reporting*, 2005.

220 The 'Responsible Care' programme had Community Advisory Panels involving members of the community.

disclosure, according to Florini.[221] The previously mentioned voluntary initiatives and the Aarhus Convention itself are said to be a part of this trend as well.[222] The underlying assumption of eco-labelling initiatives is that disclosure of the productive processes and qualities of a product will empower the public to make sustainability-sound consumption decisions.

Eco-labelling and reporting obligations for corporations, both relate to the supply of companies' environmental information to the public, the first from the perspective of a product and the other about the company itself.[223]

Eco-labelling schemes can be implemented by governments or by independent organisations like NGOs. Examples of government placed eco-labelling schemes are the EU Flower, the Nordic Swan, the German Blau Engel, the Japanese Eco Mark and the Chinese Environmental Label. Other initiatives have been adopted by non-governmental organisations such as the Forest Stewardship Council, the Marine Stewardship Council and national organisations.

In Colombia, the Colombian Environmental Seal was established by Resolution 1555 of 2005 of the Ministry of the Environment.[224] This is a voluntary certification scheme aiming to incorporate the environmental costs associated with the production process, to guide consumer's preference towards products with potential to reduce their negative effects through the life-cycle and, in this way, create incentives for environmentally-sound products in the national market. This system complies with the ISO 14024 standards.

Overall, eco-labelling schemes and other voluntary disclosure programs can be said to have a marginal effect in the context of public participation in environmental decision-making, especially regarding specific projects or activities, but they may nonetheless contribute to a positive disposition towards increased transparency and accountability from the private sector, among other positive outcomes such as the development of environmental consciousness and more sustainable production and consumption patterns.

5.3.3.3. Environmental Reporting

This section refers to environmental reporting defined as 'the various means by which companies disclose information on their environmental activities',[225] specifically mandatory programs. From an international perspective, the Escazú Agreement provides that 'each Party shall encourage public and

221 Florini, A. (2010). The National Context for Transparency-based Global Environmental Governance. *Global Environmental Politics, 10*(3), 120–131.

222 Gupta, A. (2008). Transparency Under Scrutiny: Information Disclosure in Global Forum. *Global Environmental Politics*, 8, 1–7.

223 Erlandsson, J., & Tillman, A. M. (2009). Analysing Influencing Factors of Corporate Environmental Information Collection, Management and Communication. *Journal of Cleaner Production*, 17, 800–810.

224 Resolution 1555 of 2005 'Establishing the Colombian Environmental Seal', Ministry of Environment, Housing and Territory Development, 25 October 2005.

225 Emtairah, *Review of Policy Action in Europe*, 2002, p. 7.

private companies, particularly large companies, to prepare sustainability reports that reflect their social and environmental performance'.[226] No similar provision is found in the Aarhus Convention.

Most mandatory reporting schemes in the US and Europe come originally from specific obligations placed upon private companies to report to public authorities about the use of hazardous substances or in the context of the public's 'right to know' as established in FOIAs. Examples are the US Toxic Release Inventory (TRI) established in 1986 and the EU Council Directive 90/313/EEC on access to environmental information.[227] Not surprisingly, mandatory reporting is mostly found in the framework of permitting regimes, in favour of government authorities. Active access mechanisms to disclose information directly to the public remain largely voluntary.

As a matter of fact, environmental-specific reporting requirements in the US are found spread out in several environmental acts, such as the Clean Water Act, the Clean Air Act, the CERCLA and the EPCRA among others, which usually feed into PRTRs. Importantly, the main source of disclosure obligations for the US publicly traded companies is the Securities Exchange Act of 1934 with its many regulations and administrative rules[228] which include some environmental aspects (to the extent that they have 'economic materiality' for the company's financial outlook).[229]

Colombia's Renewable Natural Resources Code established in 1974 the duty of proprietors, users, and persons otherwise entitled by a permit to use renewable natural resources, to gather and supply, at no cost, information about the use of the resource, especially the quantities consumed, for the National Environmental Information System.[230] This obligation was regulated through Decree 1600 of 1994, establishing that all information about the quality of the environment and the state of the renewable natural resources was of public interest, thus any holder of an environmental permit was under the obligation to gather and supply at no cost such information to the environmental authorities.[231]

At the EU level, environmental information from private entities may be accessed pursuant to the obligations imposed by Member States under the

226 Escazú Agreement, Article 6(13).

227 Council Directive 90/313/EEC of 7 June 1990 on the freedom of access to information on the environment [1990] O.J. L158/56/90.

228 Oesterle, D. A. (1998). The Inexorable March Toward a Continuous Disclosure Requirement for Publicly Traded Corporations: 'Are We There Yet?' *Cardozo Law Review, 20*, 135.

229 Case, *Corporate Environmental Reporting*, 2005.

230 President of Colombia, Decree – Law 2811 of 1974 'Code of Renewable Natural Resources', 18 December 1974, Article 23.

231 Decree 1600 of 1994, 'Por el cual se reglamenta parcialmente el Sistema Nacional Ambiental (SINA) en relación con los Sistemas Nacionales de Investigación Ambiental y de Información Ambiental', 27 July 1994, Article 3.

'Accounting Directives'.[232] These directives establish obligations for the preparation of annual and consolidated financial statements and related reports which, 'where appropriate and to the extent necessary for an understanding of the company's development, performance or position, (…) shall also contain non-financial information, including information relating to environment and employee matters'.[233] Furthermore, Directive 2014/95/EU on the disclosure of non-financial and diversity information entered into force on 6 December 2014. This Directive mandates for Members States to establish reporting obligations for public-interest large enterprises (*e.g.* listed companies, banks, insurance companies and other companies considered public-interest entities of more than 500 employees) covering environmental information specifically.[234] With the implementation of the Directive, an estimated 6,000 public-interest large undertakings were required to include non-financial statements in their annual reports from 2018 onwards about the policies they implement in relation to *inter alia* environmental protection, social responsibility and the treatment of employees and respect of human rights.[235]

In 2017, the European Commission issued a communication providing detailed guidelines on non-financial reporting in the framework of the EU sustainability reporting Directive, which promptly points out that companies obligated to submit their reports may do so following any international, EU-based or national framework.[236] The Commission also acknowledges the concerns that may arise in the reporting process regarding business confidentiality. To address them, it suggests providing global, summarised, or general information on sensitive issues, which may go a long way in satisfying stakeholder's needs for transparency without risking disclosure of the company's protected information. The Directive explicitly allows the exclusion of information about impending developments or matters undergoing negotiations in exceptional cases to prevent damaging the undertaking's commercial position.[237]

In summary, all systems examined provide for mandatory environmental reporting, at least from the largest, public interest enterprises (*i.e.* 'publicly traded companies' in the US); covering minimum key performance indicators such as emissions into the environment, use and management of hazardous substances (including chemicals), resource consumption patterns (energy

232 Fourth Council Directive (EC) 78/660 on the annual accounts of certain types of companies, [1978], O.J. L 222 and Seventh Council Directive (EC) 83/349 on consolidated accounts, [1983] O.J. L 193.
233 US Fourth Council Directive, Article 46(1)(b).
234 Companies concerned started applying the Directive as of 2018, on information relating to the 2017 financial year.
235 See European Commission informative website at https://ec.europa.eu/info/business-economy-euro/company-reporting-and-auditing/company-reporting/non-financial-reporting_en.
236 European Commission. (2017). *Communication 2017/C 215/01 Guidelines on non-financial reporting*, O.J. C 215, pp. 1–20.
237 European Commission. *Communication 2017/C 215/01*, 2017.

efficiency, water use, biodiversity matters) and related social issues, although to a limited extent. Most of the reporting is addressed to government agencies in two contexts: either as requirements for environmental permits for specific activities (mostly technical information for the use of environmental authorities) or as part of general reporting obligations for publicly traded companies (mostly information with financial implications of interest for investors and trading markets). The weakest system would be the Colombian regime, as it is still pending the implementation of a Pollutants Release and Transfer Register and there is no clear pathway for the public to access the reported information. In this last aspect, however, the EU and the US may also need improvement, since much of the reported information remains out of public sight, filed away in public offices,[238] or is oftentimes found to be fragmented, inaccessible and drafted in difficult technical terms. Case pointedly states in this regard:

> Environmental disclosure required under various environmental statutes and federal securities laws was not intentionally designed as informational regulation-that is, with wide- spread public information access and dissemination as primary goals. These reporting requirements are described as 'fragmentary,' 'uncoordinated,' 'chaotic,' and intended primarily to determine minimal compliance with regulatory standards. Especially with respect to information disclosed pursuant to environmental statutes, public access is generally limited and public review difficult, burdensome, and costly.[239]

5.3.3.4. Concluding Remarks

Disclosure of environmental information from private entities has been taking place for the last few decades, although the vast variations in the characteristics, scope, direction and shape of the duties to disclose makes it difficult to identify a 'regime' of access to environmental information from the private sector as a unified and comparable object of study. Some of the interesting points of evolution observed through time in the different jurisdictions relate to: (i) a tendency to extend the scope of reporting requirements, whereas they used to be almost exclusively about toxic releases in the earliest laws, some of them now require disclosure of information about internal policies and strategies, environmental liabilities and natural resources consumption and efficiency indicators; (ii) a transition towards more integrated reporting practices that show the interrelation between environmental practices and the way business is conducted in general; (iii) a change in the directionality of the information flows, from almost exclusively 'business to government' to 'business to public', as well as improvement in the dissemination mechanisms from

238 Lamdan, *Beyond FOIA*, 2017; Roesler, *Environmental Right to Know*, 2012.
239 Case, *Corporate Environmental Reporting*, 2005, p. 438.

the government to the public in terms of accessibility, availability and promotion and (iv) a refinement of the mechanisms allowing direct public access to information held by private entities in certain contexts such as environmental licencing or permitting procedures and when the private entity can be considered a public authority within the scope of transparency laws by virtue of its engagement with the public sphere.

6 The Protection of Trade Secrets and 'Confidential Business Information'

Trade secrets law has as primary concerns maintaining business ethics and encouraging the inventive spirit and innovation in business.[1] However, trade secret and 'confidential business information' – CBI – protection interferes with public access to environmental information. A main argument put forward in the present book is that this interference is sometimes justified, and sometimes it is not.

Several authors have reported on the way confidentiality interests may interfere with transparency. From the EU perspective, Tilling asserts that 'there is an inherent tension between the right of EU citizens to access environmental information and the desire of the private sector to protect commercially sensitive information such as pricing structures or intellectual property'.[2] Mason affirms that 'the well-established right to commercial confidentiality routinely disables access to information on pollutants from industrial facilities'[3] based on a 2008 survey. Roesler suggests an *interest theory of rights* to resolve conflicts arising between the right to know and the confidentiality of commercial secrets.[4] This type of conflict also occurs in the US, as many statutory regimes regulating human health and the environment allow individuals submitting information to public agencies to claim confidentiality over the information because its disclosure would affect their commercial interests, thus limiting its disclosure.

However, access to information as a right and a principle is not meant to be absolute or equally applied in all situations. Its application must be tempered by considering conflicting interests, such as the interest to keep certain

1 Levine, D. S. (2011). The Impact of Trade Secrecy on Public Transparency. In R. Dreyfuss & K. J. Strandburg (Eds.), *The Law and Theory of Trade Secrecy: A Handbook of Contemporary Research*. Edward Elgar Publishing, pp. 406–442.
2 Tilling, S. (2013). Access to commercially sensitive environmental information. *ERA Forum, 14(4)*, 493–506, 493.
3 Mason, M. (2010). Information Disclosure and Environmental Rights: the Aarhus Convention. *Global Environmental Politics, 10*(3), 10–31, 17.
4 Roesler, S. M. (2012). The Nature of the Environmental Right to Know. *Ecology Law Quarterly, 39*, 989–1040, quoting Raz, J. (1986). *The Morality of Freedom*, Oxford University Press, pp. 165–192.

DOI: 10.4324/9781003307617-6

information secret for economic or strategic purposes. Article 19 of the International Covenant on Civil and Political Rights establishes some limitations to the general rule of freedom of expression, stating that its exercise carries 'special duties and responsibilities' and may be subject to certain restrictions when necessary for respect of the rights or reputation of others, for the protection of national security or public order, health or morals. Article 10 of the ECHR similarly puts forward several grounds on which freedom of expression can be conditioned or restricted, including for the protection of the rights of third parties and to prevent the disclosure of information received in confidence.

In all the studied legal regimes there are exceptions to the general right of access to information, regardless the scope of the right, when the disclosure of such information may adversely affect legitimate economic interests of a third party for whom the information in question can be considered CBI. This chapter will start by analysing the reasons that justify CBI protection, including trade secrets, followed by the examination of the legal principles that currently support the adoption of specific mechanisms to enforce this protection. The study will then focus on the operational characteristics of the mechanisms in the different jurisdictions to provide a better understanding of the way CBI protection is interfering with the rights of access to environmental information and, ultimately, with effective public participation in certain contexts.

In a scenario where the public can request access directly to private entities, the importance of having clarity about the prevalence of confidentiality or disclosure becomes more visible and, arguably, easier to address. The point of the analysis from this perspective is to reveal the public and private interests that are really at stake. In this sense, the purpose of transparency as a tool for accountability of public spending becomes almost irrelevant, as the specific interests of the person or group requesting the information and those of the company holding it become the focus of the study.

Against this background, the following lines address the protection of trade secrets and CBI as the main counterargument for wider transparency in the private sector and the source of many current conflicts in the application of environmental transparency provisions.

6.1. Why is Business Confidentiality Worthy of Protection?

The protection of CBI can be justified for several reasons. First, it is necessary to ensure fair competition in countries with market economy systems.[5] The unauthorised use of confidential information belonging to others can be considered an unfair practice,[6] and it can interfere with market stability,

5 World Intellectual Property Organization Website. Retrieved from http://www.wipo.int/patents/en/topics/trade_secrets.html.

6 Nair, M D. (2002). Protection of Trade Secrets/Undisclosed Information. *Journal of Intellectual Property Rights*, 7, 526–529.

entrepreneurship and the legitimate exercise of business-related liberties, which eventually could adversely affect employment, consumption and economic growth.

Second, in our increasingly knowledge-based economies, the protection of confidential information is necessary to promote innovation and business competitiveness. The US Supreme Court has acknowledged the value of protecting trade secrets for innovation. In *Kewanee Oil Co. v Bicron Corp* the Court refused the argument that patent law pre-empted trade secret law, stating:

> The patent policy of encouraging invention is not disturbed by the existence of another form of incentive to invention. In this respect the two systems are not and could never be in conflict...
>
> Trade Secret law will encourage invention in areas where patent law does not reach, and will prompt the independent innovator to proceed with the discovery and exploitation of his invention. Competition is fostered and the public is not deprived of the use of valuable, if not quite patentable invention.[7]

Intangible business assets are as much worthy of legal protection as any other forms of private property[8] and often enough producing information requires a substantial investment associated with the development of new products through research and innovation processes, which should be legally protected, especially where intellectual property law remedies do not apply.[9] The protection of CBI outside intellectual property mechanisms is particularly important for small and medium business which may lack the resources to legally protect all of their creative works and commercial information through these channels. They, therefore, tend to rely heavily on general laws protecting trade and industrial secrets without the need to register under an Intellectual Property Rights (IPR) figure.

7 *Kewanee Oil Co. v Bicron Corp*, 416 US 470 (1974); cited in Lemley, M. A. (2011). The Surprising Virtues of Treating Trade Secrets as IP Rights. In R. Dreyfuss, P. Newman, & K. J. Strandburg (Eds.), The Law and Theory of Trade Secrecy. Edward Elgar Publishing, p. 122.

8 In 2009, it was estimated that intangible assets represented about 81% of the value of the S&P 500 market. European Commission. (2011). *A Single Market for Intellectual Property Rights Boosting Creativity and Innovation to Provide Economic Growth, High Quality Jobs and First Class Products and Services in Europe*. Communication From the Commission To the European Parliament, the Council, the European Economic and Social Committee and the Committee of the Regions, Brussels, 1–21.

9 The protection of test data is particularly relevant when there is no patent protection, since, if the latter exists, the title-holder may exercise exclusive rights. ICTSD-UNCTAD. (2005). *Resource Book on TRIPS and Development: An Authoritative and Practical Guide to the TRIPS Agreement*. Cambridge University Press.

The European Commission issued a communication in 2011 on the subject of a single market for Intellectual Property Rights, building on the idea of a 'virtuous IPR cycle' which would rely on a policy that 'incentivises innovation, which in turn attracts investment, thereby resulting in new products and services for new consumer demand which enhances growth and employment'.[10] The same rationale supporting the legal protection of intellectual property rights may be employed to justify the right of business owners to keep secret certain information when disclosure may adversely affect their commercial operations.[11] It should be noted, however, that the mechanisms for the defence of intellectual property rights are based on the idea of the private ownership of intellectual property, but not all of CBI may fall within the definition of 'private property'.[12]

In a somewhat counterintuitive way, trade secrets protection may also favour disclosure of information. According to Lemley, just as patent and copyright laws encourage disclosure of the inventions in several ways to ensure that the public receives the benefits of the creative work, the legal protection of CBI may also provide incentives for disclosure in two different ways. First, with proper legal protection in place, firms do not have to take extreme measures to prevent *physical* access to the information they want to protect (such as fences, roofs and increased security measures) and can be comfortable outsourcing part of their production processes and hiring new employees in a more efficient way without fear of losing their competitive advantage. Undue restrictions on the flow of information within a company and even within the same industry may slow the process of commercialisation and improvement of the secret inventions and interfere with the invention and disclosure functions of IP law.[13] In this sense, solid trade secret regimes contribute to more openness and not more secrecy. The second way in which trade secret law may lead to disclosure is in the framework of negotiations to make an idea known to someone who may be interested in its acquisition, improvement or implementation. Without trade secret protection, the negotiating parties would have to enter into intricate contracts or confidentiality agreements that may not always be practical. By creating presumptions of confidentiality in certain contexts, trade secret law contributes to the flow of ideas and business opportunities.[14]

From the above, it is possible to infer that an appropriate framework of trade secret and CBI protection may potentially increase the public availability of private information, at least for state authorities. It is possible that a poor regime of protection of trade secrets may act as a deterrent for companies against revealing important information even in the context of reporting

10 European Commission, *A Single Market for Intellectual Property*, 2011, p. 4.
11 Lemley, *The Surprising Virtues*, 2011.
12 See Aplin, T. (2013). Confidential Information as Property? *King's Law Journal, 24*, 172–201.
13 Lemley, *The Surprising Virtues*, 2011, p. 126.
14 Lemley, *The Surprising Virtues*, 2011, p. 127.

requirements to environmental authorities because of the fear of losing their trade secrets to competitors. If the information cannot be protected from misappropriation after it is submitted to the authorities, private entities are likely to submit the *minimum* information necessary to comply with their legal obligations and abstain from participating in any voluntary initiatives or other forums where information may be disclosed (public meetings, hearings, expositions etc.). This would cause a decrease in the amount of environmental information available to the public instead of an increase.

Trade secret law and IP protection is thus necessary from the perspective of innovation, competition, employee mobility, business transactions and the general health of the economic system. It is important, however, to be aware of the risks of an abusive or unbalanced IP regime.

The European Commission rightly warns in its communication about an IPR single market that a stronger framework for the protection and enforcement of IPR should be accompanied by rigorous application of competition rules to prevent the abuse of IPR, which can hamper innovation or exclude new entrants from markets.[15] With the same logic, strengthening the protection of CBI through harmonised legislation and carefully drafted exceptions in FOI laws should be accompanied by rigorous application of human rights rules safeguarding the right of access to public information and the principles of disclosure in order to avoid undermining the right of access to public information and the opportunity of the public to participate effectively in decision-making processes.

6.2. Defining 'Confidential Business Information'

When speaking of 'confidential business information' (CBI) instead of similarly used terms such as 'industrial secrets' or 'trade secrets', two aspects are taken into consideration: (i) approaching as closely as possible the terminology found in the Aarhus Convention and many of other legal instruments to refer to exceptions for the protection of legitimate commercial interests; and (ii) the need to include within the definition legally protected business information that may not be uniformly protected under the same concept in the different jurisdictions (*e.g.* trade secrets, undisclosed information, etc.).

At this point, it is important to explore the difference between 'intellectual property', 'trade secrets' and 'confidential business information' for the purposes of the forthcoming analysis. To start, it is worth noting that the Aarhus Convention establishes separate exceptions to the general right of access for the protection of intellectual property rights and for confidential business information.[16] This suggests that they are different and distinguishable concepts protecting specific

15 European Commission, *A Single Market for Intellectual Property*, 2011.

16 Convention on Access to Information, Public Participation in Decision-making and Access to Justice in Environmental Matters, Aarhus, Denmark, 25 June 1998 (entered into force 30 October 2001) 2161 UNTS 447, Article 4(3)(e) and Article 4(3)(d).

interests. 'Trade secrets' present a somewhat troublesome dilemma. Some theories assert that they are a form of intellectual property. Others argue that they can be considered 'confidential business information' but not intellectual property *stricto sensu.*[17] When referring to Intellectual Property Rights in the EU, for instance, the European Commission affirms that they include 'property rights, such as patents, trademarks, designs and geographical indications, copyright and rights related to copyright'.[18] Not, therefore, trade secrets. In its communication, the Commission refers to trade secrets as 'know-how that has not or not yet been registered as industrial property rights but that is actually or potentially valuable to its owner and not generally known or readily ascertainable by the public, and which the owner has made a reasonable effort to keep secret'.[19] It further acknowledges that the level of protection granted to trade secrets throughout the EU varies considerably.

Under the Aarhus Convention, the inclusion of 'trade secrets' as IPR or CBI is highly relevant because it determines the extent to which the protection depends on national laws and whether information about emissions can be withheld on such grounds. The protection of CBI in the Aarhus Convention is expressed in the following terms:

> 4.A request for environmental information may be refused if the disclosure would adversely affect: (…)
>
> d)The confidentiality of commercial and industrial information, where such confidentiality is protected by law in order to protect a legitimate economic interest. Within this framework, information on emissions which is relevant for the protection of the environment shall be disclosed;

The provision implies a broad scope of the concept but does not provide a definition. In fact, it relies on the domestic legislation of each of the Parties to give relevance to the exception by establishing the condition that such confidentiality is protected by law to protect a legitimate economic interest. It states, however, that information about emissions shall not be withheld on grounds of business confidentiality.

Article 4(4)(e), in turn, establishes that 'A request for environmental information may be refused if the disclosure would adversely affect: (…) (e) Intellectual property rights'. This does not condition the application of the exception to national law, nor does it make it depend on the protection of a legitimate economic interest, and it may even apply to information about emissions.

17 See i.e. Hogan Lovells (2012). *Report on Trade Secrets for the European Commission*. Study carried out for the European Commission (MARKT/2010/20/D). Retrieved from: http://ec.europa.eu/internal_market/iprenforcement/documents/index_en.htm#maincontentSec2.

18 European Commission, *A Single Market for Intellectual Property*, 2011, p. 3.

19 European Commission, *A Single Market for Intellectual Property*, 2011, p. 15.

Interestingly, the Aarhus Convention Implementation Guide suggests that trade secrets are covered by the exception protecting intellectual property rights, stating: 'The primary forms of intellectual property rights are copyright, patent, trademark (including geographical indications) and trade secret'[20] We argue that a better approach is to protect trade secrets as a subcategory of 'commercial and industrial information', under Article 4 literal d).

Taking comparable definitions in different legal instruments such as 'undisclosed information' in the Trade Organisation's Agreement on Trade-Related Aspects of Intellectual Property Rights ('TRIPS agreement') at the international level,[21] the definition of 'trade secret' in Directive 2016/943 at EU level,[22] and the definition of the same term in the US Uniform Trade Secrets Act (UTSA),[23] which are fundamentally the same and thus provide a solid basis for comparison, it may be observed that the definition of business information as a 'trade secret' will basically depend on two factors: (i) the confidential nature of the information, *i.e.* the information is not in the public domain and the owner takes 'reasonable measures' to keep it secret;[24] and (ii)

20 United Nations Economic Commission for Europe – UNECE. (2014). *The Aarhus Convention: An Implementation Guide*, 2nd ed., UN Doc. ECE/CEP/72/ Rev.1, p. 88.

21 Agreement on Trade-Related Aspects of Intellectual Property Rights, Annex 1C of the General Agreement on Tariffs and Trade (GATT), World Trade Organisation, 1994. Article 39 (2): '2. Natural and legal persons shall have the possibility of preventing information lawfully within their control from being disclosed to, acquired by, or used by others without their consent in a manner contrary to honest commercial practices so long as such information: (a) is secret in the sense that it is not, as a body or in the precise configuration and assembly of its components, generally known among or readily accessible to persons within the circles that normally deal with the kind of information in question; (b) has commercial value because it is secret; and (c) has been subject to reasonable steps under the circumstances, by the person lawfully in control of the information, to keep it secret'.

22 Directive (EU) 2016/943 on the protection of undisclosed know-how and business information (trade secrets) against their unlawful acquisition, use and disclosure, [2016] O.J. L 157/1. '1) "trade secret" means information which meets all of the following requirements: (i) is secret in the sense that it is not, as a body or in the precise configuration and assembly of its components, generally known among or readily accessible to persons within the circles that normally deal with the kind of information in question; (ii) has commercial value because it is secret; and (iii) has been subject to reasonable steps under the circumstances, by the person lawfully in control of the information, to keep it secret'.

23 US Uniform Trade Secrets Act [UTSA] § 1 (amended 1985), 14 U.L.A. 437 (2006). 'Trade secrets are [I] Information, including a formula, pattern, compilation, program device, method, technique, or process, that: i. Derives independent economic value, actual or potential, from not being generally known to, and not being readily ascertainable by proper means by, other persons who can obtain economic value from its disclosure or use, and ii. Is the subject of efforts that are reasonable under the circumstances to maintain its secrecy.'

24 Some authors suggest, under the US regime, that the requirement of secrecy of the information (*i.e.* the reasonable efforts taken by the owner to keep it secret)

this circumstance represents a competitive advantage to the owner of the information, or, in other words, its disclosure would entail a commercial disadvantage for them.

There is evident affinity between this rough definition of 'trade secrets' and 'confidential business information' in the sense of Article 4(4)(d) of the Aarhus Convention because they both reference a 'legitimate economic interest' as the underlying cause of protection and the 'secrecy' condition of 'trade secrets' can be logically construed from an ordinary reading of the term 'confidential' as a characteristic of the information to be protected under the Convention's provision. In fact, the Implementation Guide suggests that, in order to determine whether the confidentiality of certain information protects a 'legitimate economic interest', as required for the exception to apply, the authorities might assess whether the information is secret (only known by the company and the authorities) and reasonable measures have been taken to keep the secrecy, and if its disclosure would entail a significant damage to the economic interests of the holder and be useful for its competitors.[25] aspects that are clearly coincidental with the attributes of trade secrets.

This analysis suggests that, for the purposes of the exception for the protection of business confidentiality in the Aarhus Convention, CBI and trade secrets can be considered one and the same thing. Parties to the convention may however determine the limits of the CBI exception via domestic legislation.

This conclusion entails that trade secrets are *not* considered to fall within the definition of 'intellectual property rights' for the purposes of the Aarhus Convention's exceptions regime, because if this was the case, there would be a conflict between Article 4(3) literal d) and e) as they both would protect the category of 'trade secrets' to different levels. Hence, a more logical, contextual, and consistent interpretation of these provisions would be that Article 4(3)(d) allows an exception to disclosure when it would adversely affect trade secrets (the scope of protection shall be determined under domestic law) whilst Article 4(3)(e) applies for the protection of Intellectual Property Rights, such as trademarks, copyrights, and patents. Under the Convention provisions, therefore, information about emissions into the environment cannot be exempted as a trade secret, but it could if it is protected as intellectual property.[26]

should be taken more as evidenciary support of the trade secret nature of the information than as an independent requirement for the protection to operate. Some forms of torts-based relief alternatives disregard the condition that the information is secret and focus instead in the damages caused with the misappropriation (Lemley, *The Surprising Virtues*, 2011).

25 UNECE, *Aarhus Implementation Guide*, 2014.

26 European Commission officials share this interpretation (Personal Interview, 14 November 2017). It is important to note however that in the implementation of the Aarhus Convention to the EU institutions and bodies, Regulation No 1367/2006 refers to the procedures and general rules of Regulation 1049/2001, which

Another plausible interpretation would be that trade secrets are protected as intellectual property rights under lit. e) and the exception in lit. d) applies to confidential business information that would not be defined as trade secrets. This interpretation, however, raises the question of what sort of confidential business information should be kept secret to protect a legitimate economic interest of the holder and still is not considered a trade secret. Furthermore, the application of the exception would be considerably limited since it would be conditioned to the protection of such information under the domestic law of each of the Parties, and there are very few provisions protecting CBI outside the scope of IPR or trade secret laws.

Yet another interpretation would be that neither Article 4(3)(d) nor 4(3)(e) protect trade secrets from disclosure,[27] after all they are not explicitly mentioned, and exceptions are supposed to be interpreted restrictively. However, based on the previous arguments about the definitions and inclusions of CBI and IPR, this interpretation would seem to be incorrect, not least because it would be contrary to the stated intentions of the Parties to the Convention for the regime of exceptions.

Ultimately, the application of either of the exceptions in Article 4(3) to protect trade secrets will depend greatly on the legislation for the protection of confidential business information in the domestic legal systems of each of the Parties (including trade secrets, intellectual property rights and other information), since the language of the Convention leaves significant room for interpretation and does not contain any universal definition of 'confidential business information', which may be a significant impediment to the uniform application of the confidentiality exceptions.

For the previous reasons, the present study will employ the term 'confidential business information' (CBI) to generally mean 'trade secrets', thus it would be applicable to a variety of business information, including:

- technical know-how, such as design, process, formulae and other technological knowledge often resulting from experience and intellectual ability;
- data of commercial value, such as marketing plans, customers lists and other business-related information that provides an advantage over competitors;

comprises the protection of commercial information and intellectual property rights in the same exception. Article 6(1) of Regulation 1367/2006 then mandates that information about emissions into the environment cannot be withheld on grounds of this exception.

27 I strongly disagree with this interpretation of Stražišar & Kralj : 'The Aarhus Convention only protects Intellectual Property Rights and not Trade Secrets. That is acceptable as a matter of principle, since the rights to property is not absolute and needs to be balanced against other fundamental rights and public policies'. Stražišar, B., & Kralj, M. (2016). The Aarhus convention in the nuclear sector – right to information versus nonproliferation? *Journal of Radiological Protection, 36*, 160, 168.

- test and other data submitted for the approval of pharmaceutical and chemical products for agriculture.[28]

However, when the system under study provides for the protection of CBI outside the scope of trade secrets, it would be explicitly acknowledged. In the US case, for instance, trade secrets and CBI have been found by the Courts to be different concepts. Trade secrets are defined and protected under the UTSA, and they differ from other types of confidential information because businesses can derive an economic advantage from them.[29] Johnson attributes to the concept of trade secrets under the US system the core elements of *discreteness and countability* (trade secrets can be individualised whilst CBI remains a mass noun of undetermined unities of information); *spoilability* (if they are disclosed they lose all their value); having positive value for the holder (whoever that is in any given time); being a species of intellectual property (not all CBI can be considered intellectual property);[30] having a similarity to an exemplars list (*i.a.* formula, pattern, device, compilation of information, process of manufacturing, list of customers, designs, prototypes, plans, methods, techniques); allowing to 'claw back' to prevent disclosure, even from innocent third parties; having the ability to be protected through criminal law; having a transferable value; and being able to emancipate from their original owner and not lose their value.[31] The clarification of the notion of 'trade secrets' supports the argument that not all of the information that a business would like to keep for itself qualifies as a trade secret. Some statutes even provide some examples of this non-trade secret type of confidential information: salaries, certain financial information, the date of release of a new product or an announcement of a company's strategic plans.

Following this logic, it can be concluded that there is a category of business information which can be confidential for the holder due to strategic economic reasons but does not fall within the scope of 'trade secrets' (or any other category of intellectual property), whose limits are to be found in domestic legislation or even in private agreements, by virtue of which it could eventually be protected under Article 4(4)(d) of the Aarhus Convention.[32] This concept cannot be positively defined on the basis of the nature of the information and international and national laws fail to provide a definition as well. This category of CBI may be better understood as a negative concept, composed by the residual information that the holder considers confidential

28 ICTSD-UNCTAD, *Resource Book on TRIPS*, 2005.
29 US UTSA, Sec. 1(4)(i).
30 Johnson, E. (2010). Trade Secret Subject Matter. *Hamline Law Review*, 11, 545. Some authors disagree as to the inclusion of trade secrets as 'property' or 'intellectual property', but in practice it is significantly less disputed that trade secrets are a species of intellectual property.
31 Johnson, *Trade Secret Subject Matter*, 2010, p. 562.
32 In common law countries, for instance the law of confidence potentially protects all types of confidential and secret information whether it is commercial, industrial, or personal. See Hogan Lovells, *Report on Trade Secrets*, 2012.

for business reasons but does not fit into the definition of intellectual property rights or, especially, 'trade secrets'.

Uncertainty about the definition of trade secrets and CBI affects the fair and consistent application of exceptions to disclosure in the context of transparency. In the words of Levine, 'the effect of counterintuitive and ambiguous definitions is that more, and not less, information has the possibility of being protected by trade secrecy doctrine from the unfettered and easy public disclosure and examination'.[33]

Additionally, it is not the same to define trade secrets in the context of controlling misappropriation or industrial espionage as it is in the context of freedom of information regimes, particularly if the regime is exclusively about access to environmental information. Adopting a specific definition of trade secrets and CBI for the purposes of the exceptions in these cases may be recommended, ideally including mechanisms to verify that the information claimed as confidential does in fact protect the legitimate economic interests of the claimant and that disclosure could effectively harm or endanger their competitive position.

6.3. The Logic Behind the Protection of CBI

This section examines the rationale supporting the laws that establish intellectual property and trade secrecy as rights and legitimate interests worthy of protection. This sort of 'dissecting' exercise allows for the identification of the underlying interests in the legal provisions, which would be the raw material for the balancing exercise following an interpretation of the *interest theory of rights,*[34] already mentioned. By inquiring into the ultimate values or interests that support certain subjective rights (or, in this case, legal protection) it is possible to define the correlative duties associated with them and to make a better assessment about in which situations the legal protection must subside to other rights that are more important.

An overview of trade secret law provides the following rationales for protection, each of them resulting in slightly different levels of protection.

6.3.1. Trade Secrets as Property

The protection of CBI in the framework of unfair competition disregards the conception of trade secrets as a form of property. Although unfair competition rules provide remedy against dishonest commercial practices, they do not give rise to exclusive rights. Therefore, even if trade secrets can be considered

33 Levine, *The Impact of Trade Secrecy*, 2011, p. 413.

34 In an approximation to this theory, we propose identifying the underlying values protected by a right and confronting them with the (seemingly) opposite right's protected values in order to find the right balance and give proper weigh to the clashing interests at stake. See Raz, *The Morality of Freedom*, 1986.

a category of intellectual property, this does not entail property rights over undisclosed information.[35] The protection of CBI under TRIPS is afforded to the 'possession' or *de facto* 'control' rather than on basis of the ownership of said information.

The distinction of CBI and other forms of intellectual property as to the non-proprietary nature of the first, has implications *vis-à-vis* the protection mechanisms afforded to the 'owner' of the information and certainly in the way that these mechanisms apply when they appear in conflict with other rights such as public access to information. In a recent decision by the UK Court of Appeal,[36] it was held that Article 1 of Protocol 1 to the European Convention of Human Rights (ECHR), which establishes the right to the peaceful enjoyment of possessions,[37] extended to confidential information, virtually implying that there is a human right to the protection of confidential information. Even more interesting for the present study, the case in question related to the protection of commercial confidential information. The Court found that confidential information was a species of property thus it fell within Article 1 of Protocol 1 and, furthermore, that it was protected under Article 8 of the ECHR, hence, interference with this right had to be duly justified.[38] Previous decisions of the ECtHR (Grand Chamber) suggested that certain intangible rights could be protected as 'possessions' under Article 1 of Protocol 1 if they had an *economic value* (*i.e.* if they were marketable).[39] Under this criterion, CBI would qualify as a 'possession' for the purposes of Article 1 of Protocol 1 to the ECHR in certain cases, but at least one author disagrees with this conclusion, because confidential information cannot be 'sold' or 'licenced' in the same way as other types of intellectual property, instead it is shared subject to certain contractual conditions that assign economic value to the right to hold the information.[40]

However, there is little support for the defence of CBI as property, and the conceptual analysis around the theories of what constitutes 'property' and

35 Aplin, *Confidential Information as Property*? 2013.
36 UK, *Veolia ES Nottinghamshire Ltd v Nottinghamshire County Council*, [2010] EWCA Civ 1214, [2011] Env LR 12.
37 Protocol to the Convention for the Protection of Human Rights and Fundamental Freedoms as amended by Protocol No. 11, Council of Europe, 20 March 1952, Paris, France. Article 1: 'Protection of property. Every natural or legal person is entitled to the peaceful enjoyment of his possessions. No one shall be deprived of his possessions except in the public interest and subject to the conditions provided for by law and by the general principles of international law. The preceding provisions shall not, however, in any way impair the right of a State to enforce such laws as it deems necessary to control the use of property in accordance with the general interest or to secure the payment of taxes or other contributions or penalties'.
38 *Veolia v Nottinghamshire,* paras 129, 141.
39 CJEU (Grand Chamber), *Anheuser-Busch Inc v Portugal* App No 73049/01 (2007), para. 76, quoted in Aplin, *Confidential Information as Property*? 2013..
40 Aplin, *Confidential Information as Property*? 2013, p. 179.

'ownership' do not quite agree with the definition of CBI as property either. Aplin argues, for instance, that confidential information does not have the characteristics of permanence and stability, as it tends to disappear when it's made public; nor does it entail excludability in the same way as other intellectual property rights;[41] and, finally, that there are significant difficulties in the exchange and alienation of the rights associated with confidential information, since sharing the information will not automatically entail that the recipient is *entitled* to it and may thus exercise his right against others who also possess the information.

Despite this generally accepted conclusion, US Courts have assimilated 'trade secrets' to 'property' in the past. In the case of *Ruckelshaus v. Monsanto Co.*,[42] some data about a pesticide product submitted to the EPA for authorisation purposes under the Federal Insecticide, Fungicide, and Rodenticide Act (FIFRA)[43] was then employed by the agency to issue new authorisations for other applicants. Monsanto filed a request for compensation claiming that the information was a trade secret (property) and the use by the EPA was a 'taking' which would entitle Monsanto to compensation under the Fifth Amendment. The US Supreme Court asserted that

> Trade secrets have many of the characteristics of more tangible forms of property. A trade secret is assignable. A trade secret can form the *res* of a trust, and it passes to a trustee in bankruptcy.[44]

The Court also attached certain conditions to the 'property' nature of trade secrets, stating that

> the extent of the property right therein is defined by the extent to which the owner of the secret protects his interest from disclosure to others. Information that is public knowledge or that is generally known in an industry cannot be a trade secret. If an individual discloses his trade secret to others who are under no obligation to protect the confidentiality of the information, or otherwise publicly discloses the secret, his property right is extinguished.[45]

In another case, *Carpenter v United States*, the Court reasserted this position stating that 'confidential business information has long been recognised as property'.[46]

41 Aplin, *Confidential Information as Property*? 2013, p. 195.
42 *Ruckelshaus v. Monsanto Co.,* 467 U.S. 986, 104 S. Ct. 2862 (1984).
43 Federal Insecticide, Fungicide, and Rodenticide Act (amended in 1972 and 2003) 7 U.S.C. §§ 136 et seq. (1947).
44 *Ruckelshaus v. Monsanto*, p. 467 U. S. 1002.
45 *Ruckelshaus v. Monsanto*, p. 467 U. S. 1002.
46 US Supreme Court, *Carpenter v. United States,* 484 U.S. 19, 108 S. Ct. 316 (1987). See also Roesler, S. M. (2012). The Nature of the Environmental Right to Know. *Ecology Law Quarterly, 39*, 989–1040.

However clear these Court Opinions may appear at first glance, it is important to note that the definition of 'property' and other associated terms like 'proprietary rights' in these rulings may not carry the same meaning and legal implications as they do nowadays, and could also vary from one state to another, and from a common law to a civil law system. Lemley suggests that the references to 'property' in the framework of trade secrets protection are better accommodated under the assumption that trade secrets should be treated as intellectual property rights, like patents or copyrights. Contrary to traditional forms of property, the owner of a trade secret can control the information even when it has left his possession. The reason for this extended protection would be the same reason supporting patent rights and copyright law, namely, to encourage investment in the research and development that produces the information. The treatment of trade secrets as property would be in the interest of creating incentives for innovation where patent laws would come short because the information is not patentable, or the procedures result inefficient due to natural market dynamics.[47]

In conclusion, there is no agreement as to whether trade secrets can be qualified as 'property', but if, for the sake of the argument, this position is accepted, interesting issues may be raised *vis-à-vis* public access to environmental information protected as a trade secret.

First, such a conception of CBI or trade secrets would be difficult to wrap around information concerning emissions or other releases into the environment. Once the substances are in the 'public domain', the proprietary rights over the information regarding these substances is dissolved as the owner no longer has material possession of the objects to which the information refers. The same argument could be used to, eventually, access information about products or chemical substances 'released' into the public domain. In fact, information on released products that can be reversed engineered could not be protected as a trade secret because the requirement of 'secrecy' is no longer fulfilled.[48]

Second, the rights to property conventionally have attached duties of care to prevent harm to third parties, including the duty to inform or to warn about risks emerging from the property. Environmental, health or safety information attached to products may be required to be publicly disclosed because of the duty of care by the owner of the information.[49] In this context, Lyndon makes the case that 'rather than supporting secrecy, property principles compel disclosure' and 'the property frame itself, which tends to bypass complexity, reduces cases to the question of the firm's right to the information'.[50]

47 Lemley, *The Surprising Virtues*, 2011, p. 119.

48 Lyndon, M. (2014). Secrecy and access in an innovation intensive economy: reordering information privileges in environmental, health and safety law. *University of Colorado Law Review, 78*(465), 1–46.

49 Lyndon, *Reordering Information Privileges*, 2014.

50 Lyndon, *Reordering Information Privileges*, 2014, p. 461.

Third, in the framework of general transparency laws, information held by public authorities has been noted to be a 'public good'; the authorities' duty is to administer it on the public's behalf. Within this context, the information that private companies are required to submit to public entities can no longer be deemed a 'private property' and, therefore, trade secret protection would not apply to that information.

The above reflections point out that supporting trade secret protection on a theory of property rights would not be the most effective approach when the information is no longer in the possession of the owner. From the perspective of public access to environmental information, the application of property law principles to trade secrets protection could, theoretically, support broader access to the 'confidential' information held by public authorities or to the information related to substances or products already in the public domain.

6.3.2. Trade Secrets as Intellectual Property

For the purposes of this study, trade secrets are deemed to be an independent category of protectable confidential information not included in the traditional definitions of intellectual property rights (IPR). In fact, most of the transparency instruments cited throughout make a distinction between IPR and CBI in the framework of the right of access to information. The European Commission's communication on IPR does not include within its scope trade secrets or other CBI.[51] and laws pertaining to intellectual property rights regularly exclude trade secrets as well. The basic reason for this distinction is that, unlike conventional intellectual property rights, trade secrets do not emerge into the legal world following a regulated registration process, which oftentimes translates into much more complex forms of legal protection than IPR.

However, several authors have defended the virtues of classifying trade secrets in the realm of intellectual property rights along with patents or copyrights.[52] The main reason for this is their inherent connection with the protection of innovation and the competitive position of the owner, just as conventional IPR figures.

Considering that the main objections to the treatment of trade secrets as IPR are mostly related to practical aspects of regulation and application of the protection mechanisms, and the focus of this section is to identify the *underlying values* protected by trade secret legislation, the analysis of the objectives and core assumptions shared by IPR and Trade Secret law are found to be relevant in the context of this study.

Trade secret protection as a derivative of IPR law would be generally based on the need to protect confidential business information regarding a product,

51 European Commission, *A Single Market for Intellectual Property*, 2011.

52 *i.e.* Lemley, *The Surprising Virtues*, 2011 and Johnson, *Trade Secret Subject Matter*, 2010.

process, the know-how of a business, or an original idea which represents a competitive advantage in a market, but which does not fulfil all the legal requirements to be registered as a patent, protected under copyright law, or assimilated into any other IPR figure. Following an assumption that such information does, in fact, exist; and it is as worthy of protection as other inventions and intangible goods protected under IPR, it is logical that some other mechanism be developed to defend the legitimate interests embedded in IPR laws.

The implications of a view of trade secrets under the umbrella of IPR can be positive to resolve conflicts with access to information legislation to the extent that there would be a more clearly defined scope of protection, a set of specific legal principles, and legal figures and resources providing context and uniformity to the theory and practice of trade secret protection.

Taking the US as an example of an advanced legal system for the protection of trade secrets, there are many different legal pathways to enforce rules protecting the confidentiality of business information. Under the TSA, there are clear definitions, limitations and procedures in place for the protection of trade secrets, and this federal act has the added virtue of pre-empting state regulation in this subject-matter. However, some state courts have allowed legal claims for the misappropriation of CBI that does not qualify as a trade secret under the TSA, because they are being framed as torts deriving from a supposed breach of confidence, unjust enrichment, abuse of rights and other legal forms. If a conflict between the application of the US FOIA and the protection of CBI were to emerge in this legal framework, the degree of uncertainty as to the scope of protection of the CBI would be decisive in the analysis of whether the information requested should be disclosed to the public or not, regardless of other relevant factors such as the subject-matter of the documents, the public interest in disclosure and the actual harm to the interest protected with the exception (which, incidentally, would be more difficult to determine outside a framework such as the one provided by IPR laws).

This does not mean that the protection of trade secrets and CBI *needs* to be framed within the scope of IPR to apply the guidelines and principles for the application of exceptions to disclosure, but the merits of the theory are worth noting.

6.3.3. *Trade Secrets as Human Rights*

The potential implications of asserting a fundamental right to confidential information may be far-reaching. Intellectual Property Rights have been recognised as fundamental rights in several instruments, for instance in Article 17(2) of the EU Charter of Fundamental Rights, establishing under the title 'Right to Property' that 'Intellectual Property shall be protected'.[53]

53 European Charter of Human Rights (final text), [2007] O.J. C303/1.

Rather optimistically, Geiger opines, in reference to intellectual property rights, that their protection as fundamental rights offers the following advantages: (a) the high rank of fundamental rights in the hierarchy of norms, (b) the fact that fundamental rights must be considered equally and (c) the fact that fundamental rights reflect important ethical values that would have to be taken into account by legislatures and judges.[54] As to trade secrets specifically, Aplin, however, raises concerns about the potential conflicts due to the expansion of protection that would be afforded to confidentiality (particularly in favour of corporate actors) versus the actual necessity to classify the information as 'confidential'; the position of third parties *vis-à-vis* reverse engineering and other so far acceptable ways to discover confidential information; and in regards to the application of remedies such as the imposition of constructive trust over the property (confidential information).[55]

From the perspective of the research core questions, recognising the human rights status of the protection afforded to business confidentiality would imply that both access to environmental information and the protection of CBI stand at the same level in the legal hierarchy, and that the rules that usually apply for the balancing exercise of human rights would have to be observed by judges and legal operators when they clash.

Personal confidential information has already been recognised in the realm of human rights, with important consequences for the regulation of the mechanisms for the protection of privacy and the resolution of conflicts at judicial and administrative stances.[56] On this basis we could predict that the hypothetical recognition of 'confidential information' as a human right may entail similar repercussions.

In my opinion, the relatively recent recognition of access to environmental information as a human right in different legal contexts provides a minimum of grounding that was necessary to propel forward environmental participatory rights that also share a strong link with several fundamental human rights such as the right to life, freedom of expression and the right to privacy and family life. This normative support is comparatively unnecessary for 'confidential business information' to the extent that its protection is already grounded in long-standing legal principles providing for the protection of private property, intellectual property rights and fair competitive practices.

This research aims for an unbiased approach to the conflict between access to environmental information and the protection of business confidential information, but under the assumption that the general rule must be access

54 Geiger, C. (2008). The Constitutional Dimension of Intellectual Property, in P. Torremans (Ed.), *Intellectual Property and Human Rights* (pp. 101–131). Kluwer Law International.

55 Aplin, *Confidential Information as Property*? 2013.

56 Aplin points out that the process of reshaping breach of confidence principles in light of ECHR jurisprudence may be particularly traumatic and would surely entail doctrinal uncertainty and incoherence (Aplin, *Confidential Information as Property*? 2013, p. 201).

and the restriction on grounds of business confidentiality is an exception to that general rule. In that spirit, there is clearly not need to have both interests stand at the same level from a human rights perspective, but rather to have enough uniformity and clarity in each of the legal regimes to duly protect the legitimate confidentiality interests without undermining the effective exercise of access rights. To this point, there is no evidence in any of the studied jurisdictions suggesting that confidential business information qualifies as a human right in the way access to information does, this, however, does not prevent exceptions on grounds of business confidentiality to have full effect and actually counterweight the exercise of the fundamental right of access to information, which is why the formulation of general guidelines for the application of these rules is so relevant.

6.4. Statutes for the Protection of CBI

Having reviewed the theories backing up protection of CBI, this section examines the different forms this protection can take. The protection of CBI can be found in different types of legislation, for instance under privacy laws, in the framework of unfair competition regulations, breach of contracts, torts, and also in the FOI instruments themselves.[57] Furthermore, remedies for the protection of IPR and other types of industrial secrets can be found not only in civil law but also in criminal law (*e.g.* protection of trade secrets against unlawful acquisition and use).[58] The broad variety of instruments protecting CBI, many of them under different rationales and motives, contributes to a general lack of harmonisation between access to information and confidentiality regulations.[59] The present section, therefore, maps out the mechanisms provided for the protection of CBI at the different levels and jurisdictions to identify the underlying reasoning behind these provisions in order to better understand the conflicts that may arise in the application of access to information laws and possible ways forward in the balancing exercise necessary for their adequate application.

6.4.1. Trade Secrets Under International Law

At the international level, the main protection to trade secrets is found in the TRIPS agreement, which was the first international convention imposing obligations regarding undisclosed information.[60] Article 39 reads as follows:

57 Nair, *Protection of Trade Secrets*, 2002.
58 In the US, the Economic Espionage Act 1996 (EEA) grants ample powers to the Attorney General to criminally prosecute a person for appropriating trade secrets (Johnson, *Trade Secret Subject Matter*, 2010).
59 Hogan Lovells, *Report on Trade Secrets*, 2012.
60 ICTSD-UNCTAD, *Resource Book on TRIPS*, 2005.

> In the course of ensuring effective protection against unfair competition as provided in Article 10bis of the Paris Convention (1967), Members shall protect undisclosed information in accordance with paragraph 2 and data submitted to governments or governmental agencies in accordance with paragraph 3.
>
> Natural and legal persons shall have the possibility of preventing information lawfully within their control from being disclosed to, acquired by, or used by others without their consent in a manner contrary to honest commercial practices so long as such information:
>
> (a) is secret in the sense that it is not, as a body or in the precise configuration and assembly of its components, generally known among or readily accessible to persons within the circles that normally deal with the kind of information in question;
>
> (b) has commercial value because it is secret; and
>
> (c) has been subject to reasonable steps under the circumstances, by the person lawfully in control of the information, to keep it secret.
>
> Members, when requiring, as a condition of approving the marketing of pharmaceutical or of agricultural chemical products which utilise new chemical entities, the submission of undisclosed test or other data, the origination of which involves a considerable effort, shall protect such data against unfair commercial use. In addition, Members shall protect such data against disclosure, except where necessary to protect the public, or unless steps are taken to ensure that the data are protected against unfair commercial use.

It should be noted that Article 39.3 presents a sort of 'exception to the exception' of business confidentiality, by stating that the protection of data submitted for marketing approval shall not interfere with disclosure *for the protection of the public* (or for other purposes when steps are taken to ensure that data will not be used in a commercially unfair manner).

The protection afforded to trade secrets shall be framed in the 'unfair competition' practices referred to in Article 10bis of the Paris Convention:

> The countries of the Union are bound to assure to nationals of such countries effective protection against unfair competition.
>
> Any act of competition contrary to honest practices in industrial or commercial matters constitutes an act of unfair competition.
>
> The following in particular shall be prohibited:
>
> all acts of such a nature as to create confusion by any means whatever with the establishment, the goods, or the industrial or commercial activities, of a competitor;
>
> false allegations in the course of trade of such a nature as to discredit the establishment, the goods, or the industrial or commercial activities, of a competitor;

indications or allegations the use of which in the course of trade is liable to mislead the public as to the nature, the manufacturing process, the characteristics, the suitability for their purpose, or the quantity, of the goods.

Unfair competition can be defined as 'any act that a competitor or another market participant undertakes with the intention of directly exploiting another person's industrial or commercial achievement for his own business purposes without substantially departing from the original achievement.'[61] In this context, the protection applies against acts contrary to 'honest business practices', including theft, bribery, breach of contract, commercial espionage, or breach of confidence.

Article 39.3 of the TRIPS Agreement provides for the protection of 'undisclosed data' that is submitted to a government authority to obtain approval for marketing a pharmaceutical or agricultural chemical product. This protection applies when (i) there is an obligation to submit the information; (ii) the information is not publicly available; (iii) it refers to a 'new chemical entity'; and, (iv) the origination of the data involved a 'considerable effort'. This is an interesting example of the protection afforded to information that is clearly CBI and is submitted to a government authority following a legal requirement. Importantly for the Colombian case, the protection afforded in the TRIPS agreement to trade secrets may also apply to traditional knowledge, *i.e.* that of native and indigenous communities, which may be of technological and economic value.

The US was a frontrunner in the protection of test data, having adopted rules on the matter in the Pesticides Act in 1972 and established, in 1984, exclusivity provisions for medicines, which prevented the utilisation by government authorities or other interested applicants of data submitted for marketing approval in order to assess other applications of similar characteristics (*i.e.* generic versions of drugs). The EU Member States, in turn, provided exclusivity protection for test data filed in the process of marketing authorisation for pharmaceuticals in 1987.[62] Exclusivity provisions are also found in international multilateral treaties such as the Dominican Republic and Central American Free Trade Agreement[63] and bilateral agreements like the US-

61 WIPO (1994). *Protection against Unfair Competition*, Geneva, p.55.

62 ICTSD-UNCTAD, *Resource Book on TRIPS*, 2005. Directive 65/65/EEC of 26 January 1965 on the approximation of provisions laid down by Law, Regulation or Administrative Action relating to proprietary medicinal products, as amended by Directive 87/21/EEC, [1965] O.J. 22/369. Similar provisions for veterinary products are found in Directive 81/851/EEC, as amended by Directive 90/676/EC.

63 Dominic Republic and Central American Free Trade Agreement (DR-CAFTA), Washington D.C., 5 August 2004, Chapter 15, Article 15.10(1)(a). The Central American Free Trade Agreement was subscribed by the US, Costa Rica, El Salvador, Guatemala, Honduras, Nicaragua and Dominican Republic between 2004 and 2006.

Morocco and the US-Chile free trade agreements.[64] Whilst other instruments may go even further than the TRIPS agreement by establishing a minimum period of exclusivity over the information submitted for a marketing approval, like the NAFTA[65] (Sec. 1711, paras 6–7 provide for a minimum exclusivity period of five years), other instruments forego of exclusivity provisions in favour of a less stringent approach to the protection of test data, such as the Andean Community.[66] A common argument for this last approach is that it facilitates market access to generic producers, who would only have to prove bioequivalence between the generic products and the originally approved drug to rely on the test data already in possession of the authority for marketing approval. Exclusivity provisions have also been criticised because they may delay the market entry of generic versions of products for which patents have expired, affecting public access to medicines.[67]

In South America, the regulation of intellectual property rights is found in Decision 486 of 2000 of the Andean Community which establishes the regime for the protection of 'business secrets', defined as

> Any undisclosed information that a natural person or legal entity holds legitimately, which may be used in an industrial, commercial or productive activity, and is transferable to third parties, as long as it is: a) secret, in the sense that, as a whole or in the configuration and precise reunion of its components, it is not generally known or easily accessible by people found in the circles that normally deal with the respective information; b) has a commercial value because it is secret, and c) has been subject to reasonable measures by its legitimate possessor to keep it secret.[68]

Decision 486 protects against the use, diffusion, or acquisition by a third party in the framework of unfair commercial practices, in a similar manner as TRIPS. In this context, the following will be considered acts of 'unfair competition': the diffusion of secrets learned in the development of a labour or contractual relationship, the acquisition of business secrets by unlawful or dishonest means, the use of a business secret learned from another person knowing, or having to know, that the discloser obtained the information through dishonest or unlawful means, among others. Examples of 'dishonest commercial practices' included in the Decision's provisions are industrial espionage, breach of contract, abuse of confidence and breach of a loyalty

64 ICTSD-UNCTAD, *Resource Book on TRIPS*, 2005.
65 North-American Free Trade Agreement (NAFTA), Section 1711, Pars. 6 and 7.
66 Decision 486 'Common Regime on Intellectual Property', Andean Community (CAN), 14 September 2000. This Decision amended the pre-existing regulation (Decision 344) eliminating an exclusivity period for the use of test data.
67 ICTSD-UNCTAD, *Resource Book on TRIPS*, 2005, p. 537.
68 Andean Decision 486, Article 260.

duty.[69] There is no time limit to the protection afforded to business secrets, if the conditions set up above are met.[70]

The existing conflicts between an expansive interpretation of the rights of access granted under the Aarhus Convention and the protection of IPR and Trade Secrets under international conventions has been pointed out in different scholarly works.[71]

6.4.2. CBI Protection at National Level

In the US legal framework, the main instrument for the protection of trade secrets at the federal level is the Uniform Trade Secrets Act (UTSC), which provides the basis to develop a uniform body of law among the different states.[72] Trade secrets have a separate legal regime because their regulation goes beyond the contractual sphere as they may involve third parties (not bound by the contract terms), and the protection extends to situations in which there may not be a blameworthy conduct involved, thus going beyond tort law.[73] Under US legislation, the owner of a trade secret may get an injunction to prevent its disclosure when it has been known by a third party, even if no unlawful means were employed.[74] In 2016, the protection of Trade Secrets in the US system was enhanced with the adoption of the Defend Trade Secrets Act (DTSA),[75] which introduced a new civil cause of action for misappropriation of trade secrets at the federal level, allows for *ex parte* seizure of 'property necessary to prevent the propagation or dissemination of the trade secret'[76] and creates immunity from misappropriation actions for whistle-blowers. Unlike other forms of intellectual property, the regulation of trade secrets has largely been left to each state, thus, by federalising trade secret misappropriation actions, the DTSA contributes to increase the predictability in the application of trade secrets laws in general.[77] It must be

69 Andean Decision 486, Article 262.
70 Andean Decision 486, Article 263.
71 See *i.e.* Stražišar & Kralj, *Aarhus in the Nuclear Sector*, 2016; Shabalala, D. B. (2017). Access to Trade Secret Environmental Information: Are TRIPS and TRIPS-Plus Obligations a Hidden Landmine? *Columbia Journal of Transnational Law, 55*, 648–717; Garçon, G. (2012). Access to Regulatory Information on Agrochemicals – To which extent does Regulation 1107/2009 prevail over the EU Transparency Legislation? *European Journal of Risk Regulation, 10*(2), 393–400.
72 All but three states have adopted their own statute for the protection of trade secrets (Massachusetts, Texas, New York). United States Patent and Trademark Office, *Trade Secrets Protection in the U.S.* Retrieved from https://www.nist.gov/sites/default/files/documents/mep/marinaslides.pdf.
73 Johnson, *Trade Secret Subject Matter*, 2010
74 US UTSA, Sec. 2(b).
75 US Defend Trade Secrets Act [DTSA], Public Law 114 153 (2016). This act amended the Economic Espionage Act (EEA).
76 US DTSA, Sec. 2(A)(i).
77 Kaplan, S. (2017). *The Defend Trade Secrets Act of 2016 Creates a Federal Jurisdiction for Trade Secret Litigation.* Retrieved from http://www.ipwatchdog.com/

noted however that the DTSA does not pre-empt existing state trade secrets laws, but it does provide uniform definitions of 'trade secrets' (basically the same definition of the UTSA) and 'misappropriation'.

At EU level, Directive (EU) 2016/943 on the protection of undisclosed know-how and business information provides for Member States to enable mechanisms for the protection of trade secrets against their unlawful acquisition, use and disclosure. Some authors have found more than coincidental that both the US DTSA and the EU Directive 2016/943 were adopted with less than a month in-between, since they share significant similarities in purpose and content. The International Chamber of Commerce published a white paper in 2014 under the title 'Trade Secrets: Tools for Innovation and Collaboration'.[78] Both the DTSA and Directive 2016/943 took guidance from the document and included many of its recommendations. They both also aim for an international harmonisation of the protection of trade secrets to safeguard innovation at the domestic level by including provisions for extra-territorial enforcement and to increase cooperation among different jurisdictions,[79] they adopt a uniform definition of critical terms such as trade secrets and 'misappropriation', they provide for *ex-parte* measures to prevent the propagation of the trade secrets and establish the possibility to collect damages and compensation, and they even provide for mechanisms to protect trade secrets from disclosure during court proceedings.[80]

In the US, the parties to a judicial process are allowed to submit information under seal to protect trade secrets. The DTSA specifically provides that courts may not authorise the disclosure of information without first giving the opportunity to the owner of the information to submit arguments to preserve the information as confidential. Similarly, Directive 2016/943 established that an applicant for confidentiality in court proceedings must submit a 'duly reasoned' application as to why the information should be kept confidential.[81]

However, the laws for the protection of trade secrets anticipate cases in which protection must be limited to ensure the legitimate exercise of other rights. Such is the case of the protection for whistle-blowers under the DTSA and protection of collective bargaining agreements and employment contracts under Directive 2016/943 as means to ensure mobility of employees. The scope of the Directive 2016/943, like the US Act, is restricted to the occurrence of an unlawful act (without the consent of the owner and through dishonest means, illegal acts, or breach of contract), which means that disclosure of trade secrets through other means such as access to information requests, reporting requirements or journalistic works are out of the scope of protection.

2016/05/23/defend-trade-secrets-act-2016-creates-federal-jurisdiction-trade-secret-litigation/id=69245/.

78 Brant, J., and Lohse, S. (2014). *Trade Secrets: Tools for Innovation and Collaboration.* International Chamber of Commerce.

79 EU Directive 2016/943, Preamble.

80 EU Directive 2016/943, Article 9.

81 EU Directive 2016/943, Article 9(2).

Notably, misappropriation under the US TSA entails criminal consequences. The federal statute establishes criminal penalties for agency employees who disclose confidential information that:

> concerns or relates to the secrets, processes, operations, style of work, or apparatus, or to the identity, confidential statistical data, amount or source of any income profits, losses, or expenditures of any person, firm, partnership, corporation, or association.[82]

The term 'confidential' within this provision applies to information which, if released, is likely: (1) to impair the government's ability to obtain necessary information in the future; or (2) to cause substantial harm to the competitive position of the person from whom the information was obtained.[83] Note that this language extends beyond a strict definition of 'trade secrets' into the more comprehensive concept of CBI.

Including disclosure of trade secrets as a criminal offense may act as a powerful deterrent for public operators to disclose information that may be exempted under FOIA, even if the application of the exception is not completely clear or in the presence of compelling reasons of public interest to disclose. Understandably, the public servant may decide that avoiding the risk to his personal responsibility in an eventual unlawful disclosure is a more compelling argument than upholding the spirit of FOIA and allowing access to information in the public interest.

In a clear departure from the US approach, the protection of trade secrets in Colombia is largely supported in Decision 486/2000 of the Andean Community, already mentioned, and through the widespread utilisation of non-disclosure agreements in all sorts of commercial, labour, and administrative operations. Trade secrets in the Colombian legal system are assimilated to the concept of 'undisclosed information' in the TRIPS agreement, and generally referred to as *'secretos empresariales'* (business secrets) which is the term employed in Decision 486.[84] The requisites for information to be protected under these provisions is that (i) it is secret, meaning that it is not generally known or easily accessible to the persons who work in the same field, (ii) it has potential to be used in the business and (iii) the owner derives a competitive advantage from the information and takes reasonable measures to keep it secret.[85]

Under Decision 486, trade secrets can be divided in two subcategories: (i) industrial secrets and (ii) commercial secrets. The industrial secrets will be predominantly technical and scientific information about how to produce or

82 US Federal Statute, 18 U.S.C. § 1905 (2012).
83 *Guerra v. Guajardo*, 466 F. Supp. 1046 (D.C. Tex. 1978) aff'd 547 F. 2d 769.
84 Tobón Franco, N. (2018). La Protección del Know How como Secreto Empresarial en Colombia. *Foro de Derecho Mercantil, 58*, 31–52.
85 Andean Decision 486, Article 260.

transform goods and services to make them specific and characteristic to the producer. The commercial secrets, in turn, refer to general information of the business such as sales, advertising, clients and suppliers.[86] Other information, which is not strictly of a technical or commercial nature, may still be protected under the general umbrella term of 'confidential business information'.[87] In general terms, the scope of protectable information under Decision 486, and under Colombian laws, is similar to the US DTSA.

Under Colombian law, the unauthorised use of privileged information is criminally penalised as well. Article 258 of the Criminal Code establishes penalties of prison and fines to a person who

> [I]n his condition as an employee, advisor, directive or member of the board in a private organisation, to obtain a personal gain for himself or a third party, misuses information to which he has had access for reason of his position, and which is not publicly known.[88]

The characteristics of this privileged information are: (i) it must be only known by a limited number of people, by virtue of their job position, in the public or private sector, (ii) it must be suited to be used, and (iii) it must refer to concrete facts of the field in which the company operates.[89]

Additionally, Article 308 establishes prison and fines for the violation of industrial or commercial secrets to anyone that

> (…) utilises, reveals, or divulges discoveries, scientific inventions, commercial or industrial processes or applications, that came to his knowledge by reason of his employment, position, or occupation and which are protected as confidential
>
> (…)
>
> The same penalty will be imposed to anyone who unlawfully learns, copies, or obtains secrets related to discoveries, scientific inventions or commercial or industrial processes and applications.[90]

Reportedly, criminal actions are one of the most cost-effective measures for the owner of trade secrets against a person who unlawfully and knowingly uses or discloses their CBI.[91] The main purpose of these actions, however, is

86 Tobón Franco, *La Protección del Know How*, 2018.
87 Payan Rodríguez, C. F. (2011). Secreto Empresarial, vigencia como mecanismo de protección en la propiedad intelectual. *La Propiedad Inmaterial, 15*, 207–224.
88 Colombian Criminal Code, Law 599 of 2000, Article 258.
89 Colombian Superintendencia de Sociedades. (1997). Circular 20/97.
90 Colombian Criminal Code, Law 599 of 2000, Article 308.
91 Tobón Franco, N. (2019). *Sanciones por Revelar los Secretos Comerciales en Colombia*. Retrieved from https://es.scribd.com/document/206449766/Sanciones-por-Revelar-los-Secretos-Comerciales-en-Colombia-Natalia-Tobon-pdf.

to punish reproachable conduct, but not necessarily to prevent further harm or to obtain appropriate indemnification.

Article 39 of the TRIPS agreement presents the protection of trade secrets as an effective way to ensure fair competition. In a similar way, the unauthorised use of trade secrets in Colombia may constitute an unfair trade practice,[92] for instance when disclosure of CBI is made with the purpose of destabilising a company,[93] or for the mere act of disclosure or exploitation of information obtained legally (but under a duty of confidentiality) or by illegal means such as industrial espionage or similar practices.[94] Such actions may trigger the jurisdiction of the Colombian *Superintendencia de Industria y Comercio* (Superintendence of Industry and Commerce), an administrative authority holding judicial powers to prosecute and impose penalties for illegal practices against competition. Procedures before this authority allow for the imposition of interim measures to stop the harmful conduct or prevent further damages, a mechanism not foreseen by Decision 486, but available under domestic legislation.[95] Outside the scope of an unfair competition practice, the owners of trade secrets are entitled to seek remedies before civil courts through regular judicial actions.

From a domestic perspective, the Colombian regime is weak in comparison with the more developed US framework for the protection to CBI. Though both establish criminal penalties for the violation of CBI and trade secrets, only the US has a clear and integrated legal framework for the protection of business information. The Colombian system is made of piecemeal provisions in isolated laws with a strong hold on regional and international instruments, which generally lack specificity and effective enforcement mechanisms that could apply at national level. The absence of an established regime with general principles and explicit recognition of remedies for the holders of CBI may affect the efficacy of the defence mechanisms in practice, and perhaps even make a balanced application of the exceptions more difficult and interfere negatively with the balancing exercise when there are different legitimate interests at stake. Quoting Roberts,

> The task of setting limits on transparency is not qualitative different than that of making the preliminary case for transparency: in both cases an appeal to fundamental interests is necessary (…) it is this connection

92 Colombian Law 256 of 1996, 'Establishing rules on unfair competition', 15 January 1996, Article 7: unfair competitive practices include acts against honest commercial uses, against the principle of commercial good faith, acts aimed at to affect freedom of choice of consumers, and the acts affecting the general functioning of the market. See also Paris Convention (approved in Colombia by Law 178 of 1994), Article 10bis(2).

93 Superintendencia de Industria y Comercio, Resolution 11090, 29 April 2003.

94 Superintendencia de Industria y Comercio, Judgment 005, 3 April 2006.

95 Colombian Law 256 of 1996, Article 31.

> alone that gives these considerations weight in the calculation of appropriate transparency rules.[96]

If the principles and interests underlying the mechanisms for protection of CBI are not clear, setting limits becomes significantly harder.

6.4.3. CBI Not Qualifying as Trade Secrets or IP

As previously mentioned, the concept of CBI may be broader than that of trade secrets, depending on the jurisdiction, and it is clearly distinguishable from the concept of intellectual property as well. This section focuses on the laws or judicial remedies that can be applied specifically to CBI falling outside the scope of trade secret laws.

In speaking of 'protection' of CBI, the intention is to refer to legal mechanisms to prevent public disclosure of such information or to judicial remedies that can be employed to claim compensation in favour of the owner of the information and thus act as deterrents to misappropriation or unlawful disclosure. With this concept in mind, the US system offers several ways in which CBI can be protected. First, the Trade Secrets Act extends the protection against misappropriation clearly beyond the limits of the definition of trade secrets. The criminal sanctions may come to anyone who incurs in misappropriation over information which 'concerns or relates to the secrets, processes, operations, style of work, or apparatus, or to the identity, confidential statistical data, amount or source of any income profits, losses, or expenditures of any person, firm, partnership, corporation or association' (Sec 1905).

Another mechanism in the US System is to rely on tort law to claim damages based on allegations of 'unfair competition', 'breach of duty' and similar. By carefully avoiding labelling the information as a trade secret and therefore circumventing the statutory requirements for a trade secret claim and also its pre-emption clause, CBI owners have successfully obtained judicial remedy and compensation for the disclosure and utilisation of their business information.[97] But these common law remedies have been criticised for undermining the trade secret legal regime and creating uncertainty around the utilisation of business information that may otherwise be allowed, like the information obtained through reverse engineering or that it is already in the public domain. Graves summarises the problem as follows:

96 Roberts, A. (2001). Structural Pluralism and the Right to Information. *The University of Toronto Law Journal, 51*(3), 243–271, esp. 264–265.

97 Graves, C. T. (2011). Trade Secrecy and Common Law Confidentiality: the Problem of Multiple Regimes. In R. Dreyfuss & K. J. Strandburg (Eds.), *The Law and Theory of Trade Secrecy: A Handbook of Contemporary Research*. Edward Elgar Publishing, p. 92.

> In what is probably an unintended outcome, these rulings leave the plaintiff with a potentially stronger claim than would have existed had the information been found secret. The plaintiff seemingly does not have to establish secrecy, can seek punitive damages under common law instead of facing the UTSA's treble damages cap, and need not fear a ruling that the claim was brought in 'bad faith'. It is unclear what defences can be raised against 'confidential' information claims. The minority position on UTSA pre-emption, then, not only creates a second regime of protectable information, but maximises protection for weaker information that is not a trade secret.[98]

The TSA safeguard against misappropriation is regularly mentioned in labour contracts to give more teeth to the confidentiality obligations established therein. Interestingly, under the DTSA, employers must give notice to their employees of the whistle-blowers immunity, which protects them from actions for misappropriation of trade secrets within the framework of the confidentiality duties included in their employment contracts. If they fail to do so, employers may not recover double damages or attorney fees in trade secret litigation (Sec. 7).

In Colombia and the EU, this type of information is only generally protected as a corollary to the right of intimacy and through blank expressions within provisions protecting trade secrets. This makes it difficult to map out the mechanisms and protective measures available to the holders of such information. The most likely scenario is that this type of information will be protected on an *ad hoc* basis through favourable judicial interpretations. Viable preventive measures however are non-disclosure agreements (NDA), specifically drafted according to the necessities of the business, the information involved, and the nature of the transaction. NDAs usually include their own definition of 'confidential business information' and disclosure of information protected under these figures often triggers civil actions for damages, injunctions, and compensation for breach of contract, as opposed to constitutional claims or litigation in the public interest.

CBI outside the scope of trade secrets submitted to the government may be in a more precarious situation, since its protection will always depend on the existence of specific legislation supporting the claim for confidentiality, NDAs can have a very limited use in this framework, because public authorities may have little incentive to enter such contracts. The US federal legislation, however, provides specific rules for EPA to enter into confidentiality agreements to keep business information confidential when there is no alternative to compel the submission of the information.[99]

98 Graves, *Common Law Confidentiality*, 2011, p. 96.
99 Freedom of Information Act of July 4, 1966, Public Law No. 89–487, 80 Stat. 250, codified as amended at 5 U.S.C. § 552 (1994), Sec. 2.215.

Again, this case points to the conclusion that the US system provides a stronger and more comprehensive framework for the protection of business confidentiality.

6.4.4. Types of CBI and Trade Secrets with Special Protection

There are few objective restrictions to the kind of information that can be deemed to be CBI by its owners. Since its very nature is to be kept secret, it is extremely difficult to develop a catalogue of the information that should objectively be protected as a trade secret. For this reason, general criteria and some non-restrictive lists of examples have had to suffice to navigate the application of confidentiality exceptions and remedies under trade secrets protection legislation.

There are, however, a few exceptions to the rule. In the studied jurisdictions, some specific pieces of information are vested with a presumption of confidentiality because their disclosure will almost certainly adversely affect the legitimate commercial interests of the holder. An example is the information listed in Sec.14(c)(2) of the amended US TSCA[100] which, when claimed as confidential by the submitter, does not need any further substantiation. Another example, directly related to our topic, is the information about tests and technical composition of a new product or substance, which is submitted to a regulatory authority in the process of approval to enter the market.

This type of information is specifically protected in the TRIPS Agreement. Article 39(3) provides:

> Members, when requiring, as a condition of approving the marketing of pharmaceutical or of agricultural chemical products which utilize new chemical entities, the submission of undisclosed test or other data, the origination of which involves a considerable effort, shall protect such data against unfair commercial use. In addition, Members shall protect such data against disclosure, except where necessary to protect the public, or unless steps are taken to ensure that the data are protected against unfair commercial use.

The provision allows a slim opening for the hypothetical disclosure of this kind of information in order to protect the public, but its general purpose is clearly the protection of a very specific type of CBI to which public authorities will have access. This provision creates an expectation of nondisclosure for the person submitting the information,[101] which is equivalent in practice to an exclusion of this data from general access-to-information regimes.

100 Toxic Substances Control Act, 15 U.S.C. § 2613(b) (2000).
101 Shabalala, *Hidden Landmine*, 2017.

In the EU, Directive 1991/414 and Regulation (EC) 2009/1107[102] specifically provide for the confidentiality of information submitted to the competent authorities for the authorisation for the placement in the market of chemical substances, in line with Article 39 of the TRIPS agreement.

Article 63(2) of Regulation (EC) 2009/1107, reads:

> Disclosure of the following information shall normally be deemed to undermine the protection of the commercial interests or of privacy and the integrity of the individuals concerned:
> (a) the method of manufacture;
> (b) the specification of impurity of the active substance except for the impurities that are considered to be toxicologically, ecotoxicologically or environmentally relevant;
> (c) results of production batches of the active substance including impurities;
> (d) methods of analysis for impurities in the active substance as manufactured except for methods for impurities that are considered to be toxicologically, ecotoxicologically or environmentally relevant;
> (e) links between a producer or importer and the applicant or the authorisation holder;
> (f) information on the complete composition of a plant protection product;
> (g) names and addresses of persons involved in testing on vertebrate animals.

These specific provisions were deemed inapplicable by the General Court of the CJEU in the case of *Stichting Greenpeace Nederland* (2013)[103] because, in the Court's opinion, the information was related in a sufficiently direct manner to emissions into the environment and, therefore, a presumption of an overriding public interest prevailed over the protection afforded by the exception on grounds of business confidentiality under Article 6(1) of the Aarhus Regulation.[104] This position was later overturned by the Grand Chamber, but only to clarify that information 'linked' to emissions into the environment, even directly, does not fall within the definition of 'emissions into the environment'. The presumption of public interest over this

102 Regulation (EC) No 1107/2009 of the European Parliament and of the Council of 21 October 2009 concerning the placing of plant protection products on the market and repealing Council Directives 79/117/EEC and 91/414/EEC, OJ L 309.

103 CJEU (General Court), Case T-545/11, *Stichting Greenpeace Nederland v European Commission*, Judgment of 8 October 2013.

104 Regulation (EC) No 1367/2006 of the European Parliament and of the Council on the application of the provisions of the Aarhus Convention on Access to Information, Public Participation in Decision-making and Access to Justice in Environmental Matters to Community institutions and bodies, [2006] O.J. L 264/13.

information, which prevents the application of the business confidentiality exception, was upheld.[105]

The sole existence of this type of presumptions triggers conflicts of laws within a broader spectrum of applicable legislation because they create a legitimate expectation of nondisclosure for the submitter of the information and may preclude the application of balancing rules for the disclosure of information in the public interest when such a possibility has not been explicitly provided in the law.[106] The conflict then emerges between the typically constitutionally-based right of access to information against the very specific legal presumption of confidentiality of certain types of CBI, usually found in *lex specialis* like chemicals regulations, substance law protocols and technical norms. The resolution of these conflicts calls for a more comprehensive and nuanced methodology than most general guidelines of legal interpretation can provide. Domestic FOIAs and implementing legislation for international agreements that contain transparency requirements also seem to fall short in providing explicit guidelines for their solution.[107] In this scenario, the courts have to decide on a case-by-case basis which presumption to uphold: the right of access or the protection of confidentiality; and in many jurisdictions they may lack adequate legal basis for a balanced and predictable decision.

6.5. Protection of CBI and Trade Secrets Via Exceptions to Disclosure

The protection of CBI via exceptions to disclosure under the different transparency instruments operates differently than the previously explored mechanisms, although the reason behind the establishment of the exceptions of business confidentiality, trade secrets and intellectual property rights are similarly justified to protect the legitimate economic interests of private businesses and may also depend on the existence of independent legislation recognising the confidentiality of this type of information in each jurisdiction.

A first difference between the protection of CBI in the reviewed statutes and the exclusion of disclosure requirements by an exception to the general rule of public access is the threshold for the application of the exception: it is much lower for the application of the exception than the requirements for remedial action against unlawful use of CBI. For the exception to apply, it does not need to breach any legal or contractual obligations, nor does it depend on the receiver's deceitful intentions.

The exception of business confidentiality is drafted in very similar terms in different statues. The Aarhus Convention establishes in Article 4(4) that a request for information may be refused if the disclosure would adversely affect

105 CJEU, Case C-673/13 P *Commission v Stichting Greenpeace Nederland and PAN Europe*, Judgment of 23 November 2016.
106 Shabalala, *Hidden Landmine*, 2017.
107 Shabalala, *Hidden Landmine*, 2017.

(c) The confidentiality of commercial and industrial information, where such confidentiality is protected by law in order to protect a legitimate economic interest. Within this framework, however, information about emissions which is relevant for the protection of the environment shall be disclosed.
(d) Intellectual property rights.

From the text we can infer the key requisites for this exception to apply, namely, it must be protected *under the national laws* of the Party in order to safeguard a *legitimate economic interest*.

The Aarhus Implementation Guide emphasises this last condition, explaining, *e.g.*, that it would be difficult for a state-owned enterprise operating in a monopolistic manner to assert a claim of confidentiality, since there are no competitors that could gain an advantage through access to the information.[108] The Aarhus Compliance Committee expressed in its findings about non-compliance from Hungary, taking note of the fact that a company established by legislation for the construction of express highways was state-owned and would therefore fall under the definition of public authority, that 'this in itself limits the scope of application of the commercial confidentiality exemption'.[109] Ebbesson points out that 'it is not clear whether "this in itself" refers to the fact that the company was established by legislation and state-owned, or to the mere fact that the company qualified as a public authority, which could be the case also for privately owned companies'.[110] We are inclined to accept the first interpretation as correct because the second interpretation would render the CBI exception useless by implying that it can hardly apply to information from entities who are considered to fall in the definition of 'public authority' of the Convention. Moreover, this interpretation emphasises the necessary connection between the information to be protected under the CBI exception and the commercial activities of the entity thus limiting its application to prevent misuse of the exception to withhold any kind of business-related information.

The Implementation Guide makes the following suggestions to assert if the confidentiality truly serves a legitimate economic interest: establishing a special test to identify which information can legitimately be claimed as confidential, examining the actual confidentiality of the information, *i.e.* verifying that the information is not already in the public domain and the owner has taken reasonable measures to keep it secret, and determining the actual harm that the disclosure would cause to the economic interests of the owner by assisting competitors.[111]

108 UNECE, *Aarhus Implementation Guide*, 2014.
109 Case ACCC/C/2004/4 (Hungary), ECE/MP.PP/C.1/2005/2/Add.4, para. 10.
110 Ebbesson, J. (2011). Public Participation and Privatisation in Environmental Matters: An Assessment of the Aarhus Convention. *Erasmus Law Review, 4*(2), 71–72, 83 (footnote).
111 UNECE, *Aarhus Implementation Guide*, 2014.

It is important to note that these recommendations also apply to the protection of trade secrets *stricto sensu*, but they are particularly relevant where the CBI to be protected is outside the scope of the national laws protecting trade secrets (since these laws already place qualifying conditions for the protection to apply), provided that the confidentiality of such information is still protected under domestic laws. Shabalala opines that 'where different legal regimes – such as unfair competition – protect such information, it remains unclear whether those protections would be sufficient to classify the information as "protected by law" under the Convention'.[112]

Under the US FOIA, both trade secrets and other CBI are explicitly exempted from disclosure. Exemption 4 explicitly excludes from the duty of disclosure 'trade secrets and commercial or financial information obtained from a person [that is] privileged or confidential' (Sec 552(b)(4)).

The term 'trade secrets' must be interpreted in accordance with the judicial precedent established in *Public Citizen Health Research Group v FDA*, in which the D.C. Circuit rejected the application of the definition of trade secrets found in the Restatement of Torts because in its opinion the broad definition was 'inconsistent with the language of… FOIA and its underlying policies'.[113]

The way the exemption operates is the following: federal agencies must give notice to the entity that submitted the information presumed to be confidential when there is a request for that information under FOIA, and the agency considers that the information must be disclosed, after reviewing the request and the records in question. This notice applies to confidential business information whose disclosure could reasonably be expected to cause substantial competitive harm.[114] Administrative and judicial operators have frequently invoked the 'materiality' of the foreseeable harm from disclosing confidential business information as a prerequisite for the application of exceptions on grounds of business confidentiality.[115] After the notice, the submitter shall have a 'reasonable' period of time to present his objections to the disclosure of the information, and after careful consideration, the administrative authority will decide about the request. The decision shall be informed to the submitter prior to the disclosure of the information to the applicant.[116] Importantly, when the information has been found to be a trade

112 Shabalala, *Hidden Landmine*, 2017, p. 687.

113 Vladeck, D. C. (2007). Information Access – Surveying the Current Landscape of Federal Right-to-Know Laws. *Texas Law Review*, 86, 1987, citing *Public Citizen Health Research Group v FDA*, 704 F.2d 1280, 1288 (D.C. Cir. 1983), p. 1811.

114 US Executive Order No. 12,600, 5 U.S.C. § 552 note (2006), Sec. 2(a). However, in June 2019 the US Supreme Court reversed the 'substantial competitive harm' requirement for commercial information to qualify as 'confidential' under Exemption 4 (*Food Marketing Institute v. Argus Leader Media*, 2019 WL 2570624 (June 24, 2019)).

115 *i.e.* CJEU, Case C-404/10 P, *Commission v Éditions Odile Jacob*, Judgment of 28 June 2012.

116 Executive Order 12.600, Sec. 4–5.

secret, federal agencies are forbidden to disclose it by virtue of the TSA. Shabalala opines that given that the US FOIA does not explicitly provide an exception to the protection of trade secrets for public interest motives, the submitter has an expectation of nondisclosure that would prevent any balancing exercise by the administrative authority between the interests of the submitter and the applicant of the information. In this sense, the prohibition of disclosure of trade secrets under the US FOIA appears to be absolute.[117]

Regarding CBI, US Courts have read this second prong of FOIA's Exemption 4 as separate and additional to the basic trade secret exemption. The term is used to describe information claimed to be confidential by its submitter, but not meeting the legal test for trade secrecy.[118] Until the Supreme Court's decision in *Argus Leader* (2019), which reversed the 'substantial competitive harm' test to determine the confidentiality of the information, there was an objective 'test' to determine what information could be protected under this category. Commercial or financial information was only considered confidential if:

> (…) disclosure of the information is likely to have either of the following effects: (1) to impair the Government's ability to obtain necessary information in the future; or (2) to cause substantial harm to the competitive position of the person from whom the information was obtained.[119]

This 'objective' test was first adopted by the Court of Appeals for the District of Columbia Circuit in the 1974 case *National Parks & Conservation Ass'n v. Morton,* and had been recognised afterwards as the leading case in the application of Exemption 4 for over 40 years.[120] A caveat to this judicial rule was introduced later regarding information that was submitted to the government agency on a *voluntary* basis: in these cases, the commercial information was to be presumed confidential if the submitter did not customarily released it to the general public.[121] The intention of broadening the scope of the exception in this case was to protect the future availability of such information for the government.

Once certain information had been determined to be 'commercial or financial information' following the rules above, the US Trade Secrets Act applied as if it were trade secrets,[122] hence, its unauthorised disclosure could be criminally penalised.

117 Shabalala, *Hidden Landmine*, 2017, p. 690. Note that this is only in the context of FOIA, other regulatory statutes may provide exceptions to trade secret protection in certain cases.
118 Lyndon, *Reordering Information Privileges*, 2014.
119 *National Parks & Conservation Ass'n v. Morton*, 498 F.2d 765 (D.C. Cir. 1974).
120 U.S. DOJ, Department of Justice Guide to the Freedom of Information Act 2 (2016). Retrieved from https://www.justice.gov/sites/default/files/oip/legacy/2014/07/23/procedural-requirements.pdf#p9.
121 *Critical Mass Energy Project v. NRC*, 931 F.2d 939, 948 (D.C. Cir.).
122 US DOJ, *Guide to the Freedom of Information Act*, 2016.

In addition to the exemptions of the FOIA, US pollution control laws regulating the submission of environmental information from private entities to government agencies call for disclosure of records, reports and information to the public except for information that, if disclosed, would 'divulge methods or processes entitled to protection as trade secrets'.[123] In these cases, the administrator of the agency is directed to consider those records as confidential in accordance with a section of the TSA establishing criminal penalties for agency employees who disclose confidential information that:

> concerns or relates to the secrets, processes, operations, style of work, or apparatus, or to the identity, confidential statistical data, amount or source of any income profits, losses, or expenditures of any person, firm, partnership, corporation or association.[124]

US Courts have largely agreed that all the information falling within the scope of Exemption 4 also falls within the scope of the TSA,[125] but this could change after the *Argus Leader* decision. The consequence of making equivalent CBI and trade secrets for the purposes of the application of the TSA is that US agencies 'discretionary disclosure' powers can never be exercised over information falling in the scope of Exemption 4, because it is explicitly forbidden in the TSA.

Trade secrets and CBI could, theoretically, also be exempted from disclosure under Exemption 3 of the FOIA, which applies to 'information specifically exempted from disclosure by another statute',[126] but not by virtue of the TSA, which, according to settled case-law, does not qualify to prevent disclosure of information covered by the FOIA under this exemption because it does not comply with the legal requirements set in the statute for that purpose.[127]

The US FOIA also establishes an exception for the protection of geological and geophysical data concerning wells (Exception b(9)), which may eventually

123 Environmental Law Institute. (1984). *Environmental Audit Issue Paper: Duties to Report or Disclose Information on The Environmental Aspects of Business Activities*. Washington D.C.

124 US Federal Statute, 18 U.S.C. § 1905 (2012).

125 US DOJ, *Guide to the Freedom of Information Act*, 2016.

126 US FOIA, Sec. 552 (b)(3).

127 US FOIA, Sec. 552(b)(3) (2006 & Supp. IV 2010): '(b) This section does not apply to matters that are– … (3) specifically exempted from disclosure by statute … if that statute – (A)(i) requires that the matters be withheld from the public in such a manner as to leave no discretion on the issue; or (ii) establishes particular criteria for withholding or refers to particular types of matters to be withheld; and (B) if enacted after the date of enactment of the OPEN FOIA Act of 2009, specifically cites to this paragraph'.

be used to prevent disclosure of environmental information held by private entities,[128] and is likely to include CBI within its scope.

As previously noted, the US legal system provides very detailed regulations about procedural aspects of the FOIA exemptions. This level of detail is hardly found in any of the other systems.

In the EU, Directive 2003/04 establishes that Member States may provide for a request to be refused if disclosure would adversely affect

> (d) the confidentiality of commercial or industrial information where such confidentiality is provided for by national or Community law to protect a legitimate economic interest, including the public interest in maintaining statistical confidentiality and tax secrecy;
> (e) intellectual property rights;[129]

Within this framework, Member States may not authorise withholding information on emissions into the environment on grounds of protection of commercial information, nor for the protection of (i) the confidentiality of the proceeding of public authorities (when provided for by law), (ii) the confidentiality of personal data, (iii) the protection of persons who submitted the information on a voluntary basis, or (iv) the protection of the environment to which such information relates. In this aspect, the regime of exceptions in Directive 2003/4 is less restrictive to the right of access than Aarhus.

An *a priori* assessment of the way exceptions work suggests that there is an expectation of nondisclosure for the submitter of the information when it is covered by the exceptions of the access regime, but a more detailed analysis shows that this may not always be the case, especially regarding environmental information.

Sometimes, the 'exception to the exception' will be in the same regulatory instrument, like in the case of emissions into the environment in the Aarhus Convention and its implementing instruments in the EU, health and safety information in the US Clean Air Act[130] and, more generally, information of overriding public interest under Regulation No 1049/2001.[131] The use of explicit language regarding these conditionings to the application of exceptions prevents the creation of nondisclosure expectations for submitters of

128 In at least one case this exemption was used to refuse access to information about ground water. *Starkey v. U.S. Department of Interior*, 238 F. Supp. 2d 1188 (S.D. Cal. 2002).

129 Directive 2003/4/EC of the European Parliament and of the Council of 28 January 2003 on Public Access to Environmental Information and repealing Council Directive 90/313/EEC, [2003] O.J. L 41/26, Article 4.

130 US Clean Air Act [CAA], 42 U.S.C, 7401 et seq. (1970).

131 Regulation (EC) No 1049/2001 of the European Parliament and of the Council of 30 May 2001 regarding public access to European Parliament, Council and Commission documents, [2001] O.J. L 145/43, Article 2(2).

information and ensures the harmonious coexistence of trade secret protection laws and access legislation.[132]

Explicit safeguards to the rights of access are also sometimes included in trade secret laws. The EU Directive 2016/943, for instance, acknowledges the risk of affecting the right of access to environmental information through the establishment of rules for the protection of trade secrets, it therefore advises in the Preamble that the rules of the Directive 'should not affect the application of Union or national rules that require the disclosure of information, including trade secret, to the public or to public authorities', specifically mentioning Regulation (EC) No 1049/2001, Regulation No 1367/2006, and Directive 2003/4/EC.

Resuming the analysis of the exceptions, it is important to note that neither the Aarhus Convention nor Directive 2003/4 provide an override for information relating to emissions into the environment when the information must be kept secret for the protection of intellectual property rights.[133] This is different in Regulation No 1049/2010. Article 4(2) establishes the exception to public access for the protection of CBI in the following terms:

> The institutions shall refuse access to a document where disclosure would undermine the protection of:
> – commercial interests of a natural or legal person, including intellectual property,
> – court proceedings and legal advice,
> – the purpose of inspections, investigations and audits,
> unless there is an overriding public interest in disclosure.

Note that the EU institutions and bodies are not vested with a discretionary power to disclose information that is protected by one of the exceptions, on the contrary, upholding the public and private interests protected by the exceptions is mandatory, unless there is an overriding public interest in disclosure. Regulation 1367/06, applying the Aarhus Convention to the EU institutions and bodies, established an irrebuttable presumption of public interest over information relating to emissions into the environment, which means that this information must be publicly disclosed even if giving access may undermine the protection of CBI or intellectual property rights (Article 6 (1)), which, again, goes beyond the provisions in the Aarhus Convention that did not foresee a public interest override for information about emissions into the environment protected as IPR.

In practice, this difference means that authorities at Member State level may be allowed to refuse access to information about emissions into the environment that is protected as intellectual property whilst EU institutions and bodies are not. The protection of CBI, on the other hand, must always

132 Shabalala, *Hidden Landmine*, 2017.
133 Garçon, *Regulatory Information on Agrochemicals*, 2012.

relent against the public interest in information about emissions, under the Aarhus Convention, Directive 2003/4 or Regulation No 1367/2006.

The irrebuttable presumption of public interest in Article 6(1) of Regulation No 1367/2006 also pre-empts the balancing act, thus in cases regarding information about emissions into the environment, there is no place to assess the extent to which disclosure may harm the protected interests in confidentiality or any other factor usually considered in the balancing of interests.

Shabalala opines that the presumption of public interest over information about emissions into the environment 'reflects the absolute barrier that Aarhus presents to confidentiality claims related to information regarding environmental harms'.[134] To the extent the legislation and courts have so far been shy to extend a similar presumption to other types of environmental information, we generally agree with this author that confidentiality claims can justifiably be restricted in relation to information about environmental harms, human health and safety and for the protection of other prevalent interests of the public. An example of this principle is found in Colombian Law 1955/2019 (National Development Plan), providing in Article 129 that all the information about the legal strategy of the state in national and international courts will be classified as confidential, but it shall not be withheld when it is necessary evidence in favour of the petitioner of the information and it is being held by the state in exercise of its legal functions.[135] In this case, the fundamental right of access to justice of the petitioner prevails over the public interest represented in the confidentiality of the legal strategies of the state. Regarding the balancing act, the Constitutional Court has stated:

> The confidentiality of public documents in a democratic state cannot be absolute, in so far as the general rule is the principle of publicity of the authorities' activity and the exception is confidentiality; therefore, the legal operator must not only assess that a provision of law permits the confidentiality of the document, but also which constitutional rights, principles and values are affected with the restriction, because in some cases the rights, values and principles that inspire the confidentiality of the information must prevail, and in other cases, those that oppose it. In this context, weighted the interests at stake, the confidentiality of the information may prevail before rights such as the right to information; but will have to subside before others such as the right of defence and access to justice, which, *prima facie,* are of higher importance in modern democratic societies.[136]

134 Shabalala, *Hidden Landmine*, 2017, p. 685.

135 Colombian Law 1955 of 2019, 'Adopting the National Development Plan 2019–2022', 24 May 2019.

136 Colombian Constitutional Court, Case T-928/04, Judgment of 24 September 2004, M.P. Jaime Araújo Rentería.

Compared to the US and the EU, Colombia has less experience applying the exceptions of its transparency instruments, perhaps because the regulations were only recently adopted. Both the Transparency Law and the Right of Petition establish a regime of exceptions to public disclosure including for the protection of commercial and industrial secrets.

The Transparency Law provides in Article 18 the possibility for an authority to refuse access to information whose disclosure could harm the rights of third parties, including the right to commercial, industrial and professional secrets, providing sufficient motive in writing. There are two exceptions to the exception in the same article: when the natural or legal person to whom the information concerns consents to its disclosure; or when it is *clear* that the information was submitted as part of the information required to be published under the applicable regime. This last condition is somewhat vague, but it can be interpreted as applying to information that is explicitly required to be published under the Transparency Law (*e.g.* information submitted in the framework of a public procurement process).

The Right of Petition Law, in turn, provides that only documents and information whose confidentiality is explicitly established in the laws and the constitution can be exempted from the Right of Petition, especially including '(...) 6. Those protected by the commercial and industrial secret, as well as the strategic plans of the public utility companies'.[137]

According to the Constitutional Court, the term 'industrial secrets' in these provisions refers to the definition of Decision 486 of the Andean Community,[138] which is directly applicable in the Colombian legal regime and, furthermore, is the most comprehensive instrument for the protection of trade secrets at national level. As already mentioned, the scope of this definition is equivalent to that of trade secrets in the TSA and the 'undisclosed information' in the TRIPS agreement.

Regarding the inclusion of the strategic plans of public utility companies as exempted information, the Constitutional Court affirmed that the private or public nature of the person providing public services in Colombia is irrelevant, insofar as the activity was declared in the Constitution as one 'inherent to the social finality of the state'.[139] This makes public utility companies in Colombia quite *sui generis*, to the extent that special provisions based on the nature of the service they provide supersede several aspects of both private and public legal regimes generally applicable to other entities. From the viewpoint of public access to information, this condition entails that public utility companies must provide information under the transparency legislation in the same way as any other public authority, but only in relation to their

137 Law 1755 of 2015, 'Regulating the Fundamental Right of Petition and repealing a Title of the Code of Administrative Procedure', 30 June 2015, Article 24.

138 Colombian Constitutional Court, Case C-951 of 2014, Judgment of 4 December 2014, M.P. Gloria Stella Ortiz Delgado.

139 Colombian Constitutional Court Case C-951 of 2014.

activities as providers of public services, and they are also entitled to a right to commercial and industrial secrecy over their strategic plans, because they need to be able to compete in the market in the same conditions as other private companies.[140]

Although the language of the exception in the legislative instruments suggests an unconditional protection of trade secrets, the Constitutional Court opened the door to the possibility of disclosing information when a more important constitutional value is at odds with the protection afforded by the exception. In the words of the Court:

> Insofar as the limitation (exception) is funded in the satisfaction of constitutional values, and these are never absolute, the constitutionality of this provision is without prejudice to the eventual nonapplication of the protection in cases where a right or good of higher value is being affected (…) Consider, for example, constitutional goods such as **public health and environmental protection**, which could eventually render the protection of commercial and industrial secrets as disproportionate or unreasonable in a concrete case (emphasis added).[141]

The Colombian Council of State has reaffirmed that any information to be withheld under any of the exceptions in the transparency instruments must be explicitly protected by another law or by the Constitution,[142] hence, the scope of protection for CBI and trade secrets under the exceptions will ultimately depend on the existence and specificity of the other laws. Article 15 of the Constitution, for instance, provides the right of every person to intimacy and the confidentiality of private documents, which can only be required for disclosure when they are necessary for inspection, vigilance, and intervention of state authorities in the exercise of their constitutional and legal functions. The Code of Commerce provides for the confidentiality of the 'business books', defined in the text as those that businessmen must keep under the law and those ancillary that are necessary for the complete understanding of the first.[143] This would include the shareholders registry, Board meetings, General Assembly meetings and accounting registries with their additional supporting documents. The same statute provides an exception to the confidentiality of the books consisting in the possibility of administrative authorities exercising the supervision of the company to require the exhibition of the books.[144] The

140 The protection does not extend to specific investment projects of public entities, which must be publicly disclosed (Law 1474 of 2011, Article 77).

141 Colombian Constitutional Court Case C-951 of 2014, p. 163.

142 Colombian Council of State, Case 11001-03-15-000-2016-0194301, *Maria Cristina Ferrucho Porras v Tribunal Administrativo de Antioquia*. Judgment of 15 March 2018, M.P. Stella Jeannette Carvajal Basto.

143 Decree 410 of 1971, Colombian Code of Commerce, 27 March 1971, Articles 49 and 61.

144 Colombian Code of Commerce, Article 63.

revelation of this information in this context, however, does not imply that the books become public or the information is in the public domain. The authorities that have had access to the information are required to keep its confidentiality in the terms of the law.

Regarding the special case of public access to information directly from private entities when the information is necessary for the exercise of the petitioner's fundamental rights, the Constitutional Court has recently clarified that this mechanism cannot be used to circumvent the protection of trade secrets and the confidentiality of business transactions. In an important decision, the Court granted access to specific information pertaining the business of a transportation company to one of its equity holders, because the information was necessary for him to exercise his right of access to justice. The Court warned, however, that the Right of Petition before private entities does not extend to (i) information classified as confidential in another law, (ii) documents containing trade secrets and (iii) information whose divulgation could cause detriment to the company, and, in any case, the information obtained could be used only and exclusively in the materialisation of the petitioner's fundamental right.[145] Regarding this last category, it would be interesting to see how the Court would decide a conflict about disclosure of information that is of high public interest, such as risks of a product for human health and safety, and for this reason its disclosure could be detrimental for the company.

6.5.1. Concluding Remarks

The protection of trade secrets and CBI in the context of the exceptions to the right of access to information is generally an expression and a consequence of the protection afforded to that kind of information within the legal system in which the law operates and, therefore, their scope and strength will depend greatly on the mechanisms established in other laws. In the US, for instance, the prohibition to disclose CBI under the TSA makes it illegal for a federal agency to use its discretion in the application of the Exemption 4 of FOIA; once certain information has been found to be a trade secret, its unauthorised disclosure could bring criminal consequences for the public servant. In Colombia, for public authorities to refuse disclosure under the CBI exceptions of the transparency laws, the information must be explicitly protected as confidential in other laws or in the Constitution.

Nevertheless, access to information laws condition the applicability and scope of the protection established by their respective exceptions regime. When the laws provide for public interest overrides, 'harm tests' or other measures enabling the operator to balance the interest in confidentiality and the interest in disclosure, there is less of an expectation of nondisclosure for

145 Colombian Constitutional Court, Case T-317/19, Judgment of 15 July 2019, M.P. Diana Fajardo Rivera.

the entity who submits the information to the authority. In the EU, for instance, operators are aware that information relating to emissions into the environment could not be expected to be protected as CBI under transparency laws. In Colombia, even if the law does not provide for explicit exceptions to the exceptions (other than human rights violations or crimes against humanity), the Constitutional Court has made it clear that the private interests in confidentiality of commercial and industrial secrets may subside before other higher values, such as public health and environmental protection.

However, the application of the 'harm tests' and the balancing exercise that come into play when there are contradicting interests at stake should be supported within a clear conceptual and legal framework, and this aspect seems to be lacking in the studied jurisdictions. For instance, there are no uniform definitions of 'public interest', when there is a requirement of some degree of harm to the protected interest, there is no agreement as to the level and characteristics of the harm that triggers the protection, and there are no specific guidelines or system of values informing the balancing acts. The shortcomings of these tools are further explored in Chapter 7.

6.5.2. Access to Information About Emissions Into the Environment According to the CJEU

One of the first keys in the analysis of access to environmental information *versus* business confidentiality relates to the possibility of assessing the *nature* of the information in question instead of only its origin. This can be deduced from the various and distinct cases in which legislation providing for the exception of business confidential information from public disclosure, explicitly excludes information related to emissions into the environment. Logical questions in this scenario would be: why does this sort of information warrant such special treatment? And, what's the scope of the term 'emissions into the environment' in this context? The following lines will be dedicated to these questions from the perspective of the Court of Justice of the European Union.

Emissions into the environment are simply defined as the releasing of substances into the air, water or soil. A more formal definition can be found in the EU Directive on industrial emissions: 'the direct or indirect release of substances, vibrations, heat or noise from individual or diffuse sources in the installation into air, water or land'.[146] Interestingly, the Aarhus Convention Implementation Guide refers to this Directive as an auxiliary criterion for the interpretation of the definition of 'Environmental Information' in the framework of the Convention.[147]

146 Directive 2010/75/EU of the European Parliament and of the Council of 24 November 2010 on industrial emissions (integrated pollution prevention and control), [2010] O.J. L 334, Article 3(4).

147 UNECE, *Aarhus Implementation Guide*, 2014.

The CJEU recently made a decision that clarifies the scope of the concept of 'information about emissions into the environment' in Article 6(1) of Regulation No 1367/2006 (implementing the Aarhus Convention in EU's institutions and bodies) which reads:

> As regards Article 4(2), first and third indents, of Regulation (EC) No 1049/2001, with the exception of investigations, in particular those concerning possible infringements of Community law, an overriding public interest in disclosure shall be deemed to exist where the information requested relates to emissions into the environment. As regards the other exceptions set out in Article 4 of Regulation (EC) No 1049/2001, the grounds for refusal shall be interpreted in a restrictive way, taking into account the public interest served by disclosure and whether the information requested relates to emissions into the environment.[148]

On 23 November 2016, the CJEU delivered its decisions in two separate cases, appeal Case C-673/13 P *European Commission v Greenpeace Nederland and Pesticide Action Network Europe (Stichting Greenpeace Nederland)* and preliminary reference Case C-442/14 *Bayer Crop Science v College voor de toelating van gewasbeschermingsmiddelen en biociden* (Board for the authorisation of plant protection products and biocides),[149] drawing from the general idea of providing the widest possible access to environmental information and adopting a restrictive interpretation of exceptions to disclosure.

Judgment C-673/13 (*Stichting Greenpeace Nederland)* concerned a request by Greenpeace Netherlands and PAN Europe to access a 'draft assessment report' submitted by Germany to the European Commission relating to the approval of glyphosate as an active substance under EU Plant Protection legislation. The Commission refused to disclose the information under the argument that disclosure would harm the manufacturer's commercial interest by allowing competitors to copy the production method, and it did not consider the information to be related to emissions to the environment, thus no overriding public interest in disclosure was foreseen. The General Court had found in the first instance that at least part of the information had a 'sufficiently direct link' to emissions into the environment, thus, access to some documents was granted on these grounds. The Grand Chamber reversed this decision, stressing that this criterion had no basis in law and, in fact, the concept of emissions into the environment did not include information that had any link, not even *direct*, to actual emissions to the environment (para. 81). In the Grand Chamber's opinion, such a wide interpretation would render meaningless the definition of 'Environmental Information' in Article 2 (1)(d) of the Aarhus Convention, making it practically impossible to apply

148 EU Regulation No 1367/2006, Article 6(1).

149 CJEU, Case C-442/14 *Bayer CropScience and Stichting De Bijenstichting*, Judgment of 23 November 2016.

the exception for the protection of business confidential information, and also would constitute a disproportionate interference with Article 339 TFEU, which protects business and professional secrecy.

However, the Grand Chamber clarified that the concept was not restricted only to emissions from industrial facilities, but that it included 'foreseeable emissions, under normal or realistic conditions of use, from the product in question, or from the substances which that product contains, into the environment' (para. 75). In the Court's opinion, these are not merely hypothetical emissions, insofar as glyphosate was actually intended to be released into the environment by its functional design.

In line with the previous argument, the Court also issued a decision in Case C-442/14, *Bayer Cropscience*, a case related to a petition to the Dutch authority in charge of authorisations for pesticide products from an association for the protection of bees, Bijenstichting, regarding products containing imidacloprid, a compound toxic to bees. Bayer, who submitted the information in the first place as part of the authorisation process, objected to the disclosure arguing confidentiality and intellectual property rights over the information in question. In the framework of the preliminary procedure, the Dutch Court asked the CJEU whether this information could be considered to fall within the definition of 'emissions into the environment' in the sense of Article 4(2) of Directive No 2003/4.

Beyond the amplifying interpretation of the concept of 'emissions into the environment', the Court further acknowledged the purpose of access to environmental information in public participation processes, opening the door for wider access to information when it is necessary to ensure that the public understands the effects of the substances to be emitted into the environment and the elements used for the risk assessment carried out by the authorities, like any toxicity studies in the framework of decision-making processes about chemicals. According to the Court,

> Information enabling the public to check whether the assessment of actual or foreseeable emissions, on the basis of which the competent authority authorised the product or substance in question, is correct, and the data relating to the effect of those emissions on the environment (…) is included in the definition of 'emissions into the environment'.[150]

This finding has potentially far-reaching consequences not only for the future of access to information in the framework of substance legislation but as a more general parameter to be replicated in decisions regarding public participation and transparency. Indeed, if the efficacy of the legislation to fulfil its intended purpose is counted as a factor, remarkable progress could be achieved via judicial action of the CJEU and other courts following its example, though probably at the expense of legal certainty, at least initially.

150 *Bayer Cropscience*, para. 80.

On the other hand, using the same logic that justifies exempting information about emissions into the environment from the information that can be withheld on grounds of business confidentiality, additional categories of information could eventually be established as exempted. An example is information relating to the health and safety of humans and the environment, for instance in the context of chemicals or crop protection regulations. The Overarching Policy Strategy adopted by the Strategic Approach to International Chemicals Management (SAICM), an international voluntary initiative for states and organisations, establishes with regards to knowledge and information the objective to

> Ensure that, in making information available in accordance with paragraph 15(b), confidential commercial and industrial information and knowledge are protected in accordance with national laws or regulations or, in the absence of such laws or regulations, are protected in accordance with international provisions. In the context of this paragraph, information on chemicals relating to the health and safety of humans and the environment should not be regarded as confidential (emphasis added).[151]

Note that this is a statement from the perspective of the interests of the industry, and not from the perspective of the right of access to information. Lyndon sustains, from a US perspective, that health, safety, and environmental data are not in the same legal category as purely commercial information protected by in the Trade Secrets Act (TSA) or the Economic Espionage Act (EEA), she argues that

> Neither the EEA nor the TSA change the underlying law of trade secrecy, nor do they purport to criminalize the release of health and environmental or safety data. The foundational concept—trade secrets—does not include such data and incremental expansions of FOIA's Exemption 4 do not change this.[152]

The effects of the application of this interpretation of trade secret law would be the same as including health, safety, and environmental data as exceptions in the scope of application of the exception of business confidentiality under public access legislation. The rationale behind both approaches is also the same: some information is just too important to the public to be held as a business secret.

151 UNEP. (2015). *Putting Rio Principle 10: An Implementation Guide for the UNEP Bali Guidelines for the Development of National Legislation on Access to Information, Public Participation and Access to Justice in Environmental Matters.* Nairobi, p. 39 (Box 17). Retrieved from https://wedocs.unep.org/bitstream/handle/20.500.11822/11201/UNEP%20MGSB-SGBS%20BALI%20GUIDELINES-Interactive.pdf?sequence=1&isAllowed=y.

152 Lyndon, *Reordering Information Privileges*, 2014, p. 509.

7 Problems of the System for Access to Information from the Private Sector

This chapter covers the analysis of the issues emerging from the comparative study as key points of conflict between the right of access to environmental information held by the private sector and business confidentiality. These issues are examined in detail to dissect the underlying challenges preventing a harmonious regulation and application of transparency obligations to private entities in a way that ensures public access to information for effective participation and reasonably safeguards the private interests in confidentiality.

7.1. Shortcomings of the Public/Private Divide for Access to Environmental Information

7.1.1. No Clear Criteria to Assimilate Private Entities to Public Authorities

As seen in the comparative study, there are no clear criteria to define when non-government entities should fall within the definition of 'public authorities' in the different transparency statutes, either at the international level, European level or within domestic jurisdictions.

However, there is a generalised acceptance of the fact that private entities nowadays are acting in the capacity of public authorities or on their behalf and are engaging in services and functions that used to be mostly performed by state entities, such as the construction of public infrastructure, the provisions of basic public services, public transportation, administration of prisons, public education and health services. Government agencies are also contracting out large amounts of work and projects with private corporations and persons, taking out of their control information that would otherwise be publicly available under public transparency legislation. When presented with this conjunction, courts and administrative authorities struggle to draw a line for the application of disclosure requirements in a way that preserves the final purpose of transparency legislation without unduly affecting private interests, private property, intellectual property rights and business confidentiality.

But in the United States, at least ten different 'tests' are being applied by state courts to interpret the scope of their respective transparency legislation *vis-à-vis* non-governmental organisations with some degree of public

DOI: 10.4324/9781003307617-7

interference.[1] Although this could be expected in a federal model, it can be argued that virtually all the state FOI laws have the same motivations and goals, and state courts were presented with the same question in similar factual contexts, thus more uniformity could reasonably have been expected.

But even when courts and administrative authorities are applying the same rules, like the Aarhus Convention[2] or the EU's directives and regulations on access to information, no uniform criteria to determine when a private entity is performing 'public administrative functions' or is acting 'under control' of a public authority for the purposes of the right of access to environmental information has been settled. The case of the UK courts and the CJEU are an example of this discrepancy.[3]

The lack of a clear-cut standard undermines access to information across the board. Private entities are likely to opt out of the scope of transparency legislation in the face of uncertainty[4] and public officials in charge of enforcement will lack strong legal arguments to provide effective remedy.

7.1.2. Deficiencies of Corporate Transparency

From the examination of the different ways in which the public can access environmental information held by private sector through active and passive mechanisms, it can be ascertained that the current systems have deficiencies when held against the standard of transparency described in the normative framework.

Some critical points are identified in the following situations:

1 Critical technical and test data submitted by private corporations to obtain approval for a product or substance to enter the public market is kept out of public scrutiny,[5] which makes it impossible to duly assess the

1 Feiser, C. D. (2000). Protecting the Public's Right to Know: The Debate over Privatization and Access to Government Information under State Law. *Florida State University Law Review*, 27, 825–64; Capeloto, A. (2014). Transparency on Trial: A Legal Review of Public Information Access in the Face of Privatization. *Connecticut Public Interest Law Journal*, 13, 19–42.

2 Convention on Access to Information, Public Participation in Decision-making and Access to Justice in Environmental Matters, Aarhus, Denmark, 25 June 1998 (entry into force 30 October 2001) 2161 UNTS 447.

3 UK Upper Tribunal, Case No. GIA/0979/2011, *Fish Legal and Emily Shirley v Information Commissioner, United Utilities Water plc, Yorkshire Water Services Ltd, Southern Water Services Ltd and the Secretary of State for the Environment, Food and Rural Affairs*; Randhawa, R. K. (2015). *Rights of Access to Environmental Information from Privatised Companies.* Gowling WLG.

4 Bünger, D., & Schomerus, T. (2011). Private Bodies as Public Authorities under International, European, English and German Environmental Information Laws. *Journal for European Environmental & Planning Law, 8*(1), 62–81.

5 Agreement on Trade-Related Aspects of Intellectual Property Rights [TRIPS], Annex 1C of the General Agreement on Tariffs and Trade (GATT), World Trade Organisation, 1994; Shabalala, D. B. (2017). Access to Trade Secret

decision-making process carried out by the regulatory agency and to make informed decisions about exposure and consumption by the general public, which, according to the CJEU, is a fundamental aspect of the right to access environmental information under international law.[6] Presumably, relevant data to assess risks for human health and safety and the environmental impacts of certain compounds or substances are never submitted to the regulatory agencies if the product is not being marketed immediately in the specific form that it was tested, which makes it even more unlikely to ever reach the public light, despite being clearly relevant for environmental regulation and the public interest.

2 Environmental Impact Assessments may not be publicly accessible in time for effective public participation in decision-making processes on specific projects and activities; they may also fall short in providing all the *relevant* information about the project or activity (budgetary considerations, alternatives to the main project, details of the foreseeable impacts), affecting effective public participation.[7] This is currently the case in Colombia, most likely due to the fact that there are no specific provisions about the moment and manner in which operators or environmental authorities should disclose the EIA to the public in general or to the specific community in order to enable public participation in the specific project or activity.

3 Voluntary initiatives by private corporations may result in significant amounts of environmental information being publicised, and such information can be presumed to be relevant and true, but may also be partial, biased and insufficient to assess negative environmental consequences of the company's activities. At best, voluntary initiatives like eco-labelling, environmental auditing and annual reporting to the public may offer important insights on the environmental performance of a company, but the information is likely to be incomplete; and, at worst, the presence of voluntary schemes may result in a false sense of transparency that can prevent timely adoption of mandatory duties upon private actors.

4 Information produced and gathered by private entities performing an activity on behalf of a government agency will remain out of reach to the public if said entity falls out of the scope of freedom of information laws. This may affect overall state transparency, since private entities in general are not subject to the same transparency standards as public authorities, and the information they hold is, in many cases, presumed to be their private property. This has consequences for public accountability and

Environmental Information: Are TRIPS and TRIPS-Plus Obligations a Hidden Landmine? *Columbia Journal of Transnational Law*, *55*, 648–717.

6 CJEU, Case C-673/13 P *Commission v Stichting Greenpeace Nederland and PAN Europe*, Judgment of 23 November 2016.

7 Colombian Council of State, Case 11001-03-15-000-2016-0194301, *Maria Cristina Ferrucho Porras v. Tribunal Administrativo de Antioquia*. Judgment of 15 March 2018, M.P. Stella Jeannette Carvajal Basto.

control of corruption and may contribute to inefficiency in the management of public funds. From the environmental point of view, large amounts of environmental information may be out of reach for the public, *e.g.* natural resources monitoring reports held by an environmental research institute or a private laboratory.

5 Companies may raise confidentiality claims to refuse public requests for environmental information, even in cases when they are legally required to disclose, and the public may lack alternatives to challenge such claims. In the absence of a public authority controlling the information, claims for business confidentiality may remain unchecked until a court gets involved.

7.1.3. The Organic Focus of Access Laws

In connection to the above, a key issue to consider is whether the organic criterion, *i.e.* distinguishing between *public* and *private* entities, is the right approach to transparency obligations. Most access laws examined throughout the study limit their scope based on this distinction, depending on whether an organisation can be called public or private. Considering that public access to environmental information is generally the means to an end, and not an end on itself, this research employed effective public participation in decision-making processes under the Aarhus Convention as a point of reference to assess public access to environmental information held by private entities. From this perspective, public access to environmental information will *always* be in the public interest, as it materialises the aims of the states for democratic participation, protection of fundamental rights and sustainable development, and, in the framework of public participation in decision-making processes (EIA procedures, public consultation of legislative or regulatory initiatives, etc.), is a fundamental prerequisite for the exercise of the rights.

The organic focus of access laws, represented in the predilection to define their scope by virtue of the nature of the entity that holds the environmental information, generally and systematically excluding private entities, undermines the public right of access to environmental information for the purposes of effective participation. By generally excluding private entities from the scope of the laws, states are pre-emptively dismissing the fact that environmental information held by private entities can be of the upmost relevance for public participation processes and they are implicitly defending the assumption that private entities are exempted of public duties and their activities shielded from public control or scrutiny, which is not true.

Only the private operators of impactful projects and activities are guaranteed to have all the information considered to be relevant for effective public participation purposes, such as the technical details of the substances to be released into the environment, the alternatives to the projects, full account of potential impacts, the cost analysis and tests results supporting risk assessments, the results of internal environmental audits and general information about the environmental performance of the company. It might be that in very rigorous regimes public authorities would hold all this information as well, but it can hardly be ensured. In any case, a public authority will never be in the possession of more information about a certain project or product than the private entity generating the environmental information in the first place.

In the context of the right of public access to environmental information, the distinction between private and public entities seems artificial and capricious. Unlike general transparency legislation based on the ideal of open government and freedom of speech, access to environmental information in the context of participatory rights is an instrument for the public to exercise and defend other rights. It is the how to an end that transcends the idea of transparency for its own sake, it is not simply the product of a state's commitment to certain democratic or environmental values.

Leaving out information held by private entities is sometimes justified in general transparency legislation because private information in general is not a public possession, but a private entitlement; it is a legally backed expectation in any modern liberal state that recognises private property and fundamental rights to intimacy, privacy and free economic competition;[8] it is also the assumption sustaining virtually all intellectual property rights theories.

The argument put forward does not advocate for the abolishment of all barriers and distinctions between public and private, nor between public and private information; but it proposes that a different criteria should be primarily employed to determine the scope of the public's right of access to environmental information, such as the nature of the information and whether it is needed in the framework of a process of public participation in decision-making or for the defence of other fundamental rights.

This approach is not novel. Provisions aimed at making public information about 'emissions into the environment', regardless of its origin or the risk to business confidentiality, already put in place imperative criteria based on the nature of the information instead of the entity that holds it or of the private interests in confidentiality.

The distinction between public and private entities in the sphere of general transparency laws has also been called into question. As government functions are being increasingly transferred to the private sector, right-to-know laws that apply exclusively to government agencies may not make sense now that government responsibilities are not so clearly determined. Privatisation has largely led to the diminishing role of the state in the provision of critical services, which brings into question if the fact that the government is

8 See *i.e.* Colombian Constitution (1991) Article 15, establishing the right to intimacy and the presumption of privacy over information held by citizens and legal entities; the Charter of Fundamental Rights of the European Union, Article 17 protecting the right of property; the First Additional Protocol to the ECHR, Article 1, establishing the right of every person to the peaceful enjoyment of their possessions.

contracting out many of its previous functions justifies the expiration of the public's right to know about how these activities are being executed.[9]

As Roberts puts it, 'the process of restructuring the public sectors of the advanced democracies is still underway. When it is done… it may be difficult to speak intelligently about a "public sector" at all'.[10] He further argues that this restructuring process already poses a threat to existing disclosure legislation. Since most of these laws build on a classical liberal conception of the social and political world, with a stark distinction between the public and private spheres, and which, moreover, poses the defence of the private sphere from public incursions as one of the main goals of political action,[11] access to public information is seen as a tool against government abuses of power and not as an instrument of public participation.

This traditional conception of public *versus* private harms the right of access to environmental information as it has been conceptualised through this research. There is a clear contradiction between the public right of access to the environmental information necessary for effective participation in the decision-making process about any specific project or activity and the *a priori* exclusion of private entities from the scope of environmental transparency laws. Although tools for public access to environmental information held by private entities are appearing across the legal landscape, a significant intellectual inconsistency remains, as 'policy makers around the world are unable to articulate a clear explanation of the standards that should be used to determine when an organisation must be subject to disclosure rules'.[12] The lack of uniform standards is the necessary consequence of this change of political and social conditions and the profusion of isolated disclosure requirements that aim to correct the asymmetries in access to information from public and private actors but fail to provide a consistent rationale of why and how this is to be done.

Hunt coined the term 'structural formalisms' to refer to impediments in the exercise of a right for reasons such as the extent to which an organisation is connected or controlled by a government agency.[13] Colombia and a few other countries have managed to overcome such impediments by establishing a constitutional right of access to information from private entities for the protection of other (fundamental) rights. What is important about such provisions is that they shift the logic underlying most transparency laws from the conceptual dichotomy between the public and private sphere and instead focus on the constitutional aim of preventing unjustified barriers to the

9 Roberts, A. (2006). *Blacked Out: Government Secrecy in the Information Age*. Cambridge University Press.

10 Roberts, *Blacked Out*, 2006, p. 160.

11 Roberts, *Blacked Out*, 2006.

12 Roberts, *Blacked Out*, 2006, p. 162.

13 Hunt, M. (1997). Constitutionalism and Contractualisation of the Government. In M. Taggard (Ed.), *The Province of Administrative Law*. Hart Publishing, quoted in Roberts, *Blacked Out*, 2006.

exercise of basic rights. Even though a right of access to environmental information held by private entities for the protection of human rights is not explicitly recognised in any other of the examined regimes, provisions such as those pertaining to PRTRs and the obligation upon private corporations to disclose information about hazardous substances clearly aim to ensure protection of the public's basic rights to health, family life and safety. Roberts argues that these examples of isolated provisions requiring disclosure from private entities share a common logic: 'the veil that ordinarily surrounds the private sector is lifted to protect a fundamental interest – namely, the right to personal security'.[14] The same can be said about provisions on people's access to *personal* information held by private actors for the protection of their privacy, and mandatory disclosure of corporations' financial and non-financial data for the protection of shareholders' legitimate economic interests. It must be noted, too, that in all these cases ownership of the information is not an issue, neither for supporting disclosure of personal information that belongs to the applicant nor for withholding information that can be said to be the property of the private entity. The issue of whether access to information is recognised as a fundamental human right in and of itself doesn't play a significant role in these cases, either. Access to information from private entities is being provided, explicitly or implicitly, as a derivative right – as a natural consequence of the state's commitment to ensure that a range of basic human rights are operational.[15]

In this scenario, the focus on whether an entity can be considered public or private to define the scope of the public right of access to information is insufficient and backwards, even more so in the case of access to environmental information. A sounder approach will have to consider the significant changes to the traditional delimitation of the public sector, the role of private entities in modern society, and the instrumental quality of information as the key for the effective exercise of other rights, including public participation in environmental matters.

On the other hand, shifting the focus from the *public* nature of the information to be accessed as the main and sufficient cause to provide public access in a democratic state that defends government transparency to the purpose of the information as a means for the protection and defence of other basic rights, entails consequences for the scope of beneficiaries of the right, for instance by defining 'public' more restrictively, and possibly for the requirements to obtain access, *i.e.* establishing the need to state a motive or to prove a direct interest.

In defining the scope of the public right of access, it can be argued that there is an inverse relationship between the range of the obligated subjects and the level of accessibility by the public without having to state a particular interest. This relationship is moderated by the logic that underpins the

14 Roberts, *Blacked Out*, 2006, p. 165.
15 Roberts, *Blacked Out*, 2006.

disclosure law: under general transparency legislation such as the Colombian Transparency Law[16] and the EU Regulation No 1049/01,[17] access is given to any person without having to state a motive but only to information held by public entities or bodies. The US FOIA is also based on the assumption of a general right of access to public records that springs from the inherent democratic nature of the state, and an important attribute of the right is that any person can exercise it, without having to state any particular interest. If people had to prove their interest or even just state their motives to access public information held by the government, the core of the right would be undermined. These laws are based on a transparency standard that presumes public 'ownership' of all official documents and records.

Access to information held by private entities, on the other hand, depends, in the Colombian case, on who is asking for the information and for what reason. Access is provided in this case to ensure the exercise and protection of individual fundamental rights and has little to do with public transparency or the 'ownership' of the information. Providing public access to private records for no particular reason is not the general rule in a democratic state and can hardly be justified on grounds of transparency, freedom of expression or any other human right. In fact, protecting private property, even for intangible goods like information, is one of the pillars of modern liberal states, not to mention other long-standing rights such as the right to personal privacy, the protection of intellectual property, business confidentiality and professional secrecy. A general right of access to information from private entities derogates from these principles and can only be justified for the protection of other legally or constitutionally relevant principles, in this case, fundamental human rights. In western legal systems, it is expected to call upon rules of proportionality, necessity and moderation when establishing measures that derogate from constitutional liberties. This case is no different. Access to information from private entities, therefore, is subject to certain qualifications: the information must be necessary for the exercise or protection of the petitioner's fundamental rights. The general scope and accessibility of the 'access right' is significantly diminished in comparison to access from public entities but this is justified as it prevents an excessive interference with the right to private property and other privacy-related rights of these entities.

Environmental information could be the exception to this general rule for several reasons: First, activities that have a significant impact on the environment transcend the private sphere, weakening the presumption of private property over relevant environmental information held by private

16 Law 1712 of 2014 'Creating the Law of Transparency and of the Right of Access to National Public Information and other dispositions', 6 March 2014.

17 Regulation (EC) No 1049/2001 of the European Parliament and of the Council of 30 May 2001 regarding public access to European Parliament, Council and Commission documents, [2001] O.J. L 145/43.

companies;[18] second, the necessary link that exists between having access to relevant environmental information and being able to exercise other participatory rights, which apply to public and private undertakings alike;[19] third, the recognition of the right to a healthy environment as a fundamental human right and, related to this, the close relationship between environmental conditions and the effective exercise of other fundamental rights such as the right to privacy and family life, freedom of expression, and health and safety, provide strong grounds for a presumption of public interest over environmental information in general; and finally, the fact that the environment and its components are generally recognised as common goods, thus information pertaining to these common goods is clearly in the public interest.

Viewed together, these circumstances merit a revision of the positions against a general right of access to environmental information from private entities. Though not explicitly, much of this logic is already supporting access to information on emissions, risk assessments, chemical data, environmental impact assessments, test data, monitoring results etc. directly from the private entities and corporations holding it. It is a relatively small step to enable direct requests of the public to access environmental information held by private entities in specific cases, such as EIA processes, in relation to possible environmental damage, or as a way to inform consumers of the risks of a product. The application of principles of proportionality, necessity and moderation in derogating from the general right of private entities to keep information private appears to be satisfied in a significant number of scenarios. This reform would come paired with new challenges and legal issues that need to be considered, among them the risk of unduly interfering with the competitive interests of companies over their trade secrets and intellectual property rights.

7.2. Overlapping Between the Definitions of 'Environmental Information' and 'Confidential Business Information'

From the study of the definitions of 'environmental information' in the framework of access to information laws and 'confidential business information'

18 *E.g.* information about emissions into the environment loses its proprietary nature once the emissions enter the public domain. United Nations Economic Commission for Europe – UNECE. (2014). *The Aarhus Convention: An Implementation Guide*, 2nd ed., UN Doc. ECE/CEP/72/Rev.1.

19 From participation in decision-making processes for specific projects or activities to consumer's decisions based on the environmental characteristics of a product, information is the raw material for public participation. See, *i.e.*, Lamdan, S. (2017). *Environmental Information: Research, Access and Environmental Decisionmaking*. Environmental Law Institute; Lyndon, M. (2011). Trade Secrets and Information Access in Environmental Law. In R. Dreyfuss & K. J. Strandburg (Eds.), *The Law and Theory of Trade Secrecy: A Handbook of Contemporary Research*. Edward Elgar Publishing, pp. 443–466; Fung, A., Graham, M., & Weil, D. (2007). *The Perils and Promise of Transparency.* Cambridge University Press.

in the same jurisdictions, some *a priori* conflicts can be identified. The question addressed here is: are some recognised forms of CBI included within the definition of 'environmental information' in the framework of public access to information and participation in decision-making laws? The following examples shed some practical light into the so far mostly theoretical debate.

7.2.1. Cost-Benefit Analysis and Other Financial Information

Both the Aarhus Convention and Directive No 2003/4/EC[20] make specific reference to 'cost-benefit and other economic analysis and assumptions', in relation to the state of the elements of the environment and the factors likely to affect those elements, a category of 'environmental information' under these instruments. This would include qualitative and quantitative data.[21] The working definition of 'relevant environmental information' introduced in the normative framework also includes budgetary information and the cost of the different alternatives to a project or activity. Thus, can cost-benefit and other economic analysis like budgets and expenses be considered CBI? Under the domestic regimes of the US and Colombia, financial information pertaining to a business can be considered CBI and is protected under the exceptions to the right of access to information in their respective transparency laws.[22] Neither of these national regimes establish a specific right of access to this kind of information or provide exceptions to the protection afforded under confidentiality laws for purposes of public participation or other grounds. In this sense, it can be asserted that this kind of information is covered under a presumption of nondisclosure, even when held by public authorities, by virtue of the specific laws protecting CBI.

7.2.2. Technical Information About Hazardous Activities or Products

In the case of *Matky v Czech Republic*[23] the ECtHR had to consider a public request for access to technical information held by the government about a nuclear power plant. The particularities of such a project may very well fall within the definition of 'environmental information' insofar as the construction and operation of the plant is counted as a factor that is likely to affect the elements of the environment and this data can be considered of high

20 Directive 2003/4/EC of the European Parliament and of the Council of 28 January 2003 on Public Access to Environmental Information and repealing Council Directive 90/313/EEC, [2003] O.J. L 41/26.
21 Thorp, T. (2012). The Right to Know and the Duty to Disclose: Pathways to Effective Monitoring, Reporting, and Verification within the Constitutionalism of Climate Justice. *Pace Environmental Law Review*, 30, 140.
22 Colombia: Decree 410 of 1971, Colombian Code of Commerce, 27 March 1971, Article 63; US: Freedom of Information Act of July 4, 1966, Public Law No. 89–487, 80 Stat. 250, codified as amended at 5 U.S.C. § 552 (1994), Exception 4.
23 *Sdruženi Jihoðeské Matky v. Czech Republic*, App. 19101/03 (2006).

public interest to the extent that it is employed as basis for the formulation of safety protocols and emergency plans for the protection of the facilities and the community in which it operates. The Convention on the Transboundary Effects of Industrial Accidents (Helsinki, 1992) establishes obligations to disclose a minimum of information to the public in areas likely to be affected by an industrial accident arising out of a hazardous activity.[24] The same information can be considered highly confidential, not only for the company's commercial interests but also for national security reasons.

Some of the relevant information such as construction techniques, designs, layouts, materials to be employed and the general functioning of the nuclear plant is likely to be included in the EIA, because these aspects are all relevant from the environmental impact viewpoint, but they are also relevant in the framework of any other decision-making process regarding this project, in which the public should be able to participate.[25] The Aarhus Convention Compliance Committee (ACCC) has been consistent about the impossibility of withholding EIAs from the public for the protection of intellectual property rights,[26] but the precedent of disclosure is not equally clear when the relevant information is not part of the EIA.

In *Matky v Czech Republic*, the ECtHR ultimately rejected the application because it found the refusal of the information justified on the basis of the restrictions applicable to the right of freedom of expression, specifically referring to factors of national security, contractual obligations and the protection of economic confidentiality.[27] The analysis suggests that access to specific technical data about hazardous activities or products is not a prevalent interest in the same way as access to other types of environmental information, at least when there is no imminent threat.

The Aarhus Convention (Article 5(10)), the Escazú Agreement (Article 6 (5)),[28] and EU instruments implementing Aarhus obligations provide for the active dissemination of information to the public when there is a threat to public health or to the environment; in this scenario it is unlikely that any of the exceptions could be applied, due to the 'public interest test' mandated by

24 Convention on the Transboundary Effects of Industrial Accidents, UNECE, Helsinki, Finland, 17 March 1972 (amended on 15 December 2015; entered into force on 19 April 2000), Article 9(1).

25 See Convention on the Transboundary Effects of Industrial Accidents, Article 9 (2). At EU level, Directive 2012/18/EU (Seveso III Directive) requires that the public concerned be given an early opportunity to give its opinion on the planning of new upper-tier establishments, on significant modifications to existing establishments, and new developments around existing establishments that may increase the risk or consequences of a major accident (UNECE, *Aarhus Convention Implementation Guide*, 2014).

26 Case ACCC/C/2005/15 (Romania), ECE/MP.PP/2008/5/Add.7.

27 *Matky v Czech Republic*, paras 10–11.

28 United Nations, Regional Agreement on Access to Information, Public Participation and Justice in Environmental Matters in Latin America and the Caribbean, 4 March 2018 (entered into force 22 April 2021), Escazú, Costa Rica.

these instruments for the application of the exceptions.[29] In an emergency situation, even national security interests do not prevail over the protection of public health and the environment from an imminent threat. However, if a petitioner wants access to safety information before there is a threat or an emergency, this information may not be readily available because of public security considerations and business confidentiality.

Technical information about biotechnology and nanotechnology products and from the chemicals industry will frequently be deemed confidential or protected under intellectual property law and, at the same time, be critical to assert the risks of these products. Especially in the field of new technologies, it is recommended that the public gets access to basic explanatory materials when dealing with scientific and technical details of new projects.[30] This requirement should not be undermined by the extensive protection of business confidentiality over crucial technical data.

Another notable example is the case of GMOs, in which the public right of access to information would arguably outweigh confidentiality claims, at least in what concerns biosafety information,[31] and there is clearly an overlap between environmental information and trade secrets (formulae, composition of substances, processes) and even IP rights. The same argument applies to this case: with higher uncertainty, higher transparency is needed. The application of a precautionary approach in the framework of the regulation of new technologies demands increased transparency and public participation, including by enabling the public to verify the risk assessment process carried out by the public authority.

7.2.3. Chemical Substances

The case of chemical substances is particularly critical in light of the recent decisions of the CJEU stating that the concept of 'emissions into the environment' under the Aarhus Convention and EU regulatory instruments includes data about substances which, under normal conditions of use, will produce foreseeable emissions into the environment, such as pesticides and other plant protection products used on plants or soil,[32] and, considering that

29 UNECE, *Aarhus Implementation Guide*, 2014.

30 D'Silva, J., & van Calster, G. (2010). For Me to Know and You to Find Out? Participatory Mechanisms, The Aarhus Convention and New Technologies. *Studies in Ethics, Law, and Technology, 4*(2).

31 Nielsen, K. M. (2013). Biosafety Data as Confidential Business Information. *PLOS Biology, 11*(3), 1–6: 'such claims oftentimes marginally serve their legitimate purpose to protect commercial interests and unnecessarily limit transparency and public peer review of data submitted to regulatory authorities' (p. 1).

32 CJEU, Case C-442/14 *Bayer CropScience and Stichting De Bijenstichting*, Judgment of 23 November 2016. See analysis in Buonsante, V. A., & Friel, A. (2017). What is Information Relating to Emissions into the Environment? *European Journal of Risk Regulation, 8*(02), 453–460; *Commission v Stichting Greenpeace Nederland and PAN Europe.*

under the regime of exceptions of the Aarhus Convention information on 'emissions into the environment' cannot be withheld on grounds of business confidentiality, this decisions will undoubtedly bring about significant consequences for commercial interests of the companies producing chemical substances.[33]

The CEJU judgments in *Stichting Greenpeace Nederland* and *Bayer Cropscience* arguably do not offer enough elements to discern when the emissions can be considered 'foreseeable under normal conditions of use' and when they are 'merely hypothetical'. This distinction is critical, particularly taking into account that transparency obligations regarding chemical substances and registration processes for entering the market had been largely left to the specific provisions in substance law instruments, such as REACH and the US TSCA, which provide specific safeguards for the protection of sensitive commercial information and trade secrets and harmonise (to an extent) private interest protection with the public interest and minimum transparency requirements. The field of substance law and chemical regulation is also one where uniformity among jurisdictions is highly relevant and some level of cooperation between regulatory authorities in different jurisdictions is recommended. The CJEU decisions in these cases are more likely to affect foreign markets and companies operating in several countries.[34]

Adding to the debate, the European Court sustained in a recent case that information such as toxicity tests and other data on the effects and consequences of a substance is relevant from the perspective of public participation in decision-making, and that disclosure should cover not only information on the emissions as such but also about the effects and long-term consequences of these emissions on the state of the environment, in a way that enables the public to assess the risks associated with the substance.[35] In the case in question, *Tweedale v EFSA*,[36] the Court established a distinction regarding studies made in realistic conditions of use and regular doses of the substance, which were considered to be within the concept of 'emissions into the environment', and studies carried out in unrealistic conditions of use or abnormally high doses of the substance, which were related to 'hypothetical' emissions and, as such, not included within the definition. The Court clarified, however, that if the information obtained from the studies carried out

33 Von Holleben, H. (2013). Judgment of the General Court of the EU on Access to Information under Substance Law. *European Journal of Risk Regulation, 4*, 565–578.

34 In this case, several American associations and companies voiced their concerns to the Court. *Amicus Brief*, Court of Justice of the European Union, Case C-673/13, CropLife America, NAM and The American Chemistry Council. Retrieved from http://www.nam.org/Advocacy/The-Center-for-Legal-Action/Briefs-Online/2015/NAM-Amicus-Brief-in-European-Commission-v-Stichting-Greenpeace-(Court-of-Justice-of-the-European-Union).pdf.

35 *Stichting Greenpeace Nederland,* para 80; *Bayer Cropscience*, para. 86.

36 CJEU, Case T-716/14, *Anthony C. Tweedale v European Food Safety Authority (EFSA)*, Judgment of 7 March 2019.

under unrealistic conditions of use were then used to determine the safety of the product and the quantities and conditions for its actual utilisation in the market, then the information was considered relevant to determine the effects of the product's foreseeable emissions into the environment and should therefore be made publicly available.[37]

Some authors have argued that this interpretation is at odds with specific provisions of EU secondary law establishing the confidentiality of technical information submitted by private actors in the process of approval of a new product or substance to enter the market[38] which explicitly extends to *i.a.* information about impurities and the exact composition of a chemical substance.[39]

This example especially demonstrates the overlapping categories of information that are simultaneously protected by confidentiality laws and also fall into the definition of environmental information to which the public should have free access. Garçon points out that

> as agrochemicals are only authorised if registrants can demonstrate the absence of harmful effects on human or animal health nor unacceptable effects on the environment, most of the information submitted by registrants will in itself concern the elements of the environment or the state of human health or safety, and therefore be environmental information.[40]

Moreover, there could be an overlap between data protected as trade secrets and CBI and information about 'emissions into the environment', which, if held by a EU institution, is covered by an irrebuttable presumption of public interest, which means that the information must be disclosed to the public regardless of the harm to the third party's legitimate economic interests.

7.2.4. Health and Safety Data

The general category of Health, Safety and Environmental (EHS) data encompasses some of the other categories of information listed in this section. However, several authors have carried out important analysis taking the whole category as a distinguishable body of information, which should arguably be covered by a general presumption of public interest in its entirety.

37 *Tweedale v EFSA,* paras 116–119.

38 Von Holleben, *Judgment of the General Court*, 2013; CropLife America, *Amicus Brief.*

39 Regulation (EC) No 1107/2009 of the European Parliament and of the Council of 21 October 2009 concerning the placing of plant protection products on the market and repealing Council Directives 79/117/EEC and 91/414/EEC, OJ L 309, 24.11.2009, Article 63 (2).

40 Garçon, G. (2012). Access to Regulatory Information on Agrochemicals – To which extent does Regulation 1107/2009 prevail over the EU Transparency Legislation? *European Journal of Risk Regulation, 10*(2), 393–400, esp 395.

Lyndon makes the important point that 'where market actors claiming secrecy entitlement are themselves the source of EHS risks, commercial justifications for confidentiality are especially weak'.[41] She suggests that this category of information was never meant to be covered by the TSA or the confidentiality clauses of the FOIA.[42]

However, outside the valuable analysis offered by this author from a US normative perspective, there is the fact that EHS and CBI frequently overlap, thus, judges and administrators are increasingly faced with a dilemma between the protection of public and private interests.

In a 2005 case, a German Administrative Court refused an injunction requested by Monsanto to prevent German authorities from disclosing information to Greenpeace (Germany) about a study carried out as part of the risk assessment for a new genetically modified maize plant. Greenpeace had filed its request under the Environmental Information Act.[43] Monsanto's argument to refuse access to the whole study (including raw data) was that it was protected as an operating and business secret. The case was primarily decided on the basis of national law, specifically the German 'Genetic Engineering Act', which explicitly exempted from the information that could be withheld on grounds of operating or business secret the name and address of the operator and 'the evaluation of foreseeable effects, particularly pathogenic and ecologically disruptive effects'.[44] In this case, prevalence was given to the 'right to know' of the public, understood as a normative belief that those exposed to potential harm have a right to know about damaging environmental products and activities.

The importance of EHS data is increasingly being recognised in the IP and confidentiality laws themselves, where clauses exempting information about environmental impacts or threats to human health and safety are now routinely included.[45] Furthermore, the CJEU has asserted in respect to some of these confidentiality provisions that they must be interpreted as being capable

41 Lyndon, *Trade Secrets and Information*, 2011, p. 468.

42 Lyndon, *Trade Secrets and Information*, 2011, p. 509.

43 Wollenteit, U., Michéle, J. and Gebauer, J. (2006). A Strong Case for Transparency: Public Interest in Disclosure of Risk Data Prevails over Business Secrets. *Journal of European Environmental and Planning Law*, 3, 13. For a full account (and for the complete wording) of the case in German see: OVG Monster, file reference: 8 B 940/05, in Zeit- schrift fOr Umweltrecht 2005 (ZUR 2005), p. 420 et seq. and as abridgement in UPR 2005, p. 450 et seq.

44 German Genetic Engineering Act, s. 17a(2), quoted in Wollenteit, Michéle and Gebauer, Case for Transparency, 2006, p. 14.

45 See *i.e.*, Regulation 1107/09, Article 63(2), exempting from the confidentiality presumption information which is toxicologically, ecotoxicologically or environmentally relevant, and Article 63(3) mentioning that provisions on confidentiality will operate without prejudice to Directive 2003/4/EC; The US TSCA also excludes from confidentiality protection information about health and environmental studies relevant for the assessment of the substance (Toxic Substances Control Act [TSCA], 15 U.S.C. § 2613(b) (2000), Sec. 15(b)(2)).

of application only insofar as transparency obligations under other laws are not affected.[46] As pointed out throughout the present study, there are strong arguments favouring public access to this kind of information, especially when public authorities and regulators employ it for the risk assessment of the substances and products to which the general public might be exposed.

7.2.5. Environmental Impact Assessments and Other Relevant Information on Specific Projects

Environmental Impact Assessments are the typical example of 'relevant environmental information' for the purposes of effective public participation in decision-making for specific projects and activities. They may also include trade secrets and CBI, such as manufacturing processes, production data, customer's information, specifics about the supplies and raw materials used, strategic plans of the company, lay-outs of the installations and other commercially sensitive data. Even the EIA document itself could be theoretically protected by copyrights, to the extent that their content or configuration can be considered as a unique creative production of the author (*e.g.* Case ACCC/C/2005/15 (Romania)). In this context, could it be possible for the project's operator to leave confidential information outside of the EIA or to withhold part of the study from the public?

This question was presented to the Colombian Council of State, one of the highest national courts, which in a recent decision affirmed that the EIA study could not be withheld from the public on the basis of business confidentiality as a general rule, without prejudice for the protection of specific sensitive data which could be suppressed from public versions of the EIA in order to ensure the confidentiality of industrial secrets.

In the case in question, a citizen requested access to the full EIA study presented to the regional environmental authority, CORNARE, regarding a project to build a cement production plant. CORNARE granted access to a part of the environmental licence file but withheld the EIA study which, according to its own assessment, was protected from public disclosure because it was an 'industrial secret' under Decision 486 of the Andean Community (to which Colombia is a Party).[47]

Invoking the Right of Petition Law,[48] the petitioner sought recourse before the regional Administrative Tribunal, triggering its jurisdiction to make the final decision. The Judge (Tribunal Administrativo de Antioquia) agreed with CORNARE and did not order the disclosure of the EIA. The petitioner thus

46 CJEU, Case C-266/09, *Stichting Natuur en Milieu v College voor de toelating van gewerbeschermingsmiddelen en biociden*, Judgment of 16 December 2010, para 50 et seq.

47 Decision 486 'Common Regime on Intellectual Property', Andean Community (CAN), 14 September 2000.

48 Law 1755 of 2015 'Regulating the Fundamental Right of Petition and repealing a Title of the Code of Administrative Procedure', 30 June 2015.

filed a *Tutela* Action against the Tribunal based on the violation of her fundamental rights to due process, access to public information and the right of petition.

The Council of State decided that the information of the EIA should be publicly available, basically for two reasons, one formal and one more substantial. The first is that there is no specific rule in the Colombian regime that explicitly establishes that the EIA can be protected from public disclosure on commercial confidentiality or other grounds. The Court believed that the absence of such disposition made the decision of the Tribunal (and CORNARE's) illegal, because it was against the rule that mandated a restrictive interpretation of the rules establishing exceptions to disclosure of public information. The other reason, according to the Court, came from the very nature of the EIA and its importance for the protection of constitutional values. The Council of State expressed that:

> Due to the very nature of the EIA, any possibility to restrict public access must be dismissed. Restrictions must rely on a constitutionally legitimate end, important and imperative, and must be reasonable and proportional (…) The public release of the EIA serves the constitutionally legitimate purpose of [providing] access to public information in an individual and social dimension, it is important because it enables the community to participate in decisions regarding the environment and it is imperative because the previous knowledge of such information may prevent the consummation of damages not only for the environment, but for humanity. This is why such restriction is unreasonable and disproportionate.[49]

The Council of State takes a very strong position in favour of disclosure of information that is needed for the exercise of constitutionally recognised rights such as public participation in decision-making in environmental matters and access to public information.

Furthermore, in supporting its decision, the high Court relied on the opinion of the Inter-American Court of Human Rights regarding the application of Article 13 of the Inter-American Convention on Human Rights and the international standards established therein for the limitation of the right of expression and access to public information.[50]

In this case, the environmental authority had provided access to the administrative decisions regarding the application for environmental licence, but withheld the EIA and other documents containing designs, drawings, layouts and details of the cement processing plant because it considered them to be commercially sensitive and protected, therefore, under Articles 6 and 18

49 *Ferrucho v. Tribunal Administrativo de Antioquia.*

50 Inter-American Court of Human Rights, *Gomes Lund and others ('Guerrilha do Araguaia') v Brasil*, Opinion 24 November 2010.

(c) and paragraph of Law 1712 of 2014 (Transparency Law). The Council of State went into the detail of the documentation requested and clarified that not everything in the administrative file was deemed to be public because some restrictions to access for the protection of business secrecy apply, therefore, the sensitive information can be suppressed from the file for purposes of public disclosure, including some data of the EIA.

The restrictions to access on grounds of business confidentiality are based on the protection of free economic competition, economic liberties, and freedom to carry a business, values constitutionally recognised in Colombia. The Constitutional Court had already asserted on this account:

> To allow the divulgation of commercial and industrial secrets would undermine an essential aspect of the effective protection of these constitutional liberties, by favouring competitors with information that does not belong to them without a legitimate justification.[51]

The Council of State confirmed that the designs, layouts and information pertaining to the cement plant process could contain 'industrial secrets' and may be protected from disclosure under the law,[52] but the EIA, in principle, cannot be put in the same category, as it contains information of general interest to effectively assess the environmental impact of the project which does not contain vital or privileged information affecting the economic activity. Furthermore, access to the information of the EIA allows for adequate social control of industrial projects that could produce irreparable damage to the environment.

The decision of the Colombian Council of State in this case echoes doctrinal and jurisprudential theories from other sources. The importance of access to EIA studies for effective public participation in decision-making about specific projects is a generally accepted argument and can be found implicitly or explicitly stated in different laws and doctrinal sources.

51 Colombian Constitutional Court, Case C-951 of 2014, Judgment of 4 December 2014, M.P. Gloria Stella Ortiz Delgado.

52 In a subsequent petition, the owners of the project submitted another *tutela* action claiming that their fundamental rights to due process and the protection of their industrial secrets had been affected. The submission contained more detailed explanations about what part of the information included in the EIA was considered trade secrets because its disclosure could adversely affect the company's market position: information about the consumption of water and electricity and costs of production, detailed manufacturing processes and designs of the production plant were among the most sensitive components. As a result, the original decision was nullified, but only in consideration to the fact that the owner of the project had not had the opportunity to defend his interest in those procedures. Colombian Council of State, Case 11001-03-15-000-2017-01010–00 (AC), *Empresa Colombiana de Cementos S.A.S – Ecocementos S.A.S v. Sección Cuarta del Consejo de Estado*, Judgment of 25 May 2017, M.P. Carlos Enrique Moreno Rubio.

In the international landscape, the Aarhus Convention does not adopt a specific definition of EIA, however it does imply that EIA statements shall be made publicly available due to their materiality in the processes of participation in environmental decision-making.[53] An official definition can be found in the Espoo Convention,[54] which refers to EIA as 'a national procedure for evaluating the likely impact of a proposed activity on the environment' (Article 1 (vi)). The Aarhus Convention Implementation Guide highlights the importance of EIA procedures in the framework of public participation in decision-making under the Aarhus Convention, stating:

> Environmental assessment is a very useful tool in ensuring effective public participation in decision-making: without environmental assessment documentation, the public usually have no easy access to reports or studies evaluating the environmental and health risks of an activity. Thus, such documentation helps the public to develop and express their own science-based opinions on the proposed activity, plan or policy.[55]

Further reinforcing the close correlation between public participation and EIA procedures is the fact that requirements of Article 6 of the Aarhus Convention relating to public participation in decision-making about specific projects or activities are implemented in the EU through the EIA Directive[56] and the Industrial Emissions Directive.[57] Within these frameworks, public participation is mandated in the early stages of decision-making about projects that are likely to have a significant effect on the environment and thus require an EIA or a permitting procedure.

The Aarhus Convention Compliance Committee (ACCC) has also examined if claims of confidentiality on grounds of commercial secrecy and intellectual property rights could apply to EIA documentation. In case ACCC/2005/15 regarding compliance by Romania, an environmental NGO submitted a communication to the ACCC with a complaint regarding a legislative proposal from the Romanian Minister of the Environment which would

53 Aarhus Convention, Article 6(6) provides for 'all information relevant to the decision-making' to be made accessible for the public concerned as soon as it is available (without prejudice to the exceptions in Article 4).

54 UNECE Convention on Environmental Impact Assessment in a Transboundary Context, 25 February 1991 (entered into force on 10 September 1997), 1989 UNTS 309.

55 UNECE, *Aarhus Implementation Guide*, 2014, p. 123.

56 Council Directive 85/337 of 27 June 1985 on the assessment of the effects of certain public and private projects on the environment [1985] O.J. L 175/40 codified with amendments by Directive 2011/92/EU of the European Parliament and of the Council, [2012] O.J. L. 26/1, as amended by Directive 2014/52/EU of the European Parliament and of the Council, [2014] O.J. L. 124/1

57 Directive 2010/75/EU of the European Parliament and of the Council of 24 November 2010 on industrial emissions (integrated pollution prevention and control), [2010] O.J. L 334.

include the possibility for the developer of a project to request the confidentiality of any part of the EIA. In this case, the Romanian Copyright Office had informed the National Environmental Protection Agency that 'environmental impact studies were scientific studies protected by copyright law and therefore could be used, and in particular made publicly available, only with the express agreement of the author'.[58] The ACCC deemed this approach to be in non-compliance with Article 5(1) of the Convention, which requires public authorities to possess and update information relevant to their functions; as, in the opinion of the Committee, this includes, at the very least, EIA studies in their entirety. Article 6(6) (access to relevant environmental information for decision-making) was also affected in this scenario. The ACCC concluded that introducing a general rule excluding full EIA studies from public disclosure on grounds of copyright protection was against the Convention's provisions. The ACCC conceded, however, that specific parts of an EIA study could theoretically be exempted from disclosure for the protection of intellectual property rights, but this required a case-by-case assessment by the public authority considering that exceptions to disclosure must be applied restrictively and taking into account the public interest served by disclosure. In the ACCC opinion, it was doubtful that this exemption could ever be applicable in practice in connection with EIA documentation. Disclosure of EIA studies in their entirety should be considered the rule, with the possibility for exempting parts of them being the exception to the rule.

The evidence gathered in the present study supports the conclusion that information contained in an EIA, which is utilised by the authorities in their decision on whether to allow a specific activity or project, should be presumed to be public information and restrictions to disclosure on grounds of business confidentiality should be seriously reconsidered, either to establish a presumption of public interest as in the case of information about emissions into the environment in the framework of the Aarhus Convention, or, at the very least, to establish a qualified rule of full access by allowing the public that can be directly affected by the project or activity to know the full content of the EIA regardless of business confidentiality considerations.

However, the regulation of EIA remains, to a large extent, an issue of national law, and therefore, specific provisions regulating the possibility to claim the confidentiality of the information submitted in the framework of an EIA process need to be introduced in each of the jurisdictions.

7.2.6. Geotechnical Information and Locations of Natural Resources

The US FOIA establishes nine exemptions to disclosure, number nine relates to 'geological and geographical information and data, including maps, concerning wells'.[59] Reportedly, this exemption was included due to lobbying by

58 Case ACCC/2005/15 (Romania).
59 US Freedom of Information Act, Sec. 552(b)(9).

the oil industry in order to protect them from unfair competitive harm by 'speculators'.[60] Although this exemption is rarely used,[61] in at least one case it was applied preventing access to environmental information, namely, the presence and quantity of groundwater, more specifically, 'ground water inventories, [water] well yield in gallons per minute, and the thickness of the decomposed granite aquifer'.[62] Interestingly, information about water rights has been considered of a commercial nature under exemption 4 of the US FOIA that protects information 'commercial or financial, obtained from a person, which is privileged or confidential', a category beyond the definition of trade secrets.[63]

In Colombia, a similar provision was adopted in 2011, through Law 1450 (National Development Plan)[64] establishing that any geotechnical information produced by the Colombian Geological Service (INGEOMINAS) from the declaration and delimitation of Strategic Mining Areas by the regulatory mining agency, was to be kept confidential until the declaration was revoked or until the agency published the terms to bid for the right to exploit the areas (Article 108). This rule was accessory to the regulation of 'special interest areas for mining' whose main purpose was to protect the economic interests of the state in mining development.

The Constitutional Court declared this rule to be unconstitutional.[65] The Court opined that this exception to the general right of access to public documents failed the proportionality test because it posed an excessive interference with the constitutionally protected interests to open government (as reflected in the fundamental right of public access to official documents), the rights of local governments and communities to participate in decision-making about the use of the land and projects that may have a significant environmental impact, the special rights of ethnic minorities to prior consultation and participation, and, finally, the Court did not find it justifiable that information about non-renewable natural resources, which were

60 Mendel, T. (2009). *The Right to Information in Latin America. A Comparative Legal Survey,* UNESCO. Retrieved from http://portal.unesco.org/ci/en/files/26159/12054862803freedom_information_en.pdf/freedom_information_en.pdf.

61 US DOJ. (2016). *Department of Justice Guide to the Freedom of Information Act 2*. Retrieved from https://www.justice.gov/sites/default/files/oip/legacy/2014/07/23/procedural-requirements.pdf#p9.

62 *Starkey v. U.S. Department of Interior*, 238 F. Supp. 2d 1188 (S.D. Cal. 2002).

63 US DOJ, *Guide to the Freedom of Information Act*, 2016, p. 267: 'water rights themselves are an object of commerce … that is bought and sold, (…) information about the quantity available or information that creates the Tribes' negotiating position, supports their claims, or maximizes their position, is all commercial information in function' (citing *Flathead Joint Bd. of Control v. U.S. Dep't of the Interior*, 309 F. Supp. 2d 1217, 1221 (D. Mont. 2004)).

64 Colombian Law 1450 de 2011 'Por la cual se expide el Plan Nacional de Desarrollo, 2010–2014', 16 June 2011.

65 Colombian Constitutional Court, Case C-221/16, Judgment of 4 May 2016, MP Alberto Rojas Ríos.

considered a public possession, could be kept from the public. In the Court's opinion, this situation was inherently contradictory.

Furthermore, the Court opined that withholding this information from the public would prevent effective social control of the environmental performance of public and private entities carrying out mining activities, which 'regularly present problems in striking a [right] balance between land use, the environment and social development'. In a previous decision the Court had asserted as to the instrumentality of information that

> In order to ensure the materialisation of the right to participate in the decisions that may affect the legitimate interests and rights of the inhabitants of the country, State authorities are responsible for supplying timely to the public all the information which is not exempted by a constitutional or legal provision.[66]

In this sense, it is not surprising that the Constitutional Court would have taken into account the purpose of the information or the consequential benefits of disclosure for other constitutional values, in this case, environmental protection.

However, one of the Constitutional Court Justices, who saved her vote in the decision to lift the confidentiality of geological information, cautioned against the generality of the arguments presented. It was her opinion that this approach could lead to a perverse effect: it could imply a prohibition to determine the confidentiality of *any* information involving ethnic minorities or natural resources.

This is an example of the fine line that separates a justifiable exception to public disclosure and an unjustifiable one when the information in question has an inherent economic value, and how environmentally based arguments may tip the balance in favour of disclosure. The Colombian Constitutional Court said in regards to the balancing exercise:

> The confidentiality of public documents in a democratic state cannot be absolute, in so far as the general rule is the principle of publicity of the authorities' activity and the exception is confidentiality; therefore, the legal operator must not only assess that a provision of law permits the confidentiality of the document, but also which constitutional rights, principles and values are affected with the restriction, because in some cases the rights, values and principles that inspire the confidentiality of the information must prevail, and in other cases, those that oppose it. In this context, weighted the interests at stake, the confidentiality of the information may prevail before rights such as the right to information; but will have to subside before others

66 Colombian Constitutional Court, Case C-891/02, Judgment of 22 October 2002, MP Jaime Araújo Rentería.

such as the right of defence and access to justice, which, *prima facie,* are of higher importance in modern democratic societies.[67]

Regarding this type of technical information, it was deemed a rather odd exemption when it was adopted in the US FOIA in 1966,[68] but it is no longer surprising to find similar provisions in modern regulations of highly technical and environmentally impactful activities, such as shale gas; or in the field of new technologies, where high uncertainty is paired with highly valuable commercial information like algorithms, formulae and software. Among the US states, for instance, there is an abysmal difference in the treatment of disclosure of information about the chemical substances used in fracking: in California this information cannot be protected as CBI whilst in North Carolina the disclosure of the same information is considered a criminal offense.[69] The EPA reported in a EIS on the effects of hydraulic fracturing on drinking water resources that the information about the identity of chemicals, frequency of use and properties is necessary to assess how these chemicals move through the environment and interact with the human body, but well operators claimed at least one of the chemicals they use as confidential at more than 70% of wells reported.[70] This is a clear example of how confidentiality claims may interfere with the adequate assessment of environmental and health risks, particularly regarding new technologies.

7.2.6.1. Concluding Remarks

The previous examples show cases in which protectable CBI, trade secrets and IPR overlap with information of high public interest in the framework of public participation in environmental matters. Generally, data included in the definitions of 'environmental information' and 'public information' could be protected from disclosure in order to prevent harm to legitimate economic interests, but this protection can be disproportionate and unwarranted when it stands in the way of protection to other prevailing rights such as public health and safety, prevention of environmental harm, effective public participation in decision-making and the exercise of the general right-to-know of the people.

These examples demonstrate that confidentiality claims routinely interfere with the effective exercise of the right of public access to environmental information and, consequently, to participate effectively in decision making processes. This situation merits a review of the legal provisions supporting

67 Colombian Constitutional Court, Case T-928/04, Judgment of 24 September 2004, MP Jaime Araújo Rentería.

68 Mendel, *Legal Survey*, 2009.

69 Lamdan, *Environmental Information*, 2017.

70 EPA (2016). *Hydraulic Fracturing for Oil and Gas: Impacts from the Hydraulic Fracturing Water Cycle on Drinking Water Resources in the United States.* Retrieved from: https://www.epa.gov/sites/production/files/2016-12/documents/hfdwa_executive_summary.pdf.

public access and their interaction with laws providing protection for CBI and private interests, and particularly how these conflicts are being handled at the regulatory, administrative, and judicial scenarios in order to identify key issues and formulate coherent proposals for improvement.

7.3. Inconsistencies in the Applicable Laws

The general approach to the question of when private entities should disclose environmental information despite adverse effects on confidentiality interests leads to the revision of legislative and administrative instruments across the different jurisdictions: On one side, there are transparency instruments, some of them providing public access to information from the government (the majority), and others providing access to environmental information in particular. On the other side, there are instruments protecting trade secrets and establishing limitations for the dissemination of business confidential information. Somewhere in the conceptual middle lie the exceptions to public disclosure on grounds of business confidentiality and the (less common) exceptions to the protection of trade secrets and intellectual property on grounds of public transparency or environmental protection.

The profound differences in the legal nature of each of these instruments (their scope, aims, motives and methods) and perhaps the fact that their application and study is mostly carried out from diametrically opposed fields of legal research and practice (*e.g.* public v. private law; profit v. non-profit organisations; economic development v. environmental protection; business regulation v. human rights, etc.) makes it remarkably difficult to find authoritative sources on how to reconcile the two main interests at stake in a way that is consistent with the logic underlying both transparency instruments and business confidentiality regulations. Lyndon pointed out to this problem stating that 'in conflicts over secrecy and access the two sides invoke separate legal traditions and neither addresses the concerns of the other'.[71]

Yet, practical confrontations between these different normative regimes are increasingly appearing throughout the full spectrum of legal debate, from local government offices in small towns where an industrial activity may be causing pollution but the public is unable to obtain precise information about the operator's environmental practices; to the international policy-makers discussing the reporting requirements in a new environmental multilateral treaty, not to mention all the judicial, regulatory and administrative authorities in-between.

At the centre of the problem are the laws themselves, providing, with the same binding power, for the defence and protection of the contradictory interests, originating inconsistencies in the legal framework that can hardly be resolved recurring to traditional legal doctrines such as the principle of *lex specialis* or the *lex posterior derogat legi priori.* Heremans suggests a tendency

71 Lyndon, *Trade Secrets and Information*, 2011, p. 455.

of the CJEU to accept sector legislation providing for the confidentiality of certain information as prevailing over the general regime of transparency in the EU (Regulation 1049/2001), applying this principle in a way that a rebuttable presumption of confidentiality is created by the *lex specialis.*[72]

One of the most recent examples of such a conflict is the CJEU case of *Stichting Greenpeace Nederland*, where the Grand Chamber overturned an Opinion of the General Court on the interpretation of the concept of 'emissions into the environment'. Referring to specific information about impurities of the active substance glyphosate among other data, the General Court asserted that 'information with a direct link to emissions into the environment' fell within this concept and, thus, could not be withheld on grounds of business confidentiality in application of Article 6(1) of the Aarhus Regulation (Regulation 1367/2006).[73] In the second instance, the Grand Chamber took a closer look at the laws on the other side of the spectrum: those protecting business confidentiality and professional secrets. It found that such an expansive interpretation would constitute a 'disproportionate interference with the protection of business secrecy ensured by article 339 TFEU'. The Court further asserted that

> If that concept [emissions into the environment] were interpreted as covering such information, it would to a large extent deprive the concept of 'environmental information' as defined in Article 2(1)(d) of Regulation No 1367/2006 of any meaning. Such an interpretation would deprive of any practical effect the possibility, laid down in the first indent of Article 4(2) of Regulation No 1049/2001, for the institutions to refuse to disclose environmental information on the ground, inter alia, that such disclosure would have an adverse effect on the protection of the commercial interests of a particular natural or legal person and would jeopardise the balance which the EU legislature intended to maintain between the objective of transparency and the protection of those interests.[74]

In the same decision, however, the Court interpreted the definition of 'emissions into the environment' as including not only information about actual emissions or emissions from industrial facilities but also about any

72 Heremans, T. (2011). 'Optimal' versus 'Maximal' Public Access to Documents: a Brief Note on EU Case Law. *Egmont Institute*, (2), 1–7. See also Karageorgou, V. (2013). Transparency principle as an evolving principle of EU law: Regulative contours and implications. *Journal of Chemical Information and Modeling, 53*(9), 1689–1699, esp 1698.

73 Regulation (EC) No 1367/2006 of the European Parliament and of the Council on the application of the provisions of the Aarhus Convention on Access to Information, Public Participation in Decision-making and Access to Justice in Environmental Matters to Community institutions and bodies, [2006] O.J. L 264/13.

74 *Stichting Greenpeace Nederland*, para 81.

'foreseeable' emissions under normal and realistic conditions of use of a product. The placing into the market of a product does not lead to the automatic conclusion that the product will be released into the environment, this will ultimately depend, *inter alia,* on the quantity of the product to be employed by users and the exact composition of the marketed product.[75] In this context, foreseeable emissions under normal conditions of use of a product fall within the definition of 'emissions into the environment' for the purposes of the presumption of disclosure.

In this case, the first judgment of the General Court, adopted on 8 October 2013, (Case C-545/11) received considerable attention from the industry and legal practitioners in the field of substance regulation, plant protection law and IPR,[76] who claimed that the interpretation of the General Court about 'emissions into the environment' as including any information directly related with the emissions constituted an excessive limitation to the protection of commercial and industrial secrets in this context.[77] The Grand Chamber partially agreed, but it still dismissed specific legislation in the field of plant protection law establishing the confidentiality of the documents related to tests submitted to the regulator in the process for approval to enter the market (specifically, Regulation 1107/2009), asserting that these rules lacked the power to rebut the irrebuttable presumption established in Article 6(1) of Regulation No 1367/2006, according to which an overriding public interest in disclosure will be deemed to exist whenever the information relates to emissions into the environment. This means that there is no need to weigh the interest of disclosure against any others, even if the information contains commercial or industrial secrets; information about emissions into the environment must always be disclosed.[78] This presumption applies, under Regulation No 1367/2006, to information protected by the exceptions established in Article 4(2), first and third indents of Regulation No 1049/2001:

> –commercial interests of a natural or legal person, including intellectual property,
>
> (…)
>
> –the purpose of inspections, investigations and audits.

75 Buonsante & Friel, *Emissions into the Environment*, 2017.

76 The Statement of Support submitted by CropLife America, The National Association of Manufacturers of the United States of America and American Chemistry Council in support of the Commission stated: '… this case has a dramatic impact on the ability of US companies to continue marketing their products in the EU; in particular, products that are IP-intensive and involve the transmission of CBI to public authorities in order to get marketing authorization'. CropLife America, *Amicus Brief.*

77 Von Holleben, *Judgment of the General Court*, 2013.

78 Von Holleben, *Judgment of the General Court*, 2013.

According to this interpretation, EU institutions and bodies cannot withhold information relating to emissions into the environment on grounds of protection of commercial or industrial secrets, intellectual property rights, or for the protection of the confidentiality of inspections and audits.[79]

Stichting Greenpeace Nederland presented the Court with the first conflict between access to environmental information and commercial secrets in the field of substance regulation.[80] Intellectual property rights and commercial secrets are specifically protected under EU substance law legislation in the framework of certain processes such as the approval of new products to enter the market. Regulation (EC) No 1107/2009 states in Article 63 (2):

> Disclosure of the following information shall normally be deemed to undermine the protection of the commercial interests or of privacy and the integrity of the individuals concerned:
> (a) the method of manufacture;
> (b) the specification of impurity of the active substance except for the impurities that are considered to be toxicologically, ecotoxicologically or environmentally relevant;
> (c) results of production batches of the active substance including impurities;
> (d) methods of analysis for impurities in the active substance as manufactured except for methods for impurities that are considered to be toxicologically, ecotoxicologically or environmentally relevant;
> (e) links between a producer or importer and the applicant or the authorisation holder;
> (f) information on the complete composition of a plant protection product;
> (g) names and addresses of persons involved in testing on vertebrate animals.

In *Stichting Greenpeace Nederland,* the applicants requested the disclosure of information about a) identity and quantity of all the impurities in the active substance notified by each operator; b) the impurities present in the various batches and the minimum, median and maximum quantities of each of those impurities; and c) the composition of the plant protection products developed by the operators (on the basis of the active substance). All of this information falls into one of the categories in Article 63(2) of Regulation No 1107/2009, which means that they are deemed to affect the commercial interests of the holders; and all of the information was deemed to relate 'in a sufficiently direct manner' to emissions into the environment by the General Court, thus applying the presumption in Article 6(1) of Regulation No 1367/2006 to order

79 Information about investigations can still be kept from disclosure, in particular those concerning possible infringements of community law (Regulation No. 1367/2006, Article 6 (1)).

80 Von Holleben, *Judgment of the General Court*, 2013.

its disclosure without any further consideration (*e.g.,* without weighing of the conflicting interests or identifying an overriding public interest in disclosure in the specific case).

Under the General Court's viewpoint, there is clearly a clash between the provisions of Regulation No 1107/2009 because it effectively provides a legal presumption of confidentiality based on the assumption that the release of this information will almost certainly harm the commercial interests of the submitter, and Article 6(1) of the Aarhus Regulation providing a diametrically opposed presumption of public interest (*ergo* of public disclosure) over the same information.

In this case, it is the opinion of this author that the Court of first instance did not take due account of the laws protecting the commercial interests in confidentiality, of the dispositions in Regulation No 1107/2009 read in accordance with the TRIPS Agreement (Articles 39(2) and 39(3) providing for the confidentiality over trade secrets and specifically test information submitted for approval or a new product), the EU Charter of Fundamental Rights (Articles 16 and 17 about the freedom to conduct a business and the right to private property) and the TFEU (Article 339 about the protection of professional secrecy).

The Grand Chamber, in the second instance, corrected the overbroad interpretation of the concept of 'emissions into the environment' by clarifying that it does not include information 'related, even directly, with emissions into the environment',[81] but also reaffirmed that the concept of 'emissions into the environment' could not be applied restrictively,[82] as a consequence of the principle of maximum disclosure, and it therefore extends to foreseeable emissions in normal conditions of use of a product or substance.

The final decision in the case *Stichting Greenpeace Nederland* fell to the General Court (Fourth Chamber), which ultimately decided to deny access to the information in question because it was submitted in the framework of the proceedings for approval of the active substance glyphosate by the European Commission, and there was an additional procedure for the approval of the products containing the active substance which was required for the placement of the product in the market in each of the Member States. In the General Court's opinion, the information collected about the active substance in the process of approval by the Commission had at most a direct link to emissions into the environment, because the active substance still needed to be put into a product, combined with other substances and reprocessed, and only then would it be released into the environment.[83] Notably,

81 *Stichting Greenpeace Nederland*, para 54.

82 The European Commission had argued that derogations from the principle of confidentiality provided to certain information by Regulation No. 1107/09, Article 63(2), had to be interpreted restrictively. Several authors coincide with this argument (see Von Holleben, *Judgment of the General Court*, 2013 and Garçon, *Information about Agrochemicals*, 2012).

83 CJEU (General Court), Case 545/11 RENV *Stichting Greenpeace Nederland and PAN Europe v. European Commission*, 21 November 2018.

this is a radically different application of the precedent established by the Grand Chamber in its judgment of 23 November 2016 on that same case (Case C-673/13) to the one adopted by the General Court (Eighth Chamber) in cases T-716/14 *Hautala*[84] and T-329/17 *Tweedale v EFSA*,[85] in both of which the General Court decided that two toxicity studies that were used to determine the 'acceptable daily intake' of the active substance glyphosate held by the European Food Safety Authority (EFSA) had to be disclosed because they referred to *actual* emissions into the environment, thus, overruling the application of any confidentiality exceptions. Furthermore, the General Court affirmed that

> [I]nformation which relates to emissions into the environment for the purposes of Article 6(1) of Regulation No. 1367/2006 is not limited to information which makes it possible to assess the emissions as such, but also covers information relating to the effects of those emissions.[86]

The precedent of *Tweedale v EFSA* and *Hautala* now effectively extends the definition of 'emissions into the environment' for the purposes of the presumption of public interest to information about the *effects* of emissions into the environment. Interestingly, the General Court calls again on the need to provide enough information to the public to enable it to participate effectively in decision-making as the justification for providing access to this type of information regardless of the possible harm to the legitimate economic interests in confidentiality.[87]

These cases provide an example of the lack of agreement, even within the same Court, about the way these laws should be interpreted. The deficiencies come from the legal system, establishing contradictory presumptions over the same information.

The laws provide some tools for their interpretation aimed at preventing this sort of conflicts, but the inconsistence largely remains. Article 63(b) of Regulation No 1107/2009, for example, exempts from the 'presumption of confidentiality' specifications about impurities in a chemical product or their analysis methods when such information is toxicologically, eco-toxicologically or environmentally relevant. The same Regulation provides for the proactive disclosure of this information to the public (Article 63(2), Article 10) yet the language is different from that of the Aarhus Regulation and the Aarhus Convention: 'emissions into the environment' is substantially different than 'toxicologically, eco-toxicologically or environmentally relevant' information. In such a highly regulated field as substance law, discrepancy in terms may seriously impair efforts towards a unified interpretation in the scope of these provisions.

84 CJEU, Case T-329/17, *Hautala v. EFSA*, Judgment of 7 March 2019.
85 CJEU, Case T-716/14, *Anthony C. Tweedale v European Food Safety Authority (EFSA)*, Judgment of 7 March 2019.
86 *Hautala*, para 99.
87 *Hautala*, para 98.

7.4. The Current Toolbox for Solving Conflicts Between Access to Environmental Information and the Protection of CBI

Two sections of this book touched upon the rules to apply the regime of exceptions to disclosure in a way that preserves the main purpose of transparency legislation (maximum public disclosure) and still provides enough protection to conflicting interests. The first was in the comparative part of the study, when examining the nature and scope of the right of access to information in the different jurisdictions, and the second was in the analysis of the tools for the protection of CBI and trade secrets, noting how the specific interests in commercial and industrial confidentiality are balanced out in practice against provisions for public access to information. This section builds upon the previous concepts to produce a critical assessment of the current toolbox for resolving conflicts between private commercial interests and public access to environmental information.

Integrating the concepts reviewed throughout the study, the current toolbox for solving conflicts at most judicial and conceptual levels consist of the following criteria.

7.4.1. The Principle of Maximum Disclosure

In the framework of FOI laws and environmental transparency instruments, the principle of maximum disclosure establishes the presumption that all of the information and documents held by public authorities are, in principle, of a public nature and should be publicly accessible.[88] Thus, the general rule is access, and only in very specific and narrowly defined situations may the information be withheld from the public for the protection of other public or private interests.[89]

If the principle of maximum disclosure applies to environmental information in the framework of most regulatory instruments on this subject, it provides a valuable starting point for the analysis of whether or not to disclose information which is also CBI on a case-by-case basis, and this approach is also consistent with the ultimate goal of providing for effective public participation in environmental matters. The CJEU applied the principle of maximum disclosure in deciding the appeal raised by the Commission in *Stichting Greenpeace Nederland,* where the Court rejected a restrictive interpretation of the concept of 'emissions into the environment' in Article 6(1) of Regulation

88 See *i.a.* Organisation of American States - Inter-American Juridical Committee, Principles on the Right of Access to Information, CJI/RES.147 (LXXIII-O/08). Retrieved from http://www.oas.org/en/sla/dil/docs/CJI-RES_147_LXXIII-O-08_eng.pdf; Escazú Agreement, Articles 3 and 5.

89 See US Freedom of Information Act, Section 552(a)(3)(A): 'each agency … shall make [documents and other records] promptly available to any person', subject only to carefully limited exemptions listed in Section 552(b). The Aarhus Convention, Article 4, provides that exceptions 'shall be interpreted in a restrictive way'.

No 1367/2006 under the argument that the public should have the widest possible access to information held by institutions and bodies of the European Union.

As a guiding principle to the application of transparency provisions, maximum disclosure does not present significant conceptual issues. It is the starting point for the analysis of the conflicting interests, providing the background against which the merits of confidentiality exceptions must be assessed.

The practical application of this principle implies that:

- Exceptions to disclosure shall be interpreted in a restrictive manner.
- The burden of proof lies with the person/authority advocating for the application of confidentiality exceptions.
- In consonance with the above, exceptions to the exceptions (*e.g.* information about emissions into the environment) cannot be interpreted restrictively.

Notably, the principle of maximum disclosure does not apply to the right of access to information from private entities, where it exists. In Colombia, the general rule is the proprietary character of private information, and the right of public access to information is given through the right of petition law as an exception to the general rule, for the protection of the petitioner's fundamental rights.

However, in the framework of public-private associations or contracts, there is a strong case to make the principle of maximum disclosure operative over the information produced, considering the involvement of the government and the need for public transparency, even when the documents contain some commercially sensitive information from the private party.[90]

7.4.2. The 'Harm Test'

The theory behind the 'harm test' is that information covered by an exception should only be withheld when there is evidence that disclosure would actually cause harm to the interest protected by the exception. The characteristics of the harm and its proof are subject to different interpretations.

For the 'harm test' to apply, it must firstly be stipulated in the law providing for the exceptions to the general rule of transparency, or at least in authoritative interpretations by the Courts. In the Aarhus Convention, there is a built-in harm test in Article 4(4), stating: 'A request for environmental information may be refused if the disclosure would **adversely affect**…' (emphasis added). This means that information should not be withheld simply because it falls into one of the exceptions, but, as derogations to the general right of access, the exceptions must only apply when necessary to prevent unjustifiable harm to another party's protected interests.

90 Rosenblum, P., & Maples, S. (2009). *Contracts confidential: ending secret deals in the extractive industries.* Revenue Watch Institute.

The Aarhus Implementation Guide ascribes to one of the higher standards for the application of exceptions: the showing of actual harm from the release of information rather than the mere possibility thereof, as well as a demonstration that other compensatory mechanisms cannot remedy the harm.[91] Consequently, a certain level of harm is admissible in consideration to the public interest in disclosure. The Aarhus Convention Compliance Committee asserted as much in its findings about compliance by the EU:

> The Committee wishes to point out that this exemption may not be read as meaning that public authorities are only required to release environmental information where no harm to the interests concerned is identified. Such a broad interpretation of the exemption would not be in compliance with Article 4, paragraph 4, of the Convention which requires interpreting exemptions in a restrictive way, taking into account the public interest served by disclosure. Thus, in situations where there is a significant public interest in disclosure of certain environmental information and a relatively small amount of harm to the interests involved, the Convention would require disclosure.[92]

A logical implication of this idea is that for disclosures of higher public interest, a more rigorous harm standard should apply, *i.e. serious actual* harm to the interest protected by the exception.

Frequently, Courts would provide additional guidance to the application of the 'harm test' according to the legal text. In the EU, the 'harm standard' for the application of the exceptions under Regulation 1049/2001 was defined by the CJEU in the *Turco* case as 'reasonable, foreseeable, specific and effective',[93] and in the case of harm due to disclosure of CBI, it must affect the submitters' position *vis-à-vis* competitors, *i.e.* provide an unfair competitive advantage.

In Colombia, the Transparency Law establishes that exceptions to access will only be valid to prevent 'present, probable and specific harm to the protected interest, which exceeds the public's interest in accessing the information'.[94] The burden of proof in these cases belongs to the authority holding the information, which means that any refusal must refer explicitly to the legal exception that applies, the legal provisions establishing the confidentiality or protection of the specific information requested, the reasons

91 UNECE, *Aarhus Implementation Guide*, 2014; Shabalala, *Hidden Landmine*, 2017.

92 Case ACCC/C/2007/21 (European Community), Addendum: Findings with Regard to Communication ACCC/C/2007/21 Concerning the Compliance by European Community, 30(c), U.N. Doc. ECE/MP.PP/C.1/2009/2/Add.1 (8 February 2011).

93 CJEU Joined Cases C-39 & 52/05 P, *Sweden and Turco v. Council*, Judgment of 1 July 2008.

94 Colombian Transparency Law, Article 28.

that justify the withholding of the information, and the evidence that the information must be kept confidential because of the risk of a real, probable and specific harm to the protected interest, which exceeds the public interest in disclosure.[95]

In interpreting this standard, the Constitutional Court referred to the application of exceptions in the framework of the Transparency Law, stating:

> In order to validly restrict access to public information for the protection of public interests, not only is it necessary that access to that information has a **real, probable and specific possibility to harm those interests, but also that this harm is 'significant'**.[96] (emphasis added)

Unfortunately, there are no additional guidelines on how to determine if the harm is 'significant', thus, an ordinary interpretation of the word would have to suffice when applying this judicial rule.

The exemptions in the US FOIA are conceived differently. Only some of them have built-in harm tests[97] there is no general rule in the law requiring an actual harm to the protected interests, and only in 2016 an official memorandum was adopted for the application of a 'foreseeable harm test' to FOIA refusals.[98] Applying the harm standard to the trade secrets and CBI exemption under FOIA, the US judicial precedent used to be that CBI could only be considered 'confidential', and therefore qualify for protection if disclosure of the information would cause 'substantial harm to the competitive position of the person from whom the information was obtained (…) because of the affirmative use of proprietary information by competitors'.[99] The 'substantive competitive harm' test was satisfied by showing that the submitter faced 'actual competition' and a 'likelihood of substantial competitive injury' from its disclosure.[100]

This harm test however was recently debunked as the official precedent by the Supreme Court in the case of *Food Marketing Institute v Argus Leader Media*,[101] decided on June 2019. In this case, *Argus Leader Media* made a FOIA request to the US Department of Agriculture (USDA) seeking the names and addresses of all retail stores participating in the national food-stamp program (SNAP) and each store's annual SNAP redemption data from fiscal years 2005 to 2010. The USDA refused to disclose this information under FOIA's Exemption 4 (covering 'trade secrets and commercial or

95 Colombian Transparency Law, Article 29.
96 Colombian Constitutional Court, Case C-274/13, Judgment of 9 May 2013, MP Maria Victoria Calle Correa.
97 Mendel, *Legal Survey*, 2009.
98 FOIA Improvement Act of 2016, Public Law No. 114–185 (2016).
99 *National Parks & Conservation Ass'n v Morton*, 498 F.2d 765 (D.C. Cir. 1974).
100 *Gulf & W. Indus. v U.S.*, 615 F.2d 527, 530 (D.C. Cir. 1979).
101 *Food Marketing Institute v Argus Leader Media*, 2019 WL 2570624 (24 June 2019).

financial information obtained from a person and privileged or confidential'). *Argus Leader* then sued the USDA and the District Court employed the 'substantive competitive harm' test finding that the disclosure of the information, even if found to be detrimental for the financial interests of the retailers, could not be said to cause substantive competitive harm, and therefore ordering the disclosure thereof. The 8th Circuit Court of D.C. affirmed the first ruling. Before the Supreme Court, *Food Marketing Institute*, intervening as an interested party in the appeal, requested the abolishment of the 'substantial competitive harm test' to determine that CBI is 'confidential' for the purposes of Exemption 4 of the FOIA. The Supreme Court agreed with the applicant's arguments, rejecting the 'competitive harm' test as the decisive criterion to determine when financial or commercial information can be considered confidential. Instead, the Court held that where commercial or financial information is both customarily and actually treated as private by its owner, the information is 'confidential' within the meaning of Exemption 4. Even more so if the information is submitted to government agencies under an expectation of privacy, as in this case. The Court deemed it unnecessary to define if this last condition was also a requirement for determining confidentiality because in the case at hand the information clearly complied with both parameters.

The decision may not even be surprising. One current Justice of the US Supreme Court had expressed before that 'the substantive competitive harm test is an amorphous and convoluted test that, in practice, has been applied inconsistently, relies on judicial speculation, and fails to offer sufficient clarity and consistency for litigants and the Court'.[102] In the *Argus Leader Media* case, the Supreme Court referred to the standard of the harm test introduced in *National Parks* as the product of 'casual disregard of the rules of statutory interpretation' by the Courts that followed this D.C. Circuit decision in the beginning. In the Supreme Court's view, the word 'confidential' in Exemption 4 must be given the ordinary dictionary meaning, because that was most probably the intent of Congress at the time of FOIA's adoption, therefore, commercial or financial information is confidential if the person supplying it customarily keeps it private. Additional requirements for 'substantial competitive harm' to consider commercial information as confidential are thus not supported by the statute's provisions.

The Supreme Court's decision in *Argus Leader Media* changes in a significant way the scope of application of FOIA' Exemption 4, and may even affect the protection of trade secrets under federal and state misappropriation statutes which require an equivalent 'substantive competitive harm' test to

102 *New Hampshire Right to Life v. Dep't of Health & Human Servs.*, 136 S.Ct. 383, 384–85 (2015) (Thomas, J., dissenting), quoted in Weil. (2019). *FMI v. Argus Media Leader: Re-examining What Constitutes Protectable 'Confidential' and 'Trade Secret' Information.* Retrieved from https://www.weil.com/articles/fmi-v-argus-media-leader.

determine when information qualifies as a trade secret.[103] Bell brings up other possible implications of this decision: (i) it may reduce fiscal transparency, as it could lead to the application of Exemption 4 to information about government's expenditures reported by third parties; (ii) it could interfere with the application of Exemptions 6 and 7 dealing with personal privacy by introducing an alternative to protect natural persons' financial information under Exemption 4 with a lower standard that pre-empts the balancing approach applied in these cases so far; (iii) it may affect future applications of the FOIA's Improvement Act (2016) which introduced the 'foreseeable harm' standard as a general rule to allow discretionary disclosure of information otherwise falling within one of the exemption's scope when no harm to the protected interest could be envisaged from disclosure, which thus far did not apply to information protected under Exemption 4 because its disclosure was explicitly prohibited in the Trade Secrets Act. To the extent that the scope of Exemption 4 is now broader than the provision in the Trade Secrets Act, there could be room for discretionary disclosure of CBI by the agencies, but then again a definition and guidelines of the required 'foreseeable harm' to the protected interest would have to be adopted in lieu of the *National Parks* test; (iv) the decision could change the assumption that exemptions to FOIA are to be construed narrowly. This argument was brought forward by *Argus Leader* but the Court dismissed it arguing that FOIA's exemptions should be 'fairly construed' and that the same weight given to the Act's general transparency goals should be given to the policy considerations underlying the exemptions and, finally, (iv) there could be a risk that information important for the safety of consumers and welfare of employees would be shielded from disclosure by allegations of confidentiality from the company, which finds disclosure detrimental to its interests, with no room to argue the potential harm of withholding such information, insofar as the question of potential harm is 'irrelevant to the question of whether the company keeps the information closely held (…) or whether the government obtained the information under a promise of confidentiality'.[104]

Resuming the general analysis of the 'harm tests', it is interesting to note that for information to qualify for protection as a trade secret under most domestic laws, it must already comply with the requisite that its disclosure would harm the 'competitive position' of the holder.[105] To the extent that the

103 Wail, *FMI v. Argus Media Leader*, 2019.

104 Bell, B. (2019). *Food Marketing Institute: A Preliminary Assessment (Part II)*. Retrieved from https://yalejreg.com/nc/food-marketing-institute-a-preliminary-assessment-part-ii/#_ftnref10.

105 Early jurisprudence of the CJEU supported a similar interpretation of trade secrets and CBI. In Case T 198/03 *Bank Austria Creditanstalt AG v Commission* [2004] C35/16, the General Court established the following criteria for the definition of confidential information: (a) that the information should be known only to a limited number of persons; (b) that disclosure of the information must be liable to cause serious harm to the person who has provided that information or

standard of harm to the competitive position in trade secret law is the same or higher than an 'objective' standard of harm for the application of the CBI exception, the application of the harm test under the FOI law will be unnecessary once information has been determined to be a trade secret. Perhaps this explains the absence of a build-in harm test for the application of the trade secrets exemption under the US FOIA and also for the fact that agencies are forbidden to exercise their discretionary powers to release information that is protected under the TSA. The qualification of information as trade secrets under the US regime, entails a pre-emptive assessment of the actual harm to the commercial interests of the owner of the trade secrets. Notably, this would be different if the harm to the protected interest is to be relatively measured against the harm that refusal would cause to the public's interest in disclosure. In this case, even when certain information has been determined to be a trade secret because its disclosure would harm the competitive position of the submitter, the harm test must be conducted weighing this impact against the harm to the public interest in transparency in the so-called 'balancing act'.

However, because this type of information is *secret* by definition, there are serious limitations to openly assessing the actual harm that its disclosure would cause to the protected commercial interests (especially by the party asking for the information in the first place).[106]

Notably, the existence of a built-in harm test in the definition of CBI and trade secrets considerably limits the protection afforded to this kind of information in certain legal regimes, such as the US TSA. If a 'harm test' or a 'balancing act' against the interests protected by disclosure is required on a case-by-case basis to determine if certain information constitutes CBI, the protection apparently provided in legislative texts can become meaningless.[107]

On the other hand, the application of 'harm tests' in cases of access to information directly from private entities may lead to a dead-end situation where the private entity asserts its confidentiality claim over the information requested, explicitly or implicitly affirming that disclosure of the information

to third parties; and (c) that the interests liable to be harmed by disclosure must objectively be worthy of protection. The Court added referring to the third criterion: 'The assessment as to the confidentiality of a piece of information thus requires the legitimate interests opposing disclosure of the information to be weighed against the public interest that the activities of the Community institutions take place as openly as possible', effectively establishing a 'harm test' and a 'balancing act' for the very definition of any information as CBI. The General Court applied this test again in Case T-474/04 *Pergan Hilfsstoffe v Commission*, Judgment of 12 October 2007.

106 See Wagner, W. E. (2004). Commons ignorance: the failure of environmental law to produce needed information on health and the environment. *Duke Law Journal, 53*(6), 1619–1745.

107 Carlton, R., Lawrence, J., & Mcelwee, M. (2008). Confidentiality and Disclosure in European Commission Antitrust Proceedings – The Case for Clarity. *European Competition Journal, 4*, 401.

would cause substantial harm to its commercial interests, and the applicant would have no basis to argue on the contrary, precisely because they do not have access to the information that would enable them to analyse the actual harm to the protected interests of the private person. In these cases, the existence of a presumptive actual harm to the competitive position of the entity should not be the ultimate criterion, the nature of the information and the context in which it is being requested could justify at least some level of harm in certain cases.

Generally, the standards of the 'harm test' in the different jurisdictions depend for their correct application on auxiliary criteria developed by courts and legal operators that still leave significant room for subjectivity. The US case is a good example, considering also that the 'substantial competitive harm' test that has been used in the last 40 years was the product of a Court's interpretation in the first place.

In conclusion, the 'harm test' is an auxiliary tool for the application of exceptions whose objective is the preservation of the purposes of transparency legislation and the effectiveness of the exceptions only in cases where the protection of the private interests actually warrant a derogation of the general principle of maximum disclosure. Some of the shortcomings of this mechanism are: (i) by design, it must be applied on a case-by-case basis, which can become burdensome for administrative and judicial authorities and give rise to inconsistencies, unequal treatment and legal uncertainty; (ii) in most jurisdictions, there are few to none general guidelines to measure the harm in a consistent, predictable and verifiable way; (iii) the application of the 'harm test' becomes more challenging when the information sought is protected under a CBI exception, because there could be power asymmetries between the applicant and the holder of the information which prevent a meaningful exercise of the right to administrative and judicial review by the applicant, and (iv) the application of a 'harm test' by a private authority regarding its own CBI is unlikely to ever result in a decision to disclose information.

Notably, the estimation of the harm to be suffered by the protected interest in case of disclosure is also crucial for the balancing act between the public interest served by disclosure and the interest protected by the exception, which translates the potential shortcomings of the 'harm test' to the application of the 'balancing act'.

Public authorities are faced with difficult dilemmas when granting access to information could potentially affect other private and public interests, such as public safety, personal privacy and the protection of trade secrets. Their first impulse may be to withhold the information because the potential harm to the protected interests could appear to be more imminent than an abstract and distant harm to transparency and accountability.[108] This is where contextualising the request for information could be helpful. Maximum access must be the default response to requests of information when no conflict with

108 Lyndon, *Trade Secrets and Information,* 2011.

another interest can be envisaged, and the applicant should not be required to disclose any motives or to proof a specific interest, but when the information could be potentially sensitive, the applicant could be required to explain the context in which the information is sought, because only in this way is the public authority properly equipped to assess the harm to both sets of interests and perform a meaningful balancing exercise.

Information about animal welfare, for instance, may fall into the definition of 'environmental information' and be held by a public authority. Disclosure of certain data, however, like the names of the public inspectors auditing facilities where animal testing is conducted or the lay-out of the buildings could conflict with the rights to private privacy, public safety and the protection of trade secrets. In the US, the Animal Welfare Act explicitly excludes from disclosure any information of a proprietary nature (CBI or trade secrets),[109] but most regimes do not offer such specific rules for this kind of information. Knowledge about the context of the request in this case would be extremely helpful for the authorities making the decision about whether to disclose the sensitive information and may even enable additional or alternative solutions such as disclosing only the relevant information for the interest of the petitioner that solves their particular situation or establishing additional safeguards such as confidentiality agreements and restricting further use and dissemination of the disclosed information.

7.4.3. Public Interest Overrides

A 'public interest override' is the generic name for the cases in which transparency laws (or other laws) provide that disclosure will prevail even if other public or private interests may be significantly affected, for example the case of information about emissions into the environment in the Aarhus Convention against the interest in business confidentiality and the protection of trade secrets, information about crimes against humanity in the Colombian Transparency Law, and, notably, Article 6(1) of Regulation No. 1367/2006 establishing an irrebuttable presumption of public interest over information relating to emissions into the environment held by the EU institutions and bodies.[110]

109 Levine, D. S. (2011). The Impact of Trade Secrecy on Public Transparency. In R. Dreyfuss & K. J. Strandburg (Eds.), *The Law and Theory of Trade Secrecy: A Handbook of Contemporary Research*. Edward Elgar Publishing, pp. 406–442, p. 414.

110 Other examples are the US TSCA, 15 U.S.C. § 2613(b) (2000) (stating types of data of which disclosure is not prohibited); CWA, 33 U.S.C. § 1318(b) (exempting all information on 'effluent data,' standards, or limitations from protection as trade secrets); Clean Air Act [CAA], 42 U.S.C, 7401 et seq. (1970) (same for 'emission data'); CERCLA, 42 U.S.C. 42 U.S.C. § 7414(c) (2000) § 9604(e)(7)(F) (2000) (identifying 'information with respect to any hazardous substance' not entitled to protection).

Public interest overrides that are clearly defined in the law provide a somewhat certain safeguarding mechanism for the preservation of the transparency objectives of the law. In the EU case, for instance, the clear and consistent language found in the Aarhus Convention and the EU secondary legislation regarding information about emissions into the environment (even if the scope of the concept is being disputed) ensures that private companies who submit CBI to the EU institutions and bodies do not hold any nondisclosure expectations over information generally recognised as such.[111]

Like the above, FOI laws may provide for a general clause of 'public interest override'. This is found in Article 4(4) of the Aarhus Convention in relation to the application of the exceptions to access to environmental information, stating that grounds for refusal shall be interpreted in a restrictive way, 'taking into account the public interest served by disclosure'. A similar provision is found in Article 4(3) of Regulation (EC) No 1049/2001.

In Colombia, Article 21 of the Transparency Law provides that 'no authority will be allowed to refuse disclosure of a document, unless the harm caused to the protected interest is higher than the public interest in access to the information'. Under the US FOIA, there is no obligation to consider the public interest when applying the exemptions to disclosure, but the changes introduced by the 2016 amendments may play an equivalent function by establishing the application of a presumption of openness and the need to carry out a 'foreseeable harm test' before refusing access based on one of the law's exemptions. Furthermore, authors and courts have suggested that the process of drafting the law was the balancing exercise itself, where congress considered the public interest in disclosure against the interests protected with the exemptions, therefore dismissing the possibility to undertake a new balancing act for the assessment of the public interest on a case-by-case basis.[112]

But what does public interest mean in this context? The concept may have, to some degree, a political content, as the 'general interest' of society may shift according to government's priorities. Interpreting the application of this concept by the courts, it could be stated that the public interest represents what is considered to be the best option for the majority of people in a

111 Shabalala, *Hidden Landmine,* 2017.

112 Resources for the Future (2001). *Public Access to Environmental Information and Data: Practice Examples and Lessons from the United States, the European Union, and Central and Eastern Europe*, Washington D.C.: Resources for the Future; US DOJ, *Guide to the Freedom of Information Act*, 2016, citing *Public Citizen Health Research Group v. FDA:* 'the D.C. Circuit squarely rejected "a consequentialist approach to the public interest in disclosure" as "inconsistent with the 'balance of private and public interests' that Congress struck in Exemption 4.' The court went on to state that 'that balance is accurately reflected in the test of confidentiality' established by National Parks and that a requester cannot 'bolster the case for disclosure by claiming an additional public benefit in release (…) In other words, the public interest side of the balance is not a function of the identity of the requester, (…) or of any potential negative consequences disclosure may have for the public, (…) nor likewise of any collateral benefits of disclosure.'

specific society, as opposed to the particular benefit of a few or of an individual person.[113] Many times, the defence of the public interest will coincide with the aims of the government, to the extent that a major part of the government's role is to protect citizens and to ensure a viable environment for the exercise of their liberties, but this will not necessarily be always the case. In the context of transparency laws, the public interest may be at odds with the government's interest. After all, transparency is a tool for public accountability, and some public servants and public institutions may prefer to keep their actions out of public scrutiny. Furthermore, confidentiality of the information might protect the public interest better than disclosure in certain cases, such as the grounds in Article 4(1) of Regulation No.1049/2001. Even business confidentiality is ultimately linked with a public value: fair competitive practices and the protection of innovation initiatives by industries.

The application of the general clause of 'public interest override' found in many FOI laws should redefine what 'public interest' stands for in the context of a conflict between confidentiality and public disclosure. This concept goes beyond the general interest in transparency, which is already embodied in the FOI law and provides for the opportunity to ask for information in the first place. The public interest override refers to the existence of a special circumstance in which the good of the majority should be given prevalence despite the harm that this may cause to another protected right. In the environmental field, public interest references to justify broader access to information legislation are abundant. Information about hazardous substances, public health and safety, releases and emissions into the environment, toxicological characteristics of a substance, environmental impact assessments, risk assessments, public expenditure in environmental issues and geological resources have all been found at some point to be of high public interest. Besides considerations regarding the subject-matter of the information, disclosure may be considered of overriding public interest by virtue of the circumstances surrounding the petition of the information, *e.g.* when there has been an industrial accident and the community may be exposed to an imminent threat.[114]

The problem with this concept, similarly to the other criteria already mentioned, is that the appreciation of the public interest occurs on an *ad hoc* basis, after a conflict has emerged, making the outcome difficult to predict

113 Freiberg, A. (1997). Commercial Confidentiality, Criminal Justice and the Public Interest. *Current Issues in Criminal Justice, 9*(2), 125, p. 146, citing the Supreme Court of the Australian State of Victoria: 'The public interest is a term embracing matters, among others, of standards of human conduct and of the functioning of government and government instrumentalities tacitly accepted and acknowledged to be for the good order of society and for the well being of its members. The interest is therefore the interest of the public as distinct from the interest of an individual or individuals'.

114 Kravchenko, S. (2009). Is Access to Environmental Information a Fundamental Human Right? *Oregon Review of International Law, 11*, 227–266.

and seriously interfering with the expectations of confidentiality of the submitters of the information.

The drafters of FOI laws including a general 'public interest override' have chosen to safeguard public access to information at the expense of legal certainty, internal consistency of the legal system and recognised rights of confidentiality and protection of sensitive information.

Combining the 'public interest override' and the 'harm test', we now have the elements to carry out a balancing exercise in which the public interest in disclosure is weighed against the possible harm to a legitimate interest covered by one of the exceptions. If the public interest is higher than the perceived harm, information shall be disclosed despite the adverse effects to the conflicting interest.

7.4.4. The 'Balancing Act'

Every time that a FOI law provides for a public interest clause, especially in the presence of a 'harm standard' for the application of the exceptions, there is an explicit or implicit reference to a 'balancing act'. This is the process of weighing the public interest served by disclosure against the interest protected by an exception.

The Aarhus Convention Compliance Committee (ACCC) advised in its findings about compliance by the European Community that 'in situations where there is a significant public interest in disclosure of certain environmental information and a relatively small amount of harm to the interests involved, the Convention would require disclosure'.[115] The ACCC refers to this opinion as the basis for 'the balancing test that authorities must go through to weigh the public interest served by disclosure against an interest protected under one of the exceptions in subparagraphs (a) to (h)'.[116] In practice, the balancing act mandates that an analysis be made to effectively determine if the possible harm to the particular interest protected by the exception justifies the interference with the general interest served by disclosure.

From the viewpoint of business confidentiality, this means that it is not enough for the information to be considered CBI if substantial harm to the private interest cannot be foreseen because of disclosure, since refusal will always be deemed to affect the public interest. As mentioned before, not just any harm should trigger the application of the exceptions, but an actual, probable, and significant harm to the interest protected by the exception.

The CBI exception protects the legitimate economic interest of a company to keep its competitive advantage, helps to prevent unfair competition practices and, in a more general level, acts as an incentive of innovation and for

115 ACCC/C/2007/21 (European Community), Add. 1.
116 UNECE, *Aarhus Implementation Guide*, 2014, p. 91.

the private investment in research and development,[117] which has been interpreted in the past to be an aim of society in general and thus embodies certain aspects of the public interest on its own.[118] Access to information, on the other hand, represents society's interest in transparency, in the accountability of the administrative authority exercised by the state's agencies vested with the powers derived from the people through democratic participation, and ultimately the protection of the core collective values enshrined in the constitutions and international treaties.

A sensible application of the balancing test would consider these interests, but not in the same way in all the cases. It is not quite the same to assess the different interests at stake when drafting a law, since the main purpose in this case is to uphold as best as possible the integrity of the legal system whilst materialising policy objectives considered to be valuable. The analysis at this level remains theoretical and abstract, and the inherent limitations of legislative reform to foresee all possible scenarios is likely to result in general concepts that would need to be reinterpreted on application to concrete cases.

The balancing act at the application by administrative or judicial authorities, on the other hand, needs to assess the interests at stake within a predetermined factual and legal context. The aim, in these cases, is to produce material justice for the parties involved, whilst upholding the laws and safeguarding the principles that inspire them.

The balancing act in the framework of access to environmental information comes with its own special conditions. The argument can be made that environmental information is always of public interest, insofar as the environment can be considered a public good. This reasoning is always at the core of environmental transparency legislation, which, nonetheless, establishes

117 Some authors are cautious to endorse the protection of trade secrets as a positive driver for innovation due to the secrecy required by trade law, which is at odds with the divulgation of scientific discoveries for peer review and the collective construction of knowledge. See Lyndon, *Trade Secrets and Information*, 2011 and Wagner, *Commons Ignorance*, 2004.

118 *Veolia v Nottinghamshire* CC [2010] EWCA 1214 per Rix LJ: '…it is plain that there is a strong public interest in the maintenance of valuable commercial confidential information … If the penalty for contracting with public authorities were to be the potential loss of such confidential information, then public authorities and the public interest would be the losers, and the result would be potentially anti-competitive' (Hogan Lovells (2012), *Report on Trade Secrets for the European Commission*. Study carried out for the European Commission (MARKT/2010/20/D). Retrieved from: http://ec.europa.eu/internal_market/iprenforcement/documents/index_en.htm#maincontentSec2. p. 6; 'the law does not exist merely to protect confidentiality for its own sake. Rather, it is a tool in the preservation and promotion of quite diverse individual, social and public values and public interests. And it is these values, these public interests, that can provide the foundations for the transformation of confidentiality from a privacy expectation, from a matter of ethics, or whatever, into a concern of the law'. (*Finn's Liquor Shop v. State Liquor*. (1984) Auth., 24 N.Y.2d 647, 1984:498, quoted in Freiberg, *Commercial Confidentiality*, 1997, p. 130)

cases in which information may remain secret for the protection of other public and private interests. It is important, therefore, to identify if there is an overriding public interest in disclosure beyond access to information for transparency sake and access to environmental information as a matter of public ownership over common natural resources.[119] The laws providing access to environmental information and transparency in general have already accounted for these arguments of public interest, and have nonetheless established the exceptions to disclosure for the protection of other interests, the implication being that in certain cases confidentiality should prevail.

Several sources regard as good practice to perform a weighing exercise on a case-by-case basis;[120] however, this is not a general rule of practice. Under the US FOIA, for instance, the D.C. Circuit decided in *Public Citizen Health Research Group v. FDA* to dismiss the request of an applicant to 'gauge whether the competitive harm done to the sponsor of an [Investigational New Drug] by the public disclosure of confidential information is outweighed by the strong public interest in safeguarding the health of human trial participants', under the argument that Congress had already struck the appropriate balance between public and private interest and no balancing test was required for the application of Exemption 4.[121] In the absence of specific rules, administrative authorities have little basis to carry out a balancing exercise when deciding about the application of one of the exceptions. Judicial authorities may have more leeway in this regard, even if there is no substantial basis in law requiring the weighing of the contradicting interests at stake.

Importantly, a specific public interest override, such as the one provided in Article 6(1) of Regulation No. 1367/2006 (emissions into the environment), derogates from the rule requiring the weighing up of the interests due to the irrebuttable presumption of public interest that supersedes any possible outcome of the balancing act.[122] This does not mean however that the concept of public interest protected by this type of provisions would not admit interpretations. The CJEU held in Case T-716/14 (*Tweedale*) that the public interest protected by Article 6(1) of Regulation No. 1367/2006 '…is

119 CJEU (General Court), Case T-245/11, *ClientEarth v. ECHA*, Judgment of 23 September 2015, para 194: 'general considerations cannot provide an appropriate basis for establishing that the principle of transparency represents in a specific case a matter of particularly pressing concern which prevails over the reasons justifying the refusal to disclose the documents requested'.

120 CJEU, Case T-3 80/04, *Terezakis v. Commission*, Judgment of 30 January 2008, emphasized the need to conduct an individual exam for each one of the documents requested when an exception protecting the private interest would nominally apply to the information request. Adamski, D. (2009). How Wide is 'The Widest Possible'? Judicial Interpretation of the Exceptions to the Right of Access to Official Documents Revisited. *Common Market Law Review, 46*(2), 521–549, esp 529.

121 US DOJ, *Guide to the Freedom of Information Act*, 2016.

122 *Tweedale v EFSA*, para 57.

specifically to know not only what is, or foreseeably will be, released into the environment, but also to understand the way in which the environment could be affected by the emissions in question'.[123] This reading suggests that the concept of public interest for the purposes of the balancing exercise is, at least to an extent, a fluid concept.

Similarly, there will be no place for a weighing exercise when there is a presumption of confidentiality over certain information, as in Article 118(2)(d) of the REACH Regulation regarding information on links between a manufacturer or importer and his distributors or downstream users, whose disclosure is deemed to undermine the commercial interest of the submitter, when there are no arguments being put forward by the person requesting the information that could overturn the legal presumption of the law.[124] In this particular scenario, the burden of proof reverts to the person asking for the information covered by a presumption of confidentiality, and the 'harm test' over the interest protected by the exception is waived by effect of that presumption.

The balancing act will also be pre-empted when the exceptions are established in a mandatory way, as is the case for Article 4(1) of Regulation No. 1049/2001, since in this case, provided that the formal requirements for the application of an exception are in place, the authority may not use its discretion to grant disclosure even if the public servant had the opinion that the public interest in disclosure should prevail.[125] The exceptions of Article 4(1) protect the public interest as regards: (i) public security, (ii) defence and military matters, (iii) international relations and (iv) the financial, monetary or economic policy of the Community or a Member State. In this case, a new assessment of the public interest in disclosure would seem redundant, particularly given the clear language of the Regulation.[126] Notably, the grounds for exceptions under Article 4(2) of the Regulation can be appreciated cumulatively for the purposes of the balancing exercise to be carried out by the public authorities.[127]

The Colombian Constitutional Court has referred to the balancing exercise adding an extra layer to the appreciation of the public interest. In Case T-928/04, the Court asserted that

123 *Tweedale v EFSA*, para 99.

124 CJEU (General Court), Case T-245/11, *ClientEarth v. ECHA*, Judgment of 23 September 2015, para 176: 'Where the legal presumption in Article 118(2)(c) of the REACH Regulation is applicable, the authority concerned are free to take the view that disclosure would undermine the protection of the commercial interests of the persons concerned without having to make an individual assessment of the content of each of the documents disclosure of which is requested'.

125 Peers, S. (2005). *Statewatch Case Law Summary EU: Access to Documents Regulation.* Retrieved from https://www.statewatch.org/analyses/no-116-eu-case-law-summary-access-regulation.pdf, citing Case T-264/04 – *WWF v Council.*

126 Adamski, *The Widest Possible*, 2009.

127 CJEU, Case C-71/10, *Office of Communications v Information Commissioner*, Judgment of 28 July 2011.

> The confidentiality of public documents in a democratic state cannot be absolute, insofar as the general rule is the principle of publicity of the authorities' actions and the exception is secrecy. Therefore, the legal operator must assess not only the provision of law authorising the withholding of a public document, but also which rights, principles and constitutional values are affected with the restriction, because, in some cases, the rights, values and principles supporting the confidentiality of the information shall prevail, and in others those that oppose to it. In this scenario, once the interests at stake have been pondered, it may be that the confidentiality of a document prevails against rights such as information, but must give in before others such as the rights to defence (fair trial) and access to the administration of justice, which, *prima facie*, hold a higher value in modern democratic societies.[128]

The implication of this reasoning is that even within the public interest realm some interests will be more important than others, and therefore should be given more weight during the balancing act. Again, a significant drawback would be the generalised lack of agreement as to the hierarchy of public values that should be employed when confronting the public interest against the interest protected with an exception.

7.4.5. Weaknesses of the Current Toolbox

The previous examination reveals that although the tools for addressing conflicts between confidentiality and transparency are largely commonplace among the different jurisdictions, the way in which they are applied and defined in specific cases differ.

First, even if all transparency legislation is enacted with the general interest of maximum disclosure at its core, the prevalence of the maximum disclosure principle is not necessarily a given. In the US, the FOIA was enacted in 1966 and yet only in 1993 was there a guideline specifically establishing a presumption of public access.[129]

Second, regarding the 'harm test', not all FOI laws will include a provision requiring operators to verify the existence of an actual harm to the interest protected by an exception before applying it, and even those that do sometimes fail to provide specific guidelines to determine when the detriment for the protected interest merits the application of the exception. The lack of clear

128 Colombian Constitutional Court, Case T-928/04, Judgment of 24 September 2004, MP Jaime Araújo Rentería.

129 Memorandum from Janet Reno, Attorney Gen., U.S. Dep't of Justice, for Heads of Departments and Agencies, (Oct. 4, 1993). Retrieved from http://www.usdoj.gov/oip/foia_updates/Vol_XIV_3/page3.htm: 'The Department will no longer defend an agency's withholding of information merely because there is a 'substantial legal basis' for doing so. Rather, in determining whether or not to defend a nondisclosure decision, we will apply a presumption of disclosure'.

guidelines can be appreciated in the case-law of the CJEU regarding public access to administrative files. The 'harm test' can be basically waived when the information is considered to fall within certain categories for which a general presumption of harm has been established.

Thirdly, 'public interest overrides' constitute strong devices to safeguard the purposes of the legislation when there is already an agreement on the content to be protected from excessive confidentiality (*e.g.* emissions into the environment), but a general clause precluding the application of exceptions when there is an overriding public interest in disclosure may suffer from the same faults as the 'harm tests': a general lack of substantial guidelines to give flesh to the open carcass that the concept of 'public interest' represents.[130] These weaknesses manifest in the 'balancing act' employed to weigh the public interest in disclosure against the interest protected by the exception and its potential harm, ultimately producing a one-time solution for the case at hand, which, at best, will be mostly proportional and balanced and, at worst, unpredictable and arbitrary.

Thus, the first important shortcoming of the current toolbox is the absence of specific guidelines and an authoritative framework for the application of the different tools, both at the national and international level. In fact, there are no international guidelines or formal criteria regarding what constitutes legitimate CBI claims[131] which only adds to the conundrum formed by the lack of agreement on what constitutes an 'overriding public interest' and of a general hierarchy of the public and private values than come into play in these situations. The lack of uniformity can also be observed comparatively among the jurisdictions. Even if each of the concepts is found in national laws and judicial opinions of domestic courts, the similarity is more formal than substantial. Most of the current pieces of the toolbox are open-ended concepts, which is arguably necessary to apply them to a wide variety of events, the problem is that the way the concepts are being filled in by legal operators and courts in analogous situations is producing rather unequal results.[132]

This feeds into the second important weakness. There is no explicit recognition in any of the studied jurisdictions of a 'matrix of values' providing content and clear guidance. The current systems of principles are incomplete because they regularly account for a one-sided view of the problem: either

130 Adamski, *The Widest Possible*, 2009, p. 526: 'On many occasions the Court has indicated what the 'overriding public interest in disclosure' is not to mean. But never has it said what it is'.

131 Nielsen, *Biosafety Data*, 2013.

132 See, *e.g.*, the CJEU Case T-329/17 *Tweedale,* and Case T-716/14 *Hautala*, on the one hand, and Case 545/11 RENV, *Stichting Greenpeace Nederland.* In the first two, the General Court (Eight Chamber) granted access to information about the active substance glyphosate which was submitted by the producer as part of the registration process to enter the market; in the third case, the Fourth Chamber refused to grant access to analogous information on the same active substance. These judgments were issued only four months apart.

from a 'defence of the right of access' perspective or from the opposite 'protect our business secrets' perspective, and even if the 'matrix of values' can be logically deduced from the existing legislation, the regulatory instruments fail to implement it properly: most of them have shortcomings in the definition of the exceptions and integrating the other pieces of legislation that influence the exercise of access rights and the fulfilment of the laws' purposes.

A third issue is related specifically to the 'balancing act' as the default mechanism for resolving conflicts arising between the protection of CBI and the right of public access to information. It has been pointed out that this mechanism leaves significant room to the discretion of the legal operator, that the cumulative effects of the decisions remain unaccounted for, and that, in judicial settings, the more immediate interests in confidentiality (which are usually better funded) tend to prevail against the more diffuse an abstract detriment to the public interest.[133]

Additionally, in the specific case of balancing out the right of access to information against information protected as trade secrets, not all interested parties would have access to the information necessary to perform the analysis in the first place. Shabalala sharply asks: 'What is the appropriate risk calculus between the relative certainty of damage to the trade secret holder and the potential harm that can only be confirmed once the information disclosed has been assessed?'.[134] It is his opinion that the balancing act is almost impossible regarding undisclosed information, because 'the peculiar nature of the undisclosed information is that the need for disclosure directly destroys the undisclosed nature of the information and thus implicates an absolute right. In light of this inherent destruction, there can rarely be any balancing of harms'.[135]

133 Adamski, *The widest Possible*, 2009, p. 14: '[The] balancing of interests has turned to a rather token and abstract assumption, without a real impact on the interpretation of discretionary exceptions'.
134 Shabalala, *Hidden Landmine*, 2017, p. 672.
135 Shabalala, *Hidden Landmine*, 2017, p. 675.

8 Proposal to Reform Access to Environmental Information

Throughout the analysis it has become apparent that (i) private entities are increasingly being subject to transparency obligations, especially regarding environmental aspects of their activities, but there is no consensus about the relevant factors that justify their inclusion in transparency regimes, (ii) Confidential Business Information (CBI) and environmental information of high public interest regularly overlap, and claims of business confidentiality rooted in trade secret law routinely interfere with the disclosure of relevant environmental information to the public, (iii) legal frameworks for the protection of transparency and trade secrets are not harmonised and, in some cases, they contain openly contradictory provisions and (iv) the application of the current toolbox containing the methodological instruments to handle conflicts between the right of public access to environmental information and the protection of trade secrets and CBI fails to deliver predictable, consistent and coherent solutions in line with the legal principles involved, which can be appreciated from the enactment of the legislation to its interpretation by legal operators and court's adjudications.

To contribute to the debate, the following lines explain a methodological approach build as a general framework relying on what can be called modern principles of public access to environmental information, derived from court findings and scholarly contributions.

The model is described as a 'matrix of values', with the potential to be implemented through legislative reform and codes of legal practice.

8.1. Matrix of Values

The 'matrix of values' is simply a compiled set of principles that emerge as priorities in the legal instruments and which courts aim to protect in specific cases. Some of these values are expressed as general formulations, in a way that can be adapted to different legal systems.

8.1.1. Basic Precepts

Most of the substantive components of the 'matrix of values' are found in the law, the case-law, or in the legal theory and practice regarding the right of

DOI: 10.4324/9781003307617-8

access to environmental information, the others (emphasised) consist of an original proposal to extend the matrix of values in order to account for new findings related to participatory rights. These basic assumptions are summarised below:

1. The principle of maximum disclosure of public information. Disclosure must be the rule and withholding the information should be the exception.
2. In the framework of access to information, confidential business information and other proprietary information can be exempted from disclosure for the protection of the legitimate economic interests of the owner, regardless of whether the information is held by a public or a private entity.
3. As a general principle, public information held by public authorities should always be publicly available (the state only keeps information on behalf of the public, it does not 'own it').
4. As a general principle, private information held by private entities (not otherwise considered 'public authorities' for access purposes) can be kept private.
5. Certain categories of information, environmental and otherwise, must be openly available, **regardless of the person holding the information**, such as: information about violation of human rights, crimes against humanity, hazardous substances, threats to human health and safety, nature and effects of emissions into the environment and, in general, **information clearly in the public interest whose disclosure protects important constitutional values like public morality, public health, the environment and public finances.**
6. In certain circumstances, **information outside the public realm shall be made available to an applicant by virtue of the special circumstances in which the information is required**. For instance, when the information is necessary to protect and exercise the applicant's fundamental rights, as recognised in the state's constitution, they shall be able to obtain access to such information regardless of whether the information is held by a public or private entity. Special safeguards can be taken in these cases to prevent the dissemination of information considered to be sensitive under domestic laws, such as confidentiality agreements and other contractual obligations limiting the use of the information.
7. The protection of trade secrets and CBI, even if provided for in the national laws, shall not prevail over the right of public access in these four (4) cases:

    a. When the information relates to emissions into the environment.
    b. When the information **pertains to damages or to serious risk for the environment or the public health**.
    c. When the information is **necessary for communities and individuals to exercise their rights effectively, as in the framework of public**

participation in decision-making processes, public interest litigation and class actions, and the exercise of their rights as consumers.

d When **the information is being requested by a person who needs it to exercise and protect their fundamental rights effectively**. In these cases, the petitioner may be asked to sign a non-disclosure agreement or other document containing special duties to preserve the information from general knowledge and misuse by the petitioner or others.

8 In other cases, private and public persons should be **mandated to withhold** information, which has been classified as CBI or protected under trade secret or IP laws, but an administrative review mechanism shall be in place to address complains and provide final decisions in cases of refusal.

In order to prevent excessive interference with transparency rights, an official definition of 'trade secrets' and CBI for the purposes of transparency legislation should be adopted at the higher possible level. This definition should include the verification that the protection of the information serves a legitimate economic interest and should require that the person claiming confidentiality provides preliminary evidence of the potential threat that disclosure would cause to this interest.

As observed from the above, when defining if certain information should be disclosed, three factors are generally considered: (i) the nature of the entity holding the information, (ii) the nature of the information requested and (iii) the circumstances of the person requesting the information. The combined considerations of these factors provide the principles above, some of which are generally accepted and well known, and some of which are not. To justify the inclusions of the 'new' parameters, the following title explains the conceptual basis for this proposal.

8.1.2. The New Categories in the Matrix of Values

After examining the relevant laws and the most recent case-law, and observing the integrated framework of access to environmental information from the private sector under international, European and comparative (Colombia and the US) legal frameworks, a proposal is hereby introduced to include in the 'matrix of values' a new rule that gives prevalence over organic and confidentiality considerations to public access of information **necessary for communities and individuals to exercise their rights effectively, namely in the framework of public participation in decision-making processes, public interest litigation and class actions, and the exercise of their rights as consumers.**

This category should be accessible to the *public concerned*, even if held by private entities, and even if it falls under the definition of CBI, but only to the extent that it is considered *relevant* for the decision-making process. That would place it in a similar level to information about emissions to the environment, with the difference that it doesn't have to be accessible to the general public but could be restricted to the public involved in the decision-making process.

This proposition is largely based on the generally accepted premise that information is the basis for effective participation in decision-making processes and on the assumption that the nature of the information is a significant factor to determine whether public access should be granted. Under the Aarhus Convention[1] and its derived instruments, information relating to emissions into the environment cannot be withheld on grounds of protection of business confidentiality (Article 4(d)). This provision represents an underlying assumption that certain environmental information of key importance should always be publicly known, regardless of whether its disclosure may adversely affect businesses' legitimate economic interests in keeping their trade secrets safe. This is also an *objective* indicator, insofar as 'emissions into the environment' is an independent concept which, properly defined and harmonised, is an effective criterion for the consistent application of the CBI exception. Furthermore, the logic behind the emissions' exception may be employed for other environmental information in certain circumstances. Health and safety information about hazardous substances is also exempted from confidentiality claims under several international legal instruments,[2] and some states have specific provisions establishing that information about hazardous chemical substances or environmental information in general cannot be withheld on grounds of business confidentiality.[3]

The same rationale behind rules of prevalent access to information about emissions into the environment, hazardous substances that pose a risk to health or to life, and other information of public interest, can be brought forward to defend public access to environmental information that is required for effective public participation in decision-making processes. This would include EIAs with all their supportive documents and studies and information that is *relevant* to achieve meaningful and effective public participation, as described in the normative framework: detailed description of the activity, impacts, measures to mitigate or compensate the foreseeable impacts, alternatives to the project and budgetary or cost-analysis reports, in the framework of specific projects and activities. Regarding legislative or administrative

1 Convention on Access to Information, Public Participation in Decision-making and Access to Justice in Environmental Matters, Aarhus, Denmark, 25 June 1998 (entry into force 30 October 2001) 2161 UNTS 447.

2 *e.g.*, Article 17 of the Minamata Convention on Mercury stipulating that information on the health and safety of humans and the environment shall not be regarded as confidential and the Convention on Persistent Organic Pollutants, United Nations, Stockholm, Sweden, 22 May 2001 (entry into force 17 May 2004), Article 9(5) (information on health and safety of humans and the environment shall not be regarded as confidential).

3 Reportedly, the Republic of Korea and Georgia (ECLAC). (2016). *Society, Rights and the Environment: International Human Rights Standards Applicable to Access to Information, Public Participation and Access to Justice*, United Nations, p. 96).

measures, this category of information should include risk assessments,[4] information and technical data necessary to assess the safety of a new product or service,[5] and any other relevant information that is necessary for the public to understand the health and environmental consequences of the proposed measure.[6]

This proposal finds echo in some of the judgments referenced throughout the study. The CJEU has practically recognised an unconditional right of public access to information about emissions into the environment in the framework of EU law, in the understanding that it not only covers data about the nature, location and quantities of actual emissions but also about emissions which are *foreseeable under normal conditions of use of a product,* their effects for the state of the environment and, furthermore

> … Information enabling the public to check whether the assessment of actual or foreseeable emissions, on the basis of which the competent authority authorised the product or substance in question, is correct, and the data relating to the effects of those emissions on the environment.
>
> (…)
>
> The public must have access to information enabling it to ascertain whether the emissions were correctly assessed and must be given the opportunity reasonably to understand how the environment could be affected by those emissions.[7]

Within this framework, detailed information about the effects of drugs or chemical substances placed in the market should be accessible to allow consumers to make an informed decision about the risks they are willing to take and to monitor the decision-making process of public entities in charge of approving these substances.

An additional rule would provide a right of access to information held by private entities when the information is necessary to protect or defend the applicant's rights, as currently the case in Colombia. This entails an even larger shift of perspective to focus on the instrumental nature of the right of access to information in general, as a means to an end. The Colombian

4 Such as those requested by ClientEarth to the European Commission in the framework of legislative action for measures on access to justice in environmental matters and environmental inspections (CJEU, Case C-57/16, *ClientEarth v. European Commission*, Judgment of 4 September 2018).

5 Such as test results and the exact composition and purity of the chemical substances present in the products that will be released into the environment (CJEU, Case T-716/14, *Anthony C. Tweedale v European Food Safety Authority (EFSA),* Judgment of 7 March 2019; CJEU, Case T-329/17, *Hautala v. EFSA*, Judgment of 7 March 2019)

6 *E.g.* information regarding the *effects* of emissions into the environment (*Tweedale v. EFSA* and *Hautala*).

7 CJEU, Case C-673/13 P *Commission v Stichting Greenpeace Nederland and PAN Europe*, Judgment of 23 November 2016, para 80.

Constitutional Court defends this position as a way to correct power asymmetries in society,[8] human rights theory largely supports this approach as well.[9] The focus on the traditional distinction between private and public entities is shifted, in this case, in favour of a more 'subjective' approach that takes into consideration the special circumstances of the person requesting the information and the ultimate purpose the information is going to serve, namely the protection of the petitioner's fundamental rights.

In consequence, the proposal involves (i) explicitly recognising the 'matrix of values' as the current product of the international framework, regional development and national implementation of the right of access to information, (ii) updating the 'matrix of values' to include new rules giving prevalent access to information **necessary for communities and individuals to exercise their rights effectively, as in the framework of public participation in decision-making processes, public interest litigation and class actions, and the exercise of their rights as consumers;** to be disclosed to the *public concerned* regardless of whether it is held by private entities or is considered confidential and (iii) aiming to integrate these principles in existing as well as forthcoming legislation on the matter, in the manuals for the administrative application of FOI laws, and in the judicial cases dealing with this type of conflicts.

This would be done, first and foremost, by the courts, because they are better positioned to consider the evolution in the interpretation of the rights of public access in environmental law and set new standards in the absence of clearly applicable provisions, as in this case. The Courts are already doing this, to an extent, as observed in the recent case-law of the CJEU that partially supports this author's proposal. In a second stage, the new standards and methodologies can be adopted in the administrative and legislative spheres, in the form of official guidelines, administrative regulations or binding laws. At the international level, endorsement in soft laws (UN Declarations, multilateral organisms' statements) can be particularly beneficial, because national and local rules are significantly influenced by international advances in the field of environmental laws and human rights. Finally, private entities themselves can take the lead and adopt the guidelines voluntarily, which could be beneficial in terms of reputation, public acceptance, social licence to operate, market rewards, legal compliance and in diminishing liability risks for their products and activities. Increased transparency in these terms can also be an incentive for companies to update and optimise the way

8 Colombian Constitutional Court, Case C-951 of 2014, Judgment of 4 December 2014, M.P. Gloria Stella Ortiz Delgado.

9 See *i.e.* Roberts, A. (2006). *Blacked Out: Government Secrecy in the Information Age.* Cambridge University Press; ECLAC. (2016). *Society, Rights and the Environment: International Human Rights Standards Applicable to Access to Information, Public Participation and Access to Justice.* United Nations; and Report of the Independent Expert on the issue of human rights obligations relating to the enjoyment of a safe, clean, healthy and sustainable environment, John H. Knox, A/HRC/28/61, 3 February 2015.

they protect their trade secrets and CBI, perhaps encouraging the use of patents for information that could be protected under this figure and rethinking the limits and scope of their confidentiality claims.

8.2. Integrated Contextual Analysis Instead of 'Balancing of Interests'

An integrated contextual analysis is the methodological tool proposed for the application of the 'matrix of values' formulated from the lessons learned in the different cases and derived from the most common conflicts and their solutions in the different jurisdictions. Table 8.1 summarises the rules above to show the way the different factors combine to produce certain outcome. This methodology to analyse requests of access to information sets aside the 'harm test' and the 'balancing act' when CBI and other confidential information has already been recognised as such and the circumstances surrounding the petition have been demonstrated.

8.2.1. Conducting the Integrated Contextual Analysis

In order to apply the 'matrix of values', judges and other legal operators should carry out an **integrated contextual analysis** of the case, to give proper weight to the main decisive factors (who's asking for the information, for what purpose, what is the nature of the information and who's holding it) considering that access to information does not happen in a factual vacuum but within a specific context and with a clear purpose.

The examined pieces of legislation and rules establishing the protection of trade secrets and other confidential information, as well as the ones providing for public access to information, equally coincide in that their respective subject-matters are open-ended concepts and the syllogistic application of the rules is thus not plausible. The key definitions of 'trade secrets', 'confidential business information', 'environmental information' and 'public authorities' need to be interpreted and applied to specific cases following a logic that does not conflict with the purposes of the laws and which provides the best possible balance between the different interests at stake. The criteria for the application of the rules are to be found in the instruments themselves, supplemented by general legal principles.

This contextual analysis is different from the 'balancing of interests' because it can be carried out following regular rules of evidence appreciation, and once the facts of the petition have been established, there will be a clear and unequivocal pathway following the rules and exceptions set up above.

At judicial instances, courts usually enjoy a high degree of discretion to give adequate consideration to the different interests of the parties in order to deliver a substantively fair decision under the law. This faculty may not be vested upon administrative authorities, and since many cases will never reach judicial instances, it is of the utmost importance that the criteria are clearly

Table 8.1 Matrix of Values

Disclosure	Non-Disclosure	*Factor influences disclosure*	Factor influences non-disclosure
INFORMATION HELD BY A PUBLIC ENTITY			
Nature of the Information	*Context of the petition*	*Outcome of petition*	*Examples*
Public records	*Exercise freedom of information Rights*	**Disclosure – No reason needs to be stated by petitioner (unless the information is otherwise exempted)**	**Public procurement documents, minutes of meetings, public expenses.**
Records originating from private entities (not confidential)	*Exercise freedom of information Rights*	**Disclosure – No reason needs to be stated by petitioner**	**Reports, audits, technical information in the framework of permitting procedures.**
Records protected as CBI or trade secrets	Exercise freedom of information Rights	Non-Disclosure (refusal must be duly motivated and supported in the law). Administrative Review mechanisms must be available.	Commercial or industrial secrets submitted in the framework of authorising procedures, infringement procedures or other administrative processes.
	Public participation in decision-making in environmental matters	**Disclosure – may be restricted to the 'public concerned'. Only information *relevant* for the stated purpose.**	**EIAs and their supporting documentation, risk assessments, tests results, location of projects of high environmental impact, fracking chemicals.**
	Exercise or protection of the petitioner's fundamental rights	**Disclosure – may be subject to NDAs**	**Personal records of the petitioner. Information about manufacturing processes or substances.**
INFORMATION HELD BY A PRIVATE ENTITY			
Nature of the Information	*Context of the petition*	*Outcome of petition*	*Examples*
Proprietary Information	Exercise freedom of information Rights	Non-disclosure (no reason needs to be stated by the entity)	Books of commerce, private or personal documents, internal procedures, accounting records.

INFORMATION HELD BY A PRIVATE ENTITY

Nature of the Information	*Context of the petition*	*Outcome of petition*	*Examples*
Information about emissions into the environment	*Exercise the right of public access to environmental information.*	**Disclosure – no reason needs to be stated by petitioner**	**Information required under PRTRs, studies about the effects of emissions into the environment.**
Information about environmental damages or serious risks to public health or the environment.	*Exercise the right of public access to environmental information.*	**Disclosure – no reason needs to be stated by petitioner**	**Health and safety studies, risk assessments.**
Information about hazardous substances.	*Exercise the right of public access to environmental information.*	**Disclosure – no reason needs to be stated by petitioner**	**Safety sheets, emergency plans, components and impurities of a marketed product with relevant effects in human health and the environment.**
Crimes against humanity or human rights violations.	*Exercise freedom of information Rights*	**Disclosure – no reason needs to be stated by petitioner**	**Records, evidence or any documents documenting these cases.**
Records protected as CBI, trade secrets or IPR.	*Request by a public entity to exercise their functions.*	**Disclosure – the information must be treated as 'confidential' by the authority.**	**Documents required in the framework of approval of a substance.**
	Members of the public, to exercise environmental procedural rights effectively: participation in decision-making and access to justice.	**Disclosure – only information relevant for the stated purpose, may be restricted to public concerned, special conditions to disclosure may apply (NDAs).**	**EIAs, information about the nature and effects of emissions into the environment or of products marketed to the public, toxicological studies, *relevant* environmental information.**
	Exercise or protection of the petitioner's fundamental rights.	**Disclosure – may be subject to NDAs**	**Personal records of the petitioner. Information about manufacturing processes or substances.**
	All other cases	Non-disclosure	

outlined and effectively communicated to the authorities in charge of applying the laws, before the case comes to courts.

8.2.2. Examples of the Application of the Integrated Contextual Analysis

The proposed methodology requires applying the rules related to the right of access and the protection of confidentiality within a specific framework. The following cases exemplify the application of this approach in different contexts of legal practice.

8.2.2.1. Access to Information on Climate Change

Thorp examines in detail the matter of access to information in the framework of the international regime for climate change. The United Nations Framework Convention on Climate Change (UNFCCC)[10] contains substantive provisions on active and passive access to information. Article 4 for instance, establishes specific obligations to disseminate information to the public and to respond to information requests, Article 6 attains the Parties' obligations to educate the public and raise awareness around climate change and to promote public access to information, and Article 12, relates to the Parties' obligation to disclose information about Greenhouse Gas (GHG) emissions to the Conference of the Parties (COP).

Collecting and disseminating information about the sources and effects of climate change may be more challenging than managing access to other types of environmental information. First, relevant climate change related information can be very vast and far-reaching, going way beyond than GHG emissions, it ranges from information about raw materials utilised in an industrial process to financial data about public investment in climate change awareness, fossil fuels' subsidies and farming techniques. Secondly, large amounts of information would come from private entities, such as industrial facilities' operators, general product manufacturers, fossil fuels producers and farmers. Even if the entities in question perform public services (*i.a.* public transport systems operators), most of the relevant information will likely be held by non-government actors. Thirdly, the diversity of information may interfere with the effectiveness of regulatory instruments and access mechanisms due to the lack of uniformity and common frameworks, at a local, national, or international level. If there is ever a need to interpret, to process and to integrate environmental information for it to be useful for the public, it is in the field of climate change, and general regulatory instruments may fall short to effectively regulate access with such complexity. In this specific case, Thorp suggests a needs-based approach to segment the stakeholders and their relevant issues, to analyse each cluster independently. She raises the question,

10 United Nations Framework Convention on Climate Change, 5 June 1992 (entered into force on 21 March 1994), 1771 UNTS 107.

'Do all citizens need a comprehensive understanding of the technical scientific underpinnings of climate change?' and, also, 'Do potential "climate migrants" have a right to know and make informed decisions?'[11] The implication is that this differentiation will help to channel efforts in the right direction to provide information within a specific context and with clear purpose. This strategy may help greatly in the analysis of conflicts between business confidentiality and access to information.

Thorp suggests that '…universality and Interoperability requires finding the right balance between a differential needs-based approach, a common people's rights-based approach, and the respective capabilities at all levels, the national level included'.[12] She supports her argument in general principles adopted in the UNFCCC for climate change governance, such as sustainable development and 'common but differentiated responsibilities' of the Parties. From the perspective of sustainable development, the UNFCCC advises that 'policies and measures to protect the climate system against human-induced change should be appropriate for the specific conditions of each Party and should be integrated with national development programmes'.[13] Article 3(1) of the UNFCCC, in turn, refers to the need for long term cooperation to be 'guided by the principles of equity and common but differentiated responsibilities and respective capabilities.'

Resolving conflicts between access to information and confidentiality in these cases, from a hypothetical perspective through regulatory instruments, or in a specific case in a judicial scenario, could improve by including into the considerations:

i The need of the information to be disclosed (as observed by the personal situation of the petitioner and the purpose that the information is going to serve).
ii The 'floor' or minimum standard that the recognition of the right provides for the public (the degree to which access is guaranteed as a subjective entitlement of the petitioner and the limits stated in the applicable law), and
iii The capabilities of the institutions involved to manage requests for information and provide reasonable solutions to the conflicts of interests that may arise (as a way of applying the principle of common but differentiated responsibilities depending on the nature and mission of the institution in question).[14]

11 Thorp, T. (2012). The Right to Know and the Duty to Disclose: Pathways to Effective Monitoring, Reporting, and Verification within the Constitutionalism of Climate Justice. *Pace Environmental Law Review, 30*, 140, esp 201.
12 Thorp, *Pathways to Effective Monitoring*, 2012, p. 202.
13 UNFCCC, Article 3(4).
14 Thorp specifically illustrates this aspect by stating in respect to the establishment of mandatory climate change reporting obligations upon private entities in the UK: 'Differentiating the scale of obligations owed by unlisted companies *vis-à-vis*

To better illustrate the concept, let us apply it in several hypothetical scenarios.

8.2.2.2. Access to Information in Transparency Laws

In this case, the minimum standard provides a general and broad right of access to any member of the public, but only to information held by a public entity and not otherwise exempted from disclosure for the protection of other interests. No motive or interest should need to be stated to access public information held by a public entity or its equivalent. In this case, public authorities presumably have a large capacity to deal with petitions of access to information, and, therefore, a short waiting period should be observed. The contextual integrative analysis in this default scenario results in access in most cases.

8.2.2.3. Access to information within stock exchange trading systems

In this case, the information is held by a public regulatory entity, the origin of the information is generally the private sector, and the petitioners of the information are investors and other stakeholders. Disclosure in this scenario protects the public interest to have transparent and legally compliant stock market transactions and the private interest of the stakeholders. The relevant information should be actively disseminated instead of passively accessed. The capacity of the regulatory entity is limited however, thus access can be restricted to the formats in which the information is reported by the companies and be published in the terms of the reporting laws. The subjective condition of the petitioner in these cases is not as relevant, insofar as the purposes of disclosure are better served when all stakeholders have equal access to the same information. The contextual integrative analysis in this case generally results in open public access to a limited amount of information whose access ensures the realisation of clear governmental purposes.

8.2.2.4. Access to Information in Defence of Other Human Rights

This perspective strongly privileges the purpose of the information as an instrument for the realisation of other rights and the subjective situation of the person asking for the information. These facts factor in support of more access but only to the person who needs the information, disclosure is therefore subject to the motivation and proof of interest presented by the petitioner. In Colombia and South Africa, anyone in this situation can request

quoted companies does not mean that loopholes should exist *ad infinitum*. Establishing stricter disclosure requirements for quoted companies and voluntary reporting for unlisted companies is a move in the right direction' (Thorp, *Pathways to Effective Monitoring*, 2012, p. 247).

information held by private entities. Exceptions for the protection of other interests may also subside for the sake of the fundamental interests to be protected by the disclosure of the information, as in the case of Colombia's National Development Law establishing the confidentiality of the state's legal strategies, except when the information is 'necessary proof' in favour of the person requesting the information.[15] This is an example of how the fundamental right of access to justice of the individual prevails over the public interest in the confidentiality of sensitive state information. A similar argument can be read in the recent decisions of the CJEU lifting the confidentiality protection over information submitted by industries for the approval of chemical substances, when the information refers to emissions into the environment and their effects in human health and safety, because access to that information is **necessary for the public to be able to assess the effects of the substance and participate effectively in decision-making processes.** To the extent that the petitioner's rights to effective participation in decision-making and to know about potential risks affecting his private and family life can be considered fundamental human rights, access to information is strongly linked to the subjective position of the requester and the purpose that the information is going to serve. In this example, the contextual integrative analysis results in access to privileged or otherwise exempted information, but only by virtue of the special circumstances of the petitioner; hence, access is not generally supported in transparency legislation or the protection of the public interest but is better understood as an accessory prerogative in the individual's exercise of fundamental rights.

*8.2.2.5. Access to Information in Administrative or Judicial Procedures (*e.g. *Commission Competition Proceedings)*

As seen above, the right of access to justice and to a fair trial are strong individual interests generally recognised as fundamental human rights and important legal principles for the rule of law. The persons involved in an administrative or judiciary procedure, particularly involving sanctions or infringement investigations, in principle enjoy the right to access the information necessary to exercise their defence. In fact, procedural transparency in favour of the interested parties to an administrative process has been long recognised as a corollary of the principle of due process. According to Savino, the right of access in this form is 'instrumental to the broader right of each person to defend their own interests when they can be affected by an administrative act',[16] therefore implying that, in this context, the right of access is

15 Colombia Law 1955 of 2019, 'Adopting the National Development Plan 2019–2022', 24 May 2019, Article 136.

16 Savino, M. (2011). *The Right to Open Public Administrations in Europe: Emerging Legal Standards,* p. 10. Retrieved from: http://www.epsa2011.eu/files/Themes_2011/OECD Administrative Transparency 1010.pdf.

only recognised to the parties and its main purpose is guaranteeing due process in individual cases, as opposed to the goal of enhancing democracy and improving accountability and legitimacy of the state decisions of the general right of access to public information.

Regarding access by the general public, however, even if the proceedings involve public entities and a public interest in the outcome can be envisioned (*e.g.* Member States infringement proceedings under Article 258 TFEU), many documents on file are largely exempted from disclosure while the proceedings are still ongoing, in order to protect the parties' ability to exercise their defence free from external pressures.[17] Regulation 1049/2001 also provides an exception to disclosure of internal documents pertaining to the decision-making of the institutions, which would cover administrative infringement procedures carried out by the European Commission.[18] This provision is aimed to protect the Commission's ability to make its decision independently and free from interference and undue pressures from the public. Even Article 6(1) of Regulation 1367/2006 establishing the irrebuttable presumption of public access when the information relates to 'emissions into the environment' excludes from this rule information exempted because its disclosure would undermine the purposes of investigations and audits carried out by the European Commission.[19]

Only the higher interest of a concerned party in the administrative proceedings seems to prevail over the protection of independent decision-making by the institution to the extent that access to the information is necessary to ensure the party's due process.[20] However, according to the CJEU, the protection of a fair trial and the independence of the judiciary in abstract seem to be better served by secrecy.[21] This results in a seemingly paradoxical situation where disclosure would seem to undermine and strengthen the right course of justice at the same time; but this reasoning is quite plausible in the framework

17 Regulation (EC) No 1049/2001 of the European Parliament and of the Council of 30 May 2001 regarding public access to European Parliament, Council and Commission documents, [2001] O.J. L 145/43, Article 4(2). This is a discretionary exception, however, and the EU institution must carry out a balancing test to determine if there is an overriding public interest in disclosure. According to Krämer, 'There is no legitimate reason why the public should not be informed of letters of formal notice and reasoned opinion; disclosure of these documents might even accelerate compliance of the Member State in question with EU law' (Krämer, L. (2013). The EU, Access to Environmental Information and the Open Society. *ERA Forum, 14*(4), 463–474, p. 471).

18 EU Regulation 1049/2001 (Article 4(3)). This exception was successfully invoked by the Commission in CJEU Case T-403/05, *MyTravel v Commission*, Judgment of 9 September 2008.

19 EU Regulation 1049/2001, Article 6(1).

20 CJEU Case T-48/05, *Franchet and Byk v Commission*, Judgment of 8 July 2008 The Court recognised the need to reconcile the procedural rights of the parties with the need for confidentiality of the information on file.

21 CJEU, Case T-36/04, *Association de la presse internationale ASBL (API) v. Commission*, Judgment of 12 September 2007.

of a contextual integrative analysis where the individual conditions of the applicant are routinely considered into the decision.

A scenario where the conflict of interests can be clearly appreciated is in the framework of the Commission's proceedings in competition law. In these cases, sensitive commercial information is very likely to appear on the file, the applicants for access to information will most probably be private actors pursuing their individual interests,[22] and there are procedural rules on access[23] that differ from the general access regime established in Regulation 1049/2001, which, to the extent that they are not considered *lex specialis* vis-à-vis the general regime of Regulation No. 1049/2001, establish a pressing need for a harmonious interpretation of both regulatory systems in order to safeguard the purpose of transparency without undermining the interests of the parties in the competition proceedings. In the words of the CJEU, 'those regulations do not contain a provision expressly giving one regulation primacy over the other. Therefore, it is appropriate to ensure that each of those regulations is applied in a manner that is compatible with the other and which enables a coherent application of them'.[24]

Generally, the rules applying to access to the file in the different competition procedures establish (i) their own scope of beneficiaries, (ii) their own scope of materials from the file available to disclosure and (iii) their own set of exceptions to disclosure, particularly including trade secrets and CBI, internal documents of the institution and correspondence with other authorities.[25] Furthermore, the rules of access to the file extend specific obligations upon the applicant to abstain from making copies of certain documents and to use the information only for the purposes of judicial or administrative proceedings for the application of the EU competition rules.[26]

Indeed, in competition law proceedings before the European Commission, the person asking for access is extremely relevant. According to antitrust

22 Adamski, D. (2014). Access to Documents, Accountability and the Rule of Law – Do Private Watchdogs Matter? *European Law Journal, 20*(4), 520–543.

23 The file in a competition investigation (the 'file') consists of all documents (irrespective of the storage medium) which have been obtained, produced, and/or assembled by the Commission Directorate General for Competition, during the investigation. Commission Notice on the rules for access to the Commission file in cases pursuant to Articles [101 and 102 TFEU], Articles 53, 54, and 57 of the EEA Agreement and Council Regulation (EC) No 139/2004, OJ 2005/C 325/07 [Commission Notice on access to the file], par. 8. Cited in: Goddin, G. (2011). Recent Judgments Regarding Transparency and Access to Documents in the Field of Competition Law: Where Does the Court of Justice of the EU Strike the Balance? *Journal of European Competition Law & Practice, 2*(1), 10–23, esp 10.

24 Case C-477/10 P, *Commission v Agrofert Holding*, Judgment of 28 June 2012, para 52.

25 Commission Notice on access to the file, paras 8–25.

26 Access to Immunity/leniency statements and the Notice on settlement procedures in antitrust and cartel cases is only granted to the addressees of the statement of objections if they commit to these conditions (Goddin, *Recent Judgments Regarding Transparency*, 2011).

proceeding laws, there are three groups or persons entitled to different degrees of access: (i) the recipient of the statement of objections, (ii) the complainant (if any) and (iii) interested third parties. Whereas the first has the most extensive rights of access including a general access to the file and to the statement of objections[27] – understandably, since this is the party with the highest stakes in the proceedings and access is clearly supported in due process principles – interested third parties barely have any access rights to the file,[28] and complainants sit somewhere in the middle.[29] The special procedural rules aim to protect the right of due process of the recipient of the statement of objections and the expectations of confidentiality of the parties who submit information to the Commission. The CJEU has held the view, for instance, that the complainant may have access to a redacted version of the statement of objections that may content certain confidential information, but never trade secrets,[30] based on a reading of the rights of the complainant that would require access to enough information to be able to understand the basis of the Commission's decisions on the case and participate effectively to the extent that the regulation allows them.[31]

Generally speaking, when the CJEU has decided to derogate from a presumption of confidentiality (supported on specific procedural rules or on the interpretation by the Commission of the rights of access) it has done so relying heavily on the need of the information for the exercise of the petitioner's right of due process, as recognised in the European Charter of Fundamental Rights, the ECHR and the EU treaties and secondary legislation.[32] The need of the information for the exercise of the right to defence has proved to be a decisive factor in several cases as the jurisprudence has evolved, and was again employed by the CJEU in its recent decision in *UPS*

27 Commission Regulation (EC) No 773/2004 of 7 April 2004 relating to the conduct of proceedings by the Commission pursuant to Articles 81 and 82 of the EC Treaty, [2004] O.J. L 123/18 (the Implementing Regulation), Article 15.
28 Article 13(1) establishes the right of interested third parties to be informed of 'the nature and subject matter of the procedure'.
29 Carlton, R., Lawrence, J., & Mcelwee, M. (2008). Confidentiality and Disclosure in European Commission Antitrust Proceedings – The Case for Clarity. *European Competition Journal, 4*, 401.
30 CJEU, Case 53/85 *Akzo Chemie v Commission*, Judgment of 24 June 1986.
31 Carlton, Lawrence & Mcelwee, *Confidentiality and Disclosure*, 2008
32 Specifically in the Charter of Fundamental Rights of the European Union Article 7 (respect for private life, home, and communications), Article 41 (right to good administration, including inter alia the right to be heard and the right to have access to one's file), Article 47 (right to an effective remedy and to a fair trial), Article 48 (presumption of innocence and right of defence), ECHR, Article 6 (fair trial, due process); and Regulation 1/2003 Article 27 (1) and (2). For a complete analysis of the interplay between these legal provisions see. Wils, W. P. J. (2011). EU Anti-trust Enforcement Powers and Procedural Rights and Guarantees: The Interplay between EU Law, National Law, the Charter of Fundamental Rights of the EU and the European Convention On Human Rights. *World Competition, 34 (2),* 189–213.

v. Commission[33] where it confirmed the annulment of a Commission's decision to block the merger between TNT and UPS because the applicant, UPS, was not duly informed of the changes made by the Commission to the economic model analysis on which the decision to block the merger was (partially) based. The Court sustained that, to ensure that the rights of defence are not infringed, the parties to the procedure need to be given the opportunity to submit their views on all of the information on which the Commission intends to base its decision.[34] Disclosure of all the relevant information in this case is necessary to ensure that the procedure is fair in accordance with the principle of good administration. Furthermore, the Court stated that failure to give access to the information in question was enough basis for the annulment of the Commission's decision if it had been demonstrated that, had the company concerned had access to the information, 'there was even a slight chance that it would have been better able to defend itself'.[35] The Company therefore did not have the burden to prove that access to the information in question would have led to a different decision, but only that there was even the smallest chance that it would have been able to structure its defence in a better way.

From the perspective of third party access to competition files, the lack of specific EU rules on the matter led the CJEU to establish a doctrine where a case-by-case examination by the national courts was necessary, in the framework of national competition laws, conducting a balancing exercise of the individual interests of the applicant in disclosure (access to evidence for damage actions) and the interests protected by confidentiality (public enforcement of competition laws).[36] The recognition of this approach and an approximation to a legislative balance of interests came in the form of Directive 2014/104/EU on access to evidence in the framework of actions for damages,[37] which adopts a purposive approach to the right of access to information by establishing rules that support access to evidence which is necessary for the defence of the claimants' interests to obtain compensation in the judicial proceedings including CBI when it is relevant to the action for damages, provided that some measures are taken to protect the confidentiality of the information (Article 5(4)). Article 6 deals with access to the information on the file of a competition authority, providing specific criteria to be

33 CJEU, Case C-265/17 *European Commission v United Parcel Service, Inc.*, Judgment of 16 January 2019.

34 *European Commission v United Parcel Service, Inc*, para 36.

35 *European Commission v United Parcel Service, Inc*, para 56.

36 CJEU, Case C-36/09, *Pfleiderer v Bundeskartellamt*, Judgment of 14 June 2011 and Case 536/11, *Bundeswettbewerbsbehorde v Donau Chemie*, Judgment of 6 June 2013.

37 Directive 2014/104/EU of the European Parliament and of the Council on certain rules governing actions for damages under national law for infringements of the competition law provisions of the Member States and of the European Union, [2014] O.J. L 349.

applied in the balancing exercise by the national courts,[38] specifying documents that cannot be disclosed while the proceedings are still ongoing,[39] and permanently restricting access to certain documents (*e.g.* leniency statements and settlement submissions) (Article 6(6)). Importantly, the information from the file obtained by the applicant can be used in an action for damages only by himself (or his successor) (Article 7(3)).

Despite a general presumption that non-protected information on the file could be accessible under Regulation No 1049/2001 (Transparency Regulation),[40] the existence of specific provisions of secondary law establishing rules of access may interfere with the application of the transparency regulation, especially considering the lack of proper harmonisation between both regimes. In order to uphold the purpose of the specific competition laws, a careful reading of the exceptions in the Transparency Regulation is needed, in consonance with the exceptions regime included in the competition procedural rights. The interpretation by the CJEU has not been consistent, however. The General Court has applied a strict interpretation of the exceptions in Regulation No 1049/2001 in the past. For example, regarding the exception for the protection of inspections, investigations and audits,[41] regularly invoked by the Commission to refuse access to merger files, the General Court has said that the protection does not extend to the file after the proceedings have ended,[42] and the argument put forward by the Commission that disclosure could cause third parties to be more reluctant to submit information if they knew that the information could be publicly disclosed, has also been dismissed under the argument that the Commission failed to provide specific

38 EU Directive 2014/104/EU, Article 6(4): 'When assessing, in accordance with Article 5(3), the proportionality of an order to disclose information, national courts shall, in addition, consider the following: (a) whether the request has been formulated specifically with regard to the nature, subject matter or contents of documents submitted to a competition authority or held in the file thereof, rather than by a non-specific application concerning documents submitted to a competition authority; (b) whether the party requesting disclosure is doing so in relation to an action for damages before a national court; and (c) in relation to paragraphs 5 and 10, or upon request of a competition authority pursuant to paragraph 11, the need to safeguard the effectiveness of the public enforcement of competition law'.

39 EU Directive 2014/104/EU, Article 6(5): 'National courts may order the disclosure of the following categories of evidence only after a competition authority, by adopting a decision or otherwise, has closed its proceedings: (a) information that was prepared by a natural or legal person specifically for the proceedings of a competition authority; (b) information that the competition authority has drawn up and sent to the parties in the course of its proceedings; and (c) settlement submissions that have been withdrawn'.

40 EU Directive 2014/104/EU, Article 6(2). 'This Article is without prejudice to the rules and practices on public access to documents under Regulation (EC) No 1049/2001'.

41 EU Regulation No 1049/2001, Article 4(2)(3).

42 CJEU, Case C-404/10 P, *Commission v Éditions Odile Jacob*, Judgment of 28 June 2012, under appeal C-404/10.

facts and evidence of this risk.[43] Regarding the CBI exception in Regulation No 1049/2001, the General Court affirmed the need to conduct a concrete and individual examination of each document of the file to determine if it contained commercially sensitive information.[44]

In another notable case, *Commission v. MyTravel*,[45] the General Court found valid the refusal of the Commission to grant access to a report drafted by its legal services following the annulment in 2002 of the prohibition by the Commission of the Airtours/First Choice merger. The report in question was considered an internal document whose disclosure could undermine the decision-making process of the Commission. Interestingly, the Court noted that the motivation of the petitioner (MyTravel, before Airtours) was the relevance of the document for its defence in the judicial action for damages against the Commission which was pending in court, but ruled that even if the document proved to be necessary in this context, this circumstance was irrelevant for the purposes of the public interest balancing act mandated by Regulation No 1049/2001.[46] In applying the *contextual integrative analysis*, this circumstance would have been indeed relevant for the decision on whether to disclose the documents.

The Grand Chamber seems to have taken a different approach than that of the General Court in several cases. In case C-139/07 P *Commission v TGI*,[47] the Court admitted the application of the exception for the protection of inspections, investigations and audits to a State Aid file. In application of the *Turco* reasoning, the Court affirmed the need to verify that disclosure would specifically and effectively undermine the interest protected by the exception, but added that a concrete and individual examination of each document was not necessary when the information was covered by a presumption of confidentiality under other regulations, such as the State Aid Regulation, in this case. More specifically, the Grand Chamber presented the argument that State Aid regulations did not provide for a right of access to information therefore concluding that the application of Regulation No 1049/2001 to access file documents would undermine the system for the review of State Aid.[48]

Later judgments have effectively established a doctrine of categories of information that is presumed confidential, including State Aid files, merger cases and proceedings under Article 101 TFU. Regarding access to these categories of information, the authority may refuse access invoking one of the exceptions in Regulation No 1049/2001 without having to analyse and demonstrate the harm that disclosure of each document could have on the

43 CJEU, Case C-477/10 P, *Commission v Agrofert Holding*, Judgment of 28 June 2012.

44 *Commission v Agrofert Holding*, para 86.

45 CJEU Case T-403/05, *MyTravel v Commission*, Judgment of 9 September 2008.

46 *Commission v. MyTravel*, para 67.

47 CJEU Case C-139/07 P, *Commission v. Technische Glaswerke Ilmenau GmbH*, Judgment of 29 June 2010.

48 *Commission v TGI*, para 58.

protected interest. In the Court's opinion, this interpretation of the possible conflicts between the general presumption of access from the transparency regime and the protection afforded by other statutes to certain information ensures that public access is mostly provided whilst preserving the *effet utile* of the other laws.[49]

In the same way as a 'simplified' harm test is applicable in cases where the information is especially protected from disclosure, this author believes that the balancing act should also be carried out differently, if at all. When the laws provide for mandatory exceptions and clear 'exceptions to the exceptions', the analysis should be an objective one, based on the regulations and as free of discretion as possible. This is the case of the provisions regarding access to the file in antitrust proceedings, clearly establishing the grounds for refusal and its exceptions:

> The right of access to the file shall not extend to business secrets, other confidential information and internal documents of the Commission or of the competition authorities of the Member States.
>
> (…)
>
> Nothing in this Regulation prevents the Commission from disclosing and using information necessary to prove an infringement of Articles 81 or 82 of the Treaty.[50]

Notwithstanding the need for a detailed analysis when applying this provision, the decision should be objectively based on the criteria provided in the legislative instrument, which implicitly precludes any additional balancing exercise where the discretion of the operator could come into play. This is what Carlton, Lawrence & Mcelwee call a rule-based approach, in which clarity is increased but may not be well adapted to producing 'fair' results in certain cases, as opposed to a judgment-based system starring a balancing test that measures each interest's weigh into the final decision on disclosure.[51] In Directive 2014/104/EU, a hybrid approach is taken because there are provisions establishing specific documents that are exempt from disclosure but there are also criteria to be applied by the national courts in a balancing exercise to determine whether access to the information should be granted.

In the framework of conflicts between the universal right of access to documents in the EU and the interests protected by confidentiality in administrative procedures, Adamski makes an interesting contribution by distinguishing two different approaches to the conflict which have been taken by the CJEU: the 'decoupled' approach, whereby the Court disregards the values

49 Goddin, *Recent Judgments Regarding Transparency*, 2011. For an analysis of the CJEU position in this regard see also Vandenborre, I., & Goetz, T. (2012). EU Competition Law Procedure. Journal of European Competition Law & Practice, *3*(6), 578–585.

50 EU Commission Regulation (EC) No 773/2004, Articles 15(1) and (3).

51 Carlton, Lawrence & Mcelwee, *Confidentiality and Disclosure*, 2008

and interests conflicting with transparency as irrelevant, and therefore avoids the conflict altogether; and the 'linked' approach, where the Court recognises the value of the conflicting interests and gives proper consideration to the legal provisions they stem from (most often other pieces of EU secondary law). According to this author, the 'decoupled' approach maintains all the *effet utile* of the access right, resulting in the general prevalence of the maximum disclosure principle, whereas the 'linked' approach leads to the opposite result, where the right of access is overridden in order to protect other interests. When the other interests derive their protection from another piece of secondary law, the general rule of access is disabled in application of the principle of *lex specialis derogat legi generali*.[52] However, the application of this principle in all cases would result in the systematic derogation of the principle of maximum disclosure and the fundamental right of access to public information, hence, as enticing as it might be from the perspective of legal certainty, simplicity and consistency of the legal system, a different method of interpretation is necessary.[53]

Public access to information in the framework of competition law cases and access to administrative files is a clear example of the persisting conflicts inherently embedded in some of the legal regimes. To the extent that no clear hierarchy is set to establish when to apply a presumption for access and when one for confidentiality,[54] the interests protected by both regimes are at risk, and the methodological tools of interpretation appear to come short for the complexity of the conflicts.

The contextual integrative analysis in this case offers interesting alternatives to the traditional approach. By making explicit the need to consider the special circumstances surrounding a request for information,[55] courts and legal

52 Adamski, *Do Private Watchdogs Matter*? 2014.

53 Regarding the risks of relying on specialised access rules only, Heremans points out: '...since it would be naive to assume that the legislator consciously took into account the public interest in transparency when adopting these "sector instruments", as long as these special regimes are not adapted in this respect, the existence of such a *lex specialis* should probably do no more than create a "general presumption" which remains rebuttable also on the basis of an overriding public interest in transparency' (Heremans, T. (2011). *Public Access to Documents: Jurisprudence between Principle and Practice*, Egmont Paper No. 50, p. 85).

54 See De Vries, A. (2014). *Confidentiality in EU Pesticide Risk Assessment: A Violation of the Aarhus Convention?* Tilburg University; recommending the "clarification of the hierarchy between the Regulation on the registration of plant protection products and the Aarhus legislation" as a contribution to the problem of access to environmental information from risk assessments in light of the specific regulation establishing a presumption of confidentiality over part of the same information.

55 Thus far there is evidence of cases where the CJEU has pursued the examination of the requester's motivations implying that such an examination is indeed relevant. See, generally, Adamski, *Do Private Watchdogs Matter*? 2014, discussing the impact for the right of access to information when the petitioner pursues his individual interest only. There are also cases where the law requires the applicant

operators may be able to apply the principles and rules in response to the full spectrum of interests at stake in each case. A contextual integrative analysis involves the painting of a complete picture where all the relevant factors are taken into the decision-making process, including the position of the applicant and the purpose of the petition; a practice also dubbed as a 'purposive approach' to the solution of the conflict. By conducting this analysis, the legal operator is able to determine: (i) if the request of information fulfils the general requirements for the exercise of the right of public access and therefore a presumption of disclosure applies to the case, (ii) if the disclosure of the information requested may affect other protected interests, and if so, the basis for the particular protection of these interests, compliance of the protection with the exceptions to disclosure provided in the transparency regime, and whether there are any special rules mandating disclosure even in light of the harm to the protected interest (*e.g.* certain environmental information), (iii) if doubt persists, whether there are stronger reasons in the public interest (overrides) or in the private interest of the petitioner (protection of fundamental rights) that merit disclosure of the information, and finally (iv) if there is an alternative to full unconditional disclosure that would balance the need of protection of all the conflicting interests (*e.g.* restricting the use of the information by the applicant or attaching confidentiality obligations to the disclosure of the information).

The proposed system has a resemblance to the solutions formulated so far to the issue of third-party access to the file in competition cases, at the legislative level through Directive 2014/104/EU and by the courts in the cases of *Pfleiderer, Donau Chemie* and, most recently, *UPS v. Commission*: a hybrid approach, where clear rules establish the framework for an effective balancing exercise and the boundaries to the authority's discretion, bringing into account the interests of all the parties involved and providing alternative solutions through additional measures to mitigate the potential adverse effects of the decision.

to justify his request, such as the European Data Protection Regulation (Article 8, Regulation No 41/2001). In Case C-28/08, *Commission v. Bavarian Lager*, Judgment of 29 June 2010, the CJEU expressed: 'As the applicant has not provided any express and legitimate justification in order to demonstrate the necessity for those personal data to be transferred, the Commission has not been able to weigh up the various interests of the parties concerned'.

9 Conclusions and Recommendations

The present study delved into the conflict between public access to environmental information and the interests of the private sector, specifically the protection of business confidentiality. The analysis started from the recognition of the increasing importance of transparency and public participation rights as tools for environmental good governance, which can be observed at the international, regional and national levels, driven forward by initiatives of governments, industries and civil society.

With legal development in this field also come challenges to provide a fair recognition of the already existing rights, to achieve consistence and coherence of the legal regimes, and legal certainty for the different actors playing by the new rules. The review of access to environmental information from the private sector revealed the particularities of these challenges, providing key inputs to propose possible measures to overcome them.

By researching different legal regimes against a normative framework composed by transparency best practices, inspired in the international legal system, it was possible to identify and characterise several shortcomings of the existing laws.

The first issue consists of the limitations of a pure public/private approach to determine the scope of transparency legislation. In view of the privatisation phenomena taking place at virtually every level of government action, the emergence of new actors and hybrid organisations, and the changing dynamics between the public and private spheres of interests, their interplay and how they are exercised and protected under the law, the formulation of new frameworks for the appointment of transparency obligations among the full spectrum of actors is of vital importance. New factors need to be considered beside the public or private nature of the entity holding the information, such as the functions it performs (*e.g.* through a functional definition of 'public authority'), the nature of the information itself (*e.g.* information in the public interest), the purpose served with transparency in the specific case (*e.g.* democratic participation, public accountability or the protection of other rights) and the particular conditions in which access to information is sought out (*e.g.* EIA processes, registration of a new product).

DOI: 10.4324/9781003307617-9

Secondly, a *prima facie* conflict was identified by comparing the definition of environmental information and some of the examples of protected confidential information, *e.g.* economic and financial data, specific technical information about new technologies or products, information about properties of chemical substances, environmental, health and safety information and Environmental Impact Assessments (EIAs). The clash between the public interest in disclosure and the private interest in confidentiality is clearly visible in these cases, whose study provides strong arguments for a regulation that takes into consideration the nature of the information to be disclosed, irrespective of the private or public nature of the holder.

A third problematic issue is the inconsistency of the legal regimes *vis-à-vis* their general and sectoral transparency regulations. The EU is a clear example: against the backdrop of the general, all-encompassing transparency regime established by Regulation No. 1049/2001, several sectoral regulations determine their own access to information schemes, some of them providing broader public access (*e.g.* Aarhus legislation) and some considerably limiting the scope of action of the general regime (*e.g.* Regulation 1107/09 on the registration of plant protection products). Without a clear hierarchy or criteria to determine which one of them prevails in specific cases, the result is an incoherent bundle of case-by-case decisions that, at best, provide fair solutions to the parties in the immediate conflict, but that taken together fail to provide the certainty and predictability desirable for any legal framework.

The fourth issue relates to the weaknesses of the current toolbox for the solution of these conflicts. Separately and combined, the principle of 'maximum disclosure', the 'harm test' and the 'balancing act' come short in the face of the complexity and variety of the conflicts between disclosure and confidentiality. They not only seem to be defined differently in each of the jurisdictions, but also seem to operate in a normative vacuum, as specific guidelines and consistent frameworks seem to be lacking.

In this scenario, a proposal is introduced to aid the creation and reform of policy and legislative instruments on public access to environmental information from the private sector. This proposal consists of two main components: (i) a reformed matrix of values and (ii) a methodology for the application of the matrix of values, the 'integrated contextual analysis'.

The matrix of values comprises the distilled findings emerging from international and national legislative instruments, case-law and codes of best practice giving prevalence to certain societal values regarding transparency. One conclusion was the instrumental quality of access to environmental information when it is given in the framework of a decision-making process, where the effectiveness of public participation clearly depends on the public's ability to get access to all the *relevant* information that enables it to make a reasoned assessment of the factors influencing the decision. Another notable example is access to information that is deemed necessary (or even just useful) for the exercise of the applicant's fundamental rights, *e.g.* the right to due process and access to justice. A form of this doctrine can be observed in the

EU provisions and case law regarding third party access to the file in competition cases. The enhanced importance of transparency in certain circumstances warrants a different treatment of confidentiality provisions.

When established in the law, the matrix of values is simply a balancing act taken at a higher level, in the hope of increasing consistency and facilitating the fair application of the laws in specific cases, at the administrative and judicial levels. The specific contribution that this research presents is the inclusion of a new category into the matrix of values, providing public access to information considered necessary for communities and individuals to exercise their rights effectively, as in the framework of public participation in decision-making processes, public interest litigation and class actions, and the exercise of their rights as consumers.

The 'integrated contextual analysis', on the other hand, proposes a methodology to apply the matrix of values where all the relevant factors for the decision are properly weighed in: the nature of the entity holding the information, the nature of the information itself, the purpose that disclosure is going to serve or the framework in which it is being requested, and the special circumstances of the petitioner that may merit disclosure.

In order to preserve the private interests in confidentiality, the matrix of values clearly delineates the cases in which a legitimate expectation of confidentiality can be created in favour of the person submitting information, and therefore, also makes it clear when such an expectation is unfounded. This will enable companies and other actors with a private interest in the confidentiality of information to know what to expect and to take any additional precautions that are considered appropriate for the specific case. Additionally, special measures to protect the private interests can be ordered by the authorities when allowing disclosure, such as the prohibition to communicate the information to other parties or to exploit it commercially, and the obligation to keep the confidentiality and to use the information only for the purpose that justified disclosure in the first place.

The implementation of the recommendations of the present study would entail different changes at each of the jurisdictions under study. A brief analysis of these implications follows.

9.1. Colombia

As mentioned in the comparative section, the Colombian regime presents two significant shortcomings: one, access to environmental information is not integrated in a system of public participation in environmental matters, and two, there is no specific regime for the protection of business confidentiality at the national level (the protection is mostly supported in the regional regime of intellectual property of the Andean Community and, to an extent, in isolated provisions of the Code of Commerce). The lack of more specific rules and guiding principles leads to deficiencies for the effective exercise of the rights of access and uncertainty about the expectations of confidentiality for private entities that may eventually result in the violation of their rights.

For Colombia, adapting the recommendations of this study would generally entail:

1 Ratifying the Escazú Agreement.
2 Enacting national legislation implementing its obligations under the Escazú Agreement amending the public participation section of the General Environmental Law which would be *lex specialis* vis-à-vis the Transparency Law and the Right of Petition Law.
3 The new legislation should include a section about the right of access to environmental information from private entities, adapting the constitutional and legal provisions providing access for the protection of fundamental rights to cases of environmental collective and individual interests. It should include specific rules about the form and means in which the information should be made available considering the needs and characteristics of the communities, such as translation into their native language, making non-technical summaries of EIA studies mandatory, enabling online access, and improving electronic databases to be more user-friendly.
4 Establishing a clear, detailed, and specific regime of exceptions to access, which make explicit mention of the laws (international, regional or national) on which trade secrets and other CBI is protected. In this context, a specific definition of 'trade secrets' and CBI should be drafted for the purposes of transparency legislation.
5 Including specific public interest overrides for certain categories of environmental information.
6 Providing for the application of a 'integrated contextual analysis' or a similar procedure to ensure the adequate application of the law.
7 Explicitly recognising public participation in environmental matters as a fundamental right derived from international treaties ratified by Colombia, therefore enabling the exercise of the tutela action for the protection of these rights.

9.2. The US

The study of the US regime shows an impressive development of legislation protecting trade secrets and CBI, while specific subjective environmental rights are virtually absent and public access to information is not considered a constitutional right. The public right of access to environmental information is exercised, however, mostly through the provisions of the federal and state FOIAs and, to some extent, of specific environmental statutes providing for reporting and disclosure duties upon public and private organisations.

To apply the recommendations of the present study, the US should:

1 Promote the recognition of substantive environmental rights, on which procedural environmental rights can find support.
2 Enact federal regulations that harmonise access to information from private entities in certain cases.
3 Amend the federal FOIA by adopting a section specifically dealing with access to environmental information from private and public actors, comprising information from statutory laws and duties derived from tort law and common law, *e.g.* regarding dangerous substances, consumer products and risks for the environment or to human life and health.
4 Regulate, through executive orders, the application of presumptions of disclosure and confidentiality in the context of FOIA by federal employees. A comprehensive analysis must be encouraged, duly accounting for the interests of all the parties concerned.
5 Establish a definition of CBI and trade secrets exclusively in the context of FOIA. Alternatively, additional measures can be adopted to ensure that the information claimed as confidential is in fact of a competitive value and its disclosure could cause harm to the legitimate economic interests of the submitter. This could be done following the example of the amended TSCA.
6 Improve the system of EIA by establishing a scheme for public participation in the assessment of environmental impacts. A step forward would be to establish federal rules requiring EIAs to be conducted by the private operators of projects or activities and not only public authorities. EIA studies should also be made more suitable for the understanding of the public and accessibility to electronic databases should be improved to be more user-friendly.
7 It is recommended to adopt mandatory guidelines for voluntary environmental reporting that may ensure the quality, comparability, integrity, and accessibility of the information.

9.3. The EU

The EU system most closely resembles the international regime employed as the normative framework for this study. However, there are significant issues affecting the efficacy and application of the rights of access to environmental information and the protection of CBI. In the EU the conflict is most evident between laws providing for public disclosure of information and the laws protecting the confidentiality of business secrets and other IPR, and, so far, the efforts of the CJEU to provide legal guidelines to solve these conflicts have fallen short.

In the field of substance law, the problem is more acute, as recent case-law has debunked previous interpretations of the laws establishing the confidentiality of the information submitted in the process of approval of plant protection products, but even within the same court, the arguments for doing so seem to be mutually contradictory. Legal uncertainty seems to be the most serious issue with the EU legislative regime for access to environmental information, particularly affecting private parties' interests.

To implement the recommendations of this study, the EU could:

1 Adopt a matrix of values and a 'integrative contextual analysis' that harmonise the principles of the international and regional legislative instruments and the guidelines for their application in a unified, coherent way. This could be done via amendments to the existing legislation implementing the Aarhus Convention which is the most specialised instrument regarding public access to environmental information.
2 To the extent that the Aarhus Convention is a floor and not a ceiling in the matter it regulates, the EU (and Member States) could establish broader access to information held by private entities in the cases referred in this study.
3 The amended legislation should specifically determine when this general legal regime prevails over specialised sectoral rules. By doing so, it would clarify in which cases more specific legislation can derogate from the regime of access to environmental information, considering that the Aarhus Convention prevails over regional or national regimes and thus conformity with the Convention must be the prime guiding principle.
4 The CJEU may take the opportunity to unify a position regarding access to environmental information and business confidentiality, particularly in the framework of substance law (REACH) and within the limits and purposes of effective public participation in decision-making. A few steps have been taken in this direction already, and a judicial solution could go a long way in providing legal certainty in the meantime until legislative reforms are adopted.
5 Progress on the uniform protection of trade secrets and CBI at the EU level would provide clarity and consistence to the application of the exceptions under Aarhus and the European legislation. The EU should consider adopting specific guidelines or reform the current transparency regime on the protection of confidentiality for third party entities taking into account the international conventions (*e.g.* TRIPS) and unifying recent CJEU case-law on the subject.

Index

NB Page numbers in **bold** indicate tables

www.ingramcontent.com/pod-product-compliance
Lightning Source LLC
LaVergne TN
LVHW021120300926
849160LV00010B/797